Chevrolet Cruze Automotive Repair Manual

by Jeff Killingsworth and John H Haynes

Member of the Guild of Motoring Writers

Models covered:

Chevrolet Cruze - 2011 through 2019
Does not include information specific to diesel engine models

J H Haynes & Co. Ltd. (24044-2AA5)
Sparkford Nr Yeovil ABCDE
Somerset BA22 7JJ England FGHIJ
KL

Haynes North America, Inc
2801 Townsgate Road, Suite 340
Thousand Oaks, CA 91361 USA

www.haynes.com

Acknowledgements

Technical writers who contributed to this project include John Wegmann and Bob Henderson.

© Haynes North America, Inc. 2015, 2019

With permission from J.H. Haynes & Co. Ltd.

A book in the Haynes Automotive Repair Manual Series

Printed in India

ISBN-10: 1-62092-382-3
ISBN-13: 978-1-62092-382-5

Library of Congress Control Number: 2019953914

While every attempt is made to ensure that the information in this manual is correct, no liability can be accepted by the authors or publishers for loss, damage or injury caused by any errors in, or omissions from, the information given.

Contents

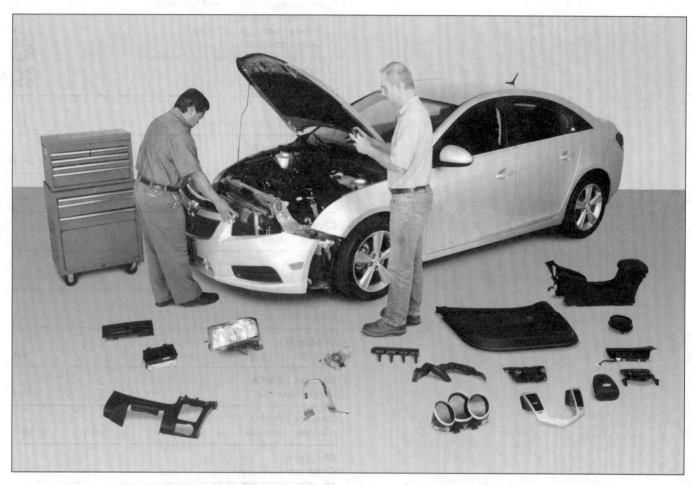

Haynes mechanic and photographer with a 2013 Chevrolet Cruze

About this manual

Its purpose

The purpose of this manual is to help you get the best value from your vehicle. It can do so in several ways. It can help you decide what work must be done, even if you choose to have it done by a dealer service department or a repair shop; it provides information and procedures for routine maintenance and servicing; and it offers diagnostic and repair procedures to follow when trouble occurs.

We hope you use the manual to tackle the work yourself. For many simpler jobs, doing it yourself may be quicker than arranging an appointment to get the vehicle into a shop and making the trips to leave it and pick it up. More importantly, a lot of money can be saved by avoiding the expense the shop must pass on to you to cover its labor and overhead costs. An added benefit is the sense of satisfaction and accomplishment that you feel after doing the job yourself.

Using the manual

The manual is divided into Chapters. Each Chapter is divided into numbered Sections, which are headed in bold type between horizontal lines. Each Section consists of consecutively numbered paragraphs.

The reference numbers used in illustration captions pinpoint the pertinent Section and the Step within that Section. That is, illustration 3.2 means the illustration refers to Section 3 and Step (or paragraph) 2 within that Section.

Procedures, once described in the text, are not normally repeated. When it's necessary to refer to another Chapter, the reference will be given as Chapter and Section number. Cross references given without use of the word "Chapter" apply to Sections and/or paragraphs in the same Chapter. For example, "see Section 8" means in the same Chapter.

References to the left or right side of the vehicle assume you are sitting in the driver's seat, facing forward.

Even though we have prepared this manual with extreme care, neither the publisher nor the author can accept responsibility for any errors in, or omissions from, the information given.

NOTE

A **Note** provides information necessary to properly complete a procedure or information which will make the procedure easier to understand.

CAUTION

A **Caution** provides a special procedure or special steps which must be taken while completing the procedure where the Caution is found. Not heeding a Caution can result in damage to the assembly being worked on.

WARNING

A **Warning** provides a special procedure or special steps which must be taken while completing the procedure where the Warning is found. Not heeding a Warning can result in personal injury.

Introduction

These models are available only in a sedan body style. They feature transversely mounted four-cylinder engines.

2015 and earlier models are equipped with an electronically controlled Sequential Fuel Injection (SFI) system. 2016 and later models are equipped with an electronically controlled Direct Injection (DI) fuel injection system. The 1.4L four-cylinder DOHC engine is turbocharged, while the 1.8L engine is normally aspirated.

The engine transmits power to the front wheels through either a six-speed manual transaxle or a six-speed automatic transaxle, via independent driveaxles.

The front suspension is a MacPherson strut design. The rear suspension employs two arms connected by a stamped-steel axle that pivots on bushings on the underbody, a Watts linkage, and a shock absorber and coil spring at the rear of each arm.

The rack-and-pinion steering unit is mounted behind the engine on the front suspension subframe, and is power-assisted on all models by an electric speed-proportional power-steering system.

All models are equipped with power assisted front disc and rear disc or drum brakes, with an Anti-lock Brake System (ABS) as standard equipment.

Vehicle identification numbers

Modifications are a continuing and unpublicized process in vehicle manufacturing. Since spare parts manuals and lists are compiled on a numerical basis, the individual vehicle numbers are essential to correctly identify the component required.

Vehicle Identification Number (VIN)

This very important identification number is stamped on a plate attached to the dashboard inside the windshield on the driver's side of the vehicle (see illustration). It can also be found on the certification label located on the driver's side door post. The VIN also appears on the Vehicle Certificate of Title and Registration. It contains information such as where and when the vehicle was manufactured, the model year and the body style.

On the models covered by this manual the model year codes are:

B   2011
C   2012
D   2013
E   2014
F   2015
G   2016
H   2017
J   2018
K   2019

On the models covered by this manual the engine codes are:

9   1.4L (LUJ) four-cylinder DOHC turbo charged engine (2011)
C   1.4L (LUJ) four-cylinder DOHC turbocharged engine (2012)
B   1.4L (LUV) four-cylinder DOHC turbo-charged, VVT engine (2013 through 2015)
M   1.4L (LE2) four-cylinder DI, DOHC, VVT engine (2016 and later)
H   1.8L (LUW) four-cylinder DOHC, Dual fuel engine (2013 through 2015)
G   1.8L (LWE) four-cylinder DOHC, VVT engine (2013 through 2015)

Certification label

The certification label is attached to the driver's door post (see illustration). The plate contains the name of the manufacturer, the month and year of production, the Gross Vehicle Weight Rating (GVWR), the Gross Axle Weight Rating (GAWR) and the certification statement.

Engine identification numbers

The engine serial number can be found on a machined surface at the rear of the engine, near the oil filter housing and the transaxle (see illustration).

Transmission identification

The transmission identification is listed on a Manufacturer's RPO code list or on a sticker attached to the transmission (see illustration). The codes are as follows:

M20/32	6-speed manual transaxle
AF40	6-speed automatic transaxle
6T30/35	6-speed automatic transaxle
6T40/45/50	6-speed automatic transaxle

The Vehicle Identification Number (VIN) is visible through the driver's side of the windshield

The Manufacturer's Certification Regulation label is located on the driver's door opening

The engine identification code date can be found stamped on the front side of the engine block, near the transaxle (1.4L engine shown, 1.8L engine similar)

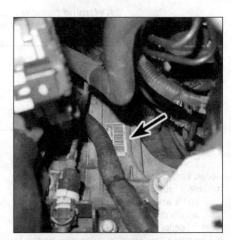

The transaxle identification label is affixed to the top of the transaxle

Recall information

Vehicle recalls are carried out by the manufacturer in the rare event of a possible safety-related defect. The vehicle's registered owner is contacted at the address on file at the Department of Motor Vehicles and given the details of the recall. Remedial work is carried out free of charge at a dealer service department.

If you are the new owner of a used vehicle which was subject to a recall and you want to be sure that the work has been carried out, it's best to contact a dealer service department and ask about your individual vehicle - you'll need to furnish them your Vehicle Identification Number (VIN).

The table below is based on information provided by the National Highway Traffic Safety Administration (NHTSA), the body which oversees vehicle recalls in the United States. The recall database is updated constantly. For the latest information on vehicle recalls, check the NHTSA website at www.nhtsa.gov, www.safercar.gov, or call the NHTSA hotline at 1-888-327-4236.

Recall date	Recall campaign number	Model(s) affected	Concern
April 06, 2011	11V221000	2011 - Cruze	GM is recalling certain models that during manufacturing the steering wheel could have been improperly fastened and may detach from the steering column. Should the steering wheel detach from the steering column while driving, the driver could lose the ability to steer the vehicle, increasing the risk of a crash.
May 06, 2011	11V270000	2011 - Cruze	GM is recalling certain models that the bolt attaching the intermediate steering shaft to the steering gear input shaft may not have been properly installed. This could allow the shafts to separate, resulting in the loss of steering. Loss of steering control may increase the risk of a crash.
May 06, 2011	11V273000	2011 - Cruze	GM is recalling certain models equipped with an automatic transmissionfor failing to comply with Federal Motor Vehicle Safety Standard No. 102, 'transmissionshift lever sequence, starter interlock, and transmission braking effect,' and Federal Motor Vehicle Safety Standard No. 114, 'theft protection.' These vehicles may have been built with a transmission shift linkage that is not properly installed. If the linkage is not properly installed, the PRNDL shift lever may not accurately reflect the position of the transmission gear. With this condition, the driver could move the shifter to park and remove the ignition key, but the transmission gear may not be in park. The driver may not be able to restart the vehicle and the vehicle could roll away after the driver has exited the vehicle, resulting in a possible crash.
June 22, 2012	12V288000	2011, 2012 - Cruze	GM is recalling certain model years that spilled or dripping oil (such as after an oil change) may collect in the under-vehicle splash shield near hot engine or exhaust system surfaces. As a result, the oil and the engine shield may ignite and burn. Either condition could result in an engine compartment fire, possibly causing injury or death.
June 22, 2012	12V289000	2011, 2012 - Cruze	GM is recalling certain model years, with attachment welds for the fuel tank strap secondary brackets that may have been omitted. The fuel tank could come loose in a crash, possibly allowing fuel to leak from the tank. A fuel leak in the presence of an ignition source could result in a fire.

Recall date	Recall campaign number	Model(s) affected	Concern
October 31, 2012	12V522000	2012 - Cruze	GM is recalling certain vehicles, with a driver side frontal airbag that has a shorting bar which may intermittently contact the air bag terminals. If the bar and terminals are contacting each other at the time of a crash necessitating deployment of the driver's frontal airbag, that airbag will not deploy, increasing the driver's risk of injury.
January 24, 2013	13V023000	2012 - Cruze	GM is recalling certain vehicles that the driver side frontal air bag has a shorting bar which may intermittently contact the air bag terminals. If the bar and terminals are contacting each other at the time of a crash necessitating deployment of the driver's frontal air bag, that air bag will not deploy, increasing the driver's risk of injury.
August 15, 2013	13V360000	2011, 2012 - Cruze	GM is recalling certain vehicles equipped with 1.4L DOHC gasoline turbo engines and 6T40 automatic transmissions and equipped with an electric vacuum pump to provide supplemental vacuum for brake assist, when needed. In the affected vehicles, the pump may not activate, resulting in an intermittent reduction or loss of brake assist. A loss of braking assistance will require extra pedal force and/or distance to bring the vehicle to a stop, increasing the risk of a crash.
September 23, 2013	13V452000	2013, 2014 - Cruze	GM is recalling certain vehicles equipped with manual transmissions (MF3/MR5); the right front driveaxle may fracture and separate. If the driveaxle fractures and separates while driving, the vehicle would lose power and coast to a stop. If a vehicle with a fractured driveaxle is parked without the parking brake applied, the vehicle could move unexpectedly. Either condition increases the risk of a crash.
February 21, 2014	14V092000	2014 - Cruze	GM is recalling certain vehicles equipped with automatic transmissions where the transmission shift cable adjuster may disengage from the transmission shift lever. As such, these vehicles do not conform to Federal Motor Vehicle Safety Standard (FMVSS) number 102, "Transmission Shift Lever Sequence, Starter Interlock, and Transmission Braking Effect." They also fail to conform to FMVSS number 114, "Theft Protection and Rollaway Prevention." If a vehicle's shift cable disengages from the transmission shift lever, a driver may be unable to shift gear positions and the indicated shift position may not represent the gear position the vehicle is in. Should a disengagement occur while the vehicle is being driven, when the driver goes to stop and park the vehicle, the driver may be able to shift the lever to the "PARK" position, but the vehicle transmission may not be in the "PARK" gear position. If the vehicle is not in the "PARK" position there is a risk the vehicle will roll away as the driver and other occupants exit the vehicle or anytime thereafter. A vehicle rollaway increases the risk of injury to exiting occupants and bystanders

Recall date	Recall campaign number	Model(s) affected	Concern
March 31, 2014	14V151000	2013, 2014 - Cruze	GM is recalling certain vehicles equipped with a 1.4L turbo engines, the right front driveaxle may fracture and separate. If the driveaxle fractures and separates while driving, the vehicle would lose power and coast to a stop. If a vehicle with a fractured driveaxle is parked without the parking brake applied, the vehicle could move unexpectedly. Either condition increases the risk of a crash.
June 06, 2014	14V300000	2012 - Cruze	GM is recalling certain vehicles with driver side frontal airbag that has a shorting bar which may intermittently contact the airbag terminals. If the bar and terminals are contacting each other at the time of a crash necessitating deployment of the driver's frontal airbag, that airbag will not deploy, increasing the driver's risk of injury.
June 26, 2014	14V372000	2013, 2014 - Cruze	GM is recalling certain vehicles where the driver's front airbag inflator may have been manufactured with an incorrect part. In the event of a crash necessitating deployment of the driver's airbag, the air bag's inflator may rupture and the air bag may not inflate. The rupture could cause metal fragments to strike and potentially seriously injure the vehicle occupants. Additionally, if the airbag does not inflate, the driver is at an increased risk of injury
July 02, 2014	14V417000	2013, 2014 - Cruze	GM is recalling certain vehicles equipped with a Calix oil pan/block heater. In cold temperatures, the insulation on the engine block heater cord can become damaged, allowing the wires to be exposed. Exposed wires increase the risk of electrical shock and personal injury if the cord is handled while it is plugged in.
February 27, 2015	15V113000	2015 - Cruze	GM is recalling certain vehicles where the left-rear or right-rear parking brake cable brackets may not have been properly fastened during the assembly process. As a result, the fastening bolts may back out completely, causing the parking brake bracket to separate and the parking brake to not hold the vehicle in place. As such, these vehicles fail to comply with the requirements of Federal Motor Vehicle Safety Standard (FMVSS) No. 135, "Light Vehicle Brake Systems." If the parking brake bracket separates, the parking brake may not hold the vehicle, increasing the risk of a vehicle roll away and a crash
July 10, 2015	15V442000	2014, 2015 - Cruze	GM is recalling certain vehicles where the inner tie-rod may not be tightened to specification allowing the tie-rod to separate from the steering gear. Separation of the tie-rod from the steering gear could result in the loss of steering, increasing the risk of a crash.

Recall date	Recall campaign number	Model(s) affected	Concern
December 23, 2015	15V876000	2015 - Cruze	On some models, one of the driver's-side seat belt assembly bolts may not be properly tightened. An insufficiently torqued bolt may prevent the seat belt from holding the required load in a crash, increasing the risk of injury.
July 01, 2016	16V498000	2016 - Cruze	On some models, the headlight assemblies are not marked with a three-digit identifier code used to properly aim the headlights. Without the identification code, the headlights may be improperly aimed during service, reducing nighttime visibility and increasing the risk of a crash.
July 05, 2016	16V502000	2011, 2012, 2013, 2014, 2015, 2016 - Cruze	On some models, the electronic park lock lever may allow the ignition key to be removed without the transmission being in PARK. Also, some models may have been serviced with similar defective replacement electronic park lock levers. If the key is removed without the transmission in PARK, the vehicle may roll away as occupants are exiting, increasing the risk of injury.
January 26, 2017	17V057000	2016, 2017 - Cruze	On some models, a bracket used in the driver or front passenger seat-back recliner mechanism may have been incorrectly welded to the seat-back frame. As a result, in the event of a crash, the head-restraints may not function properly. In a crash, the seat-backs for the front seats may break, increasing the risk of injury to the occupants.
May 10, 2018	18V304000	2016, 2017, 2018 - Cruze	GM is recalling certain vehicles, equipped with a gasoline engine and a tire inflator kit instead of a spare tire. The vehicles may leak gasoline following a rear-impact crash and a rollover. A fuel leak, in the presence of an ignition source, increases the risk of a fire.
August 30, 2018	18V576000	2018, 2019 - Cruze	On some models, the rear brake caliper pistons may have an insufficient coating causing gas pockets to form, potentially reducing rear brake performance. A reduction of braking performance can increase the risk of a crash.

Buying parts

Replacement parts are available from many sources. Our advice concerning them is as follows:

Retail auto parts stores: Good auto parts stores will stock frequently needed components which wear out relatively fast, such as clutch components, exhaust systems, brake parts, tune-up parts, etc. These stores often supply new or reconditioned parts on an exchange basis, which can save a considerable amount of money. Discount auto parts stores are often very good places to buy materials and parts needed for general vehicle maintenance such as oil, grease, filters, spark plugs, belts, touch-up paint, bulbs, etc. They also usually sell tools and general accessories, have convenient hours, charge lower prices and can give you knowledgeable answers to your questions. To be sure of obtaining the correct parts, have engine and chassis numbers available and, if possible, take the old parts along for positive identification.

Authorized dealer parts department: This is the best source for parts which are unique to the vehicle and not generally available elsewhere. Prices for most parts tend to be higher than at retail auto parts stores.

Auto recyclers or salvage yards: Auto recyclers and salvage yards are good sources for components that are specific to the vehicle and not subject to wear, such as fenders, bumpers, trim pieces, etc. You can expect substantial savings by going this route, and self-service salvage yards offer still more savings if you're willing to bring your own tools and pull the part(s) yourself.

Warranty information: If the vehicle is still covered under warranty, be sure that any replacement parts purchased - regardless of the source - do not invalidate the warranty! In most cases, replacement parts, even from aftermarket suppliers, are designed to meet manufacturer specifications. If in doubt, check with the parts supplier.

Because of a Federally mandated extended warranty that covers the emissions control system components, check with your dealer about warranty coverage before working on any emissions-related systems.

Discount auto parts stores provide a wide variety of parts, and the knowledgeable counter-people found there are an excellent resource

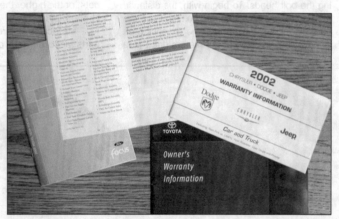

You'll find the details of your vehicle's warranty coverage in the warranty book provided by the manufacturer

Maintenance techniques, tools and working facilities

Maintenance techniques

There are a number of techniques involved in maintenance and repair that will be referred to throughout this manual. Application of these techniques will enable the home mechanic to be more efficient, better organized and capable of performing the various tasks properly, which will ensure that the repair job is thorough and complete.

Fasteners

Fasteners are nuts, bolts, studs and screws used to hold two or more parts together. There are a few things to keep in mind when working with fasteners. Almost all of them use a locking device of some type, either a lockwasher, locknut, locking tab or thread adhesive. All threaded fasteners should be clean and straight, with undamaged threads and undamaged corners on the hex head where the wrench fits. Develop the habit of replacing all damaged nuts and bolts with new ones. Special locknuts with nylon or fiber inserts can only be used once. If they are removed, they lose their locking ability and must be replaced with new ones.

Rusted nuts and bolts should be treated with a penetrating fluid to ease removal and prevent breakage. Some mechanics use turpentine in a spout-type oil can, which works quite well. After applying the rust penetrant, let it work for a few minutes before trying to loosen the nut or bolt. Badly rusted fasteners may have to be chiseled or sawed off or removed with a special nut breaker, available at tool stores.

If a bolt or stud breaks off in an assembly, it can be drilled and removed with a special tool commonly available for this purpose. Most automotive machine shops can perform this task, as well as other repair procedures, such as the repair of threaded holes that have been stripped out.

Flat washers and lockwashers, when removed from an assembly, should always be replaced exactly as removed. Replace any damaged washers with new ones. Never use a lockwasher on any soft metal surface (such as aluminum), thin sheet metal or plastic.

Fastener sizes

For a number of reasons, automobile manufacturers are making wider and wider use of metric fasteners. Therefore, it is important to be able to tell the difference between standard (sometimes called U.S. or SAE) and metric hardware, since they cannot be interchanged.

All bolts, whether standard or metric, are sized according to diameter, thread pitch and length. For example, a standard 1/2 - 13 x 1 bolt is 1/2 inch in diameter, has 13 threads per inch and is 1 inch long. An M12 - 1.75 x 25 metric bolt is 12 mm in diameter, has a thread pitch of 1.75 mm (the distance between threads) and is 25 mm long. The two bolts are nearly identical, and easily confused, but they are not interchangeable.

In addition to the differences in diameter, thread pitch and length, metric and standard bolts can also be distinguished by examining the bolt heads. To begin with, the distance across the flats on a standard bolt head is measured in inches, while the same dimension on a metric bolt is sized in millimeters (the same

is true for nuts). As a result, a standard wrench should not be used on a metric bolt and a metric wrench should not be used on a standard bolt. Also, most standard bolts have slashes radiating out from the center of the head to denote the grade or strength of the bolt, which is an indication of the amount of torque that can be applied to it. The greater the number of slashes, the greater the strength of the bolt. Grades 0 through 5 are commonly used on automobiles. Metric bolts have a property class (grade) number, rather than a slash, molded into their heads to indicate bolt strength. In this case, the higher the number, the stronger the bolt. Property class numbers 8.8, 9.8 and 10.9 are commonly used on automobiles.

Strength markings can also be used to distinguish standard hex nuts from metric hex nuts. Many standard nuts have dots stamped into one side, while metric nuts are marked with a number. The greater the number of dots, or the higher the number, the greater the strength of the nut.

Metric studs are also marked on their ends according to property class (grade).

Larger studs are numbered (the same as metric bolts), while smaller studs carry a geometric code to denote grade.

It should be noted that many fasteners, especially Grades 0 through 2, have no distinguishing marks on them. When such is the case, the only way to determine whether it is standard or metric is to measure the thread pitch or compare it to a known fastener of the same size.

Standard fasteners are often referred to as SAE, as opposed to metric. However, it should be noted that SAE technically refers to a non-metric fine thread fastener only. Coarse thread non-metric fasteners are referred to as USS sizes.

Since fasteners of the same size (both standard and metric) may have different strength ratings, be sure to reinstall any bolts, studs or nuts removed from your vehicle in their original locations. Also, when replacing a fastener with a new one, make sure that the new one has a strength rating equal to or greater than the original.

Grade 1 or 2   Grade 5   Grade 8

Bolt strength marking (standard/SAE/USS; bottom - metric)

Grade	Identification
Hex Nut Grade 5	3 Dots
Hex Nut Grade 8	6 Dots

Standard hex nut strength markings

Grade	Identification
Hex Nut Property Class 9	Arabic 9
Hex Nut Property Class 10	Arabic 10

Metric hex nut strength markings

Class 10.9   Class 9.8   Class 8.8

Metric stud strength markings

00-1 HAYNES

Tightening sequences and procedures

Most threaded fasteners should be tightened to a specific torque value (torque is the twisting force applied to a threaded component such as a nut or bolt). Overtightening the fastener can weaken it and cause it to break, while undertightening can cause it to eventually come loose. Bolts, screws and studs, depending on the material they are made of and their thread diameters, have specific torque values, many of which are noted in the Specifications at the beginning of each Chapter. Be sure to follow the torque recommendations closely. For fasteners not assigned a specific torque, a general torque value chart is presented here as a guide. These torque values are for dry (unlubricated) fasteners threaded into steel or cast iron (not aluminum). As was previously mentioned, the size and grade of a fastener determine the amount of torque that can safely be applied to it. The figures listed here are approximate for Grade 2 and Grade 3 fasteners. Higher grades can tolerate higher torque values.

Fasteners laid out in a pattern, such as cylinder head bolts, oil pan bolts, differential cover bolts, etc., must be loosened or tightened in sequence to avoid warping the component. This sequence will normally be shown in the appropriate Chapter. If a specific pattern is not given, the following procedures can be used to prevent warping.

Initially, the bolts or nuts should be assembled finger-tight only. Next, they should be tightened one full turn each, in a criss-cross or diagonal pattern. After each one has been tightened one full turn, return to the first one and tighten them all one-half turn, following the same pattern. Finally, tighten each of them one-quarter turn at a time until each fastener has been tightened to the proper torque. To loosen and remove the fasteners, the procedure would be reversed.

Metric thread sizes	Ft-lbs	Nm
M-6	6 to 9	9 to 12
M-8	14 to 21	19 to 28
M-10	28 to 40	38 to 54
M-12	50 to 71	68 to 96
M-14	80 to 140	109 to 154

Pipe thread sizes		
1/8	5 to 8	7 to 10
1/4	12 to 18	17 to 24
3/8	22 to 33	30 to 44
1/2	25 to 35	34 to 47

U.S. thread sizes		
1/4 - 20	6 to 9	9 to 12
5/16 - 18	12 to 18	17 to 24
5/16 - 24	14 to 20	19 to 27
3/8 - 16	22 to 32	30 to 43
3/8 - 24	27 to 38	37 to 51
7/16 - 14	40 to 55	55 to 74
7/16 - 20	40 to 60	55 to 81
1/2 - 13	55 to 80	75 to 108

Standard (SAE and USS) bolt dimensions/grade marks

- G Grade marks (bolt strength)
- L Length (in inches)
- T Thread pitch (number of threads per inch)
- D Nominal diameter (in inches)

Metric bolt dimensions/grade marks

- P Property class (bolt strength)
- L Length (in millimeters)
- T Thread pitch (distance between threads in millimeters)
- D Diameter

00-2 HAYNES

Micrometer set

Dial indicator set

Component disassembly

Component disassembly should be done with care and purpose to help ensure that the parts go back together properly. Always keep track of the sequence in which parts are removed. Make note of special characteristics or marks on parts that can be installed more than one way, such as a grooved thrust washer on a shaft. It is a good idea to lay the disassembled parts out on a clean surface in the order that they were removed. It may also be helpful to make sketches or take instant photos of components before removal.

When removing fasteners from a component, keep track of their locations. Sometimes threading a bolt back in a part, or putting the washers and nut back on a stud, can prevent mix-ups later. If nuts and bolts cannot be returned to their original locations, they should be kept in a compartmented box or a series of small boxes. A cupcake or muffin tin is ideal for this purpose, since each cavity can hold the bolts and nuts from a particular area (i.e. oil pan bolts, valve cover bolts, engine mount bolts, etc.). A pan of this type is especially helpful when working on assemblies with very small parts, such as the carburetor, alternator, valve train or interior dash and trim pieces. The cavities can be marked with paint or tape to identify the contents.

Whenever wiring looms, harnesses or connectors are separated, it is a good idea to identify the two halves with numbered pieces of masking tape so they can be easily reconnected.

Gasket sealing surfaces

Throughout any vehicle, gaskets are used to seal the mating surfaces between two parts and keep lubricants, fluids, vacuum or pressure contained in an assembly.

Many times these gaskets are coated with a liquid or paste-type gasket sealing compound before assembly. Age, heat and pressure can sometimes cause the two parts to stick together so tightly that they are very difficult to separate. Often, the assembly can be loosened by striking it with a soft-face hammer near the mating surfaces. A regular hammer can be used if a block of wood is placed between the hammer and the part. Do not hammer on cast parts or parts that could be easily damaged. With any particularly stubborn part, always recheck to make sure that every fastener has been removed.

Avoid using a screwdriver or bar to pry apart an assembly, as they can easily mar the gasket sealing surfaces of the parts, which must remain smooth. If prying is absolutely necessary, use an old broom handle, but keep in mind that extra clean up will be necessary if the wood splinters.

After the parts are separated, the old gasket must be carefully scraped off and the gasket surfaces cleaned. Stubborn gasket material can be soaked with rust penetrant or treated with a special chemical to soften it so it can be easily scraped off. **Caution:** *Never use gasket removal solutions or caustic chemicals on plastic or other composite components.* A scraper can be fashioned from a piece of copper tubing by flattening and sharpening one end. Copper is recommended because it is usually softer than the surfaces to be scraped, which reduces the chance of gouging the part. Some gaskets can be removed with a wire brush, but regardless of the method used, the mating surfaces must be left clean and smooth. If for some reason the gasket surface is gouged, then a gasket sealer thick enough to fill scratches will have to be used during reassembly of the components. For most applications, a non-drying (or semi-drying) gasket sealer should be used.

Hose removal tips

Warning: *If the vehicle is equipped with air conditioning, do not disconnect any of the A/C hoses without first having the system depressurized by a dealer service department or a service station.*

Hose removal precautions closely parallel gasket removal precautions. Avoid scratching or gouging the surface that the hose mates against or the connection may leak. This is especially true for radiator hoses. Because of various chemical reactions, the rubber in hoses can bond itself to the metal spigot that the hose fits over. To remove a hose, first loosen the hose clamps that secure it to the spigot. Then, with slip-joint pliers, grab the hose at the clamp and rotate it around the spigot. Work it back and forth until it is completely free, then pull it off. Silicone or other lubricants will ease removal if they can be applied between the hose and the outside of the spigot. Apply the same lubricant to the inside of the hose and the outside of the spigot to simplify installation.

As a last resort (and if the hose is to be replaced with a new one anyway), the rubber can be slit with a knife and the hose peeled from the spigot. If this must be done, be careful that the metal connection is not damaged.

If a hose clamp is broken or damaged, do not reuse it. Wire-type clamps usually weaken with age, so it is a good idea to replace them with screw-type clamps whenever a hose is removed.

Tools

A selection of good tools is a basic requirement for anyone who plans to maintain and repair his or her own vehicle. For the owner who has few tools, the initial investment might seem high, but when compared to the spiraling costs of professional auto maintenance and repair, it is a wise one.

To help the owner decide which tools are needed to perform the tasks detailed in this manual, the following tool lists are offered: *Maintenance and minor repair, Repair/overhaul* and *Special.*

The newcomer to practical mechanics should start off with the *maintenance and minor repair* tool kit, which is adequate for the simpler jobs performed on a vehicle. Then, as confidence and experience grow, the owner can tackle more difficult tasks, buying additional tools as they are needed. Eventually the basic kit will be expanded into the *repair and overhaul* tool set. Over a period of time, the experienced do-it-yourselfer will assemble a tool set complete enough for most repair and overhaul procedures and will add tools from the special category when it is felt that the expense is justified by the frequency of use.

Dial caliper

Hand-operated vacuum pump

Timing light

Tachometer and dwellmeter

Fuel pressure guage set

Trouble code reader

Compression gauge

Cooling system pressure tester

Damper and steering wheel puller

Maintenance and minor repair tool kit

The tools in this list should be considered the minimum required for performance of routine maintenance, servicing and minor repair work. We recommend the purchase of combination wrenches (box-end and open-end combined in one wrench). While more expensive than open end wrenches, they offer the advantages of both types of wrench.

Combination wrench set
(1/4-inch to 1 inch or 6 mm to 19 mm)
Adjustable wrench, 8 inch

Spark plug wrench with rubber insert
Spark plug gap adjusting tool
Feeler gauge set
Brake bleeder wrench
Standard screwdriver
(5/16-inch x 6 inch)
Phillips screwdriver (No. 2 x 6 inch)
Combination pliers - 6 inch
Hacksaw and assortment of blades
Tire pressure gauge
Grease gun
Oil can
Fine emery cloth
Wire brush

Battery post and cable cleaning tool
Oil filter wrench
Funnel (medium size)
Safety goggles
Jackstands (2)
Drain pan

Note: *If basic tune-ups are going to be part of routine maintenance, it will be necessary to purchase a good quality stroboscopic timing light and combination tachometer/dwell meter. Although they are included in the list of special tools, it is mentioned here because they are absolutely necessary for tuning most vehicles properly.*

Electrical multimeter

Balljoint separator

General purpose puller

Brake hold-down spring tool

Impact screwdriver

Tap and die set

Clutch plate alignment tool

Torque angle gauge

Valve spring compressor

Repair and overhaul tool set

These tools are essential for anyone who plans to perform major repairs and are in addition to those in the maintenance and minor repair tool kit. Included is a comprehensive set of sockets which, though expensive, are invaluable because of their versatility, especially when various extensions and drives are available. We recommend the 1/2-inch drive over the 3/8-inch drive. Although the larger drive is bulky and more expensive, it has the capacity of accepting a very wide range of large sockets. Ideally, however, the mechanic should have a 3/8-inch drive set and a 1/2-inch drive set.

Socket set(s)
Reversible ratchet
Extension - 10 inch
Universal joint
Torque wrench
(same size drive as sockets)
Ball peen hammer - 8 ounce
Soft-face hammer (plastic/rubber)
Standard screwdriver (1/4-inch x 6 inch)
Standard screwdriver (stubby - 5/16-inch)
Phillips screwdriver (No. 3 x 8 inch)
Phillips screwdriver (stubby - No. 2)
Pliers - vise grip

Pliers - lineman's
Pliers - needle nose
Pliers - snap-ring (internal and external)
Cold chisel (1/2-inch)
Scribe
Scraper (made from flattened
copper tubing)
Centerpunch
Pin punches (1/16, 1/8, 3/16-inch)
Steel rule/straightedge (12 inch)
Allen wrench set (1/8 to 3/8-inch or
4 mm to 10 mm)
A selection of files

Valve spring compressor

Piston ring removal and installation tool

Piston ring compressor

Cylinder hone

Piston ring groove cleaning tool

Wire brush (large)
Jackstands (second set)
Jack (scissor or hydraulic type)

Note: *Another tool which is often useful is an electric drill with a chuck capacity of 3/8-inch and a set of good quality drill bits.*

Special tools

The tools in this list include those which are not used regularly, are expensive to buy, or which need to be used in accordance with their manufacturer's instructions. Unless these tools will be used frequently, it is not very economical to purchase many of them. A consideration would be to split the cost and use between yourself and a friend or friends. In addition, most of these tools can be obtained from a tool rental shop on a temporary basis.

This list primarily contains only those tools and instruments widely available to the public, and not those special tools produced by the vehicle manufacturer for distribution to dealer service departments. Occasionally, references to the manufacturer's special tools are included in the text of this manual. Generally, an alternative method

of doing the job without the special tool is offered. However, sometimes there is no alternative to their use. Where this is the case, and the tool cannot be purchased or borrowed, the work should be turned over to the dealer service department or an automotive repair shop.

Valve spring compressor
Piston ring groove cleaning tool
Piston ring compressor
Piston ring installation tool
Cylinder compression gauge
Cylinder ridge reamer
Cylinder surfacing hone
Cylinder bore gauge
Micrometers and/or dial calipers
Hydraulic lifter removal tool
Balljoint separator
Universal-type puller
Impact screwdriver
Dial indicator set
Stroboscopic timing light (inductive pickup)
Hand operated vacuum/pressure pump
Tachometer/dwell meter
Universal electrical multimeter
Cable hoist
Brake spring removal and installation tools
Floor jack

Buying tools

For the do-it-yourselfer who is just starting to get involved in vehicle maintenance and repair, there are a number of options available when purchasing tools. If maintenance and minor repair is the extent of the work to be done, the purchase of individual tools is satisfactory. If, on the other hand, extensive work is planned, it would be a good idea to purchase a modest tool set from one of the large retail chain stores. A set can usually be bought at a substantial savings over the individual tool prices, and they often come with a tool box. As additional tools are needed, add-on sets, individual tools and a larger tool box can be purchased to expand the tool selection. Building a tool set gradually allows the cost of the tools to be spread over a longer period of time and gives the mechanic the freedom to choose only those tools that will actually be used.

Tool stores will often be the only source of some of the special tools that are needed, but regardless of where tools are bought, try to avoid cheap ones, especially when buying screwdrivers and sockets, because they won't last very long. The expense involved in replacing cheap tools will eventually be greater than the initial cost of quality tools.

Keep your tools clean and organized – you'll spend less time under the hood, and the time spent will be more pleasant

Thread repair kits like this one can be purchased at your local auto parts store

Care and maintenance of tools

Good tools are expensive, so it makes sense to treat them with respect. Keep them clean and in usable condition and store them properly when not in use. Always wipe off any dirt, grease or metal chips before putting them away. Never leave tools lying around in the work area. Upon completion of a job, always check closely under the hood for tools that may have been left there so they won't get lost during a test drive.

Some tools, such as screwdrivers, pliers, wrenches and sockets, can be hung on a panel mounted on the garage or workshop wall, while others should be kept in a tool box or tray. Measuring instruments, gauges, meters, etc. must be carefully stored where they cannot be damaged by weather or impact from other tools.

When tools are used with care and stored properly, they will last a very long time. Even with the best of care, though, tools will wear out if used frequently. When a tool is damaged or worn out, replace it. Subsequent jobs will be safer and more enjoyable if you do.

How to repair damaged threads

Sometimes, the internal threads of a nut or bolt hole can become stripped, usually from overtightening. Stripping threads is an all-too-common occurrence, especially when working with aluminum parts, because aluminum is so soft that it easily strips out.

Usually, external or internal threads are only partially stripped. After they've been cleaned up with a tap or die, they'll still work. Sometimes, however, threads are badly damaged. When this happens, you've got three choices:

1) *Drill and tap the hole to the next suitable oversize and install a larger diameter bolt, screw or stud.*
2) *Drill and tap the hole to accept a threaded plug, then drill and tap the plug to the original screw size. You can also buy a plug already threaded to the original size. Then you simply drill a hole to the specified size, then run the threaded plug into the hole with a bolt and jam nut. Once the plug is fully seated, remove the jam nut and bolt.*

3) *The third method uses a patented thread repair kit like Heli-Coil or Slimsert. These easy-to-use kits are designed to repair damaged threads in straight-through holes and blind holes. Both are available as kits which can handle a variety of sizes and thread patterns. Drill the hole, then tap it with the special included tap. Install the Heli-Coil and the hole is back to its original diameter and thread pitch.*

Regardless of which method you use, be sure to proceed calmly and carefully. A little impatience or carelessness during one of these relatively simple procedures can ruin your whole day's work and cost you a bundle if you wreck an expensive part.

Working facilities

Not to be overlooked when discussing tools is the workshop. If anything more than routine maintenance is to be carried out, some sort of suitable work area is essential.

It is understood, and appreciated, that many home mechanics do not have a good workshop or garage available, and end up removing an engine or doing major repairs outside. It is recommended, however, that the overhaul or repair be completed under the cover of a roof.

A clean, flat workbench or table of comfortable working height is an absolute necessity. The workbench should be equipped with a vise that has a jaw opening of at least four inches.

As mentioned previously, some clean, dry storage space is also required for tools, as well as the lubricants, fluids, cleaning solvents, etc. which soon become necessary.

Sometimes waste oil and fluids, drained from the engine or cooling system during normal maintenance or repairs, present a disposal problem. To avoid pouring them on the ground or into a sewage system, pour the used fluids into large containers, seal them with caps and take them to an authorized disposal site or recycling center. Plastic jugs, such as old antifreeze containers, are ideal for this purpose.

Always keep a supply of old newspapers and clean rags available. Old towels are excellent for mopping up spills. Many mechanics use rolls of paper towels for most work because they are readily available and disposable. To help keep the area under the vehicle clean, a large cardboard box can be cut open and flattened to protect the garage or shop floor.

Whenever working over a painted surface, such as when leaning over a fender to service something under the hood, always cover it with an old blanket or bedspread to protect the finish. Vinyl covered pads, made especially for this purpose, are available at auto parts stores.

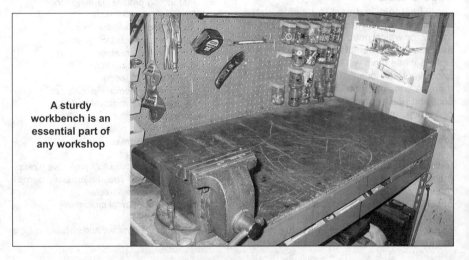

A sturdy workbench is an essential part of any workshop

Automotive chemicals and lubricants

A number of automotive chemicals and lubricants are available for use during vehicle maintenance and repair. They include a wide variety of products ranging from cleaning solvents and degreasers to lubricants and protective sprays for rubber, plastic and vinyl.

Cleaners

Carburetor cleaner and choke cleaner is a strong solvent for gum, varnish and carbon. Most carburetor cleaners leave a dry-type lubricant film which will not harden or gum up. Because of this film it is not recommended for use on electrical components.

Brake system cleaner is used to remove brake dust, grease and brake fluid from the brake system, where clean surfaces are absolutely necessary. It leaves no residue and often eliminates brake squeal caused by contaminants.

Electrical cleaner removes oxidation, corrosion and carbon deposits from electrical contacts, restoring full current flow. It can also be used to clean spark plugs, carburetor jets, voltage regulators and other parts where an oil-free surface is desired.

Demoisturants remove water and moisture from electrical components such as alternators, voltage regulators, electrical connectors and fuse blocks. They are non-conductive and non-corrosive.

Degreasers are heavy-duty solvents used to remove grease from the outside of the engine and from chassis components. They can be sprayed or brushed on and, depending on the type, are rinsed off either with water or solvent.

Lubricants

Motor oil is the lubricant formulated for use in engines. It normally contains a wide variety of additives to prevent corrosion and reduce foaming and wear. Motor oil comes in various weights (viscosity ratings) from 0 to 50. The recommended weight of the oil depends on the season, temperature and the demands on the engine. Light oil is used in cold climates and under light load conditions. Heavy oil is used in hot climates and where high loads are encountered. Multi-viscosity oils are designed to have characteristics of both light and heavy oils and are available in a number of weights from 0W-20 to 20W-50.

Gear oil is designed to be used in differentials, manual transmissions and other areas where high-temperature lubrication is required.

Chassis and wheel bearing grease is a heavy grease used where increased loads and friction are encountered, such as for wheel bearings, balljoints, tie-rod ends and universal joints.

High-temperature wheel bearing grease is designed to withstand the extreme temperatures encountered by wheel bearings in disc brake equipped vehicles. It usually contains molybdenum disulfide (moly), which is a dry-type lubricant.

White grease is a heavy grease for metal-to-metal applications where water is a problem. White grease stays soft under both low and high temperatures (usually from -100 to +190-degrees F), and will not wash off or dilute in the presence of water.

Assembly lube is a special extreme pressure lubricant, usually containing moly, used to lubricate high-load parts (such as main and rod bearings and cam lobes) for initial start-up of a new engine. The assembly lube lubricates the parts without being squeezed out or washed away until the engine oiling system begins to function.

Silicone lubricants are used to protect rubber, plastic, vinyl and nylon parts.

Graphite lubricants are used where oils cannot be used due to contamination problems, such as in locks. The dry graphite will lubricate metal parts while remaining uncontaminated by dirt, water, oil or acids. It is electrically conductive and will not foul electrical contacts in locks such as the ignition switch.

Moly penetrants loosen and lubricate frozen, rusted and corroded fasteners and prevent future rusting or freezing.

Heat-sink grease is a special electrically non-conductive grease that is used for mounting electronic ignition modules where it is essential that heat is transferred away from the module.

Sealants

RTV sealant is one of the most widely used gasket compounds. Made from silicone, RTV is air curing, it seals, bonds, waterproofs, fills surface irregularities, remains flexible, doesn't shrink, is relatively easy to remove, and is used as a supplementary sealer with almost all low and medium temperature gaskets.

Anaerobic sealant is much like RTV in that it can be used either to seal gaskets or to form gaskets by itself. It remains flexible, is solvent resistant and fills surface imperfections. The difference between an anaerobic sealant and an RTV-type sealant is in the curing. RTV cures when exposed to air, while an anaerobic sealant cures only in the absence of air. This means that an anaerobic sealant cures only after the assembly of parts, sealing them together.

Thread and pipe sealant is used for sealing hydraulic and pneumatic fittings and vacuum lines. It is usually made from a Teflon compound, and comes in a spray, a paint-on liquid and as a wrap-around tape.

Chemicals

Anti-seize compound prevents seizing, galling, cold welding, rust and corrosion in fasteners. High-temperature anti-seize, usually made with copper and graphite lubricants, is used for exhaust system and exhaust manifold bolts.

Anaerobic locking compounds are used to keep fasteners from vibrating or working loose and cure only after installation, in the absence of air. Medium strength locking compound is used for small nuts, bolts and screws that may be removed later. High-strength locking compound is for large nuts, bolts and studs which aren't removed on a regular basis.

Oil additives range from viscosity index improvers to chemical treatments that claim to reduce internal engine friction. It should be noted that most oil manufacturers caution against using additives with their oils.

Gas additives perform several functions, depending on their chemical makeup. They usually contain solvents that help dissolve gum and varnish that build up on carburetor, fuel injection and intake parts. They also serve to break down carbon deposits that form on the inside surfaces of the combustion chambers. Some additives contain upper cylinder lubricants for valves and piston rings, and others contain chemicals to remove condensation from the gas tank.

Miscellaneous

Brake fluid is specially formulated hydraulic fluid that can withstand the heat and pressure encountered in brake systems. Care must be taken so this fluid does not come in contact with painted surfaces or plastics. An opened container should always be resealed to prevent contamination by water or dirt.

Weatherstrip adhesive is used to bond weatherstripping around doors, windows and trunk lids. It is sometimes used to attach trim pieces.

Undercoating is a petroleum-based, tar-like substance that is designed to protect metal surfaces on the underside of the vehicle from corrosion. It also acts as a sound-deadening agent by insulating the bottom of the vehicle.

Waxes and polishes are used to help protect painted and plated surfaces from the weather. Different types of paint may require the use of different types of wax and polish. Some polishes utilize a chemical or abrasive cleaner to help remove the top layer of oxidized (dull) paint on older vehicles. In recent years many non-wax polishes that contain a wide variety of chemicals such as polymers and silicones have been introduced. These non-wax polishes are usually easier to apply and last longer than conventional waxes and polishes.

Jacking and towing

Warning: *The jack supplied with the vehicle should only be used for changing a tire or placing jackstands under the frame. Never work under the vehicle or start the engine while this jack is being used as the only means of support.*

Note: *Not all models are equipped with a jack and spare tire. Instead, some are equipped with a tire sealant and inflator (compressor) kit.*

The vehicle should be on level ground. Place the shift lever in Park, if you have an automatic, or Reverse if you have a manual transmission. Block the wheel diagonally opposite the wheel being changed. Set the parking brake.

Remove the spare tire and jack from stowage. Remove the wheel cover and trim ring (if so equipped) with the tapered end of the lug nut wrench by inserting and twisting the handle and then prying against the back of the wheel cover. Loosen, but do not remove, the lug nuts (one-half turn is sufficient).

Place the scissors-type jack under the vehicle and adjust the jack height until it engages with the proper jacking point on the unibody seam. There is a front and rear jacking point on each side of the vehicle (see illustration).

Turn the jack handle clockwise until the tire clears the ground. Remove the lug nuts and pull the wheel off, then install the spare.

Install the lug nuts with the beveled edges facing in. Tighten them snugly. Don't attempt to tighten them completely until

the vehicle is lowered or it could slip off the jack. Turn the jack handle counterclockwise to lower the vehicle. Remove the jack and tighten the lug nuts in a diagonal pattern.

Stow the tire, jack and wrench. Unblock the wheels.

Towing

Manual transaxle models can be towed with all four wheels on the ground, provided the following:

The shift lever is placed in Neutral.
The ignition key is turned to ACC.
Fuse nos. 22, 23, 24 and 25 are removed from the instrument panel fuse/relay box.
Towing speeds do not exceed 65 mph (105 km/h).

Automatic transaxle models must be towed with the drive (front) wheels off the ground, using either a wheel-lift tow truck or a towing dolly. A flat-bed car carrier is the preferred method.

Front and rear jacking points

Booster battery (jump) starting

Observe these precautions when using a booster battery to start a vehicle:

a) *Before connecting the booster battery, make sure the ignition switch is in the Off position.*

b) *Turn off the lights, heater and other electrical loads.*

c) *Your eyes should be shielded. Safety goggles are a good idea.*

d) *Make sure the booster battery is the same voltage as the dead one in the vehicle.*

e) *The two vehicles MUST NOT TOUCH each other!*

f) *Make sure the transaxle is in Neutral (manual) or Park (automatic).*

g) *If the booster battery is not a maintenance-free type, remove the vent caps and lay a cloth over the vent holes.*

Connect the red jumper cable to the positive (+) terminals of each vehicle (see illustrations).

Note: *On 2016 and later models, the battery is located in the trunk or rear hatch area. A remote positive terminal for jump starting is located under the hood, at the rear of the fuse/relay box* near the coolant expansion tank. A grounding lug for the negative jumper cable is located on the left (driver's side) strut tower.

Connect one end of the black jumper cable to the negative (-) terminal of the booster battery. The other end of this cable should be connected to a good ground on the vehicle to be started, such as a bolt or bracket on the body.

Start the engine using the booster battery, then, with the engine running at idle speed, disconnect the jumper cables in the reverse order of connection.

Make the booster battery connections in the numerical order shown

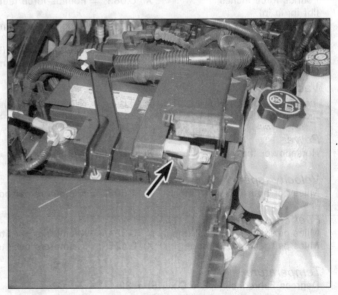

Flip up the plastic cover to access the positive terminal of the battery (2015 and earlier models)

Conversion factors

Length (distance)

Inches (in)	X	25.4	= Millimeters (mm)	X	0.0394	= Inches (in)
Feet (ft)	X	0.305	= Meters (m)	X	3.281	= Feet (ft)
Miles	X	1.609	= Kilometers (km)	X	0.621	= Miles

Volume (capacity)

Cubic inches (cu in; in³)	X	16.387	= Cubic centimeters (cc; cm³)	X	0.061	= Cubic inches (cu in; in³)
Imperial pints (Imp pt)	X	0.568	= Liters (l)	X	1.76	= Imperial pints (Imp pt)
Imperial quarts (Imp qt)	X	1.137	= Liters (l)	X	0.88	= Imperial quarts (Imp qt)
Imperial quarts (Imp qt)	X	1.201	= US quarts (US qt)	X	0.833	= Imperial quarts (Imp qt)
US quarts (US qt)	X	0.946	= Liters (l)	X	1.057	= US quarts (US qt)
Imperial gallons (Imp gal)	X	4.546	= Liters (l)	X	0.22	= Imperial gallons (Imp gal)
Imperial gallons (Imp gal)	X	1.201	= US gallons (US gal)	X	0.833	= Imperial gallons (Imp gal)
US gallons (US gal)	X	3.785	= Liters (l)	X	0.264	= US gallons (US gal)

Mass (weight)

Ounces (oz)	X	28.35	= Grams (g)	X	0.035	= Ounces (oz)
Pounds (lb)	X	0.454	= Kilograms (kg)	X	2.205	= Pounds (lb)

Force

Ounces-force (ozf; oz)	X	0.278	= Newtons (N)	X	3.6	= Ounces-force (ozf; oz)
Pounds-force (lbf; lb)	X	4.448	= Newtons (N)	X	0.225	= Pounds-force (lbf; lb)
Newtons (N)	X	0.1	= Kilograms-force (kgf; kg)	X	9.81	= Newtons (N)

Pressure

Pounds-force per square inch (psi; lbf/in²; lb/in²)	X	0.070	= Kilograms-force per square centimeter (kgf/cm²; kg/cm²)	X	14.223	= Pounds-force per square inch (psi; lbf/in²; lb/in²)
Pounds-force per square inch (psi; lbf/in²; lb/in²)	X	0.068	= Atmospheres (atm)	X	14.696	= Pounds-force per square inch (psi; lbf/in²; lb/in²)
Pounds-force per square inch (psi; lbf/in²; lb/in²)	X	0.069	= Bars	X	14.5	= Pounds-force per square inch (psi; lbf/in²; lb/in²)
Pounds-force per square inch (psi; lbf/in²; lb/in²)	X	6.895	= Kilopascals (kPa)	X	0.145	= Pounds-force per square inch (psi; lbf/in²; lb/in²)
Kilopascals (kPa)	X	0.01	= Kilograms-force per square centimeter (kgf/cm²; kg/cm²)	X	98.1	= Kilopascals (kPa)

Torque (moment of force)

Pounds-force inches (lbf in; lb in)	X	1.152	= Kilograms-force centimeter (kgf cm; kg cm)	X	0.868	= Pounds-force inches (lbf in; lb in)
Pounds-force inches (lbf in; lb in)	X	0.113	= Newton meters (Nm)	X	8.85	= Pounds-force inches (lbf in; lb in)
Pounds-force inches (lbf in; lb in)	X	0.083	= Pounds-force feet (lbf ft; lb ft)	X	12	= Pounds-force inches (lbf in; lb in)
Pounds-force feet (lbf ft; lb ft)	X	0.138	= Kilograms-force meters (kgf m; kg m)	X	7.233	= Pounds-force feet (lbf ft; lb ft)
Pounds-force feet (lbf ft; lb ft)	X	1.356	= Newton meters (Nm)	X	0.738	= Pounds-force feet (lbf ft; lb ft)
Newton meters (Nm)	X	0.102	= Kilograms-force meters (kgf m; kg m)	X	9.804	= Newton meters (Nm)

Vacuum

Inches mercury (in. Hg)	X	3.377	= Kilopascals (kPa)	X	0.2961	= Inches mercury
Inches mercury (in. Hg)	X	25.4	= Millimeters mercury (mm Hg)	X	0.0394	= Inches mercury

Power

Horsepower (hp)	X	745.7	= Watts (W)	X	0.0013	= Horsepower (hp)

Velocity (speed)

Miles per hour (miles/hr; mph)	X	1.609	= Kilometers per hour (km/hr; kph)	X	0.621	= Miles per hour (miles/hr; mph)

Fuel consumption*

Miles per gallon, Imperial (mpg)	X	0.354	= Kilometers per liter (km/l)	X	2.825	= Miles per gallon, Imperial (mpg)
Miles per gallon, US (mpg)	X	0.425	= Kilometers per liter (km/l)	X	2.352	= Miles per gallon, US (mpg)

Temperature

Degrees Fahrenheit = ($°C$ x 1.8) + 32   Degrees Celsius (Degrees Centigrade; °C) = ($°F$ - 32) x 0.56

*It is common practice to convert from miles per gallon (mpg) to liters/100 kilometers (l/100km), where mpg (Imperial) x l/100 km = 282 and mpg (US) x l/100 km = 235

DECIMALS to MILLIMETERS

Decimal	mm	Decimal	mm
0.001	0.0254	0.500	12.7000
0.002	0.0508	0.510	12.9540
0.003	0.0762	0.520	13.2080
0.004	0.1016	0.530	13.4620
0.005	0.1270	0.540	13.7160
0.006	0.1524	0.550	13.9700
0.007	0.1778	0.560	14.2240
0.008	0.2032	0.570	14.4780
0.009	0.2286	0.580	14.7320
		0.590	14.9860
0.010	0.2540		
0.020	0.5080		
0.030	0.7620		
0.040	1.0160	0.600	15.2400
0.050	1.2700	0.610	15.4940
0.060	1.5240	0.620	15.7480
0.070	1.7780	0.630	16.0020
0.080	2.0320	0.640	16.2560
0.090	2.2860	0.650	16.5100
		0.660	16.7640
0.100	2.5400	0.670	17.0180
0.110	2.7940	0.680	17.2720
0.120	3.0480	0.690	17.5260
0.130	3.3020		
0.140	3.5560		
0.150	3.8100		
0.160	4.0640	0.700	17.7800
0.170	4.3180	0.710	18.0340
0.180	4.5720	0.720	18.2880
0.190	4.8260	0.730	18.5420
		0.740	18.7960
0.200	5.0800	0.750	19.0500
0.210	5.3340	0.760	19.3040
0.220	5.5880	0.770	19.5580
0.230	5.8420	0.780	19.8120
0.240	6.0960	0.790	20.0660
0.250	6.3500		
0.260	6.6040		
0.270	6.8580	0.800	20.3200
0.280	7.1120	0.810	20.5740
0.290	7.3660	0.820	20.8280
		0.830	21.0820
0.300	7.6200	0.840	21.3360
0.310	7.8740	0.850	21.5900
0.320	8.1280	0.860	21.8440
0.330	8.3820	0.870	22.0980
0.340	8.6360	0.880	22.3520
0.350	8.8900	0.890	22.6060
0.360	9.1440		
0.370	9.3980		
0.380	9.6520		
0.390	9.9060	0.900	22.8600
0.400	10.1600	0.910	23.1140
0.410	10.4140	0.920	23.3680
0.420	10.6680	0.930	23.6220
0.430	10.9220	0.940	23.8760
0.440	11.1760	0.950	24.1300
0.450	11.4300	0.960	24.3840
0.460	11.6840	0.970	24.6380
0.470	11.9380	0.980	24.8920
0.480	12.1920	0.990	25.1460
0.490	12.4460	1.000	25.4000

FRACTIONS to DECIMALS to MILLIMETERS

Fraction	Decimal	mm	Fraction	Decimal	mm
1/64	0.0156	0.3969	33/64	0.5156	13.0969
1/32	0.0312	0.7938	17/32	0.5312	13.4938
3/64	0.0469	1.1906	35/64	0.5469	13.8906
1/16	0.0625	1.5875	9/16	0.5625	14.2875
5/64	0.0781	1.9844	37/64	0.5781	14.6844
3/32	0.0938	2.3812	19/32	0.5938	15.0812
7/64	0.1094	2.7781	39/64	0.6094	15.4781
1/8	0.1250	3.1750	5/8	0.6250	15.8750
9/64	0.1406	3.5719	41/64	0.6406	16.2719
5/32	0.1562	3.9688	21/32	0.6562	16.6688
11/64	0.1719	4.3656	43/64	0.6719	17.0656
3/16	0.1875	4.7625	11/16	0.6875	17.4625
13/64	0.2031	5.1594	45/64	0.7031	17.8594
7/32	0.2188	5.5562	23/32	0.7188	18.2562
15/64	0.2344	5.9531	47/64	0.7344	18.6531
1/4	0.2500	6.3500	3/4	0.7500	19.0500
17/64	0.2656	6.7469	49/64	0.7656	19.4469
9/32	0.2812	7.1438	25/32	0.7812	19.8438
19/64	0.2969	7.5406	51/64	0.7969	20.2406
5/16	0.3125	7.9375	13/16	0.8125	20.6375
21/64	0.3281	8.3344	53/64	0.8281	21.0344
11/32	0.3438	8.7312	27/32	0.8438	21.4312
23/64	0.3594	9.1281	55/64	0.8594	21.8281
3/8	0.3750	9.5250	7/8	0.8750	22.2250
25/64	0.3906	9.9219	57/64	0.8906	22.6219
13/32	0.4062	10.3188	29/32	0.9062	23.0188
27/64	0.4219	10.7156	59/64	0.9219	23.4156
7/16	0.4375	11.1125	15/16	0.9375	23.8125
29/64	0.4531	11.5094	61/64	0.9531	24.2094
15/32	0.4688	11.9062	31/32	0.9688	24.6062
31/64	0.4844	12.3031	63/64	0.9844	25.0031
1/2	0.5000	12.7000	1	1.0000	25.4000

Safety first!

Regardless of how enthusiastic you may be about getting on with the job at hand, take the time to ensure that your safety is not jeopardized. A moment's lack of attention can result in an accident, as can failure to observe certain simple safety precautions. The possibility of an accident will always exist, and the following points should not be considered a comprehensive list of all dangers. Rather, they are intended to make you aware of the risks and to encourage a safety conscious approach to all work you carry out on your vehicle.

Essential DOs and DON'Ts

DON'T rely on a jack when working under the vehicle. Always use approved jackstands to support the weight of the vehicle and place them under the recommended lift or support points.

DON'T attempt to loosen extremely tight fasteners (i.e. wheel lug nuts) while the vehicle is on a jack - it may fall.

DON'T start the engine without first making sure that the transmission is in Neutral (or Park where applicable) and the parking brake is set.

DON'T remove the radiator cap from a hot cooling system - let it cool or cover it with a cloth and release the pressure gradually.

DON'T attempt to drain the engine oil until you are sure it has cooled to the point that it will not burn you.

DON'T touch any part of the engine or exhaust system until it has cooled sufficiently to avoid burns.

DON'T siphon toxic liquids such as gasoline, antifreeze and brake fluid by mouth, or allow them to remain on your skin.

DON'T inhale brake lining dust - it is potentially hazardous (see *Asbestos* below).

DON'T allow spilled oil or grease to remain on the floor - wipe it up before someone slips on it.

DON'T use loose fitting wrenches or other tools which may slip and cause injury.

DON'T push on wrenches when loosening or tightening nuts or bolts. Always try to pull the wrench toward you. If the situation calls for pushing the wrench away, push with an open hand to avoid scraped knuckles if the wrench should slip.

DON'T attempt to lift a heavy component alone - get someone to help you.

DON'T rush or take unsafe shortcuts to finish a job.

DON'T allow children or animals in or around the vehicle while you are working on it.

DO wear eye protection when using power tools such as a drill, sander, bench grinder, etc. and when working under a vehicle.

DO keep loose clothing and long hair well out of the way of moving parts.

DO make sure that any hoist used has a safe working load rating adequate for the job.

DO get someone to check on you periodically when working alone on a vehicle.

DO carry out work in a logical sequence and make sure that everything is correctly assembled and tightened.

DO keep chemicals and fluids tightly capped and out of the reach of children and pets.

DO remember that your vehicle's safety affects that of yourself and others. If in doubt on any point, get professional advice.

Steering, suspension and brakes

These systems are essential to driving safety, so make sure you have a qualified shop or individual check your work. Also, compressed suspension springs can cause injury if released suddenly - be sure to use a spring compressor.

Airbags

Airbags are explosive devices that can **CAUSE** injury if they deploy while you're working on the vehicle. Follow the manufacturer's instructions to disable the airbag whenever you're working in the vicinity of airbag components.

Asbestos

Certain friction, insulating, sealing, and other products - such as brake linings, brake bands, clutch linings, torque converters, gaskets, etc. - may contain asbestos or other hazardous friction material. Extreme care must be taken to avoid inhalation of dust from such products, since it is hazardous to health. If in doubt, assume that they do contain asbestos.

Fire

Remember at all times that gasoline is highly flammable. Never smoke or have any kind of open flame around when working on a vehicle. But the risk does not end there. A spark caused by an electrical short circuit, by two metal surfaces contacting each other, or even by static electricity built up in your body under certain conditions, can ignite gasoline vapors, which in a confined space are highly explosive. Do not, under any circumstances, use gasoline for cleaning parts. Use an approved safety solvent.

Always disconnect the battery ground (-) cable at the battery before working on any part of the fuel system or electrical system. Never risk spilling fuel on a hot engine or exhaust component. It is strongly recommended that a fire extinguisher suitable for use on fuel and electrical fires be kept handy in the garage or workshop at all times. Never try to extinguish a fuel or electrical fire with water.

Fumes

Certain fumes are highly toxic and can quickly cause unconsciousness and even death if inhaled to any extent. Gasoline vapor falls into this category, as do the vapors from some cleaning solvents. Any draining or pouring of such volatile fluids should be done in a well ventilated area.

When using cleaning fluids and solvents, read the instructions on the container carefully. Never use materials from unmarked containers.

Never run the engine in an enclosed space, such as a garage. Exhaust fumes contain carbon monoxide, which is extremely poisonous. If you need to run the engine, always do so in the open air, or at least have the rear of the vehicle outside the work area.

The battery

Never create a spark or allow a bare light bulb near a battery. They normally give off a certain amount of hydrogen gas, which is highly explosive.

Always disconnect the battery ground (-) cable at the battery before working on the fuel or electrical systems.

If possible, loosen the filler caps or cover when charging the battery from an external source (this does not apply to sealed or maintenance-free batteries). Do not charge at an excessive rate or the battery may burst.

Take care when adding water to a non maintenance-free battery and when carrying a battery. The electrolyte, even when diluted, is very corrosive and should not be allowed to contact clothing or skin.

Always wear eye protection when cleaning the battery to prevent the caustic deposits from entering your eyes.

Household current

When using an electric power tool, inspection light, etc., which operates on household current, always make sure that the tool is correctly connected to its plug and that, where necessary, it is properly grounded. Do not use such items in damp conditions and, again, do not create a spark or apply excessive heat in the vicinity of fuel or fuel vapor.

Secondary ignition system voltage

A severe electric shock can result from touching certain parts of the ignition system (such as the spark plug wires) when the engine is running or being cranked, particularly if components are damp or the insulation is defective. In the case of an electronic ignition system, the secondary system voltage is much higher and could prove fatal.

Hydrofluoric acid

This extremely corrosive acid is formed when certain types of synthetic rubber, found in some O-rings, oil seals, fuel hoses, etc. are exposed to temperatures above 750-degrees F (400-degrees C). The rubber changes into a charred or sticky substance containing the acid. *Once formed, the acid remains dangerous for years. If it gets onto the skin, it may be necessary to amputate the limb concerned.*

When dealing with a vehicle which has suffered a fire, or with components salvaged from such a vehicle, wear protective gloves and discard them after use.

Troubleshooting

Contents

This section provides an easy reference guide to the more common problems which may occur during the operation of your vehicle. These problems and their possible causes are grouped under headings denoting various components or systems, such as Engine, Cooling system, etc. They also refer you to the chapter and/or section which deals with the problem.

Remember that successful troubleshooting is not a mysterious black art practiced only by professional mechanics. It is simply the result of the right knowledge combined with an intelligent, systematic approach to the problem. Always work by a process of elimination, starting with the simplest solution and working through to the most complex - and never overlook the obvious. Anyone can run the gas tank dry or leave the lights on overnight, so don't assume that you are exempt from such oversights.

Finally, always establish a clear idea of why a problem has occurred and take steps to ensure that it doesn't happen again. If the electrical system fails because of a poor connection, check the other connections in the system to make sure that they don't fail as well. If a particular fuse continues to blow, find out why - don't just replace one fuse after another. Remember, failure of a small component can often be indicative of potential failure or incorrect functioning of a more important component or system.

Engine

1 Engine will not rotate when attempting to start

1 Battery terminal connections loose or corroded (Chapter 1).
2 Battery discharged or faulty (Chapters 1 and 5).
3 Automatic transaxle not completely engaged in Park (Chapter 7A) or clutch pedal not completely depressed (Chapter 6).
4 Broken, loose or disconnected wiring in the starting circuit (Chapters 5 and 12).
5 Starter motor pinion jammed in flywheel ring gear (Chapter 5).
6 Starter solenoid faulty (Chapter 5).
7 Starter motor faulty (Chapter 5).
8 Ignition switch faulty (Chapter 12).
9 Starter pinion or flywheel teeth worn or broken (Chapter 5).

2 Engine rotates but will not start

1 Fuel tank empty.
2 Battery discharged (engine rotates slowly) (Chapter 5).
3 Battery terminal connections loose or corroded (Chapter 1).
4 Leaking fuel injector(s), faulty fuel pump, pressure regulator, etc. (Chapter 4).
5 Broken timing chain (Chapter 2A).
6 Ignition components damp or damaged (Chapter 5).
7 Worn, faulty or incorrectly-gapped spark plugs (Chapter 1).
8 Broken, loose or disconnected wiring in the starting circuit (Chapter 5).
9 Broken, loose or disconnected wires at the ignition coil or faulty coil (Chapter 5).
10 Defective crankshaft or camshaft sensor (Chapter 6).

3 Engine hard to start when cold

1 Battery discharged or low (Chapter 1).
2 Malfunctioning fuel system (Chapter 4).
3 Faulty coolant temperature sensor or intake air temperature sensor (Chapter 6).
4 Faulty ignition system (Chapter 5).

4 Engine hard to start when hot

1 Air filter clogged (Chapter 1).
2 Fuel not reaching the fuel injection rail (Chapter 4).
3 Corroded battery connections (Chapter 1).
4 Faulty coolant temperature sensor or intake air temperature sensor (Chapter 6).

5 Starter motor noisy or excessively rough in engagement

1 Pinion or flywheel gear teeth worn or broken (Chapter 5).
2 Starter motor mounting bolts loose or missing (Chapter 5).

6 Engine starts but stops immediately

1 Insufficient fuel reaching the fuel injector(s) (Chapters 1 and 4).
2 Vacuum leak at the gasket between the intake manifold/plenum and throttle body (Chapter 4).

7 Oil puddle under engine

1 Oil pan gasket and/or oil pan drain bolt washer leaking (Chapter 2A).
2 Oil pressure sending unit leaking (Chapter 2A).
3 Valve cover leaking (Chapter 2A).
4 Engine oil seals leaking (Chapter 2A).
5 Timing chain cover leaking (Chapter 2A).

8 Engine lopes while idling or idles erratically

1 Vacuum leakage (Chapters 2A and 4).
2 Leaking EGR valve (Chapter 6).
3 Air filter clogged (Chapter 1).
4 Malfunction in the fuel injection or engine control system (Chapters 4 and 6).
5 Leaking head gasket (Chapter 2A).
6 Timing chain and/or sprockets worn (Chapter 2A).
7 Camshaft lobes worn (Chapter 2A).

9 Engine misses at idle speed

1 Spark plugs worn or not gapped properly (Chapter 1).
2 Faulty coil(s) (Chapter 1).
3 Vacuum leaks (Chapter 1).
4 Uneven or low compression (Chapter 2A).
5 Problem with the fuel injection system (Chapter 4).

10 Engine misses throughout driving speed range

1 Fuel filter clogged and/or impurities in the fuel system (Chapters 1 and 4).
2 Low fuel pressure (Chapter 4).
3 Faulty or incorrectly gapped spark plugs (Chapter 1).
4 Faulty engine management system components (Chapter 6).
5 Low or uneven cylinder compression pressures (Chapter 2A).
6 Weak or faulty ignition system (Chapter 5).
7 Vacuum leak in fuel injection system, intake manifold, air control valve or vacuum hoses (Chapters 4 and 6).

11 Engine stumbles on acceleration

1 Spark plugs fouled (Chapter 1).
2 Problem with fuel injection or engine control system (Chapters 4 and 6).
3 Fuel filter clogged (Chapters 1 and 4).
4 Intake manifold air leak (Chapters 2A and 4).
5 Problem with the emissions control system (Chapter 6).

12 Engine surges while holding accelerator steady

1 Intake air leak (Chapter 4).
2 Fuel pump or fuel pressure regulator faulty (Chapter 4).
3 Problem with the fuel injection system (Chapter 4).
4 Problem with the emissions control system (Chapter 6).

13 Engine stalls

1 Idle speed incorrect (Chapter 1).
2 Fuel filter clogged and/or water and impurities in the fuel system (Chapters 1 and 4).
3 Faulty emissions system components (Chapter 6).
4 Faulty or incorrectly gapped spark plugs (Chapter 1).
5 Vacuum leak in the fuel injection system, intake manifold or vacuum hoses (Chapters 2A and 4).

14 Engine lacks power

1 Obstructed exhaust system (Chapter 4).
2 Faulty or incorrectly gapped spark plugs (Chapter 1).
3 Problem with the fuel injection system (Chapter 4).
4 Dirty air filter (Chapter 1).
5 Brakes binding (Chapter 9).
6 Automatic transaxle fluid level incorrect (Chapter 1).
7 Clutch slipping (Chapter 8).
8 Fuel filter clogged and/or impurities in the fuel system (Chapters 1 and 4).
9 Emission control system not functioning properly (Chapter 6).
10 Low or uneven cylinder compression pressures (Chapter 2A).

15 Engine backfires

1 Emission control system not functioning properly (Chapter 6).
2 Problem with the fuel injection system (Chapter 4).
3 Vacuum leak at fuel injector(s), intake manifold or vacuum hoses (Chapters 2A and 4).
4 Valve sticking (Chapter 2A).

16 Pinging or knocking engine sounds during acceleration or uphill

1 Incorrect grade of fuel.
2 Fuel injection system faulty (Chapter 4).
3 Improper or damaged spark plugs or wires (Chapter 1).
4 Knock sensor defective (Chapter 6).
5 EGR valve not functioning (Chapter 6).
6 Vacuum leak (Chapters 2A and 4).

17 Engine runs with oil pressure light on

1 Low oil level (Chapter 1).
2 Idle rpm below specification (Chapter 1).
3 Short in wiring circuit (Chapter 12).
4 Faulty oil pressure sender (Chapter 2A).

5 Worn engine bearings and/or oil pump (Chapter 2A).

18 Engine continues to run after switching off

1 Defective ignition switch (Chapter 12).
2 Faulty Powertrain Control Module (Chapter 6).
3 Faulty Body Control Module.
4 Leaking fuel injector (Chapter 4).

Engine electrical systems

19 Battery will not hold a charge

1 Drivebelt or tensioner defective (Chapter 1).
2 Battery electrolyte level low (Chapter 1).
3 Battery terminals loose or corroded (Chapter 1).
4 Alternator not charging properly (Chapter 5).
5 Loose, broken or faulty wiring in the charging circuit (Chapter 5).
6 Short in vehicle wiring (Chapter 12).
7 Internally defective battery (Chapters 1 and 5).

20 Alternator light fails to go out

1 Faulty alternator or charging circuit (Chapter 5).
2 Drivebelt or tensioner defective (Chapter 1).

21 Alternator light fails to come on when key is turned on

1 Instrument cluster defective (Chapter 12).
2 Fault in the wiring harness (Chapter 12).

Fuel system

22 Excessive fuel consumption

1 Dirty air filter element (Chapter 1).
2 Emissions system not functioning properly (Chapter 6).
3 Fuel injection system not functioning properly (Chapter 4).
4 Low tire pressure or incorrect tire size (Chapter 1).

23 Fuel leakage and/or fuel odor

1 Leaking fuel line (Chapters 1 and 4).
2 Tank overfilled.

3 Evaporative emissions control system problem (Chapters 1 and 6).
4 Problem with the fuel injection system (Chapter 4).

Cooling system

24 Overheating

1 Insufficient coolant in system (Chapter 1).
2 Water pump drivebelt defective or out of adjustment (Chapter 1).
3 Radiator core blocked or grille restricted (Chapter 3).
4 Thermostat faulty (Chapter 3).
5 Electric cooling fan inoperative or blades broken (Chapter 3).
6 Expansion tank cap not maintaining proper pressure (Chapter 3).

25 Overcooling

1 Faulty thermostat (Chapter 3).
2 Inaccurate temperature gauge sending unit (Chapter 3).

26 External coolant leakage

1 Deteriorated/damaged hoses; loose clamps (Chapters 1 and 3).
2 Water pump defective (Chapter 3).
3 Leakage from radiator core or coolant expansion tank (Chapter 3).
4 Engine drain or water jacket core plugs leaking (Chapter 2A).

27 Internal coolant leakage

1 Leaking cylinder head gasket (Chapter 2A).
2 Cracked cylinder bore or cylinder head (Chapter 2A).

28 Coolant loss

1 Too much coolant in reservoir (Chapter 1).
2 Coolant boiling away because of overheating (Chapter 3).
3 Internal or external leakage (Chapter 3).
4 Faulty radiator cap (Chapter 3).

29 Poor coolant circulation

1 Inoperative water pump (Chapter 3).
2 Restriction in cooling system (Chapters 1 and 3).
3 Drivebelt or tensioner defective (Chapter 1).
4 Thermostat sticking (Chapter 3).

Clutch

30 Pedal travels to floor - no pressure or very little resistance

1 Master or release cylinder faulty (Chapter 8).
2 Hose/pipe burst or leaking (Chapter 8).
3 Connections leaking (Chapter 8).
4 No fluid in reservoir (Chapter 8).
5 If fluid level in reservoir rises as pedal is depressed, master cylinder center valve seal is faulty (Chapter 8).
6 Broken release bearing or fork (Chapter 8).
7 Faulty pressure plate diaphragm spring (Chapter 8).

31 Fluid in area of master cylinder dust cover and on pedal

Piston primary seal failure in master cylinder (Chapter 8).

32 Fluid on release cylinder

Release cylinder plunger seal faulty (Chapter 8).

33 Pedal feels spongy when depressed

Air in system (Chapter 8).

34 Unable to select gears

1 Faulty transaxle (Chapter 7A).
2 Faulty clutch disc or pressure plate (Chapter 8).
3 Faulty release lever or release bearing (Chapter 8).
4 Faulty shift lever assembly or control cables (Chapter 8).

35 Clutch slips (engine speed increases with no increase in vehicle speed)

1 Clutch plate worn (Chapter 8).
2 Clutch plate is oil soaked by leaking rear main seal (Chapters 2A and 8).
3 Clutch plate not seated (Chapter 8).
4 Warped pressure plate or flywheel (Chapter 8).
5 Weak diaphragm springs (Chapter 8).
6 Clutch plate overheated. Allow to cool.

36 Grabbing (chattering) as clutch is engaged

1 Oil on clutch plate lining, burned or glazed facings (Chapter 8).
2 Worn or loose engine or transaxle mounts (Chapter 2A).
3 Worn splines on clutch plate hub (Chapter 8).
4 Warped pressure plate or flywheel (Chapter 8).
5 Burned or smeared resin on flywheel or pressure plate (Chapter 8).

37 Transaxle rattling (clicking)

1 Release lever loose (Chapter 8).
2 Clutch plate damper spring failure (Chapter 8).

38 Noise in clutch area

1 Fork shaft improperly installed (Chapter 8).
2 Faulty bearing (Chapter 8).

39 Clutch pedal stays on floor

1 Clutch master cylinder piston binding in bore (Chapter 8).
2 Broken release bearing or fork (Chapter 8).

40 High pedal effort

1 Piston binding in bore (Chapter 8).
2 Pressure plate faulty (Chapter 8).
3 Incorrect size master or release cylinder (Chapter 8).

Manual transaxle

41 Knocking noise at low speeds

Worn input shaft bearing (Chapter 7A).*

42 Noise most pronounced when turning

Rear differential gear noise (Chapter 10).*

43 Clunk on acceleration or deceleration

1 Loose engine or transaxle mounts (Chapter 2A).

2 Worn differential pinion shaft in case.*
3 Worn side gear shaft counterbore in rear differential case (Chapter 10).*

44 Clicking noise in turns

Worn or damaged outboard CV joint (Chapter 8).

45 Vibration

1 Rough wheel bearing (Chapter 10).
2 Damaged driveshaft (Chapter 8).
3 Out-of-round tires (Chapter 1).
4 Tire out of balance (Chapters 1 and 10).
5 Worn driveshaft joints (Chapter 8).

46 Noisy in neutral with engine running

1 Damaged input gear bearing (Chapter 7A).*
2 Damaged clutch release bearing (Chapter 8).

47 Noisy in one particular gear

1 Damaged or worn constant mesh gears (Chapter 7A).*
2 Damaged or worn synchronizers (Chapter 7A).*
3 Bent reverse fork (Chapter 7A).*
4 Damaged fourth/fifth speed gear or output gear (Chapter 7A).*
5 Worn or damaged reverse idler gear or idler bushing (Chapter 7A).*

48 Noisy in all gears

1 Insufficient lubricant (Chapter 7A).
2 Damaged or worn bearings (Chapter 7A).*
3 Worn or damaged input gear shaft and/or output gear shaft (Chapter 7A).*

49 Slips out of gear

1 Worn or improperly adjusted linkage (Chapter 7A).
2 Shift linkage does not work freely, binds (Chapter 7A).
3 Input gear bearing retainer broken or loose (Chapter 7A).*
4 Worn or bent shift fork (Chapter 7A).*

50   Leaks lubricant

1   Side gear shaft seals worn (Chapter 7A).
2   Excessive amount of lubricant in transaxle (Chapters 1 and 7A).
3   Loose or broken input gear shaft bearing retainer (Chapter 7A).*
4   Input gear bearing retainer O-ring and/or lip seal damaged (Chapter 7A).*

51   Locked in gear

1   Lock pin or interlock pin missing (Chapter 7A).*
2   * Although the corrective action necessary to remedy the symptoms described is beyond the scope of this manual, the above information should be helpful in isolating the cause of the condition so that the owner can communicate clearly with a professional mechanic.

Automatic transaxle

52   Fluid leakage

1   Automatic transmission fluid is a deep red color. Fluid leaks should not be confused with engine oil, which can easily be blown onto the transaxle by air flow.
2   To pinpoint a leak, first remove all built-up dirt and grime from the transaxle housing with degreasing agents and/or steam cleaning. Then drive the vehicle at low speeds so air flow will not blow the leak far from its source. Raise the vehicle and determine where the leak is coming from. Common areas of leakage are:
    Transaxle oil lines (Chapter 7A).
    Speed sensor (Chapter 6).
    Driveaxle oil seal (Chapter 7A).

53   Transmission fluid brown or has a burned smell

    Transmission fluid overheated (Chapter 1).

54   General shift mechanism problems

1   Chapter 7A , Part B, deals with checking and adjusting the shift linkage on automatic transaxles. Common problems which may be attributed to poorly adjusted linkage are:
    Engine starting in gears other than Park or Neutral.
    Indicator on shifter pointing to a gear other than the one actually being used.
    Vehicle moves when in Park.
2   Refer to Chapter 7B for the shift linkage adjustment procedure.

55   Transaxle slips, shifts roughly, is noisy or has no drive in forward or reverse gears

    There are many probable causes for the above problems, but the home mechanic should be concerned with only one possibility - fluid level. Before taking the vehicle to a repair shop, check the level and condition of the fluid as described in Chapter 1. Correct the fluid level as necessary or change the fluid and filter if needed. If the problem persists, have a professional diagnose the cause.

Driveaxles

56   Clicking noise in turns

    Worn or damaged outboard CV joint (Chapter 8).

57   Shudder or vibration during acceleration

1   Excessive toe-in (Chapter 10).
2   Worn or damaged inboard or outboard CV joints (Chapter 8).
3   Sticking inboard CV joint assembly (Chapter 8).

58   Vibration at highway speeds

1   Out-of-balance front wheels and/or tires (Chapters 1 and 10).
2   Out-of-round front tires (Chapters 1 and 10).
3   Worn CV joint(s) (Chapter 8).

Brakes

59   Vehicle pulls to one side during braking

1   Incorrect tire pressures (Chapter 1).
2   Front end out of alignment (have the front end aligned).
3   Front, or rear, tire sizes not matched to one another.
4   Restricted brake lines or hoses (Chapter 9).
5   Malfunctioning caliper assembly (Chapter 9).
6   Loose suspension parts (Chapter 10).
7   Excessive wear of pad material or disc on one side (Chapter 9).
8   Contamination (grease or brake fluid) of brake pad material or disc on one side (Chapter 9).

60   Noise (high-pitched squeal or grinding when the brakes are applied)

    Brake pads or shoes worn out. Replace pads or shoes with new ones immediately. Also inspect the discs/drums (Chapter 9).

61   Brake roughness or chatter (pedal pulsates)

1   Excessive lateral runout (Chapter 9).
2   Uneven pad wear (Chapter 9).
3   Defective disc (Chapter 9).

62   Excessive brake pedal effort required to stop vehicle

1   Malfunctioning power brake booster (Chapter 9).
2   Malfunctioning vacuum pump (Ch 9 apter)
3   Partial system failure (Chapter 9).
4   Excessively worn pads (Chapter 9).
5   Piston in caliper stuck or sluggish (Chapter 9).
6   Brake pads contaminated with oil or grease (Chapter 9).
7   Brake disc grooved and/or glazed (Chapter 9).

63   Excessive brake pedal travel

1   Partial brake system failure (Chapter 9).
2   Insufficient fluid in master cylinder (Chapters 1 and 9).
3   Air trapped in system (Chapter 9).

64   Dragging brakes

1   Incorrect adjustment of brake light switch (Chapter 9).
2   Master cylinder pistons not returning correctly (Chapter 9).
3   Caliper piston stuck (Chapter 9).
4   Restricted brakes lines or hoses (Chapter 9).
5   Incorrect parking brake adjustment (Chapter 9).

65   Grabbing or uneven braking action

1   Malfunction of proportioning valve (Chapter 9).
2   Binding brake pedal mechanism (Chapter 9).
3   Contaminated brake linings (Chapter 9).

66 Brake pedal feels spongy when depressed

1   Air in hydraulic lines (Chapter 9).
2   Master cylinder mounting bolts loose (Chapter 9).
3   Master cylinder defective (Chapter 9).

67 Brake pedal travels to the floor with little resistance

1   Little or no fluid in the master cylinder reservoir caused by leaking caliper piston(s) or wheel cylinder(s) (Chapter 9).
2   Loose, damaged or disconnected brake lines (Chapter 9).

68 Parking brake does not hold

Parking brake improperly adjusted (Chapter 9).

Suspension and steering systems

69 Vehicle pulls to one side

1   Mismatched or uneven tires (Chapter 10).
2   Broken or sagging springs (Chapter 10).
3   Wheel alignment incorrect. Have the wheels professionally aligned.
4   Front brake dragging (Chapter 9).

70 Abnormal or excessive tire wear

1   Wheel alignment out-of-specification. Have the wheels aligned.
2   Sagging or broken springs (Chapter 10).
3   Tire out-of-balance (Chapter 10).
4   Worn strut damper or shock absorber (Chapter 10).
5   Overloaded vehicle.
6   Tires not rotated regularly.

71 Wheel makes a thumping noise

1   Blister or bump on tire (Chapter 10).
2   Improper strut damper action (Chapter 10).

72 Shimmy, shake or vibration

1   Tire or wheel out-of-balance or out-of-round (Chapter 10).
2   Loose or worn wheel bearings (Chapter 10).
3   Worn tie-rod ends (Chapter 10).
4   Worn balljoints (Chapters 1 and 10).
5   Excessive wheel runout (Chapter 10).
6   Blister or bump on tire (Chapter 10).

73 Hard steering

1   Worn balljoints and/or tie-rod ends (Chapter 10).
2   Wheel alignment out-of-specifications. Have the wheels professionally aligned.
3   Low tire pressure(s) (Chapter 1).
4   Worn steering gear (Chapter 10).

74 Poor returnability of steering to center

1   Worn balljoints or tie-rod ends (Chapter 10).
2   Worn steering gear assembly (Chapter 10).
3   Wheel alignment out-of-specifications. Have the wheels professionally aligned.

75 Abnormal noise at the front end

1   Worn balljoints or tie-rod ends (Chapter 10).
2   Damaged shock absorber mounting (Chapter 10).
3   Worn control arm bushings or tie-rod ends (Chapter 10).
4   Loose stabilizer bar (Chapter 10).
5   Loose wheel nuts (Chapter 1).
6   Loose suspension bolts (Chapter 10).

76 Wander or poor steering stability

1   Mismatched or uneven tires (Chapter 10).
2   Worn balljoints or tie-rod ends (Chapters 1 and 10).
3   Worn struts or shock absorbers (Chapter 10).
4   Broken or sagging springs (Chapter 10).
5   Wheels out of alignment. Have the wheels professionally aligned.

77 Erratic steering when braking

1   Wheel bearings worn (Chapter 10).
2   Broken or sagging springs (Chapter 10).
3   Leaking wheel cylinder or caliper (Chapter 10).
4   Excessive brake disc runout (Chapter 9).

78 Excessive pitching and/or rolling around corners or during braking

1   Loose stabilizer bar or worn stabilizer bar bushings (Chapter 10).
2   Worn strut dampers or mountings (Chapter 10).
3   Broken or sagging springs (Chapter 10).
4   Overloaded vehicle.

79 Suspension bottoms

1   Overloaded vehicle.
2   Sagging springs (Chapter 10).

80 Cupped tires

1   Wheel alignment out-of-specifications. Have the wheels professionally aligned.
2   Worn shock absorbers (Chapter 10).
3   Wheel bearings worn (Chapter 10).
4   Excessive tire or wheel runout (Chapter 10).
5   Worn balljoints (Chapter 10).

81 Excessive tire wear on outside edge

1   Inflation pressures incorrect (Chapter 1).
2   Excessive speed in turns.
3   Wheel alignment incorrect (excessive toe-in). Have professionally aligned.
4   Suspension arm bent or twisted (Chapter 10).

82 Excessive tire wear on inside edge

1   Inflation pressures incorrect (Chapter 1).
2   Wheel alignment incorrect (toe-out). Have professionally aligned.
3   Loose or damaged steering components (Chapter 10).

83 Tire tread worn in one place

1   Tires out-of-balance.
2   Damaged or buckled wheel. Inspect and replace if necessary.
3   Defective tire (Chapter 1).

84 Excessive play or looseness in steering system

1   Wheel bearing(s) worn (Chapter 10).
2   Tie-rod end loose (Chapter 10).
3   Steering gear loose (Chapter 10).
4   Worn or loose steering intermediate shaft U-joint (Chapter 10).

85 Rattling or clicking noise in steering gear

1   Steering gear loose (Chapter 10).
2   Steering gear defective.

Chapter 1
Tune-up and routine maintenance

Contents

Specifications

Recommended lubricants and fluids

Note: *Listed here are manufacturer recommendations at the time this manual was written. Manufacturers occasionally upgrade their fluid and lubricant specifications, so check with your local auto parts store for current recommendations.*

Engine oil
    Type   API "certified for gasoline engines" (dexos 1 certification)
    Viscosity

1.4L (turbocharged) engine	SAE-5W-30
1.8L (non-turbocharged) engine	SAE 0W-30, 0W-40, 5W-30 and 5W-40
Fuel	Unleaded gasoline, 87 octane minimum
Automatic transaxle fluid	DEXRON VI automatic transmission fluid
M32, manual transaxle lubricant	
2011 models	Castrol BOT 402 (SAE 75W-85)
2012 and later models	Castrol BOT 303 (SAE 70W)
Brake fluid	DOT 3 brake fluid
Clutch fluid	DOT 3 brake fluid
Engine coolant	50/50 mixture of DEX-COOL coolant and de-ionized water

Capacities*

Engine oil (including filter)	
1.4L engine	4.25 quarts (4.0 liters)
1.8L engine	
2011 and 2012 models	4.5 quarts (4.76 liters)
2013 and later models	4.25 quarts (4.0 liters)
Coolant	
2012 and earlier models	
1.4L engine	7.5 quarts (7.1 liters)
1.8L engine	7.2 quarts (6.8 liters)
2013 and 2014 models	
1.4L engine	6.6 quarts (6.2 liters)
1.8L engine	6.6 quarts (6.2 liters)
2015 models	
1.4L engine	6.6 quarts (6.2 liters)
1.8L engine	5.92 quarts (5.6 liters)
2016 1.4L engine	5.5 quarts (5.2 liters)
2017 and later 1.4L engine	6.3 quarts (6.0 liters)
Automatic transmission (drain and refill)	4.2 to 6.3 quarts (4.0 to 6.0 liters)
Manual transaxle	1.9 quarts (1.8 liters)

Note: *All capacities approximate. Add as necessary to bring up to appropriate level.*

Ignition system

Spark plug type and gap	
Type	
1.4L engine	
2015 and earlier models.................	AC 41-121 or equivalent
2016 and later models...................	AC 41-103 or equivalent
1.8L engine	AC 41122 or equivalent
Gap	0.028 inch (0.70 mm)
Engine firing order, all models	1-3-4-2

FRONT OF VEHICLE

1-3-4-2

Cylinder locations and firing order

Brakes

Disc brake pad lining thickness (minimum)	1/8 inch (3 mm)
Drum brake shoe lining thickness (minimum)........................	1/16 inch (1.5 mm)
Parking brake adjustment...	3 to 4 clicks

Torque specifications

	Ft-lbs (unless otherwise indicated)	Nm

Note: *One foot pound (ft-lb) of torque is equivalent to 12 inch-pounds (in-lbs) of torque. Torque values below approximately 15 ft-lbs are expressed in inch-pounds, since most foot-pound torque wrenches are not accurate at these smaller values.*

	Ft-lbs	Nm
Engine oil drain plug		
2015 and earlier models.....................	124 in-lbs	14
2016 and later models........................	18	25
Engine oil filter cap (2015 and earlier models)	18	25
Automatic transaxle fluid drain and check plug	106 in-lbs	12
Manual transaxle plugs		
Drain plug..	15	20
Fill plug...	22	30
Spark plugs		
2015 and earlier models.....................	18	25
2016 and later models........................	156 in-lbs	17
Drivebelt tensioner bolt		
1.4L engine		
2015 and earlier models		
M8 bolt..................................	16	22
M10 bolt................................	41	55
2016 and later models	43	58
1.8L engine	41	55
Wheel lug nuts...	103	140

Engine compartment layout (2013 1.4L engine shown, others similar)

1	Engine oil dipstick	5	Windshield washer fluid reservoir	8	Engine coolant expansion tank
2	Engine oil filler cap	6	Underhood fuse/relay block	9	Brake fluid reservoir
3	Engine oil filter cap	7	Battery fuse/relay block	10	Air filter housing
4	Battery				

Under vehicle engine compartment layout (2013 1.4L engine shown, others similar)

1	Engine oil pan drain plug	4	Steering gear boot	7	Strut and coil spring assembly
2	Drivebelt	5	Brake disc	8	Front disc brake caliper
3	Driveaxle inner boot	6	Driveaxle outer boot	9	Transaxle drain plug

Typical rear underside components

1	Fuel tank	3	Coil spring	5	Rear disc brake caliper
2	Muffler	4	Shock absorber		

1 Maintenance schedule

The maintenance intervals in this manual are provided with the assumption that you, not the dealer, will be doing the work. These are the minimum maintenance intervals recommended by the factory for vehicles that are driven daily. If you wish to keep your vehicle in peak condition at all times, you may wish to perform some of these procedures even more often. Because frequent maintenance enhances the efficiency, performance and resale value of your car, we encourage you to do so. If you drive in dusty areas, tow a trailer, idle or drive at low speeds for extended periods or drive for short distances (less than four miles) in below freezing temperatures, shorter intervals are also recommended.

When your vehicle is new, it should be serviced by a factory authorized dealer service department to protect the factory warranty. In many cases, the initial maintenance check is done at no cost to the owner.

Every 250 miles (400 km) or weekly, whichever comes first

Check the engine oil level (Section 4)
Check the engine coolant level (Section 4)
Check the brake and clutch fluid level (Section 4)
Check the windshield washer fluid level (Section 4)
Check the power steering fluid level (Section 4)
Check the tires and tire pressures (Section 5)

Every 3000 miles (4800 km) or 3 months, whichever comes first

All items listed above plus:
Change the engine oil and oil filter (Section 6)

Every 6000 miles (10,000 km) or 6 months, whichever comes first

All items listed above plus:
Inspect (and replace, if necessary) the windshield wiper blades (Section 7)
Check and service the battery (Section 8)
Check the cooling system (Section 9)
Rotate the tires (Section 10)
Check the seat belts (Section 11)
Inspect the brake system (Section 12)

Every 15,000 miles (24,000 km) or 12 months, whichever comes first

All items listed above plus:
Replace the interior ventilation filter (Section 13)
Check all underhood hoses (Section 14)
Inspect the suspension, steering components and driveaxle boots (Section 15)
Check the exhaust system (Section 16)
Check the fuel system (Section 17)
Check the engine drivebelts (Section 18)

Every 30,000 miles (48,000 km) or 24 months, whichever comes first

All items listed above plus:
Check (and replace, if necessary) the air filter (Section 19)*
Service the cooling system (drain, flush and refill) (Section 20)
Change the brake fluid (Section 21)

Every 97,500 miles (156,000 km)

Replace the timing belt (1.8L engine; see Chapter 2A)

Every 100,000 miles (166,000 km)

Replace the automatic transaxle fluid (Section 22)**
Replace the manual transaxle lubricant (Section 23)
Replace the spark plugs (Section 24)

*This item is affected by "severe" operating conditions as described below. If your vehicle is operated under "severe" conditions, perform all maintenance indicated with an asterisk (*) at 3000 mile/3 month intervals. Severe conditions are indicated if you mainly operate your vehicle under one or more of the following conditions:
  a) Operating in dusty areas
  b) Towing a trailer
  c) Idling for extended periods and/or low speed operation

** If operated under one or more of the following conditions, change the manual or automatic transaxle fluid lubricant every 50,000 miles:
  a) In heavy city traffic where the outside temperature regularly reaches 90-degrees F (32-degrees C) or higher
  b) In hilly or mountainous terrain
  c) Frequent towing of a trailer

2 Introduction

1   This Chapter is designed to help the home mechanic maintain the Chevrolet Cruze with the goals of maximum performance, economy, safety and reliability in mind.

2   Included is a master maintenance schedule, followed by procedures dealing specifically with each item on the schedule. Visual checks, adjustments, component replacement and other helpful items are included. Refer to the accompanying illustrations of the engine compartment and under the vehicle, for the locations of various components.

3   Servicing the vehicle, in accordance with the mileage/time maintenance schedule and the step-by-step procedures will result in a planned maintenance program that should produce a long and reliable service life. Keep in mind that it is a comprehensive plan, so maintaining some items but not others at the specified intervals will not produce the same results.

4   As you service the vehicle, you will discover that many of the procedures can - and should - be grouped together because of the nature of the particular procedure you're performing or because of the close proximity of two otherwise unrelated components to one another.

5   For example, if the vehicle is raised for chassis lubrication, you should inspect the exhaust, suspension, steering and fuel systems while you're under the vehicle. When you're rotating the tires, it makes good sense to check the brakes since the wheels are already removed. Finally, let's suppose you have to borrow or rent a torque wrench. Even if you only need it to tighten the spark plugs, you might as well check the torque of as many critical fasteners as time allows.

6   The first step in this maintenance program is to prepare yourself before the actual work begins. Read through all the procedures you're planning to do, then gather up all the parts and tools needed. If it looks like you might run into problems during a particular job, seek advice from a mechanic or an experienced do-it-yourselfer.

Owner's Manual and VECI label information

7   Your vehicle owner's manual was written for your year and model and contains very specific information on component locations, specifications, fuse ratings, part numbers, etc. The Owner's Manual is an important resource for the do-it-yourselfer to have; if one was not supplied with your vehicle, it can generally be ordered from a dealer parts department.

8   Among other important information, the Vehicle Emissions Control Information (VECI) label contains specifications and procedures for applicable tune-up adjustments and, in some instances, spark plugs (see Chapter 6 for more information on the VECI label). The information on this label is the exact maintenance data recommended by the manufac-

turer. This data often varies by intended operating altitude, local emissions regulations, month of manufacture, etc.

9   This Chapter contains procedural details, safety information and more ambitious maintenance intervals than you might find in manufacturer's literature. However, you may also find procedures or specifications in your Owner's Manual or VECI label that differ with what's printed here. In these cases, the Owner's Manual or VECI label can be considered correct, since it is specific to your particular vehicle.

3 Tune-up general information

1   The term tune-up is used in this manual to represent a combination of individual operations rather than one specific procedure.

2   If, from the time the vehicle is new, the routine maintenance schedule is followed closely and frequent checks are made of fluid levels and high wear items, as suggested throughout this manual, the engine will be kept in relatively good running condition and the need for additional work will be minimized.

3   More likely than not, however, there will be times when the engine is running poorly due to lack of regular maintenance. This is even more likely if a used vehicle, which has not received regular and frequent maintenance checks, is purchased. In such cases, an engine tune-up will be needed outside of the regular routine maintenance intervals.

4   The first step in any tune-up or diagnostic procedure to help correct a poor running engine is a cylinder compression check. A compression check (see Chapter 2B) will help determine the condition of internal engine components and should be used as a guide for tune-up and repair procedures. If, for instance, a compression check indicates serious internal engine wear, a conventional tune-up will not improve the performance of the engine and would be a waste of time and money. Because of its importance, the compression check should be done by someone

with the right equipment and the knowledge to use it properly.

5   The following procedures are those most often needed to bring a generally poor running engine back into a proper state of tune.

Minor tune-up

Check all engine related fluids (Section 4)
Clean, inspect and test the battery (Section 8)
Check the cooling system (Section 9)
Check all underhood hoses (Section 14)
Check the fuel system (Section 17)
Check the drivebelt (Section 18)
Check the air filter (Section 19)

Major tune-up

Replace the air filter (Section 19)
Replace the spark plugs (Section 24)

4 Fluid level checks (every 250 miles [400 km] or weekly)

1   Fluids are an essential part of the lubrication, cooling, brake and windshield washer systems. Because the fluids gradually become depleted and/or contaminated during normal operation of the vehicle, they must be periodically replenished. See Recommended lubricants and fluids in this Chapter's Specifications before adding fluid to any of the following components.

Note: *The vehicle must be on level ground when fluid levels are checked.*

Engine oil

2   The oil level is checked with a dipstick, which extends down into the oil pan (see illustration).

3   The oil level should be checked before the vehicle has been driven, or about 5 minutes after the engine has been shut off. If the oil is checked immediately after driving the vehicle, some of the oil will remain in the upper part of the engine, resulting in an inaccurate reading on the dipstick.

4   Pull the dipstick out and wipe all the oil from the end with a clean rag or paper

4.2 The engine oil dipstick is located on the forward side of the engine (1.4L shown)

4.4 The oil level should be in the safe range - if it's below the MIN or ADD area (A), add enough oil to bring it up to or near the MAX or FULL area (B)

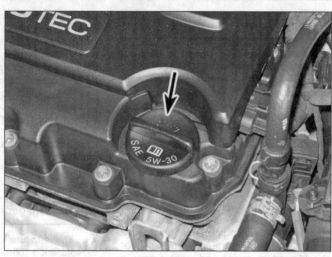

4.6 The oil filler cap is located on the valve cover - always make sure the area around the opening is clean before unscrewing the cap to prevent dirt from contaminating the engine

4.8 The coolant expansion tank is located at the rear of the engine compartment

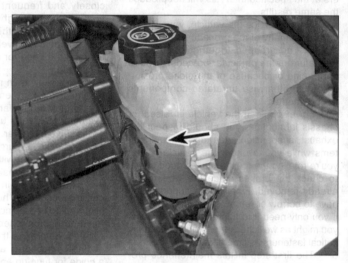

4.9 When the engine is cold, the engine coolant level should be at the Fill line

towel. Insert the clean dipstick all the way back in and pull it out again. Note the oil at the end of the dipstick. At its highest point, the level should be between the MIN and MAX marks on the dipstick (see illustration).

5   It takes one quart of oil to raise the level from the MIN mark to the MAX mark on the dipstick. Do not allow the level to drop below the MIN mark or oil starvation may cause engine damage. Conversely, overfilling the engine (adding oil above the MAX mark) may cause oil fouled spark plugs, oil leaks or oil seal failures. Maintaining the oil level above the MAX mark can cause excessive oil consumption.

6   To add oil, remove the filler cap from the valve cover (see illustration). After adding oil, wait a few minutes to allow the level to stabilize, then pull out the dipstick and check the level again. Add more oil if required. Install the filler cap and tighten it by hand only.

7   Checking the oil level is an important preventive maintenance step. A consistently low oil level indicates oil leakage through damaged seals, defective gaskets or past worn rings or valve guides. If the oil looks milky in color or has water droplets in it, the cylinder head gasket(s) may be blown or the head(s) or block may be cracked. The engine should be checked immediately. The condition of the oil should also be checked. Whenever you check the oil level, slide your thumb and index finger up the dipstick before wiping off the oil. If you see small dirt or metal particles clinging to the dipstick, the oil should be changed (see Section 6).

Engine coolant

Warning: *Do not allow antifreeze to come in contact with your skin or painted surfaces of the vehicle. Flush contaminated areas immediately with plenty of water. Don't store new coolant or leave old coolant lying around where it's ac-*

cessible to children or pets - they're attracted by its sweet smell. Ingestion of even a small amount of coolant can be fatal! Wipe up garage floor and drip pan spills immediately. Keep antifreeze containers covered and repair cooling system leaks as soon as they're noticed.

Warning: *Do not remove the expansion tank cap when the engine is warm!*

8   All models covered by this manual are equipped with a pressurized coolant recovery system. The coolant expansion tank is located at the left rear of the engine compartment and is connected by hoses to the cooling system (see illustration). As the engine heats up during operation, the level in the tank rises.

9   The coolant level should be checked regularly. It must be at the COLD FILL line on the tank when the engine is cold (see illustration). If it isn't, allow the fluid in the tank to cool, then remove the cap from the reservoir and add coolant to bring the level up to the line. Use only the type of coolant listed in this

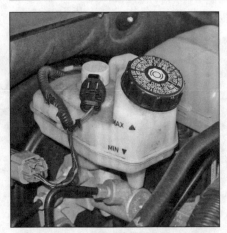

4.14 The brake fluid level should be kept between the MIN and MAX marks on the translucent plastic reservoir; with manual transaxles, the brake fluid reservoir is connected to the clutch master cylinder by a hose

4.21 The windshield washer fluid reservoir is located in the left front corner of the engine compartment

5.2 A tire tread depth indicator should be used to monitor tire wear - they are available at auto parts stores andservice stations and cost very little

Chapter's Specifications. Do not use supplemental inhibitors or additives. If only a small amount of coolant is required to bring the system up to the proper level, water can be used. However, repeated additions of water will dilute the recommended antifreeze and water solution. In order to maintain the proper ratio of antifreeze and water, it is advisable to top up the coolant level with the correct mixture.

Warning: *Never remove the pressure cap when the engine is running or has just been shut down, because the cooling system is hot. Escaping steam and scalding liquid could cause serious injury. If it is necessary to open the pressure cap, wait until the system has cooled completely, then wrap a thick cloth around the cap and slowly unscrew it. If you hear hissing or any steam escapes, wait until the system has cooled further, then remove the cap.*

10   If the coolant level drops within a short time after replenishment, there may be a leak in the system. Inspect the radiator, hoses, engine coolant pressure cap, drain plugs, and water pump. If no leak is evident, have the pressure cap pressure tested.

11   When checking the coolant level, always note its condition. It should be relatively clear. If it is brown or rust colored, the system should be drained, flushed and refilled. Even if the coolant appears to be normal, the corrosion inhibitors wear out with use, so it must be replaced at the specified intervals.

12   Do not allow antifreeze to come in contact with your skin or painted surfaces of the vehicle. Flush contacted areas immediately with plenty of water.

Brake and clutch fluid

13   The brake master cylinder is mounted on the front of the power booster unit in the engine compartment. The hydraulic clutch master cylinder used on manual transaxle models is located to the right and below the master cylinder.

14   The brake master cylinder and the clutch master cylinder share a common reservoir. To check the fluid level of either system, simply look at the MAX and MIN marks on the brake fluid reservoir (see illustration).

15   If the level is low, wipe the top of the reservoir cover with a clean rag to prevent contamination of the brake system before lifting the cover.

16   Add only the specified brake fluid to the reservoir (refer to Recommended lubricants and fluids in this Chapter's Specifications or to your owner's manual). Mixing different types of brake fluid can damage the system. Fill the brake master cylinder reservoir only to the MAX line.

Warning: *Be careful when filling the reservoir - brake fluid can harm your eyes and damage painted surfaces. Do not use brake fluid that is more than one year old or has been left open. Brake fluid absorbs moisture from the air. Excess moisture can cause a dangerous loss of braking.*

17   While the reservoir cap is removed, inspect the master cylinder reservoir for contamination. If deposits, dirt particles or water droplets are present, the system should be drained and refilled.

18   After filling the reservoir to the proper level, make sure the cap is properly seated to prevent fluid leakage.

19   The fluid in the brake master cylinder will drop slightly as the brake pads at each wheel wear down during normal operation. If the master cylinder requires repeated replenishing to keep it at the proper level, this is an indication of leakage in the brake or clutch system, which should be corrected immediately. If the brake system shows an indication of leakage check all brake lines and connections, along with the calipers, wheel cylinders and booster (see Section 12 for more information). If the hydraulic clutch system shows an indication of leakage, check all clutch lines and connec-

tions, along with the clutch release cylinder (see Chapter 8 for more information).

20   If, upon checking the brake or clutch master cylinder fluid level, you discover the reservoir empty or nearly empty, the systems should be checked, repaired and bled (see Chapters 8 and 9).

Windshield washer fluid

21   Fluid for the windshield washer system is stored in a plastic reservoir located at the left front of the engine compartment (see illustration).

22   In milder climates, plain water can be used in the reservoir, but it should be kept no more than 2/3 full to allow for expansion if the water freezes. In colder climates, use windshield washer system antifreeze, available at any auto parts store, to lower the freezing point of the fluid. Mix the antifreeze with water in accordance with the manufacturer's directions on the container.

Caution: *Do not use cooling system antifreeze - it will damage the vehicle's paint.*

5   Tire and tire pressure checks (every 250 miles [400 km] or weekly)

1   Periodic inspection of the tires may spare you the inconvenience of being stranded with a flat tire. It can also provide you with vital information regarding possible problems in the steering and suspension systems before major damage occurs.

2   The original tires on this vehicle are equipped with 1/2-inch wide bands that will appear when tread depth reaches 1/16-inch, at which point they can be considered worn out. Tread wear can be monitored with a simple, inexpensive device known as a tread depth indicator (see illustration).

UNDERINFLATION

CUPPING

Cupping may be caused by:
- Underinflation and/or mechanical irregularities such as out-of-balance condition of wheel and/or tire, and bent or damaged wheel.
- Loose or worn steering tie-rod or steering idler arm.
- Loose, damaged or worn front suspension parts.

OVERINFLATION

INCORRECT TOE-IN OR EXTREME CAMBER

FEATHERING DUE TO MISALIGNMENT

5.3 This chart will help you determine the condition of your tires, the probable cause(s) of abnormal wear and the corrective action necessary

3   Note any abnormal tread wear (see illustration). Tread pattern irregularities such as cupping, flat spots and more wear on one side than the other are indications of front end alignment and/or balance problems. If any of these conditions are noted, take the vehicle to a tire shop or service station to correct the problem.

4   Look closely for cuts, punctures and embedded nails or tacks. Sometimes a tire will hold air pressure for a short time or leak down very slowly after a nail has embedded itself in the tread. If a slow leak persists, check the valve stem core to make sure it is tight (see illustration). Examine the tread for an object that may have embedded itself in

the tire or for a "plug" that may have begun to leak (radial tire punctures are repaired with a plug that is installed in a puncture). If a puncture is suspected, it can be easily verified by spraying a solution of soapy water onto the puncture area (see illustration). The soapy solution will bubble if there is a leak. Unless the puncture is unusually

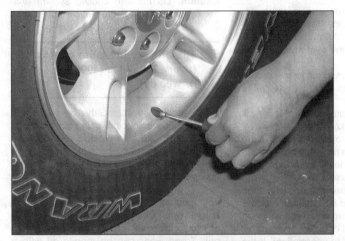

5.4a If a tire loses air on a steady basis, check the valve core first to make sure it's snug (special inexpensive wrenches are commonly available at auto parts stores)

5.4b If the valve core is tight, raise the corner of the vehicle with the low tire and spray a soapy water solution onto the tread as the tire is turned slowly - slow leaks will cause small bubbles to appear

5.8 To extend the life of your tires, check the air pressure at least once a week with an accurate gauge (don't forget the spare!)

6.7 Use a proper size box-end wrench or socket to remove the oil drain plug and avoid rounding it off

large, a tire shop or service station can usually repair the tire.

5 Carefully inspect the inner sidewall of each tire for evidence of brake fluid leakage. If you see any, inspect the brakes immediately.

6 Correct air pressure adds miles to the life span of the tires, improves mileage and enhances overall ride quality. Tire pressure cannot be accurately estimated by looking at a tire, especially if it's a radial. A tire pressure gauge is essential. Keep an accurate gauge in the glove compartment. The pressure gauges attached to the nozzles of air hoses at gas stations are often inaccurate.

7 Always check tire pressure when the tires are cold. Cold, in this case, means the vehicle has not been driven over a mile in the three hours preceding a tire pressure check. A pressure rise of four to eight pounds is not uncommon once the tires are warm.

8 Unscrew the valve cap protruding from the wheel or hubcap and push the gauge firmly onto the valve stem (see illustration). Note the reading on the gauge and compare the figure to the recommended tire pressure shown on the tire placard on the driver's side door. Reinstall the valve cap to keep dirt and moisture out of the valve stem mechanism. Check all four tires and, if necessary, add enough air to bring them up to the recommended pressure.

9 Don't forget to keep the spare tire inflated to the specified pressure (refer to the pressure molded into the tire sidewall).

6 Engine oil and filter change (every 3000 miles [5000 km] or 3 months)

Note: *These vehicles are equipped with an oil life indicator system that illuminates a light or message on the instrument panel when the system deems it necessary to change the oil. A number of factors are taken into consideration to determine when the oil should be considered worn out. Generally, this system will allow the vehicle to accumulate more miles between oil changes*

than the traditional 3000 mile interval, but we believe that frequent oil changes are cheap insurance and will prolong engine life. If you do decide not to change your oil every 3000 miles and rely on the oil life indicator instead, make sure you don't exceed 7,500 miles before the oil is changed, regardless of what the oil life indicator shows.

1 Frequent oil changes are the most important preventive maintenance procedures that can be done by the home mechanic. As engine oil ages, it becomes diluted and contaminated, which leads to premature engine wear.

2 Make sure that you have all the necessary tools before you begin this procedure. You should also have plenty of rags or newspapers handy for mopping up oil spills.

3 Access to the oil drain plug and filter will be improved if the vehicle can be lifted on a hoist, driven onto ramps or supported by jackstands.

Warning: *Do not work under a vehicle supported only by a jack - always use jackstands!*

4 If you haven't changed the oil on this vehicle before, get under it and locate the oil drain plug and the oil filter. The exhaust components will be warm as you work, so note how they are routed to avoid touching them when you are under the vehicle.

5 Start the engine and allow it to reach normal operating temperature - oil and sludge will flow out more easily when warm. If new oil, a filter or tools are needed, use the vehi-

cle to go get them and warm up the engine/oil at the same time. Park on a level surface and shut off the engine when it's warmed up. Remove the oil filler cap from the valve cover.

6 Raise the vehicle and support it securely on jackstands.

7 Being careful not to touch the hot exhaust components, position a drain pan under the plug in the bottom of the engine, then remove the plug (see illustration). It's a good idea to wear a rubber glove while unscrewing the plug the final few turns to avoid being scalded by hot oil.

8 It may be necessary to move the drain pan slightly as oil flow slows to a trickle. Inspect the old oil for the presence of metal particles.

9 After all the oil has drained, wipe off the drain plug with a clean rag. Any small metal particles clinging to the plug would immediately contaminate the new oil.

10 Clean the area around the drain plug opening, reinstall the plug and tighten it to the torque listed in this Chapter's Specifications.

2015 and earlier 1.4L and 1.8L models

11 Move the drain pan into position under the oil filter. The canister-type oil filter is located at the front left side of the engine and is accessible from the top of the engine compartment (see illustration).

6.11 Unscrew the cap to access the oil filter

6.12a Remove the filter cartridge. . .

6.12b. . . then separate the element from the cap

6.21 Typical DIC controls on the turn signal stalk

1   *Menu button*
2   *Scroll wheel*
3   *SET/CLR button*

12   Unscrew the oil filter cap (using a large socket, not an open-end wrench) and withdraw it, together with the element (see illustrations).
13   Use a clean rag to remove all oil, dirt and sludge from the oil filter housing and cap.
14   Install a new O-ring seal in the groove on the retaining cap, then install the new element in the cap and insert them both in the filter housing. Screw on the cap and tighten it to the torque listed in this Chapter's Specifications.

2016 and later 1.4L models

15   Move the drain pan into position under the oil filter.
16   Loosen the oil filter by turning it counter-clockwise with a filter wrench. Any standard filter wrench will work.
17   Once the filter is loose, use your hands to unscrew it from the block. Just as the filter is detached from the block, immediately tilt the open end up to prevent the oil inside the filter from spilling out.
18   Using a clean rag, wipe off the mounting surface on the block. Also, make sure that none of the old gasket remains stuck to the mounting surface. It can be removed with a scraper if necessary.
19   Compare the old filter with the new one to make sure they are the same type. Smear some engine oil on the rubber gasket of the new filter and screw it into place. Overtighten-

ing the filter will damage the gasket, so don't use a filter wrench. Most filter manufacturers recommend tightening the filter by hand only. Normally they should be tightened 3/4-turn after the gasket contacts the block, but be sure to follow the directions on the filter or container.

All models

20   Remove all tools and materials from under the vehicle, being careful not to spill the oil in the drain pan, then lower the vehicle.
21   Add new oil to the engine through the oil filler cap. Use a funnel to prevent oil from spilling onto the top of the engine. Pour four quarts of fresh oil into the engine, wait a few minutes to allow the oil to drain into the pan, then check the level on the dipstick (see Section 4 if necessary). If the oil level is in the OK range, install the filler cap.
22   Start the engine and run it for about a minute. Check for leaks at the oil pan drain plug and around the oil filter.
23   Wait a few minutes, then recheck the level on the dipstick. Add oil as necessary to bring the level into the OK range.
24   During the first few trips after an oil change, make it a point to check frequently for leaks and proper oil level.
25   The old oil drained from the engine cannot be reused in its present state and should be disposed of. Check with your local auto parts

store, disposal facility or environmental agency to see if they will accept the oil for recycling. After the oil has cooled it can be drained into a container (capped plastic jugs, topped bottles, milk cartons, etc.) for transport to one of these disposal sites. Don't dispose of the oil by pouring it on the ground or down a drain!

Engine oil life system reset

26   Resetting the "Change Engine Oil" light is among several information displays you can access through the Driver Information Center (DIC) on the instrument panel, using the buttons and scroll wheel on the turn signal stalk (see illustration).
27   Turn the igniton to the RUN position, then press the Menu button.
28   Use the scroll wheel to select REMAINING OIL LIFE on the DIC.
29   Push the SET/CLR button to change the oil life to 100%. Use the scroll wheel to select YES, then push the SET/CLR button.
Note: *If the "CHANGE OIL SOON" message appears, the system was not reset and the procedure must be repeated.*

7   Windshield wiper and rear wiper blade inspection and replacement (every 6000 miles [10,000 km] or 6 months)

1   The wiper and blade assembly(ies) should be inspected periodically for damage, loose components and cracked or worn blade elements.
2   Road film can build up on the wiper blades and affect their efficiency, so they should be washed regularly with a mild detergent solution.
3   If the wiper blade elements are cracked, worn or warped, or no longer clean adequately, they should be replaced with new ones.
4   Lift the arm assembly away from the glass for clearance, depress the release lever, then slide the wiper blade assembly out of the hook in the end of the arm (see illustrations).
5   Attach the new wiper to the arm and push it into place. Connection can be confirmed by an audible click.

7.4a To release the blade holder, depress the release tab. . .

7.4b. . . and pull the wiper blade in the direction of the windshield to separate it from the arm

8.1 Tools and materials required for battery maintenance

1   *Face shield/safety goggles* - When removing corrosion with a brush, the acidic particles can easily fly up into your eyes
2   *Baking soda* - A solution of baking soda and water can be used to neutralize corrosion
3   *Petroleum jelly* - A layer of this on the battery posts will help prevent corrosion
4   *Battery post/cable cleaner* - This wire brush cleaning tool will remove all traces of corrosion from the battery posts and cable clamps
5   *Treated felt washers* - Placing one of these on each post, directly under the cable clamps, will help prevent corrosion
6   *Puller* - Sometimes the cable clamps are very difficult to pull off the posts, even after the nut/bolt has been completely loosened. This tool pulls the clamp straight up and off the post without damage
7   *Battery post/cable cleaner* - Here is another cleaning tool that is a slightly different version of Number 4 above, but it does the same thing
8   *Rubber gloves* - Another safety item to consider when servicing the battery; remember that's acid inside the battery!

8   Battery check, maintenance and charging (every 6000 miles [10,000 km] or 6 months)

Warning: *Certain precautions must be followed when checking and servicing the battery. Hydrogen gas, which is highly flammable, is always present in the battery cells, so keep lighted tobacco and all other open flames and sparks away from the battery. The electrolyte inside the battery is actually dilute sulfuric acid, which will cause injury if splashed on your skin or in your eyes. It will also ruin clothes and painted surfaces. When removing the battery cables, always detach the negative cable first and hook it up last!*

Check and maintenance
Note: *On 2016 and later models, the battery is located in the rear of the vehicle under the trunk*

8.6a Battery terminal corrosion usually appears as light, fluffy powder

8.7a When cleaning the cable clamps, all corrosion must be removed

or rear hatch floor compartment trim panel.

1   A routine preventive maintenance program for the battery in your vehicle is the only way to ensure quick and reliable starts. But before performing any battery maintenance, make sure that you have the proper equipment necessary to work safely around the battery (see illustration).

2   There are also several precautions that should be taken whenever battery maintenance is performed. Before servicing the battery, always turn the engine and all accessories off and disconnect the cable from the negative terminal of the battery.

3   The battery produces hydrogen gas, which is both flammable and explosive. Never create a spark, smoke or light a match around the battery. Always charge the battery in a ventilated area.

4   Electrolyte contains poisonous and corrosive sulfuric acid. Do not allow it to get in your eyes, on your skin on your clothes. Never ingest it. Wear protective safety glasses when working near the battery. Keep children away from the battery.

5   Note the external condition of the battery. If the positive terminal and cable clamp on your vehicle's battery is equipped with a rubber protector, make sure that it's not torn or damaged. It should completely cover the terminal. Look for any corroded or loose connections, cracks in the case or cover or loose hold-down clamps.

8.6b Removing a cable from the battery post with a wrench - sometimes a pair of special battery pliers are required for this procedure if corrosion has caused deterioration of the nut hex (always remove the ground (-) cable first and hook it up last!)

8.7b Regardless of the type of tool used to clean the battery posts, a clean, shiny surface should be the result

Also check the entire length of each cable for cracks and frayed conductors.

6   If corrosion, which looks like white, fluffy deposits (see illustration) is evident, particularly around the terminals, the battery should be removed for cleaning. Loosen the cable clamp bolts with a wrench, being careful to remove the ground cable first, and slide them off the terminals (see illustration). Then disconnect the hold-down clamp bolt and nut, remove the clamp and lift the battery from the compartment (see Chapter 5).

7   Clean the cable clamps thoroughly with a battery brush or a terminal cleaner and a solution of warm water and baking soda (see illustration). Wash the terminals and the top of the battery case with the same solution but make sure that the solution doesn't get into the battery. When cleaning the cables, terminals and battery top, wear safety goggles and rubber gloves to prevent any solution from coming in contact with your eyes or hands. Wear old clothes too - even diluted, sulfuric acid splashed onto clothes will burn holes in them. If the terminals have been extensively corroded, clean them up with a terminal cleaner (see illustration). Thoroughly wash all cleaned areas with plain water.

8   Make sure that the battery tray is in good condition and the hold-down clamp bolts are tight. If the battery is removed from the tray, make sure no parts remain in the bottom of the tray when the battery is reinstalled. When reinstalling the hold-down clamp bolts, do not overtighten them.

9   Any metal parts of the vehicle damaged by corrosion should be covered with a zinc-based primer, then painted.

10   Information on removing and installing the battery can be found in Chapter 5. Information on jump starting can be found at the front of this manual. For more detailed battery checking procedures, refer to the Haynes Automotive Electrical Manual.

Charging

Warning: *When batteries are being charged, hydrogen gas, which is very explosive and flammable, is produced. Do not smoke or allow open flames near a charging or a recently charged battery. Wear eye protection when near the battery during charging. Also, make sure the charger is unplugged before connecting or disconnecting the battery from the charger.*

Note: *The manufacturer recommends the battery be removed from the vehicle for charging because the gas that escapes during this procedure can damage the paint. Fast charging with the battery cables connected can result in damage to the electrical system.*

11   Slow-rate charging is the best way to restore a battery that's discharged to the point where it will not start the engine. It's also a good way to maintain the battery charge in a vehicle that's only driven a few miles between starts. Maintaining the battery charge is particularly important in the winter when the battery must work harder to start the engine and electrical accessories that drain the battery are in greater use.

12   It's best to use a one or two-amp battery charger (sometimes called a "trickle" charger). They are the safest and put the least strain on the battery. They are also the least expensive. For a faster charge, you can use a higher amperage charger, but don't use one rated more than 1/10th the amp/hour rating of the battery. Rapid boost charges that claim to restore the power of the battery in one to two hours are hardest on the battery and can damage batteries not in good condition. This type of charging should only be used in emergency situations.

13   The average time necessary to charge a battery should be listed in the instructions that come with the charger. As a general rule, a trickle charger will charge a battery in 12 to 16 hours.

14   Remove all the cell caps (if equipped) and cover the holes with a clean cloth to prevent spattering electrolyte. Disconnect the negative battery cable and hook the battery charger cable clamps up to the battery posts (positive to positive, negative to negative), then plug in the charger. Make sure it is set at 12-volts if it has a selector switch.

15   If you're using a charger with a rate higher than two amps, check the battery regularly during charging to make sure it doesn't overheat. If you're using a trickle charger, you can safely let the battery charge overnight after you've checked it regularly for the first couple of hours.

16   If the battery has removable cell caps, measure the specific gravity with a hydrometer every hour during the last few hours of the charging cycle. Hydrometers are available inexpensively from auto parts stores - follow the instructions that come with the hydrometer. Consider the battery charged when there's no change in the specific gravity reading for two hours and the electrolyte in the cells is gassing (bubbling) freely. The specific gravity reading from each cell should be very close to the others. If not, the battery probably has a bad cell(s).

17   Some batteries with sealed tops have built-in hydrometers on the top that indicate the state of charge by the color displayed in the hydrometer window. Normally, a bright-colored hydrometer indicates a full charge and a dark hydrometer indicates the battery still needs charging.

18   If the battery has a sealed top and no built-in hydrometer, you can hook up a digital voltmeter across the battery terminals to check the charge. A fully charged battery should read at least 12.66 volts.

19   Further information on the battery and jump-starting can be found in Chapter 5 and at the front of this manual.

9   Cooling system check (every 6000 miles [10,000 km] or 6 months)

Warning: *Wait until the engine is completely cool before beginning this procedure.*

1   Many major engine failures can be caused by a faulty cooling system.

2   The engine must be cold for the cooling system check, so perform the following procedure before the vehicle is driven for the day or after it has been shut off for at least three hours.

3   Remove the pressure cap from the coolant expansion tank. Clean the cap thoroughly, inside and out, with clean water. The presence of corrosion on the underside of the cap or in the hose adapter means the coolant should be changed (see Section 20). The coolant inside the reservoir should be relatively clean and transparent. If it's not, drain the system and refill it with new coolant of the proper type.

4   Carefully check the radiator hoses and the smaller diameter heater hoses. Inspect each coolant hose along its entire length, replacing any hose which is cracked, swollen or deteriorated (see illustration). Cracks will show up better if the hose is squeezed. Pay close attention to hose clamps that secure the hoses to cooling system components. Hose clamps can pinch and puncture hoses, resulting in coolant leaks.

5   Make sure that all hose connections are tight. A leak in the cooling system will usually show up as white, bluish or brown colored deposits on the area adjoining the leak.

Check for a chafed area that could fail prematurely.

Check for a soft area indicating the hose has deteriorated inside.

Overtightening the clamp on a hardened hose will damage the hose and cause a leak.

Check each hose for swelling and oil-soaked ends. Cracks and breaks can be located by squeezing the hose.

9.4 Hoses, like drivebelts, have a habit of failing at the worst possible time - to prevent the inconvenience of a blown radiator or heater hose, inspect them carefully as shown here

6   Clean the front of the radiator and air conditioning condenser with compressed air, if available, or a soft brush. Remove all bugs, leaves, etc. embedded in the radiator fins. Be extremely careful not to damage the cooling fins or cut your fingers on them.

7   If the coolant level has been dropping consistently and no leaks are detectable, have the expansion tank cap and cooling system pressure checked at a service station.

10   Tire rotation (every 6000 miles [10,000 km] or 6 months)

1   The tires should be rotated at the specified intervals and whenever uneven wear is noticed. Since the vehicle will be raised and the tires removed anyway, check the brakes also (see Section 12).

2   Radial tires must be rotated in a specific pattern (see illustration).

10.2 The recommended four-tire rotation pattern

3   Refer to the information in Jacking and towing at the front of this manual for the proper procedure to follow when raising the vehicle and changing a tire. If the brakes must be checked, don't apply the parking brake as stated.

4   The vehicle must be raised on a hoist or supported on jackstands to get all four wheels off the ground. Make sure the vehicle is safely supported!

5   After the rotation procedure is finished, check and adjust the tire pressures as necessary and check the lug nut tightness.

11   Seat belt check (every 6000 miles [10,000 km] or 6 months)

1   Check seat belts, buckles, latch plates and guide loops for obvious damage and signs of wear.

2   See if the seat belt reminder light comes on when the key is turned to the Run or Start position. A chime should also sound.

3   The seat belts are designed to lock up during a sudden stop or impact, yet allow free movement during normal driving. Make sure the retractors return the belt against your chest while driving and rewind the belt fully when the buckle is unlatched.

4   If any of the above checks reveal problems with the seat belt system, replace parts as necessary.

12   Brake check (every 6000 miles [10,000 km] or 6 months)

Warning: *The dust created by the brake system is harmful to your health. Never blow it out with compressed air and don't inhale any of it. An approved filtering mask should be worn when working on the brakes. Do not, under any circumstances, use petroleum-based solvents to clean brake parts. Use brake system cleaner only!*

Note: *For detailed photographs of the brake system, refer to Chapter 9.*

1   In addition to the specified intervals, the brakes should be inspected every time the wheels are removed or whenever a defect is suspected.

2   Any of the following symptoms could indicate a potential brake system defect: The vehicle pulls to one side when the brake pedal is depressed; the brakes make squealing or dragging noises when applied; brake pedal travel is excessive; the pedal pulsates; or brake fluid leaks, usually onto the inside of the tire or wheel.

3   Disc brakes can be visually checked without removing any parts except the wheels. To check the drum brake show linings, the brake drums will have to be removed. Remove the hub caps (if applicable) and loosen the wheel lug nuts a quarter turn each.

4   Raise the vehicle and place it securely on jackstands.

Warning: *Never work under a vehicle that is supported only by a jack!*

Disc brakes

5   Remove the wheels. Now visible is the disc brake caliper that contains the pads. There is an outer brake pad and an inner pad. Both must be checked for wear.

6   Measure the thickness of the outer pad at each end of the caliper and the inner pad through the inspection hole in the caliper body (see illustration). Compare the measurement with the limit given in this Chapter's Specifications; if any brake pad thickness is less than specified, then all brake pads must be replaced (see Chapter 9).

7   If you're in doubt as to the exact pad thickness or quality, remove them for measurement and further inspection (see Chapter 9).

8   Check the disc for score marks, wear and burned spots. If any of these conditions exist, the disc should be removed for servicing or replacement (see Chapter 9).

9   Before installing the wheels, check all the brake lines and hoses for damage, wear, deformation, cracks, corrosion, leakage, bends and twists, particularly in the vicinity of the rubber hoses and calipers.

10   Install the wheels, lower the vehicle and tighten the wheel lug nuts to the torque given in this Chapter's Specifications.

Drum brakes (2015 and earlier models)

11   Remove the wheels, make sure the parking brake is off, then tap on the outside of the drum with a rubber mallet to loosen it.

12   Remove the brake drums. If the drum still won't come off, refer to Chapter 9.

13   With the drums removed, carefully clean the brake assembly with brake system cleaner.

Warning: *Don't blow the dust out with compressed air and don't inhale any of it (it is harmful to your health).*

14   Note the thickness of the lining material on both front and rear brake shoes (see illustration). Compare the measurement with the limit given in this Chapter's Specifications; if any lining thickness is less than specified, then all of the brake shoes must be replaced

12.6 You will find an inspection hole like this in each caliper through which you can view the thickness of remaining friction material for the inner pad

12.14 If the lining is bonded to the brake shoe, measure the lining thickness from the outer surface to the metal shoe, as shown here; if the lining is riveted to the shoe, measure from the lining outer surface to the rivet head

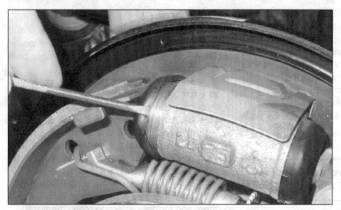

12.16 Carefully peel back the wheel cylinder boot and check for leaking fluid, indicating that the cylinder must be replaced

13.3 Release the tabs on the ventilation filter housing and swing the door down

(see Chapter 9). The shoes should also be replaced if they're cracked, glazed (shiny areas), or covered with brake fluid.

15   Make sure all the brake assembly springs are connected and in good condition.

16   Check the brake components for signs of fluid leakage. With your finger or a small screwdriver, carefully pry back the rubber cups on the wheel cylinder located at the top of the brake shoes (see illustration). Any leakage here is an indication that the wheel cylinders should be replaced immediately (see Chapter 9). Also, check all hoses and connections for signs of leakage.

17   Wipe the inside of the drum with a clean rag and denatured alcohol or brake cleaner. Again, be careful not to breathe the dangerous brake dust.

18   Check the inside of the drum for cracks, score marks, deep scratches and hard spots which will appear as small discolored areas. If imperfections cannot be removed with fine emery cloth, the drum must be taken to an automotive machine shop for resurfacing.

19   Repeat the procedure for the remaining wheel. If the inspection reveals that all parts are in good condition, reinstall the brake drums, install the wheels and lower the vehicle to the ground.

Brake booster check

20   Sit in the driver's seat and perform the following sequence of tests.

21   With the brake fully depressed, start the engine - the pedal should move down a little when the engine starts.

22   With the engine running, depress the brake pedal several times - the travel distance should not change.

23   Depress the brake, stop the engine and hold the pedal in for about 30 seconds - the pedal should neither sink nor rise.

24   Restart the engine, run it for about a minute and turn it off. Then firmly depress the brake several times - the pedal travel should decrease with each application.

25   If your brakes do not operate as described, the brake booster has failed. Refer to Chapter 9 for the replacement procedure.

13   Interior ventilation filter replacement (every 15,000 miles [24,000 km] or 12 months)

1   These models are equipped with an air filtering element for the interior ventilation system. The access panel is located behind the glove box.

2   Release the stops and lower the glove box door (see Chapter 11 , if necessary).

3   Release the tabs on the filter cover, then lower the cover for access to the filter (see illustration).

4   Slide the filter straight out (see illustration).

5   Clean out any leaves or other debris from the housing.

6   Installation is the reverse of the removal procedure. Make sure the arrow indicating AIR FLOW is pointing downward when you push the new filter in.

14   Underhood hose check and replacement (every 15,000 miles [24,000 km] or 12 months)

Warning: *Never remove air conditioning components or hoses until the refrigerant has been recovered by a licensed air conditioning technician.*

13.4 Remove the element from the housing

General

1   High temperatures under the hood can cause deterioration of the rubber and plastic hoses used for engine, accessory and emission systems operation. Periodic inspection should be made for cracks, loose clamps, material hardening and leaks.

2   Information specific to the cooling system hoses can be found in Section 9.

3   Most (but not all) hoses are secured to the fittings with clamps. Where clamps are used, check to be sure they haven't lost their tension, allowing the hose to leak. If clamps aren't used, make sure the hose has not expanded and/or hardened where it slips over the fitting, allowing it to leak.

PCV system hose

4   To reduce hydrocarbon emissions, crankcase blow-by gas is vented through the PCV valve in the valve arm cover to the intake manifold via a rubber hose on most models. The blow-by gases mix with incoming air in the intake manifold before being burned in the combustion chambers.

5   Check the PCV hose for cracks, leaks and other damage. Disconnect it from the valve cover and the intake manifold and check the inside for obstructions. If it's clogged, clean it out with solvent.

Vacuum hoses

6   It's quite common for vacuum hoses, especially those in the emissions system, to be color coded or identified by colored stripes molded into them. Various systems require hoses with different wall thickness, collapse resistance and temperature resistance. When replacing hoses, be sure the new ones are made of the same material.

7   Often the only effective way to check a hose is to remove it completely from the vehicle. If more than one hose is removed, label the hoses and fittings to ensure correct installation.

8   When checking vacuum hoses, include any plastic T-fittings in the check. Inspect the fittings for cracks and the hose where it fits over each fitting for distortion, which could cause leakage.

9   A small piece of vacuum hose (1/4-inch inside diameter) can be used as a stethoscope to detect vacuum leaks. Hold one end of the hose to your ear and probe around vacuum hoses and fittings, listening for the hissing sound characteristic of a vacuum leak. **Warning:** *When probing with the vacuum hose stethoscope, be careful not to come into contact with moving engine components such as drivebelts, the cooling fan, etc.*

Fuel hose

Warning: *Gasoline is flammable, so take extra precautions when you work on any part of the fuel system. Don't smoke or allow open flames or bare light bulbs near the work area, and don't work in a garage where a gas-type appliance (such as a water heater or clothes dryer) is present. Since fuel is carcinogenic, wear fuel-resistant gloves when there's a possibility of being exposed to fuel, and, if you spill any fuel on your skin, rinse it off immediately with soap and water. Mop up any spills immediately and do not store fuel-soaked rags where they could ignite. The fuel system is under constant pressure, so, if any fuel lines are to be disconnected, the fuel pressure in the system must be relieved first (see Chapter 4 for more information). When you perform any kind of work on the fuel system, wear safety glasses and have a Class B type fire extinguisher on hand.*

10   The fuel lines are usually under pressure, so if any fuel lines are to be disconnected be prepared to catch spilled fuel. **Warning:** *Your vehicle is equipped with fuel injection and you must relieve the fuel system pressure before servicing the fuel lines. Refer to Chapter 4 for the fuel system pressure relief procedure.*

11   Check all flexible fuel lines for deterioration and chafing. Check especially for cracks in areas where the hose bends and just before fittings, such as where a hose attaches to the fuel pump, fuel filter and fuel injection unit.

12   When replacing a hose, use only hose that is specifically designed for your fuel injection system.

13   Spring-type clamps are sometimes used on fuel return or vapor lines. These clamps often lose their tension over a period of time, and can be sprung during removal. Replace all spring-type clamps with screw clamps whenever a hose is replaced. Some fuel lines use spring-lock type couplings, which require a special tool to disconnect. See Chapter 4 for more information on this type of coupling.

Metal lines

14   Sections of metal line are often used for fuel line between the fuel pump and the fuel injection unit. Check carefully to make sure the line isn't bent, crimped or cracked.

15   If a section of metal fuel line must be replaced, use seamless steel tubing only, since copper and aluminum tubing do not have the strength necessary to withstand vibration caused by the engine.

16   Check the metal brake lines where they enter the master cylinder and brake propor-

15.4 Check the struts and shock absorbers for leakage

tioning unit (if used) for cracks in the lines and loose fittings. Any sign of brake fluid leakage calls for an immediate thorough inspection of the brake system.

---

15   Steering, suspension and driveaxle boot check (every 15,000 miles [24,000 km] or 12 months)

Note: *For detailed illustrations of the steering and suspension components, refer to Chapter 10.*

With the wheels on the ground

1   With the vehicle stopped and the front wheels pointed straight ahead, rock the steering wheel gently back and forth. If freeplay is excessive, a front wheel bearing, steering shaft universal joint or lower arm balljoint is worn or the steering gear is out of adjustment or broken. Refer to Chapter 10 for the appropriate repair procedure.

2   Other symptoms, such as excessive vehicle body movement over rough roads, swaying (leaning) around corners and binding as the steering wheel is turned, may indicate faulty steering and/or suspension components.

3   Check the shock absorbers by pushing down and releasing the vehicle several times at each corner. If the vehicle does not come back to a level position within one or two bounces, the shocks/struts are worn and must be replaced. When bouncing the vehicle up and down, listen for squeaks and noises from the suspension components.

4   Check the struts and shock absorbers for evidence of fluid leakage (see illustration). A light film of fluid is no cause for concern. Make sure that any fluid noted is from

15.10 To check a balljoint for wear, try to pry the control arm up and down to make sure there is no play in the balljoint (if there is, replace it)

the struts/shocks and not from some other source. If leakage is noted, replace the struts/shocks as a set.

5   Check the struts and shocks to be sure they are securely mounted and undamaged. Check the upper mounts for damage and wear. If damage or wear is noted, replace the shocks as a set (front and rear).

6   If the shocks must be replaced, refer to Chapter 10 for the procedure.

Under the vehicle

7   Raise the vehicle with a floor jack and support it securely on jackstands.

8   Check the tires for irregular wear patterns and proper inflation. See Section 5 for information regarding tire wear and Chapter 10 for information on wheel bearing replacement.

9   Inspect the universal joint between the steering shaft and the steering gear housing. Check the steering gear housing for lubricant leakage. Make sure that the dust seals and boots are not damaged and that the boot clamps are not loose. Check the steering linkage for looseness or damage. Check the tie-rod ends for excessive play. Look for loose bolts, broken or disconnected parts and deteriorated rubber bushings on all suspension and steering components. While an assistant turns the steering wheel from side to side, check the steering components for free movement, chafing and binding. If the steering components do not seem to be reacting with the movement of the steering wheel, try to determine where the slack is located.

10   Check the balljoints for wear by trying to move each control arm up and down with a prybar (see illustration) to ensure that its balljoint has no play. If any balljoint does have play, replace it. See Chapter 10 for the balljoint replacement procedure.

15.11 Check the balljoint boot for damage

15.14 Flex the driveaxle boots by hand to check for cracks and/or leaking grease

16.2 Check each exhaust system rubber hanger for damage

11   Inspect the balljoint boots for damage and leaking grease (see illustration). Replace the balljoints with new ones if they are damaged (see Chapter 10).

12   At the rear of the vehicle, inspect the suspension arm bushings for deterioration. Additional information on suspension components can be found in Chapter 10.

Driveaxle boot check

Note: *For detailed illustrations of the driveaxles, refer to Chapter 8.*

13   The driveaxle boots are very important because they prevent dirt, water and foreign material from entering and damaging the constant velocity (CV) joints. Oil and grease can cause the boot material to deteriorate prematurely, so it's a good idea to wash the boots with soap and water. Because it constantly pivots back and forth following the steering action of the front hub, the outer CV boot wears out sooner and should be inspected regularly.

14   Inspect the boots for tears and cracks as well as loose clamps (see illustration). If there is any evidence of cracks or leaking lubricant, they must be replaced as described in Chapter 8.

16   Exhaust system check (every 15,000 miles [24,000 km] or 12 months)

1   With the engine cold (at least three hours after the vehicle has been driven), check the complete exhaust system from the engine to the end of the tailpipe. Ideally, the inspection should be done with the vehicle on a hoist to permit unrestricted access. If a hoist isn't available, raise the vehicle and support it securely on jackstands.

2   Check the exhaust pipes and connections for evidence of leaks, severe corrosion and damage. Make sure that all brackets and hangers are in good condition and tight (see illustration).

3   At the same time, inspect the underside of the body for holes, corrosion, open seams,

etc. which may allow exhaust gases to enter the passenger compartment. Seal all body openings with silicone or body putty.

4   Rattles and other noises can often be traced to the exhaust system, especially the mounts and hangers. Try to move the pipes, muffler and catalytic converter. If the components can come in contact with the body or suspension parts, secure the exhaust system with new mounts.

5   Check the running condition of the engine by inspecting inside the end of the tailpipe. The exhaust deposits here are an indication of engine state-of-tune. If the pipe is black and sooty or coated with white deposits, the engine may need a tune-up, including a thorough engine management and fuel system inspection.

17   Fuel system check (every 15,000 miles [24,000 km] or 12 months)

Warning: *Gasoline is flammable, so take extra precautions when you work on any part of the fuel system. Don't smoke or allow open flames or bare light bulbs near the work area, and don't work in a garage where a gas-type appliance (such as a water heater or clothes dryer) is present. Since fuel is carcinogenic, wear fuel-resistant gloves when there's a possibility of being exposed to fuel, and, if you spill any fuel on your skin, rinse it off immediately with soap and water. Mop up any spills immediately and do not store fuel-soaked rags where they could ignite. When you perform any kind of work on the fuel system, wear safety glasses and have a Class B type fire extinguisher on hand. The fuel system is under constant pressure, so, before any lines are disconnected, the fuel system pressure must be relieved (see Chapter 4).*

1   If you smell gasoline while driving or after the vehicle has been sitting in the sun, inspect the fuel system immediately.

2   Remove the fuel filler cap and inspect it for damage and corrosion. The gasket should

have an unbroken sealing imprint. If the gasket is damaged or corroded, install a new cap.

3   Inspect the fuel feed line for cracks. Make sure that the connections between the fuel lines and the fuel injection system and between the fuel lines and the in-line fuel filter are tight.

Warning: *Your vehicle is fuel injected, so you must relieve the fuel system pressure before servicing fuel system components. The fuel system pressure relief procedure is outlined in Chapter 4.*

4   Since some components of the fuel system - the fuel tank and part of the fuel feed line, for example - are underneath the vehicle, they can be inspected more easily with the vehicle raised on a hoist. If that's not possible, raise the vehicle and support it on jackstands.

5   With the vehicle raised and safely supported, inspect the gas tank and filler neck for punctures, cracks and other damage. The connection between the filler neck and the tank is particularly critical. Sometimes a rubber filler neck will leak because of loose clamps or deteriorated rubber. Inspect all fuel tank mounting brackets and straps to be sure that the tank is securely attached to the vehicle.

Warning: *Do not, under any circumstances, try to repair a fuel tank (except rubber components). A welding torch or any open flame can easily cause fuel vapors inside the tank to explode.*

6   Carefully check all rubber hoses and metal lines leading away from the fuel tank. Check for loose connections, deteriorated hoses, crimped lines and other damage. Repair or replace damaged sections as necessary (see Chapter 4).

18   Drivebelt check and replacement/ tensioner replacement (every 15,000 miles [24,000 km] or 12 months)

Drivebelt

1   A single serpentine drivebelt is located at the front of the engine and plays an important

ACCEPTABLE

Cracks Running Across "V" Portions of Belt

Missing Two or More Adjacent Ribs 1/2" or longer

1/2"

UNACCEPTABLE

Cracks Running Parallel to "V" Portions of Belt

18.3 Here are some of the more common problems associated with drivebelts (check the belts very carefully to prevent an untimely breakdown)

18.4 On 2015 and earlier models, remove the fasteners from the front half of the splash shield, then pull the shield back far enough to access the tensioner

role in the overall operation of the engine and its components. Due to its function and material make up, the belt is prone to wear and should be periodically inspected. The serpentine belt drives the alternator and air conditioning compressor. Although the belt should be inspected at the recommended intervals, replacement may not be necessary for more than 100,000 miles.

Check

2   With the engine stopped, inspect the full length of the drivebelt for cracks and separation of the belt plies. It will be necessary to turn the engine (using a wrench or socket and bar on the crankshaft pulley bolt) in order to move the belt from the pulleys so that the belt can be inspected thoroughly. Twist the belt between the pulleys so that both sides can be viewed. Also check for fraying, and glazing which gives the belt a shiny appearance. Check the pulleys for nicks, cracks, distortion and corrosion.

3   Note that it is not unusual for a ribbed belt to exhibit small cracks in the edges of the belt ribs, and unless these are extensive or very deep, belt replacement is not essential (see illustration).

Replacement

4   Loosen the right front wheel lug nuts, then raise the front of the vehicle and support it on jackstands. Remove the right front wheel and, on 2015 and earlier models, the front half of the inner fender splash shield (see illustration). On 2016 and later models, remove the right-side splash shield fasteners and remove the splash shield from under the vehicle.

2015 and earlier models

5   Note how the drivebelt is routed, then place a socket with a 3/8-inch drive breaker bar onto the tensioner pulley center bolt. Rotate the arm clockwise on 1.4L engines (see illustration) or counterclockwise on 1.8L engines, then insert a punch through the tensioner and into

18.5a Rotate the tensioner arm to relieve belt tension. . .

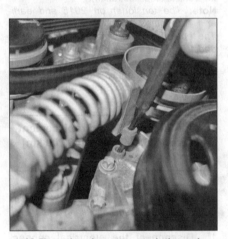

18.5b. . . then insert a punch through the tensioner and into the timing chain cover to lock the tensioner in place - 2015 and earlier models, 1.4L engine shown

the timing chain cover (see illustration) to lock the tensioner into the released position, then remove the belt from the pulleys.

6   If you're working on a 1.4L engine, support the engine from below with a floor jack and block of wood, or from above with an engine support fixture, then remove the right-side engine mount (see Chapter 2A).

2016 and later models

7   Insert a 3/8-inch drive ratchet or breaker bar into the square hole on the tensioner and rotate the handle counterclockwise to release tension on the drivebelt.

8   Once tension has been released, remove the belt from the pulleys.

All models

9   Fit the new drivebelt onto the crankshaft, alternator, water pump and air conditioning compressor pulleys, as applicable, then turn the tensioner and locate the drivebelt on the tensioner pulley. Make sure that the drivebelt

is correctly seated in all of the pulley grooves, then release the tensioner.

10   Install the fenderwell splash shield and wheel, then lower the car to the ground. Tighten the lug nuts to the torque listed in this Chapter's Specifications.

Tensioner replacement

11   Remove the drivebelt as described previously, then, on 2015 and earlier models, place a socket with a 3/8-inch drive breaker bar onto the tensioner pulley center bolt and rotate the tensioner until the punch can be removed and slowly allow the tensioner to rotate back until all the pressure is released and remove the socket and breaker bar.

12   On 2015 and earlier 1.4L models, remove the front engine mount and bracket (see Chapter 2A).

18.11 Drivebelt tensioner bolts (1.4L engine)

13   Unscrew the tensioner mounting bolt(s) and remove the tensioner from the bottom of the vehicle (see illustration).
Note: *The tensioner on 2015 and earlier 1.4L engines is mounted with two bolts. The tensioner on 2016 and later 1.4L engines and 1.8L engines has only one bolt.*
14   Installation is the reverse of removal. Tighten the tensioner bolt(s) to the torque listed in this Chapter's Specifications.

19   Air filter check and replacement (every 30,000 miles [48,000 km] or 24 months)

Caution: *Never drive the vehicle with the air filter element removed. Excessive engine wear could result and backfiring could even cause a fire under the hood.*

1   Disconnect the electrical connector from the Mass Air Flow (MAF) sensor, loosen the inlet duct hose clamp and

20.3 The radiator drain valve is located on the right end of the radiator. Attach a length of hose to the spigot (A) and direct it into a drain pan, then turn the drain valve knob (B)

19.1 Mass Air Flow (MAF) sensor electrical connector (A), inlet duct hose clamp (B) and housing cover screws (C) - 2015 and earlier 1.4L engine shown, other models similar

unscrew the filter housing cover screws (see illustration).
2   Lift up the cover and remove the filter element from the housing (see illustration).
3   Inspect the outer surface of the filter element. If it is dirty, replace it. If it is only moderately dusty, it can be reused by blowing it clean from the back to the front surface with compressed air. Because it is a pleated paper type filter, it cannot be washed or oiled. If it cannot be cleaned satisfactorily with compressed air, discard it and install a new one. While the cover is off, be careful not to drop anything down into the housing.
4   Wipe out the inside of the filter housing.
5   Place the new filter into the housing, making sure it seats properly.
6   The remainder of installation is the reverse of removal.

20   Cooling system servicing (draining, flushing and refilling) (every 30,000 miles [48,000 km] or 24 months)

Warning: *Do not allow antifreeze to come in contact with your skin or painted surfaces of the vehicle. Rinse off spills immediately with plenty of water. Antifreeze is highly toxic if ingested. Never leave antifreeze lying around in an open container or in puddles on the floor; children and pets are attracted by its sweet smell and may drink it. Check with local authorities on disposing of used antifreeze. Many communities have collection centers that will see that antifreeze is disposed of safely.*
Warning: *Wait until the engine is completely cool before beginning this procedure.*
Note: *Non-toxic antifreeze is now manufactured and available at local auto parts stores, but even this type should be disposed of properly.*

19.2 Lift the housing cover up, then remove the filter from the housing

Draining

1   Periodically, the cooling system should be drained, flushed and refilled to replenish the antifreeze mixture and prevent formation of rust and corrosion, which can impair the performance of the cooling system and cause engine damage. When the cooling system is serviced, all hoses and the expansion tank cap should be checked and replaced if necessary.
2   Apply the parking brake and block the wheels. Raise the front of the vehicle and support it securely on jackstands, then remove the under-vehicle splash shield.
Warning: *If the vehicle has just been driven, wait several hours to allow the engine to cool down before beginning this procedure.*
3   Move a large container under the radiator drain to catch the coolant. The coolant is drained by turning the knob on the radiator drain valve (see illustration). Remove the expansion tank cap and allow the coolant to drain. When the flow of coolant has stopped, close the drain plug.
4   While the coolant is draining, check the condition of the radiator hoses, heater hoses and clamps (refer to Section 9 if necessary). Replace any damaged clamps or hoses.

Flushing

5   Fill the cooling system with clean water, following the Refilling procedure (see Step 11).
6   Start the engine and allow it to reach normal operating temperature, then rev up the engine a few times.
7   Turn the engine off and allow it to cool completely, then drain the system as described earlier.
8   Repeat Steps 3, 6 and 7 until the water being drained is free of contaminants.
9   In severe cases of contamination or clogging of the radiator, remove the radiator (see Chapter 3) and have a radiator repair facility clean and repair it if necessary.
10   When the coolant is regularly drained and the system refilled with the correct antifreeze/water mixture, there should be no need to use chemical cleaners or descalers. The

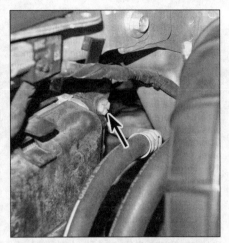

20.13 Radiator vent screw location

22.5 Location of the transaxle drain plug

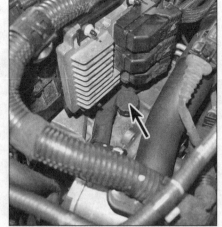

22.7 Location of the automatic transaxle vent/fill cap

manufacturer states that chemical flushing solutions should not be used.

Refilling

11   Close and tighten the radiator drain.

12   Place the heater temperature control in the maximum heat position.

13   Locate the vent screw (see illustration) at the top corner of the radiator. Remove the screw, then reinsert it into the hole and tighten it one full turn.

14   Slowly add new coolant (a 50/50 mixture of water and DEX-COOL antifreeze) to the coolant reservoir until fluid starts to come out of the vent screw, then tighten the screw and continue to fill the reservoir until the level is at the COLD FILL mark.

15   Install the expansion tank cap and run the engine at idle in a well-ventilated area for five minutes.

16   Turn the engine off and let it cool. Remove the pressure cap from the reservoir and add more coolant mixture to the reservoir until it's level with the COLD FILL mark.

17   Squeeze the upper radiator hose to expel air, then add more coolant mixture if necessary. Reinstall the expansion tank cap.

18   Start the engine and run it at idle for another five minutes. Also, set the heater and blower controls to the maximum setting and check to see that the heater output from the air ducts is warm. This is a good indication that all air has been purged from the cooling system.

21   Brake fluid change (every 30,000 miles [48,000 km] or 24 months)

Warning: *Brake fluid can harm your eyes and damage painted surfaces, so use extreme caution when handling or pouring it. Do not use brake fluid that has been standing open or is more than one year old. Brake fluid absorbs moisture from the air. Excess moisture can cause a dangerous loss of braking effectiveness.*

1   At the specified intervals, the brake fluid should be drained and replaced. Since the brake fluid may drip or splash when pouring it, place plenty of rags around the master cylinder to protect any surrounding painted surfaces.

2   Before beginning work, purchase the specified brake fluid (see Recommended lubricants and fluids in this Chapter's Specifications).

3   Remove the cap from the master cylinder reservoir.

4   Using a hand-operated suction pump or similar device, withdraw the fluid from the master cylinder reservoir.

5   Add new fluid to the master cylinder until it rises to the base of the filler neck.

6   Bleed the brake system as described in Chapter 9 at all four brakes until new and uncontaminated fluid is expelled from the bleeder screw. Maintain the fluid level in the master cylinder as you perform the bleeding process. If you allow the master cylinder to run dry, air will enter the system.

7   Refill the master cylinder with fluid and check the operation of the brakes. The pedal should feel solid when depressed, with no sponginess.

Warning: *Do not operate the vehicle if you are in doubt about the effectiveness of the brake system.*

22   Automatic transaxle fluid change (see Maintenance schedule for service intervals)

Fluid change

1   At the specified time intervals, the transaxle fluid should be drained and replaced. Since the fluid will remain hot long after driving, perform this procedure only after everything has cooled down completely.

2   Before beginning work, purchase the specified transaxle fluid (see *Recommended lubricants and fluids* in this Chapter's Specifications).

3   Other tools necessary for this job include jackstands to support the vehicle in a raised position, a drain pan capable of holding several quarts, newspapers and clean rags.

4   Raise and support the vehicle on jackstands.

5   With a drain pan in place, remove the fluid drain plug (see illustration) and allow the fluid to drain for approximately 10 minutes.

6   Install the drain plug and tighten it to the toque listed in this Chapter's Specifications.

7   Remove the the vent/fill cap (see illustration). Some models are equipped with a vent hose attached to the cap; if so, disconnect it.

Note: *On some models it may be necessary to reposition the PCM (without disconnecting the electrical connectors) for access to the cap.*

8   Using a long funnel, add the specified amount of automatic transmission fluid through the vent/fill cap hole and check the fluid level (see below).

Fluid level check

Warning: *This procedure is potentially dangerous and is best left to a professional shop with a safe lifting apparatus. The vehicle must be kept level while being safely raised high enough for access to the check plug on the transaxle.*

9   The manufacturer states that routine checks of the automatic transaxle fluid are not necessary; this procedure should only be used when refilling the transaxle after the fluid has been drained, unless an obvious leak has been detected. Low fluid level can lead to slipping or loss of drive, while overfilling can cause foaming and loss of fluid.

10   With the vehicle raised and safely supported, start the engine, then move the shift lever through all the gear ranges, ending in Park.

Note: *Incorrect fluid level readings will result if the vehicle has just been driven at high speeds for an extended period, in hot weather in city traffic, or if it has been pulling a trailer. If any of these conditions apply, wait until the fluid has cooled (about 30 minutes).*

22.11 The automatic transaxle check plug is located near the driver's side driveaxle.

24.3 Tools required for changing spark plugs

1 **Spark plug socket** - *This will have special padding inside to protect the spark plug porcelain insulator*
2 **Torque wrench** - *Although not mandatory, use of this tool is the best way to ensure that the plugs are tightened properly*
3 **Ratchet** - *Standard hand tool to fit the plug socket*
4 **Extension** - *Depending on model and accessories, you may need special extensions and universal joints to reach one or more of the plugs*
5 **Spark plug gap gauge** - *This gauge for checking the gap comes in a variety of styles. Make sure the gap for your engine is included*

11 Remove the vent/fill cap (see illustration 22.7). With the engine running and the transaxle at normal operating temperature (having idled for 3 to 5 minutes), locate the check plug on the transaxle (see illustration).
12 Place a container under the check plug and remove it. Observe the fluid as it drips into the pan, indicating correct fluid level.
13 The fluid level should be at the bottom of the check hole. If fluid pours out excessively, the transaxle is overfilled. Double-check to

make sure the vehicle is level. If no fluid drips from the check hole, add small amounts of fluid through the vent/fill cap at the top of the transaxle until it does, indicating the level is at the bottom of the check hole. A long-necked funnel will be necessary to add fluid (through the vent/fill opening).
14 The condition of the fluid should also be checked along with the level. If the fluid in the drain pan is a dark reddish-brown color, or if the fluid has a burned smell, the fluid should be changed (see above). If you're in doubt about the condition of the fluid, purchase some new fluid and compare the two for color and smell.
15 Install the check plug and tighten it securely.
16 Check under the vehicle for leaks after the first few trips.
17 The old fluid drained from the transaxle cannot be reused in its present state and should be disposed of. Check with your local auto parts store, disposal facility or environmental agency to see if they will accept the fluid for recycling. After the fluid has cooled it can be drained into a container (capped plastic jugs, topped bottles, milk cartons, etc.) for transport to one of these disposal sites. Don't dispose of the fluid by pouring it on the ground or down a drain!

23 Manual transaxle lubricant level check and change (every 100,000 miles [166,000 km])

Check

1 The manual transaxle does not have a dipstick or a check/fill plug. The fluid can only be replaced with the same amount that was measured once it has been drained (unless, of course, there was a leak). In the event of a leak, the fluid must be completely drained and refilled using the quantity listed in this Chapter's Specifications.

Change

Warning: *The manufacturer recommends changing the fluid only after it has been warmed to operating temperature. Be careful when draining the hot fluid.*
2 Loosen the left front wheel lug nuts, raise the vehicle and support it securely on jackstands. Remove the engine splash shield fasteners and splash shield from under the vehicle.
3 Move a drain pan, rags, newspapers and wrenches under the transaxle.
4 Remove the transaxle the drain plug from the lower side of the case, then allow the lubricant to drain into the pan for approximetly 10 minutes..
Caution: *The drain plug must be replaced with a new one once it has been removed.*
5 After the lubricant has drained completely, measure the amount of fluid that has been drained (if there was no apparent leak). Coat the new drain plug with thread lock-

ing compound, install it, then tighten it to the torque listed in this Chapter's Specifications.
6 Remove the PCM mounting nuts (see Chapter 6), without disconnecting the electrical connectors, and move the PCM out of the way.
7 Clean the area around the transaxle fill plug, then remove it.
8 Insert a funnel into the fill plug hole.
9 Compare the measured amount fluid that was drained to the quantity listed in the specifications and refill the tranaxle to the correct level.
10 Reinstall the fill plug and tighten it securely.
11 Reinstall the PCM (see Chapter 6) and the engine splash shield.
12 Lower the vehicle.
13 Drive the vehicle for a short distance, then check the drain and fill plugs for leakage.
14 The old lubricant drained from the transaxle cannot be reused in its present state and should be disposed of. Check with your local auto parts store, disposal facility or environmental agency to see if they will accept the lubricant for recycling. After the lubricant has cooled it can be drained into a container (capped plastic jugs, topped bottles, milk cartons, etc.) for transport to one of these disposal sites. Don't dispose of the lubricant by pouring it on the ground or down a drain!

24 Spark plug check and replacement (every 100,000 miles [166,000 km])

Warning: *Because of the very high voltage generated by the ignition system, use extreme care when you're servicing ignition components such as the ignition coil(s) and spark plugs.*
Caution: *Don't remove the spark plugs when the engine is hot; damage to the threads in the cylinder head might result.*
1 Disconnect the cable from the negative battery terminal (see Chapter 5).
2 Remove the ignition coil assembly (see Chapter 5).
Note: *On 2016 and later 1.4L engines, remove the oil filler cap and engine cover fasteners. Lift the engine cover and valve cover insulator up and off of the valve cover (it may be necessary to remove the cover and insulator separately), then reinstall the oil filler cap.*
3 In most cases, the tools necessary for spark plug replacement include a spark plug socket which fits onto a ratchet (spark plug sockets are padded inside to prevent damage to the porcelain insulators on the new plugs), various extensions and a gap gauge to check and adjust the gaps on the new plugs (see illustration). A torque wrench should be used to tighten the new plugs.
4 The best approach when replacing the spark plugs is to purchase the new ones in advance, adjust them to the proper gap and replace the plugs one at a time. When buying the new spark plugs, obtain the correct plug

24.6a The manufacturer recommends using a wire-type thickness gauge when checking the gap - if the wire does not just fit between the electrodes, adjustment is required

24.6b To change the gap, bend the side electrode only, and be very careful not to crack or chip the porcelain insulator surrounding the center electrode

24.8 Use a ratchet and extension to remove the spark plugs

type for your particular engine. This information can be found in the Specifications Section in this Chapter or in your Owner's manual.

5   Allow the engine to cool completely before attempting to remove any of the plugs. These engines are equipped with aluminum cylinder heads, which can be damaged if the spark plugs are removed when the engine is hot. While you are waiting for the engine to cool, check the new plugs for defects and adjust the gaps.

6   The gap is checked by inserting the proper-thickness gauge between the electrodes at the tip of the plug (see illustration). The gap between the electrodes should be the same as the one specified on the Emissions Control Information label or in this Chapter's Specifications. The gauge should just fit between the electrodes. If the gap is incorrect, use the adjuster on the gauge body to bend the curved side electrode slightly until the proper gap is obtained (see illustration). If the side electrode is not exactly over the center electrode, bend it with the adjuster until it is. Check for cracks in the porcelain insulator (if any are found, the plug should not be used).

Caution: *Don't force the gauge into the gap, as the coating on the electrodes could be scraped.*

Note: *The manufacturer recommends using a wire-type thickness gauge when checking platinum or iridium-type spark plugs. Other types of gauges may scrape the thin coating from the electrodes, thus dramatically shortening the life of the plugs.*

24.10 A length of snug-fitting rubber hose will save time and prevent damaged threads when installing the spark plugs

7   If compressed air is available, use it to blow any dirt or foreign material away from the spark plug hole. The idea here is to eliminate the possibility of debris falling into the cylinder as the spark plug is removed.

8   Place the spark plug socket over the plug and remove it from the engine by turning it in a counterclockwise direction (see illustration).

9   Whether you are replacing the plugs at this time or intend to reuse the old plugs, compare each old spark plug to those shown in the photos located on the inside back cover of this book to determine the overall running condition of the engine.

10   Install one of the new plugs into the hole

until you can no longer turn it with your fingers, then tighten it with a torque wrench (if available) to the torque listed in this Chapter's Specifications, or the ratchet. It is a good idea to slip a length of rubber hose over the end of the plug to use as a tool to thread it into place (see illustration). The hose will grip the plug well enough to turn it, but will start to slip if the plug begins to cross-thread in the hole - this will prevent damaged threads and the accompanying repair costs.

11   Repeat the procedure for the remaining spark plugs.

12   After replacing all the plugs, install the ignition coil pack (see Chapter 5).

Service record

Date	Mileage/hours	Work performed

Service record

Date	Mileage/hours	Work performed

Notes

Chapter 2 Part A Engines

Contents

Specifications

General

Firing order	1-3-4-2
Compression ratio	
1.4L engine	
2015 and earlier models	9.5:1
2016 and later models	10.0:1
1.8L engine	10.5:1
Compression pressure	See Chapter 2B
Bore	
1.4L engine	
2015 and earlier models	2.854 inches (72.5 mm)
2016 and later models	2.91 inches (74 mm)
1.8L engine	3.169 inches (80.5 mm)
Stroke	
1.4L engine	
2015 and earlier models	2.854 inches (72.5 mm)
2016 and later models	3.200 inches (81.3 mm)
1.8L engine	3.472 inches (88.2 mm)
Displacement	
1.4L engine	
2015 and earlier models	83.24 cubic inches
2016 and later models	85 cubic inches
1.8L engine	109.59 cubic inches
Oil pressure	See Chapter 2B

FRONT OF VEHICLE → ①②③④

1-3-4-2

Cylinder locations and firing order

Camshafts

Lobe lift	Not available
Allowable lobe lift variation	0.005 inch (0.127 mm)
Endplay	
1.4L engine	
2015 and earlier models	0.0005 to 0.0089 inch (0.013 to 0.225 mm)
2016 and later models	0.0016 to 0.0260 inch (0.040 to 0.660 mm)
1.8L engine	Not available
Journal diameter	
1.4L engine	
2015 and earlier models	1.0605 to 1.0615 inches (26.9365 to 23.9625 mm)
2016 and later models	
Journal 1	1.2179 to 1.2189 inches (30.935 to 30.960 mm)
Journal 2 through 6	0.9423 to 0.9433 inch (23.935 to 23.960 mm)
1.8L engine	Not available
Camshaft bearing oil clearance	Not available

Oil pump

2015 and earlier models 1.4L engine	
Timing chain cover-to-vane rotor clearance	0.004 inch (0.01 mm)
Timing chain cover-to-vane clearance	0.0035 inch (0.09 mm)
Timing chain cover-to-vane ring clearance	0.016 inch (0.04 mm)
Timing chain cover-to-oil pump slide clearance	0.0031 inch (0.08 mm)
Timing chain cover-to-oil pump slide seal clearance	0.0035 inch (0.09 mm)
Oil pump vane rotor-to-oil pump vane clearance	0.002 inch (0.05 mm)
Oil pump vane-to-oil pump slide clearance	0.008 inch (0.2 mm)
Oil pump slide spring length	2.4016 inches (61 mm)
1.8L engine	
Rotor-to-cover clearance	0.00079 to 0.00228 inch (0.02 to 0.058 mm)

Torque specifications

	Ft-lbs (unless otherwise indicated)	Nm

Note: *One foot-pound (ft-lb) of torque is equivalent to 12 inch-pounds (in-lbs) of torque. Torque values below approximately 15 ft-lbs are expressed in inch-pounds, since most foot-pound torque wrenches are not accurate at these smaller values.*

	Ft-lbs (unless otherwise indicated)	Nm
Camshaft sproket/actuator bolts (intake and exhaust)		
1.4L engine		
2015 and earlier models		
Step 1	37	50
Step 2	Tighten an additional 60-degrees	
2016 and later models		
Step 1	15	20
Step 2	Tighten an additional 90-degrees	
1.8L engine		
2011		
Step 1	48	65
Step 2	Tighten an additional 120-degrees	
Step 3	Tighten an additional 15-degrees	
2012 and later		
Step 1	37	50
Step 2	Tighten an additional 150-degrees	
Step 3	Tighten an additional 15-degrees	
Camshaft adjuster sprocket closure plugs (1.8L engine)	22	30
Camshaft position actuator solenoid valve bolts (intake and exhaust)		
1.4L engine		
2015 and earlier (over sprocket-type)	71 in-lbs	8
2016 and later (traditional solenoid-type)	89 in-lbs	10
1.8L engine (traditional solenoid-type)	53 in-lbs	6
Camshaft bearing cap bolts (in sequence)		
2015 and earlier models (see illustrations 11.22a or 11.27)	71 in-lbs	8
2016 and later models (see illustration 11.22b)	106 in-lbs	12
Crankshaft pulley bolt*		
1.4L engine		
2015 and earlier models		
Step 1	111	150
Step 2	Tighten an additional 45 to 60-degrees	
2016 and later models		
Step 1	74	100
Step 2	Loosen 360 degrees	
Step 3	74	100
Step 4	Tighten an additional 180-degrees	
1.8L engine		
Step 1	70	95
Step 2	Tighten an additional 45-degrees	
Step 3	Tighten an additional 15-degrees	
Cylinder head bolts*		
1.4L engine		
2015 and earlier models (in sequence - see illustration 12.17a)		
Step 1	26	35
Step 2	Tighten an additional 180-degrees	
2016 and later models (in sequence - see illustration 12.17c)		
Step 1	18	25
Step 2	22	30
Step 3	Tighten an additional 240-degrees	
1.8L engine (in sequence - see illustration 12.17b)		
Step 1	18	25
Step 2	Tighten an additional 90-degrees	
Step 3	Tighten an additional 90-degrees	
Step 4	Tighten an additional 90-degrees	
Step 5	Tighten an additional 45-degrees	
Drivebelt tensioner bolt	See Chapter 1	
Driveplate bolts* (automatic transaxle)		
1.4L engine		
2015 and earlier models		
Step 1	26	35
Step 2	Tighten an additional 30-degrees	
Step 3	Tighten an additional 15-degrees	
2016 and later models		
Step 1	15	20
Step 2	22	30
Step 3	Tighten an additional 70-degrees	
1.8L engine	44	60
Flywheel bolts* (manual transaxle)		
2015 and earlier models		
Step 1	44	60
Step 2	Tighten an additional 45-degrees	
Step 3	Tighten an additional 15-degrees	
2016 and later models		
Step 1	15	20
Step 2	22	30
Step 3	Tighten an additional 70-degrees	
Exhaust manifold/catalytic converter-to-cylinder head nuts (1.8L engine)	15	20
Exhaust pipe-to-manifold nuts (1.8L engine)	16	22

* Bolt(s) must be replaced.

Torque specifications (continued)

	Ft-lbs (unless otherwise indicated)	Nm
Timing chain cover (1.4L engine)		
M6 bolts	71 in-lbs	8
M10 bolts	26	35
Engine mount (passenger's side)		
2015 and earlier		
Mount-to-body bolts/nut	46	62
Mount-to-engine mount bracket bolts		
Step 1	37	50
Step 2	Tighten an additional 60 to 70-degrees	
2016 and later (all bolts)		
Step 1	74	100
Step 2	Tighten an additional 60 to 75-degrees	
Engine mount bracket bolts		
2015 and earlier models		
Step 1	45	60
Step 2	Tighten an additional 45 to 60-degrees	
2016 and later models		
Step 1	43	58
Step 2	Tighten an additional 60 to 75-degrees	
Transaxle (driver's side) mount		
2015 and earlier models		
Mount-to-body bolts and nut	46	62
Mount-to-transaxle bolts		
Manual transaxle (and 2013 and earlier auto transaxle)		
Step 1	37	50
Step 2	Tighten an additional 60 to 75-degrees	
Automatic transaxle (2014 and 2015)		
Step 1	59	80
Step 2	Tighten an additional 60 to 75-degrees	
2016 and later models		
Mount-to-body and mount-to-transaxle bolts		
Step 1	74	100
Step 2	Tighten an additional 60 to 75-degrees	
Mount through-bolt	43	58
Transaxle mount bracket bolts		
2015 and earlier models	74	100
2016 and later models		
Step 1	74	100
Step 2	Tighten an additional 60 to 75-degrees	
Transaxle front and rear mount fasteners (2015 and earlier models)		
Rear mount		
Mount-to-subframe bolts/nuts	82	110
Mount-to-transaxle bracket through-bolt/nut	74	100
Mount-to-transaxle bracket	74	100
Front mount		
Automatic transaxle		
Mount-to-transaxle bolts	46	62
Mount through-bolt	74	100
Manual transaxle (all bolts)	74	100
Transaxle rear mount strut fasteners (2016 and later models)		
Mount strut bracket-to-transaxle bolts		
Step 1	74	100
Step 2	Tighten an additional 60 to 75-degrees	
Mount strut through-bolt-to-bracket		
Step 1	74	100
Step 2	Tighten an additional 90 to 105-degrees	
Mount strut through-bolt-to-subframe		
Step 1	74	100
Step 2	Tighten an additional 120 to 135-degrees	
Intake manifold nuts/bolts		
2015 and earlier models	15	20
2016 and later models	132 in-lbs	15
Oil pan(s)		
Oil pan-to-engine block bolts	89 in-lbs	10
Oil pan-to-transaxle bolts		
Manual transaxle	30	40
Automatic transaxle	43	58
Lower oil pan-to-upper oil pan bolts (2016 and later 1.4L engine)	89 in-lbs	10
Oil pump bolts (2016 and later 1.4L engine)	89 in-lbs	10
Oil pump/front cover-to-engine bolts (1.8L engine)	15	20
Oil pump cover screws (2015 and earlier 1.4L engine)	71 in-lbs	8
Timing chain tensioner bolts (1.4L engine)		
2015 and earlier models	71 in-lbs	8
2016 and later models	18	25
Timing chain guide bolts (2015 and earlier 1.4L engine)		
Left side guide bolt	15	20
Right side (Fixed) guide bolts	71-lbs	8
Upper guide bolts	71 in-lbs	8
Upper timing chain guide bolts	89 in-lbs	10

Torque specifications (continued)

Note: *One foot-pound (ft-lb) of torque is equivalent to 12 inch-pounds (in-lbs) of torque. Torque values below approximately 15 ft-lbs are expressed in inch-pounds, since most foot-pound torque wrenches are not accurate at these smaller values.*

	Ft-lbs (unless otherwise indicated)	Nm
Timing chain guide bolts (2016 and later 1.4L engine)	18	25
Upper chain guide bolts (2016 and later 1.4L engine)	89 in-lbs	10
Timing chain guide access hole plug (1.4L engine)	37	50
Crankcase hole plug (1.4L engine)	30	40
Timing belt (1.8L engine)		
Idler pulley and tensioner center bolt*		
Step 1	15	20
Step 2	Tighten an additional 120-degrees	
Step 3	Tighten an additional 15-degrees	
Timing belt cover bolts	53 in-lbs	6
Timing chain cover-to-block bolts		
2015 and earlier	53 in-lbs	6
2016 and later	43	58
Timing chain cover-to-oil pan bolts		
2015 and earlier	132 in-lbs	10
2016 and later	43	15
Valve cover bolts		
2015 and earlier models	71 in-lbs	8
2016 and later models	132 in-lbs	15
Valve cover ground strap bolt	89 in-lbs	10
Water pump bolts	See Chapter 3	

* Bolt(s) must be replaced.

1   General Information

1   The Chevrolet Cruze has been equipped with either a 1.4L or a 1.8L engine. This Part of Chapter 2A is devoted to in-vehicle repair procedures for these DOHC (Double Overhead Camshaft) four-cylinder engines. Information concerning engine removal and installation and engine overhaul can be found in Part B of this Chapter.

2   The 1.4L engine is equipped with a single timing chain to drive the camshafts, and the 1.8L engine is equipped with a single timing belt to drive the camshafts.

3   The Specifications included in this Part of Chapter 2A apply only to the procedures contained in this Part. Specifications related to engine removal and installation or overhaul can be found in Chapter 2A , Part B.

3.4 On the 2015 and earlier 1.4L engine, the hole in the crankshaft pulley must align with the pointer on the timing chain cover

2   Repair operations possible with the engine in the vehicle

1   Many major repair operations can be accomplished without removing the engine from the vehicle.

2   Clean the engine compartment and the exterior of the engine with some type of degreaser before any work is done. It will make the job easier and help keep dirt out of the internal areas of the engine.

3   Depending on the components involved, it may be helpful to remove the hood to improve access to the engine as repairs are performed (refer to Chapter 11 if necessary). Cover the fenders to prevent damage to the paint. Special pads are available, but an old bedspread or blanket will also work.

4   If vacuum, exhaust, oil or coolant leaks develop, indicating a need for gasket or seal replacement, the repairs can generally be made with the engine in the vehicle. The intake and exhaust manifold gaskets, oil pan gasket, crankshaft oil seals and cylinder head gasket are all accessible with the engine in place.

5   Exterior engine components, such as the intake and exhaust manifolds, the oil pan, the oil pump, the water pump, the starter motor, the alternator and the fuel system components can be removed for repair with the engine in place.

6   Since the cylinder head can be removed without pulling the engine, camshaft and valve component servicing can also be accomplished with the engine in the vehicle. Replacement of the timing chain or timing belt, and sprockets is also possible with the engine in the vehicle.

7   In extreme cases caused by a lack of necessary equipment, repair or replacement of piston rings, pistons, connecting rods and rod bearings is possible with the engine in the vehicle. However, this practice is not recommended because of the cleaning and preparation work that must be done to the components involved.

3   Top Dead Center (TDC) for number one piston - locating

1   Top Dead Center (TDC) is the highest point in the cylinder that each piston reaches as it travels up-and-down during crankshaft rotation. Each piston reaches TDC on the compression stroke and again on the exhaust stroke, but TDC generally refers to piston position on the compression stroke.

2   Positioning the piston(s) at TDC is an essential part of certain other repair procedures discussed in this manual.

3   Before beginning this procedure, place the transmission in Park or Neutral and apply the parking brake or block the rear wheels. Remove the spark plugs (see Chapter 1).

4   Insert a compression gauge into the number one cylinder spark plug hole. Turn the crankshaft using a ratchet or breaker bar and socket (normal direction of rotation is clockwise) until compression registers on the gauge, then turn it slowly until the TDC mark on the timing chain cover (1.4L engine) or timing belt cover (1.8L engine) is aligned with the hole or notch on the crankshaft pulley (see illustration).

Note: *On 1.4L engines, there is a hole in the crankshaft pulley that must align with the pointer on the timing chain cover. On 1.8L engines, the notch on the crankshaft pulley must align with the notch in the lower timing belt cover in the 6 o'clock position.*

5   After the number one piston has been positioned at TDC on the compression stroke, TDC for any of the remaining pistons can be located by turning the crankshaft and following the firing order. Divide the crankshaft pulley into two equal sections with chalk marks at each point, each indicating 180-degrees of crankshaft rotation. Rotating the engine past TDC no. 1 to the next mark will place the engine at TDC for cylinder no. 3.

4.20 Install the gasket into the grooved recess in the valve cover

4.21 Apply a bead of sealant to the joints where the timing chain cover meets the cylinder head (2015 and earlier 1.4L engine shown, later models similar)

4.23a Valve cover bolt tightening sequence (2015 and earlier 1.4L engine)

4.23b Valve cover bolt tightening sequence (2016 and later 1.4L engine)

4 Valve cover - removal and installation

Removal

2015 and earlier models

1 Disconnect the cable from the negative battery terminal (see Chapter 5). Remove the ignition coil assembly from the valve cover (see Chapter 5).

2 On 1.8L engines, detach the PCV hose from the valve cover. On 1.4L engines, detach the PCV hose from the routing clips on the cover.

3 On 1.4L engines, disconnect the electrical connectors from the camshaft position (CMP) sensors, camshaft position actuator solenoids, engine coolant temperature (ECT) sensor, the oil pressure sensor, then unclip the harness from the valve cover and move the harness out of the way. On 1.8L engines, detach the ECM wiring harness guide from the back of the valve cover and reposition it.

4 On 1.4L engines, remove the oil dipstick.

5 Remove the valve cover bolts, then lift the valve cover off. Tap gently with a soft-face hammer, if necessary, to break the gasket seal.

2016 and later models

Warning: *Wait until the engine is completely cool before beginning this procedure.*

6 Relieve the fuel pressure (see Chapter 4), then disconnect the cable from the negative terminal of the battery (see Chapter 5).

7 Remove the oil filler cap and engine cover fasteners. Lift the engine cover and valve cover insulator up and off of the valve cover (it may be necessary to remove the cover and insulator separately), then reinstall the oil filler cap.

8 Drain the cooling system (see Chapter 1).

9 Remove the vacuum pump (see Chapter 9).

10 Remove the ignition coils (see Chapter 5), then remove the fuel rail and fuel injectors (see Chapter 4).

11 Disconnect the PCV tube quick-connect fitting.

12 Detach the wiring harness retainers, then disconnect the connector ends from the various sensors and move the harness out of the way.

13 Remove the turbocharger coolant return pipe (see Chapter 4).

14 Disconnect the coolant line from the coolant expansion tank.

15 Remove the engine lifting bracket bolts and bracket.

16 Remove the oil level dipstick.

17 Disconnect the camshaft position actuator solenoid valve electrical connectors.

18 Remove the valve cover mounting bolts and remove the valve cover.

Installation

19 Clean the gasket surfaces on the intake manifold, cylinder head and valve cover. Use a shop rag and brake cleaner to wipe off all residue and gasket material from the sealing surfaces.

20 Insert a new valve cover gasket into the grooved recess in the valve cover. Make sure the gasket is positioned properly in the groove (see illustration).

21 If you're working on a 1.4L engine, apply a bead of RTV sealant to the areas where the timing chain cover and cylinder head meet (see illustration).

22 If you're working on a 1.8L engine, apply sealant to the center bolt at the right end of the engine (next to the timing belt rear cover).

23 The remainder of installation is the reverse of removal. If you're working on a 1.4L engine, tighten the valve cover bolts in the recommended sequence (see illustrations) to the torque listed in this Chapter's Specifications. If you're working on a 1.8L

5.10 Intake manifold bolt locations (2015 and earlier 1.4L engine shown, later models similar)

6.5 Soak the exhaust pipe retaining nuts with penetrating oil, then unscrew them

engine, tighten the valve cover bolts evenly, starting with the center bolts and working outward, to the torque listed in this Chapter's Specifications.

24 Reconnect the battery (see Chapter 5).

5 Intake manifold - removal and installation

Warning: *Wait until the engine is completely cool before beginning this procedure.*

1.4L engine

Removal

1 Disconnect the cable from the negative battery terminal (see Chapter 5).
2 Remove the engine cover.
3 Detach the charge air cooler outlet pipe from the throttle body (see Chapter 4).
4 Disconnect any electrical connectors that would interfere with manifold removal. Open the wiring harness clips and detach all wiring harnesses from the manifold.
5 Disconnect any vacuum hoses connected to the manifold, including the hose leading to the brake booster. Mark the hoses, if necessary, to ensure correct reassembly.
6 Relieve the system fuel pressure (see Chapter 4).
7 Disconnect the PCV hose from the intake manifold.
8 Detach the fuel feed line from the fuel rail (see Chapter 4).
9 Disconnect the vent line from the EVAP canister purge solenoid valve (see Chapter 6).
10 Remove the intake manifold mounting bolts (see illustration).
11 Detach the intake manifold from the cylinder head.

Installation

12 Install a new gasket to the manifold.
Note: *Make sure the mating surfaces of the manifold and cylinder head are clean.*
13 Place the manifold against the cylinder

head and install the bolts, but only finger-tight.
14 Tighten the bolts to the torque listed in this Chapter's Specifications, starting with the center bolts and working towards the ends.
15 The remainder of installation is the reverse of removal.
16 Reconnect the battery (see Chapter 5).
17 Run the engine and check for vacuum and fuel leaks.

1.8L engine

Removal

18 Disconnect the cable from the negative battery terminal (see Chapter 5), then relieve the fuel system pressure (see Chapter 4).
19 Remove the air intake duct, throttle body, fuel rail and fuel injectors (see Chapter 4).
20 Disconnect any electrical connectors that would interfere with manifold removal. Open the wiring harness clips and detach all wiring harnesses from the manifold.
21 Disconnect any vacuum hoses connected to the manifold, including the hose leading to the brake booster. Mark the hoses, if necessary, to ensure correct reassembly.
22 Disconnect the PCV hose from the valve cover.
23 Remove the intake manifold brace from under the manifold.
24 Remove the intake manifold mounting bolts.
25 Detach the intake manifold from the cylinder head.

Installation

26 Install new gaskets to the manifold.
Note: *Make sure the mating surfaces of the manifold and cylinder head are clean.*
27 Place the manifold against the cylinder head and install the bolts, but only finger tight.
28 Tighten the bolts to the torque listed in this Chapter's Specifications, starting with the center bolts and working towards the ends.
29 The remainder of installation is the reverse of removal.
30 Reconnect the battery (see Chapter 5).
31 Run the engine and check for vacuum and fuel leaks.

6 Exhaust manifold - removal and installation

Warning: *Wait until the engine is completely cool before starting this procedure.*

1.4L engine

Note: *On 2016 and later models, there is no exhaust manifold (it is integral to the cylinder head).*

1 On 1.4L engines, the turbocharger is integrated into the exhaust manifold and cannot be serviced separately. To remove the turbocharger/exhaust manifold assembly see Chapter 4.

1.8L engine

Note: *The catalytic converter is integrated into the exhaust manifold and cannot be serviced separately.*

Removal

2 Disconnect the cable from the negative battery terminal (see Chapter 5).
3 Remove the exhaust manifold heat shield.
4 Raise the vehicle and support it securely on jackstands.
5 Detach the exhaust pipe from the manifold/catalytic coverter (see illustration).
6 Follow the lead from the oxygen sensor up to its electrical connector, then unplug the connector. Also detach the lead from its retaining clip.
7 Remove the exhaust manifold support bracket bolts-to-engine block but leave the support bracket attached to the converter.
8 Remove the exhaust manifold mounting nuts and detach the manifold assembly from the cylinder head.

Installation

9 Using a scraper, thoroughly clean the mating surfaces on the cylinder head, manifold and exhaust pipe. Remove the residue with brake system cleaner.
10 Check that the mating surfaces are perfectly flat and not damaged in any way. A warped or damaged manifold may require machining or, if severe enough, replacement. Install the new

7.14 Location of the lower crankcase hole plug

8.8 Upper timing chain guide bolts

gasket to the cylinder head studs and place the manifold on the cylinder head. Tighten the nuts evenly, working from the center outwards, to the torque listed in this Chapter's Specifications.

11   Connect the exhaust pipe to the manifold and tighten the nuts evenly to the torque listed in this Chapter's Specifications.

12   The remainder of installation is the reverse of removal.

13   Reconnect the battery (see Chapter 5).

14   Run the engine and check for exhaust leaks.

7   Timing chain cover (1.4L engine) - removal and installation

Caution: *This is a difficult procedure requiring several special tools. Read through the entire procedure before attempting the job.*

Removal

1   Disconnect the cable from the negative battery terminal (see Chapter 5).

2   Remove the air filter housing (see Chapter 4).

3   Set the engine to TDC (see Section 3).

4   Loosen the right front wheel lug nuts, then raise the front of the vehicle and support it securely on jackstands. Remove the right front wheel.

5   Drain the engine oil and coolant (see Chapter 1).

6   Remove the drivebelt and tensioner (see Chapter 1).

7   Remove the alternator (see Chapter 5).

8   Remove the air conditioning compressor (see Chapter 3) and support it out of the way, then remove the compressor mounting bracket bolts and bracket.

Warning: *Don't disconnect the refrigerant lines from the compressor.*

9   Remove the crankshaft pulley (see Section 10).

10   Remove the oil pan (see Section 13).

11   Remove the water pump (see Chapter 3).

12   Remove the camshaft position actuator solenoid valves (see Chapter 6).

13   Remove both camshaft position sensors (see Chapter 6).

14   On 2015 and earlier models, remove the lower crankcase hole plug (see illustration), then insert special tool EN-952 locating pin (or equivalent) into the hole to lock the engine at TDC for 1 cylinder.

15   On 2015 and earlier models, hold each of the camshafts in place, using a wrench of the flat spots of the camshaft just behind the sprocket(s), then use a socket and ratchet to loosen the sprocket bolt until the CMP sensor exciter wheel can spin freely. Hold the camshafts on the hex again, then rotate the camshafts slightly, if necessary, until special tool EN-953-A (or equivalent) can be installed easily onto the the ends of the camshafts. Remove the upper timing chain guide.

Note: *The tool should fit easily onto the ends of the camshafts and lay flat against the cylinder head.*

16   Support the engine with an engine hoist or engine support fixture and remove the right side engine mount (see Section 17) and engine mount bracket.

17   Loosen the timing chain cover bolts gradually and evenly, then remove them.

Note: *Draw a sketch of the engine cover and cover fasteners. Identify the location of all bolts for installation in their original locations.*

18   Remove the timing chain cover.

19   Remove the timing chain (see Section 8) to get access to the timing chain cover gasket, then remove the gasket.

Installation

20   Inspect and clean all sealing surfaces of the timing chain cover and the block.

Note: *Be very careful when scraping on aluminum engine parts. Aluminum is soft and gouges easily. Severely gouged parts may require replacement.*

21   If necessary, replace the crankshaft front oil seal (see Section 10).

22   Apply a small 2 mm bead of RTV sealant at the outside corners where the cylinder head meets the cylinder block, then install a new gasket.

Note: *Once the sealant has been applied, the timing chain cover must be installed within a 10*

minute period or the sealant must be removed and applied again.

23   Install the timing chain (see Section 8).

24   Install the timing chain cover and fasteners. Make sure the hub on the oil pump inner rotor is aligned with the flats on the crankshaft and the cover fasteners are in their original locations. Tighten the fasteners by hand until the cover is contacting the block around its entire edge.

25   Tighten the 13 M6 cover bolts to the torque listed in this Chapter's Specifications.

26   Tighten the two M10 bolts to the torque listed in this Chapter's Specifications.

27   Install the upper timing chain guide, then tighten the camshaft sprockets (see Section 8).

28   Install the camshaft position actuator solenoid valves (see Chapter 6).

29   Install the water pump (see Chapter 3).

30   Install the crankshaft pulley (see Section 10).

31   Reinstall the remaining parts in the reverse order of removal.

32   Fill the crankcase with the recommended oil (see Chapter 1).

33   Refill the cooling system (see Chapter 1).

34   Reconnect the battery (see Chapter 5).

35   Start the engine and check for leaks. Check all fluid levels.

8   Timing chain and sprockets (1.4L engine) - removal, inspection and installation

Removal

Caution: *The timing system is complex. Severe engine damage will occur if you make any mistakes. Do not attempt this procedure unless you are highly experienced with this type of repair. If you are at all unsure of your abilities, consult an expert. Double-check all your work and be sure everything is correct before you attempt to start the engine.*

Note: *This is a difficult procedure, involving special tools. Read through the entire Section and obtain the necessary tools before beginning the procedure. New camshaft sprocket bolts must be purchased ahead of time.*

1   Disconnect the cable from the negative battery terminal (see Chapter 5). Remove the spark plugs (see Chapter 1).

2   Remove the valve cover (see Section 4).

3   Drain the engine oil (see Chapter 1).

4   Remove the drivebelt (see Chapter 1).

5   Remove the drivebelt tensioner (see Chapter 1).

2015 and earlier models

6   Remove the timing chain cover (see Section 7).

7   Compress the timing chain tensioner until special tool EN-955-10 (or a small Allen wrench) can be inserted into the tensioner, locking the tensioner in place.

8   Remove the upper timing chain guide bolts and guide from the top of the cylinder head (see illustration).

8.13 Use a wrench on the hex on the camshaft to prevent the camshaft from turning while loosening the sprocket bolt

9   Remove the right side timing chain guide bolts and guide.

10   Remove the left side timing chain guide bolt from the bottom of the guide and remove the guide.

11   Remove the timing chain and crankshaft sprocket.

12   Remove the timing chain tensioner bolts and tensioner.

13   Use a wrench on the intake or exhaust cam hex to hold the camshaft, and remove the camshaft sprocket bolt(s) (see illustration) and slide the sprocket(s) off the end of the camshaft(s). Discard the bolt and install a new one on reassembly.

2016 and later models

14   Remove the valve cover (see Section 4).

15   Rotate the crankshaft pulley until the marks on the crankshaft pulley and timing cover are aligned.

16   Install special holder tool no. EN-51367 over the flats on the front of the camshafts to hold the camshafts in place.

17   Remove the timing chain cover (see Section 7).

18   Remove the timing chain upper guide bolts from the top of the cylinder head.

Note: *This engine has one of two timing chain tensioner designs. Both designs have a different release mechanism and position.*

19   If your model has the first design, push the plunger in slightly until the locking lever can be moved down the depress the plunger and insert a drill bit through the hole in the lever and into the tensioner body. If your model has the second design, push the plunger in slightly then insert a drill bit into hole in the tensioner body.

20   Once the tensioner is in the locked position, remove the mounting bolts and tensioner.

21   Remove the timing chain guide bolts and guides from each side of the timing chain.

22   Remove the timing chain and tensioner gasket. Be sure to replace the tensioner gasket upon assembly.

23   Use a wrench on the intake or exhaust camshaft hex towards the middle of the camshafts to hold the camshaft, then remove the camshaft position actuator bolt(s) and slide the actuator sprocket(s) off of the camshaft(s). Always replace the camshaft actuator bolts with new ones.

Inspection

24   Clean all parts with solvent and dry with compressed air, if available.

25   Inspect the chain tensioner for excessive wear or other damage. Drain all the oil out of the chain tensioner if it is to be reused.

26   Inspect the timing chain guides for deep grooves, excessive wear, or other damage.

27   Inspect the timing chain for excessive wear or damage.

28   Inspect the crankshaft and camshaft sprockets for chipped or broken teeth, excessive wear, or damage.

29   Replace any component that is in questionable condition.

Installation

Caution: *Before starting the engine, carefully rotate the crankshaft by hand through at least two full revolutions (use a socket and breaker bar on the crankshaft pulley center bolt). If you feel any resistance, STOP! There is something wrong most likely, valves are contacting the pistons. You must find the problem before proceeding.*

2015 and earlier models

30   Slide the camshaft sprockets onto the end of the camshafts, then place the exciter wheels on to each camshaft. Install new camshaft sprocket bolts, but only finger-tight at this time.

Note: *The camshaft sprockets should be able to freewheel at this time.*

31   Apply a small 2 mm bead of RTV at the outside corners where the cylinder head meets the cylinder block, then install a new timing chain cover gasket.

32   Install the front cover gasket to the cylinder block and cylinder head.

33   Place the crankshaft sprocket into the bottom of the chain loop, then drape the chain over the camshaft sprockets and slide the crankshaft sprocket onto the end of the crankshaft.

34   Install the timing chain tensioner and tighten the bolts to the torque listed in this Chapter's Specifications.

35   Install the left-side timing chain guide and guide bolt then tighten the bolt to the torque listed in this Chapter's Specifications.

36   Install the right-side timing chain guide and guide bolts then tighten the bolts to the torque listed in this Chapter's Specifications.

37   Push the left guide towards the tensioner until the locking pin can be removed, then pull the pin out from the tensioner.

38   Use a wrench on the intake or exhaust cam hex to hold the camshaft, then rotate the camshafts until special tool EN-953-A can be installed onto the the ends of the camshafts (this only applies if the camshafts were removed; otherwise, the tool will still be in place).

39   Install special tool EN-49977-200 between the camshaft adjuster sprockets where the upper timing chain guide sits and tighten the bolts securely. Adjust the tool towards the intake camshaft until the teeth on the tool engage the teeth on the intake camshaft sprocket, then lock the tool adjustment bolt in place.

40   Install special tool EN-49977-100 over the camshaft sprocket, aligning the exciter wheels to the tool as it is seated on the cylinder head, then tighten the tool-to-cylinder head mounting bolts securely.

Caution: *The tool must fit flush against the curved sections of the cylinder or the exciter wheels will be installed incorrectly.*

41   Hold the intake camshaft with a wrench on the camshaft's hex to prevent it from turning, then tighten the intake camshaft sprocket bolt to the torque listed in this Chapter's Specifications.

42   Hold the exhaust camshaft with a wrench on the camshaft's hex to prevent it from turning, then tighten the exhaust camshaft sprocket bolt to the torque listed in this Chapter's Specifications.

43   Remove both EN-49977-100 and EN-49977-200 tools, then install the upper timing chain guide and bolts, tightening the bolts to the torque listed in this Chapter's Specifications.

44   Remove the EN-953-A tool from the ends of the camshafts, then remove the EN-952 pin from the crankcase hole. Using a socket and breaker bar on the crankshaft pulley bolt, turn the crankshaft slowly (clockwise) through two complete revolutions (720-degrees) and verify the special tool can be installed again following Steps 28 through 30.

2016 and later models

45   Slide the camshaft actuator sprocket onto the camshafts and align the dowels on the camshafts with the locating hole on the actuator sprockets then insert the new camshaft actuator bolts and tighten the actuator bolts hand tight.

46   With the timing marks on the camshaft sprocket actuator at the 12 o'clock position and the crankshaft sprocket mark at the 3 o'clock position, place the timing chain around the crankshaft sprocket, aligning the color

9.12 Install the special tool to lock the camshaft adjuster sprockets in place

1	Special tool EN-6340	3	Intake camshaft
2	Exhaust camshaft alignment mark	4	Exhaust camshaft

9.17 Rotate the crankshaft from TDC back 60-degrees

1 Approximate 60-degree location

plated link of the timing chain with the crankshaft sprocket timing mark.

47 Loop the timing chain up onto the exhaust camshaft sprocket, then the intake camshaft sprocket, aligning the colored links of the chain with the camshaft sprocket timing marks (12 o'clock position).

48 Install the right chain guide and tighten the mounting bolt to the torque listed in this Chapter's Specifications.

49 With all three marks aligned, install the new timing chain tensioner gasket, tensioner and mounting bolts, then tighten the bolts to the torque listed in this Chapter's Specifications.

50 Install the left chain guide and tighten the mounting bolt to the torque listed in this Chapter's Specifications, then remove the pin from the timing chain tensioner.

51 Remove the special holder tool no. EN-51367 from the camshafts.

52 Install the upper chain guide and bolts, then tighten the bolts to the torque listed in this Chapter's Specifications.

53 Temporarily install the timing chain cover and crankshaft pulley and verify the notch on the pulley is aligned with the TDC mark on the timing chain cover. If the marks are aligned, remove the cover and verify the timing chain marks are all aligned.

54 Use a wrench on the intake or exhaust camshaft hex towards the middle of the camshafts to hold the camshaft from rotating, then tighten the camshaft position actuator bolt(s) to the torque listed in this Chapter's Specifications.

All models

55 Install the timing chain cover (see Section 7).

56 Install the valve cover (see Section 4).

57 The remainder of installation is the reverse of removal. Install a new oil filter and refill the crankcase with oil (see Chapter 1).

58 Refill the cooling system (see Chapter 1).

59 Reconnect the battery (see Chapter 5).

60 Run the engine and check for leaks.

9 Timing belt and sprockets (1.8L engine) - removal, inspection and installation

Caution: *The timing system is complex. Severe engine damage will occur if you make any mistakes. Do not attempt this procedure unless you are highly experienced with this type of repair. If you are at all unsure of your abilities, consult an expert. Double-check all your work and be sure everything is correct before you attempt to start the engine.*

Note: *This is a difficult procedure, involving special tools. Read through the entire Section and obtain the necessary tools before beginning the procedure. New camshaft sprocket bolts must be purchased ahead of time.*

Removal

1 Disconnect the cable from the negative terminal of the battery (see Chapter 5).

2 Remove the engine cover.

3 Remove the air filter housing (see Chapter 4).

4 Loosen the right front wheel lug nuts, then raise the front of the vehicle and support it securely on jackstands. Apply the parking brake and block the rear wheels. Remove the wheel.

5 Remove the inner fender splash shield (see Chapter 11). Also remove the under-vehicle splash shield.

6 Remove the drivebelt and drivebelt tensioner (see Chapter 1).

7 Remove the upper timing belt cover bolts and cover.

8 If you're working on a vehicle with a manual transaxle, remove the transaxle front mount (see Section 17).

9 Set the engine at TDC for number one cylinder (see Section 3)

10 Install a flywheel/driveplate locking tool. If you're working on a model with a manual transaxle, remove the transaxle-to-engine nut and bolt from the front of the bellhousing, mid-way up, near the catalytic converter. If you're working on a model with an automatic transaxle, remove the engine-to-transaxle bolt near the transaxle front mount. On all models, engage flywheel/driveplate locking tool no. EN-6625 (or equivalent) with the ring gear teeth, then reinstall the bolt and tighten it securely.

11 Remove the crankshaft pulley (see Section 10) and the lower timing belt cover.

12 Install special tool EN-6340 (or equivalent) in between the camshaft adjuster sprockets (see illustration) to lock the sprockets/adjuster wheels in place. Make sure the mark on the exhaust camshaft adjuster is aligned with the groove in the special tool.

13 Insert an Allen wrench into the timing belt tensioner and rotate the tensioner clockwise until lock pin tool EN-6333 (or equivalent) can be inserted into the back side of the tensioner.

14 Remove the idler pulley center bolt and idler pulley.

Note: *The idler pulley bolt must be replaced.*

15 If you intend to reuse the belt, mark it with an arrow indicating direction of travel and put match marks from the belt to the sprockets so it can be realigned easily.

16 Remove the timing belt and the tensioner. Always replace the tensioner bolt with a new one during reassembly.

17 To remove the camshaft adjuster sprockets, loosen special tool EN-6340, then insert the crankshaft pulley bolt and rotate the crankshaft 60-degrees (counterclockwise) before TDC (see illustration).

Note: *When the engine is turned back 60-degrees, a small amount of oil will come out of the camshaft adjuster sprockets.*

9.32 Align the crankshaft sprocket mark with the TDC mark on the oil pump housing

1   *TDC mark on the oil pump housing*
2   *Crankshaft alignment mark*

9.22 Check the timing belt for cracked or missing teeth; if the belt is cracked or worn, also check the pulleys for nicks or burrs - wear on one side of the belt indicates pulley misalignment problems

18   Remove the valve cover (see Section 4).
19   Rotate the camshafts by the hex areas until the slots on the end of the camshafts are parallel with the cylinder head, then install special tool EN-6628-A or a metal bar that can be inserted into the slots with little play, and long enough to reach to both camshafts.
20   The camshaft adjuster sprockets can be removed now, if necessary. Hold the hex area of the camshaft securely with a wrench, remove the outer closure plugs (the sealing "caps" over the sprocket bolts), then remove the camshaft adjuster sprocket bolts. Replace the sprocket bolts with new ones.
21   Remove the camshaft adjuster sprockets from the end of the camshafts.

Inspection

22   Check the belt for the presence of oil or dirt, and inspect for visible defects (see illustration).
23   Check that the tensioner and idler pulley turn smoothly.

Installation

24   Remove all dirt, oil and grease from the timing belt area at the front of the engine.
25   Install the camshaft sprocket(s) (if they were removed) on the camshaft(s) with new bolts, finger tight.
26   Install special tool EN-6340 onto the camshaft adjuster sprockets (see illustration 9.12), making sure the exhaust camshaft adjuster mark is aligned.
27   Hold the hex area of the camshaft securely with a wrench, then tighten the adjuster sprocket bolts to the torque listed in this Chapter's Specifications.
Caution: *Do not use special tool EN-6628-A to hold the camshafts while tightening the bolts - the camshafts could be damaged.*
28   Hold the hex area of the camshaft securely with a wrench, then install and tighten the adjuster sprocket closure plugs to the torque listed in this Chapter's Specifications.

29   Remove special tool EN-6628-A from the ends of the camshafts.
30   Install the timing belt tensioner with a new bolt and tighten the bolt to the torque listed in this Chapter's Specifications.
31   Install the idler pulley with a new bolt and tighten the bolt to the torque listed in this Chapter's Specifications.
32   Slide the crankshaft sprocket onto the end of the crankshaft, making sure the keyway (and sprocket mark) and TDC marks are aligned (see illustration).
33   Cover half of the timing belt with tape, then thread the timing belt through the engine mount bracket. Once the belt is through the the bracket you can remove the tape.
Note: *The timing belt can be cut when threading it through the engine mount bracket; it is a good idea to cover the belt before trying to slide it through the bracket.*
34   Verify the crankshaft timing mark is at 6 o'clock position (see illustration 9.32). Now align the camshaft sprockets with special tool EN-6340 (see illustration 9.12) and install the timing belt.
35   Insert an Allen wrench into the front of the tensioner and rotate the tensioner clockwise until the locking pin installed in Step 8 can be removed.
36   Using a socket and breaker bar on the crankshaft pulley bolt, turn the crankshaft slowly (clockwise) through two complete revolutions (720-degrees), positioning the crankshaft sprocket timing mark at the 6 o'clock position, with the marks lined up (see illustration 9.32). Insert special tool EN-6340-A between the camshaft adjuster sprockets, then try to install special tool EN-6628-A into the slots at the rear of the camshafts.
Caution: *Stop turning the crankshaft immediately if you feel resistance; the valves could be contacting the pistons.*
37   If the timing marks are not aligned exactly, repeat the timing belt installation procedure. DO NOT start the engine until

you're absolutely certain that the timing belt is installed correctly. Serious and costly engine damage could occur if the belt is installed incorrectly.
38   The remainder of installation is the reverse of removal.

10   Crankshaft pulley and front oil seal - removal and installation

Crankshaft pulley

1   Disconnect the cable from the negative battery terminal (see Chapter 5).
2   Remove the drivebelt (see Chapter 1).
3   Raise the vehicle and support it securely on jackstands.
4   Remove the under-vehicle splash shield.
5   Remove the inner fender splash shield (see Chapter 11).
6   If you're removing the crankshaft pulley as part of the timing chain or timing belt removal procedure, set the engine at TDC for cylinder no. 1 (see Section 3).

1.4L engine
2015 and earlier models
7   Remove the drivebelt tensioner (see Chapter 1).
8   Rotate the engine until the hole in the crankshaft pulley is aligned with the mark on the engine cover (approximately the 2 o'clock position) (see illustration 3.4).
Caution: *The crankshaft pulley can be incorrectly installed 180-degrees out. Be sure to note the location of the alignment hole before removing or installing the crankshaft pulley.*
9   Prevent the pulley from turning by holding it with a pin spanner that engages with the slots in the pulley hub, then use a large ratchet or breaker bar and socket to unscrew the crankshaft pulley center bolt (see illustration). Discard the bolt and obtain a new one for installation.

10.9 A large pin spanner can be used to prevent the pulley from rotating while the bolt is loosened

10.33 Use a seal puller to remove the old crankshaft seal, taking care not to damage the crankshaft or the seal bore in the cover

10.35 Driving the new seal in with a seal driver until the seal is flush with the surface of the timing chain cover (1.4L engine) or oil pump (1.8L engine).

10   Slide the pulley off the nose of the crankshaft.

11   If you're replacing the crankshaft front oil seal, proceed to Step 33.

12   Lubricate the hub of the pulley with clean engine oil, then slide it onto the crankshaft. The pulley flange must fit into the hexagon section of the oil pump rotor and to the flats of the crankshaft. The TDC markings on crankshaft pulley and timing marks on the timing chain cover must align. Carefully press the pulley into position. When installed, the distance between the timing chain cover and the edge of the crankshaft pulley should be 7/32-inch (5.5 mm).

13   Install a NEW bolt and, holding the pulley with a pin spanner to immobilize it, tighten the bolt to the torque listed in this Chapter's Specifications.

14   The remainder of installation is the reverse of removal.

15   Reconnect the battery (see Chapter 5).

2016 and later models

16   Prevent the engine from rotating by installing flywheel/driveplate locking tool no. EN-51760 or using the crankshaft pulley retaining tool no. EN 44226-1 and remove the crankshaft center bolt using a large ratchet or breaker bar and socket to unscrew the bolt. Obtain a new crankshaft pulley bolt and discard the old bolt.

17   Install a machined dowel or special tool no. EN-44226-5 onto the end of the crankshaft, then install a three-jaw puller or special puller set no. EN-44226-1, EN-44226-2 and EN-44226-3 and pull the crankshaft pulley off the nose of the crankshaft.

Caution: *Be sure to use the proper adapter on the end of the crankshaft to prevent damage to the threads of the crankshaft.*

18   If you're replacing the crankshaft front oil seal, proceed to Step 33.

19   Lubricate the inside of the crankshaft pulley and nose of the crankshaft with clean engine oil, then align the notch in the pulley with the key in the crankshaft.

20   Insert the special installer tool no. EN-51368 and seat the crankshaft pulley onto the crankshaft.

21   Install a NEW crankshaft pulley bolt, then prevent the engine from rotating by engaging flywheel/driveplate locking tool no. EN-51760 or using the crankshaft pulley retaining tool no. EN 44226-1 and tighten the crankshaft center bolt to the torque listed in this Chapter's Specifications.

22   The remainder of installation is the revers of removal.

1.8L engines

23   If you're working on a model with a manual transaxle, remove the transaxle front mount (see Section 17).

24   Install a flywheel/driveplate locking tool. If you're working on a model with a manual transaxle, remove the transaxle-to-engine nut and bolt from the front of the bellhousing, midway up, near the catalytic converter. If you're working on a model with an automatic transaxle, remove the engine-to-transaxle bolt near the transaxle front mount. On all models, engage flywheel/driveplate locking tool no. EN-6625 (or equivalent) with the ring gear teeth, then reinstall the bolt and tighten it securely.

25   Using a large ratchet or breaker bar and socket, unscrew the crankshaft pulley center bolt. Discard the bolt and obtain a new one for installation.

26   Slide the pulley off the nose of the crankshaft.

27   If you are going to replace the crankshaft front oil seal, remove the timing belt (see Section 9) and slide the crankshaft sprocket off the nose of the crankshaft, then proceed to Step 34.

28   Lubricate the hub of the pulley with clean engine oil, then slide it onto the crankshaft.

29   Install a NEW bolt and tighten it to the torque listed in this Chapter's Specifications.

30   The remainder of installation is the reverse of removal.

31   Reconnect the battery (see Chapter 5).

Crankshaft front oil seal replacement

32   Remove the crankshaft pulley.

33   Use a seal removal tool to pry the seal out (see illustration).

34   Clean the seal bore and check it for nicks or gouges. Also examine the area of the hub that rides in the seal for signs of abnormal wear or scoring.

35   Coat the lip of the new seal with clean engine oil and drive it into the bore with a seal driver (see illustration). The open side of the seal faces into the engine.

36   Using clean engine oil, lubricate the sealing surface of the crankshaft pulley hub.

37   Install the crankshaft pulley.

11   Camshafts and hydraulic lash adjusters - removal, inspection and installation

Note: *This is a difficult procedure, involving special tools. Read through the entire Section and obtain the necessary tools before beginning the procedure. New camshaft sprocket bolts must be purchased ahead of time.*

1   Disconnect the cable from the negative battery terminal (see Chapter 5).

2   Remove the valve cover (see Section 4).

Removal

1.4L engine

3   Remove the timing chain and and camshaft sprockets (see Section 8).

4   Each camshaft cap should be marked for location and direction prior to disassembly. A little at time, loosen each bearing cap bolt slowly and evenly in reverse order of the tightening sequence (see illustrations 11.22a or 11.22b). Lift the camshaft(s) from the cylinder head, parallel to the head surface.

Caution: *The caps must be installed in their original locations. Keep all parts from each*

11.5 Remove each rocker arm

**11.6 Store the rocker arms in an organized manner so they
can be returned to their original locations**

**11.7 Pull the lash adjusters from their bores in the head and store
them along with their corresponding rocker arms**

**11.11 Camshaft bearing cap removal order sequence -
1.8L engines**

**11.13 On 1.4L engines, check the rocker
arms and lash adjusters for wear
at the indicated points**

camshaft together; never mix parts from one
camshaft with those for another.

5   Remove the rocker arms (see illustration).

6   Place the rocker arms in a suitable container, in order, so they can be reinstalled in
their original positions (see illustration).

7   Remove the hydraulic lash adjusters
from their bores in the cylinder head (see illustration). Store these with their corresponding
rocker arms so they can be reinstalled in their
original locations.

1.8L engine

8   Remove the timing belt and camshaft
adjuster sprockets (see Section 9).

9   If not already removed, remove both
camshaft position sensors (see Chapter 6).

10   Remove the special tool EN-6628-A (or
flat bar) from the ends of the camshafts.

11   Each camshaft cap should be marked
for location and direction. Loosen each bearing cap bolt slowly and evenly, a half turn at

a time in the order of the removal sequence
(see illustration). Lift the camshaft from the
cylinder head, parallel to the head surface.
Caution: The caps must be installed in their
original locations. Keep all parts from each
camshaft together; never mix parts from one
camshaft with those for another.

12   Remove the lifters (tappets) from their
bores in the cylinder head. Identify and
arrange the lifters so they can be reinstalled in
their original locations.

Inspection

13   On 1.4L engines, check each hydraulic
lash adjuster for excessive wear, scoring, pitting, or an out-of-round condition (see illustration). Replace as necessary.

14   On 1.8L engines, check the lifters for
scuffing and wear marks and replace as necessary.

15   If the adjusters or the cylinder head
bores are excessively worn, new adjusters or a new cylinder head, or both, may be

11.17 Check the cam lobes for pitting, excessive wear, and scoring. If scoring is excessive, as shown here, replace the camshaft

11.18 Measure each camshaft lobe height with a micrometer

24044-2a-11.24 HAYNES

11.22a Camshaft bearing cap tightening sequence - 2015 and earlier 1.4L engines

24044-2a-11.22b HAYNES

11.22b Camshaft bearing cap tightening sequence - 2016 and later 1.4L engine

required. If the valve train is noisy, particularly if the noise persists after a cold start, you can suspect a faulty lash adjuster.

16   On 1.4L engines, inspect the rocker arms for signs of wear or damage. The areas of wear are the tip that contacts the valve stem, the socket that contacts the lash adjuster and the roller that contacts the camshaft (see illustration 11.13).

17   Examine the camshaft lobes for scoring, pitting, galling (wear due to rubbing), and evidence of overheating (blue, discolored areas). Look for flaking of the hardened surface layer of each lobe (see illustration). If any such wear is evident, replace the camshaft.

18   Measure the lobe height of each cam lobe on the intake camshaft, and record your measurements (see illustration). Compare t he measurements for excessive variation; if the lobe heights vary more than 0.005 inch (0.125 mm), replace the camshaft. Compare the lobe height measurements on the exhaust camshaft and follow the same procedure. Do not com-

pare intake camshaft lobe heights with exhaust camshaft lobe heights, as they are different. Only compare intake lobes with intake lobes and exhaust lobes with exhaust lobes.

19   Inspect the camshaft bearing journals and the cylinder head bearing surfaces for pitting or excessive wear. If any such wear is evident, replace the component concerned. **Note:** *The manufacturer does not furnish camshaft journal diameter specifications.*

Installation

1.4L engine

20   Lubricate the rocker arms and hydraulic lash adjusters with engine assembly lubricant or fresh engine oil. Install the adjusters into their original bores, then install the rocker arms in their correct locations.

21   Lubricate the camshafts with camshaft installation lubricant and install them in their correct locations.

22   Install the camshaft bearing caps in their

correct locations. Install the cap bolts and tighten by hand until snug. Tighten the bolts in four to five steps, starting with the center cap and working to the outside caps (see illustrations), to the torque listed in this Chapter's Specifications.

23   Reinstall the camshaft actuators and the timing chain (see Section 8).

24   Rotate the engine by hand two revolutions - if you feel any resistance, stop and find out why.

1.8L engine

25   Lubricate the lifters with engine assembly lubricant or fresh engine oil. Install the lifters into their original bores.

26   Lubricate the camshafts with camshaft installation lubricant and install them in their correct locations. The camshaft lobes for cylinder no. 1 must be pointing away from the lifters, and the slots at the rear of the shafts must be parallel (or nearly parallel with the surface of the cylinder head.

**11.27 Camshaft bearing cap tightening sequence -
1.8L engines**

**12.17a Cylinder head bolt tightening sequence -
2015 and earlier 1.4L engine**

27   Install the camshaft bearing caps in order, and tighten the caps slowly and evenly in order of the tightening sequence (see illustration). When installing the first camshaft bearing cap, apply anaerobic sealant to the sealing surfaces of the cap, making sure the sealant does not block the oil passages.

28   Coat the lips of the new camshaft oil seals with clean engine oil and drive them into their bores with a seal driver or a socket slightly smaller in diameter than the seal. The open side of the seal faces into the cylinder head.

29   Using a wrench on the hex section of the camshaft, rotate the intake camshaft counterclockwise and install special tool EN-6628-A into the rear of the intake camshaft, then rotate the exhaust camshaft counterclockwise until special tool EN-6628-A can be installed into the end of the camshaft. The tool should fit into both camshafts and be flush against the cylinder head.

Note: *It may be necessary to use a second wrench on the intake camshaft and slightly take the pressure off of the special tool to allow it to seat in both camshafts.*

30   The remainder of installation is the reverse of removal.

31   Reconnect the battery (see Chapter 5).

12   Cylinder head - removal and installation

Caution: *The engine must be completely cool when the head is removed. Failure to allow the engine to cool off could result in head warpage. New head bolts should be purchased ahead of time.*

Removal

1   Disconnect the cable from the negative battery terminal (see Chapter 5).

2   Wait until the engine is completely cool, then drain the cooling system (see Chapter 1).

3   Remove the drivebelt and the drivebelt tensioner (see Chapter 1).

4   On 1.4L engines, remove the turbocharger assembly (see Chapter 4).

5   On 1.8L models, remove the exhaust manifold (see Section 6).

6   Remove the intake manifold (see Section 5).

7   Remove the timing chain (1.4L engine, see Section 8) or timing belt (1.8L engine, see Section 9).

Caution: *On 2015 and earlier 1.4L engines it is possible to remove the cylinder head without removing the timing chain, using special tools EN-952, EN-953 and EN-955-10. If tension is lost on the chain at any point during the procedure, the timing chain will have to be removed. We recommend removing the timing chain and cover to prevent any debris or possible timing problems from occurring.*

8   Label and disconnect the electrical connectors from the cylinder head that will interfere with removal. Use tape and mark each connector to insure correct reassembly.

9   Remove the cylinder head bolts and discard them, following the reverse of the tightening sequence (see illustration 12.17a, 12.17b or 12.17c). Loosen the bolts in sequence 1/4-turn then a 1/2-turn at a time. If the head is to be completely overhauled, refer to Section 11 for removal of the camshafts, rocker arms, (if equipped) and hydraulic lash adjusters or lifters.

10   Use a prybar at the corners of the head-to-block mating surface to break the gasket seal. Do not pry between the cylinder head and engine block in the gasket sealing area.

11   Lift the cylinder head off the engine. If resistance is felt, place a wood block against the end and strike the wood block with a hammer. Store the cylinder head on wood blocks to prevent damage to the gasket sealing surfaces.

12   Remove the old cylinder head gasket. Before removing, note the correct orientation of the gasket for correct installation.

Installation

13   The mating surfaces of the cylinder head and block must be perfectly clean when the head is installed. Use a gasket scraper to remove all traces of carbon and old gasket material, then clean the mating surfaces with brake system cleaner. If there's oil on the mating surfaces when the cylinder head is installed, the gasket may not seal correctly and leaks may develop. When working on the engine block, cover the open areas of the engine with shop rags to keep debris out during repair and reassembly. Use a vacuum cleaner to remove any debris that falls into the cylinders.

14   Check the engine block and cylinder head mating surfaces for nicks, deep scratches and other damage.

15   Use a tap of the correct size to chase the threads in the cylinder head bolt holes. Dirt, corrosion, sealant and damaged threads will affect torque readings.

16   Make sure the new gasket is located on the dowels in the block.

17   Carefully position the cylinder head on the engine block without disturbing the gasket. Install new cylinder head bolts and, following the recommended sequence (see illustrations), tighten the bolts to the torque listed in this Chapter's Specifications.

Note: *The method used for the head bolt tightening procedure is referred to as a "torque-angle" method. A special torque angle gauge (available at most auto parts stores) is available to attach to a breaker bar and socket for better accuracy during the tightening procedure.*

18   Install the timing chain (see Section 8) or timing belt (see Section 9).

24044-2a-12.17b HAYNES

24044-2a-12.17c HAYNES

12.17b Cylinder head bolt tightening sequence - 1.8L engine

12.17c Cylinder head tightening bolt sequence - 2016 and later 1.4L engine

19 Install the turbocharger (1.4L engine, see Chapter 4) or exhaust manifold (see Section 6).

20 Install the intake manifold (see Section 5).

21 The remaining installation steps are the reverse of removal.

22 Reconnect the battery (see Chapter 5).

23 Change the engine oil and filter and refill the cooling system (see Chapter 1), then start the engine and check carefully for oil and coolant leaks.

13 Oil pan - removal and installation

Removal

Note: *On 2016 and later 1.4L engines, there are two oil pans: an upper oil pan and a lower oil pan. The lower oil pan must be removed first to access the upper oil pan. 2015 and earlier models use one oil pan mounted to the lower crankcase and on later models the upper oil pan is mounted to the lower crankcase.*

1 Drain the engine oil and remove the drivebelt (see Chapter 1).

2 On 1.8L models, loosen the right-front wheel lug nuts.

3 Raise the front of the vehicle and support it securely on jackstands.

4 On 1.8L models, remove the right-front wheel and the inner fender splash shield (see Chapter 11).

5 On 1.4L models, remove the exhaust system and catalytic converter (see Chapter 6).

6 On 2016 and later 1.4L engines, remove the lower oil pan mounting bolts and remove the lower oil pan from the upper oil pan.

7 On 2016 and later 1.4L engines, disconnect the electrical connector from the oil pump flow control solenoid harness connec-

tor on the outside of the upper oil pan, then disconnect the electrical connector from the oil pump flow control solenoid on the oil pump inside the oil pan. Remove the harness connector mounting bolt and pull the harness connector out of the upper oil pan.

8 On 1.8L models, disconnect the exhaust system from the exhaust manifold (see Chapter 2A).

9 Remove the engine oil heater fastener and move the heater away from the oil pan, if equipped.

10 On 1.8L engines, remove the dipstick and the dipstick tube (the tube is bolted to the intake manifold).

11 Remove the oil pan-to-transaxle bolts.

12 Loosen the oil pan bolts a little at a time, in a criss-cross pattern, until they can be removed.

13 Carefully remove the oil pan from the lower crankcase.

Caution: *If the oil pan is difficult to separate from the lower crankcase, use a rubber mallet or a block of wood and a hammer to jar it loose. If it's stubborn and still won't come off, pry carefully on casting protrusions (not the mating surfaces!).*

Caution: *On 1.8L engines, there is an oil screen mounted in the oil pan; as the pan is lowered, make sure the screen stays in the oil pan or it can get caught on the engine block and be damaged.*

Installation

14 Using a gasket scraper, thoroughly clean all old gasket material from the lower crankcase and oil pan. Remove residue and oil film with a solvent such as brake system cleaner.

15 On 1.8L engines, make sure the oil screen is seated properly in the oil pan.

16 Apply a 5/64-inch (2 mm) bead of RTV sealant (2015 and earlier 1.4L engines), or

a 3/16-inch (2.25 mm) bead of sealant (2016 and later 1.4L engines) or 1/8-inch (3.5 mm) bead of sealant (1.8L engine) to the perimeter of the oil pan, inboard of the bolt holes, and on 2015 and earlier 1.4L engines, around the oil suction port. Allow the sealant to set-up before installing the oil pan to the engine (but be sure to install the pan within the time given by the sealant manufacturer).

17 On 2015 and earlier 1.4L engines, also apply a bead of sealant to the groove at the bottom of the timing chain cover and around the bolt hole of the rear main bearing tie-plate.

18 On 1.8L engines, also apply extra beads of sealant to the joints where the oil pump and rear main oil seal retainer meet the engine block.

19 Install the oil pan and bolts, tightening them to approximately 18 in-lbs (2 Nm), then tighten the oil pan-to-transaxle bolts to the torque listed in this Chapter's Specifications. Finally, tighten the oil pan bolts a little at a time, starting from the center bolts and working outward, to the torque listed in this Chapter's Specifications.

20 On 2016 and later 1.4L engines, install the oil pump flow control solenoid harness into the oil pan, then install the bolt, tightening it securely. Connect both ends of the connector.

21 On 2016 and later 1.4L engines, apply a 3/16-inch (2.25mm) bead of sealant to the lower oil pan and install the lower oil pan to the upper oil pan, then tighten the bolts in a criss-cross pattern to the torque listed in this Chapter's Specifications.

22 The remaining installation is the reverse of removal. Tighten the wheel lug nuts to the torque listed in the Chapter 1 Specifications.

23 Refill the engine with oil and install a new oil filter (see Chapter 1), then run the engine and check for leaks.

14   Oil pump - removal, inspection and installation

Removal

1   Drain the engine oil (see Chapter 1).
2   Remove the drivebelt (see Chapter 1).
3   Loosen the right-front wheel lug nuts, raise the front of the vehicle and support it securely on jackstands. Remove the right front wheel.

2015 and earlier 1.4L engine

4   Remove the timing chain cover (see Section 7).
5   Working on the backside of the timing chain cover, loosen the eight oil pump cover screws a little at a time until they're all loose. When all of the screws are loose, remove the cover.
6   Use a screwdriver to compress the pump slide spring, then remove the spring and spring pin.
Warning: *Cover the spring with a rag to prevent the spring from flying out and possibly causing injury while its being compressed.*

2016 and later 1.4L engine

7   Remove the upper oil pan (see Section 13).
8   Disconnect the electrical connector from the oil pump flow control solenoid.
9   Make a mark the oil pump drive gear to the oil pump chain so it can be reinstalled in the same position.
10   Remove the four oil pump mounting bolts and the retainers.
Note: *Once the bolts and retainers are removed, the retainers must be replaced.*
11   With the help of an assistant, pull back on the oil pump chain tensioner then lower the rear of the oil pump and lift the oil pump drive gear out of the timing chain.
12   Remove and replace the two O-ring type oil pump gaskets.
13   To remove the oil pump flow control solenoid, slide the retaining clip out from the pump body, then using a slight twisting motion, withdraw the solenoid valve out from the pump body.

1.8L engine

Warning: *Wait until the engine is completely cool before beginning this procedure.*
14   Drain the engine coolant (see Chapter 1).
15   Remove the exhaust manifold (see Section 6).
16   Remove the air conditioning compressor mounting bolts (see Chapter 3), without disconnecting the lines, and secure the compressor out of the way.
17   Remove the alternator (see Chapter 5).
18   Remove the camshaft actuator sprockets (see Section 9), then remove the timing belt rear cover bolts and cover.
19   Remove the oil pan (see Section 13).
20   Loosen the hose clamp and detach the radiator hose from the water pump.

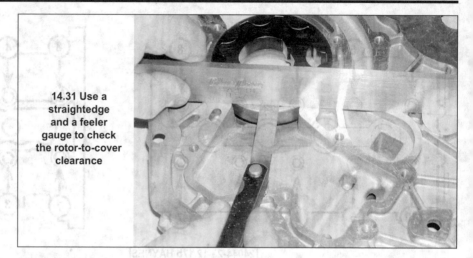

14.31 Use a straightedge and a feeler gauge to check the rotor-to-cover clearance

21   Remove the engine oil cooler inlet and outlet pipe bolts and push the pipes towards the oil cooler housing.
22   Remove the oil pump/front cover bolts, then remove the pump assembly from the front of the engine block and discard the gaskets.

Inspection

2015 and earlier 1.4L engine

23   Disassemble the oil pump by removing the oil pump outer vane ring, the oil pump vane rotor, the seven oil pump vanes, the oil pump inner vane ring, the oil pump slide, slide seals and slide seal springs.
24   Thoroughly clean and dry the components.
25   Inspect the front cover for damage and the oil pump cover mating area for flatness, the oil pump cover for flatness, the vanes, vane rotor, vane rings and pump slide for wear. Also check that the pump slide pin seats squarely and firmly in the cover.
26   Inspect the vane rotors for obvious wear or damage. The slide spring pin, slide spring, slide seal and slide seal spring can be individually replaced. If any other parts are scored or damaged, the complete oil pump assembly must be replaced. Use feeler gauges and a straghtedge to check the pump clearances.
27   Using compressed air, blow out the oil passages and main bore in the cover.

2016 and later 1.4L engine

28   The oil pump is not serviceable. If there is a problem with the pump it must be replaced.

1.8L engine

29   Note any identification marks on the rotors and withdraw the rotors from the pump body. If no marks can be seen, use a permanent marker and make your own to ensure that they will be installed correctly.
30   Thoroughly clean and dry the components.
31   Inspect the rotors for obvious wear or damage. If either rotor, the pump body or the cover is scored or damaged, the complete oil pump assembly must be replaced. Also check the

rotor-to-cover side clearance (see illustration).
32   If the oil pump components are in acceptable condition, dip the rotors in clean engine oil and install them into the pump body with any identification marks positioned as noted during disassembly.

Installation

2015 and earlier 1.4L engine

33   Install the oil pump slide into the front cover, then place the inner vane ring into the center of the slide. Set the vane rotor into the slide, making sure the mark on the vane rotor is in the 3 o'clock position.
34   Install the seven oil pump vanes into the vane rotor, making sure the wear spots from the vane rings are installed in the same positions.
35   Place the outer vane ring onto the assembly, then install the slide seals with the rounded edge facing up, and the slide seal springs with the center (hump) against the bottom of the slide seal.
36   Install the slide spring pin, with the flat side of the pin facing upward and the oil pump slide spring into the cover against the oil pump slide.
Caution: *Using tape and cardboard, protect the edges of the timing chain cover when trying to install the oil ump slide spring to prevent damage to the cover sealing surfaces.*
37   Once all the components are in the pump, apply engine oil to the vanes, rotor and slide spring, then allow the oil to fill the chambers between the vanes.
38   Install the oil pump cover and tighten the screws securely.
39   Insert the crankshaft pulley into the front cover, making sure the flats on the pulley are seated into the oil pump rotor. Turn the crankshaft pulley counterclockwise to make sure the pump spins easily.
40   Install the timing chain cover (see Section 7).
41   The reminder of installation is the reverse of removal.

2016 and later 1.4L engine

42   Install the new oil pump O-ring gaskets into the pump body.

43   With the help of an assistant, release the chain tensioner by pulling it back, then place the oil pump drive gear into the chain, aligning the marks made in Step 9. Hold the pump up against the lower crankcase then install the pins and mounting bolts.

44   Tighten the oil pump mounting bolts to the torque listed in this Chapter's Specifications.

45   Install the oil pump flow control solenoid into the oil pump then insert the retaining clip.

46   Make sure the clip is fully seated, then connect the electrical connector.

47   Install the oil pan (see Section 13).

48   The remainder of installation is the reverse of removal.

49   Refill the engine with oil and coolant (see Chapter 1). Run the engine and check for oil and coolant leaks. Also check the oil pressure as described in Chapter 2B if necessary.

1.8L engine

50   Install the rotors into the housing with the hub of the inner rotor facing the engine front cover. The inner rotor hub must be installed correctly or the engine front cover/gerotor cover will not fasten properly.

51   Pack the recesses between the rotors with petroleum jelly.

52   Install the oil pump cover and screws and tighten the screws securely.

53   Install the front cover and oil pump assembly, using a new gasket. Tighten the bolts a little at a time to the torque listed in this Chapter's Specifications.

54   Remaining installation is the reverse of removal.

All models

55   Fill the engine with fresh engine oil (see Chapter 1). Install a new oil filter.

56   If you're working on a 1.8L model, refill the cooling system (see Chapter 1).

57   Start the engine and check for leaks.

58   Run the engine and make sure oil pressure comes up to normal quickly. If it doesn't, stop the engine and find out the cause. Severe engine damage can result from running an engine with insufficient oil pressure!

---

15   Flywheel/driveplate - removal and installation

Removal

1   Remove the transaxle (see Chapter 7A or 7B). If it's leaking, now would be a very good time to replace the front pump seal/O-ring (automatic transaxle only).

2   If you're working on a manual transaxle equipped vehicle, remove the pressure plate and clutch disc (see Chapter 8). Now is a good time to check/replace the clutch components.

3   Use a center punch or paint to make alignment marks on the flywheel/driveplate and crankshaft to ensure correct alignment during reinstallation.

4   Remove the bolts that secure the fly-wheel/driveplate to the crankshaft. Wedge a screwdriver in the ring gear teeth to prevent the crankshaft from turning.

5   Remove the flywheel/driveplate from the crankshaft. Since the flywheel is fairly heavy, support it while removing the last bolt. If an automatic transaxle-equipped vehicle has a spacer between the crankshaft and the drive-plate, note which way it was installed.

Note: *On 1.8L engines, an encoder wheel and reluctor ring for the crankshaft position sensor are mounted directly to the end of the crankshaft.*

Installation

6   Clean the flywheel to remove grease and oil. Inspect the surface for cracks, rivet grooves, burned areas and score marks. Light scoring can be removed with emery cloth. Check for cracked and broken ring gear teeth. Lay the flywheel on a flat surface and use a straightedge to check for warpage.

7   Clean and inspect the mating surfaces of the flywheel/driveplate and the crankshaft. If the crankshaft rear seal is leaking, replace it before reinstalling the flywheel/driveplate (see Section 16).

8   Position the flywheel/driveplate against the crankshaft, installing the spacer if one was present originally. Align the mating marks made during removal. Note that some engines have an alignment dowel or staggered bolt holes to ensure correct installation. Before installing the bolts, apply thread locking compound to the threads.

9   Wedge a screwdriver in the ring gear teeth to keep the flywheel/driveplate from turning and tighten the bolts to the torque listed in this Chapter's Specifications. Work up to the final torque in three or four steps.

10   The remainder of installation is the reverse of removal.

---

16   Rear main oil seal - replacement

1   The one-piece rear main oil seal is pressed into the engine block and the crank-case reinforcement section. Remove the transaxle (see Chapter 7A or 7B), the clutch components, if equipped (see Chapter 8) and the flywheel/driveplate (see Section 15).

2   On 2016 and later 1.4L and all 1.8L engines, remove the crankshaft position sensor (see Chapter 6). Once the flywheel is removed, remove the crankshaft position sensor encoder wheel and reluctor ring from the end of the crankshaft.

Caution: *Do not place the crankshaft encoder wheel on or near any magnets or magnetic field. Also, the wheel is easily cut. If the encoder wheel is cut or comes in contact with a magnetic field, it must be replaced.*

3   Pry out the old seal with a special seal removal tool or a flat-blade screwdriver.

Caution: *To prevent an oil leak after the new seal is installed, be very careful not to scratch or otherwise damage the crankshaft sealing surface or the bore in the engine block.*

4   Clean the crankshaft and seal bore in the block thoroughly, then de-grease these areas by wiping them with a rag soaked in brake system cleaner. Lubricate the lip of the new seal and the outer diameter of the crankshaft with clean engine oil.

5   Position the new seal onto the crankshaft. Make sure the edges of the new oil seal are not rolled over. Use a special rear main oil seal installation tool or a socket with the exact diameter of the seal to drive the seal in place. Make sure the seal is not offset; it must be flush along the entire circumference of the engine block and the crankcase reinforcement section.

Caution: *When installing the new seal, if so marked, the words THIS SIDE OUT on the seal must face out, toward the rear of the engine.*

6   The remainder of installation is the reverse of removal.

---

17   Powertrain mounts - check and replacement

Check

1   Engine mounts seldom require attention, but broken or deteriorated mounts should be replaced immediately or the added strain placed on the driveline components may cause damage or wear.

2   During the check, the engine must be raised slightly to remove the weight from the mounts.

3   Raise the vehicle and support it securely on jackstands, then position a jack under the engine oil pan. Place a large block of wood between the jack head and the oil pan, then carefully raise the engine just enough to take the weight off the mounts.

Warning: *DO NOT place any part of your body under the engine when it's supported only by a jack!*

4   Check the mounts to see if the rubber is cracked, hardened or separated from the bushing in the center of the mount.

5   Check for relative movement between the mount and the engine or frame (use a large screwdriver or prybar to attempt to move the mounts). If movement is noted, tighten the mount fasteners.

Replacement

6   Disconnect the negative battery cable (see Chapter 5). If you're replacing the right-side engine mount, remove the air filter housing (see Chapter 4). if you're removing the left-side transaxle mount, remove the battery and the battery tray (see Chapter 5).

7   If you're replacing the front or rear transaxle mount, raise the vehicle and support it securely on jackstands.

8   Place a block of wood between the jack head and the oil pan, then carefully raise the engine or transaxle just enough to take the weight off the mounts.

Caution: *Do not disconnect more than one mount at a time unless the engine will be removed from the vehicle.*

17.9a Right-side engine mounting fasteners

1 *Mount-to-body bolts/nut*
2 *Mount-to-mount bracket bolts*
3 *Mount bracket-to-engine bolts (lower bolt not visible)*

17.9b Left-side transaxle mounting fasteners

1 *Mount-to-transaxle bolts*
2 *Mount-to-chassis bolts*
3 *Mount-to-chassis nut*

17.9c Transaxle rear mount fasteners

1 *Mount-to-subframe bolts*
2 *Through-bolt*
3 *Bracket-to-transaxle bolts*

17.9d Transaxle front mount through-bolt

9   Refer to the accompanying illustrations for the locations of the powertrain mount fasteners (see illustrations).
10   Remove the fasteners holding the mount to the bracket.
11   Installation is the reverse of removal. Proceed to Step 12.

Powertrain/mount balancing

Note: *The engine/transaxle assembly must be aligned and balanced in its weight distribution among the powertrain mounts, before the mounting bolts are tightened.*
12   Raise the vehicle and support it securely on jackstands, if not already done.
13   Loosen the front and rear transaxle mount through-bolts (see illustrations 17.9c and 17.9d).

14   Lower the vehicle, then using two floor jacks, support the engine and transaxle.
Caution: *Place blocks of wood on the heads of the floor jacks to protect the engine and transaxle.*
15   Loosen the transaxle mount-to-transaxle bolts (see illustration 17.9b).
16   Loosen the engine mount-to-mount bracket bolts (see illustration 17.9a).
17   Lower the floor jacks so there is a 1/4-inch gap between the engine mount and its bracket and the transaxle mount and the transaxle.
18   The front and rear transaxle mounts must be centered in their brackets; if not, use a prybar to adjust the powertrain to achieve this.

19   Once alignment has been achieved, tighten the transaxle mount-to-transaxle bolts to the torque listed in this Chapter's Specifications.
20   Tighten the engine mount-to-mount bracket to the torque listed in this Chapter's Specifications.
21   Lower the floor jacks, then raise the vehicle and support it securely on jackstands.
22   Shake the engine and transaxle back and forth, then tighten the transaxle rear through-bolt, then the front through-bolt, in that order, to the torque listed in this Chapter's Specifications.
23   Install the under-vehicle splash shield, then lower the vehicle.
24   Reconnect the battery (see Chapter 5).

Chapter 2 Part B
General engine overhaul procedures

Contents

Specifications

General
Displacement
    1.4L engine
        2015 and earlier models .... 83.24 cubic inches
        2016 and later models .... 85 cubic inches
    1.8L engine .... 109.59 cubic inches
Bore
    1.4L engine
        2015 and earlier models .... 2.854 inches (72.5 mm)
        2016 and later models .... 2.91 inches (74 mm)
    1.8L engine .... 3.169 inches (80.5 mm)
Stroke
    1.4L engine
        2015 and earlier models .... 2.854 inches (72.5 mm)
        2016 and later models .... 3.200 inches (81.3 mm)
    1.8L engine .... 3.472 inches (88.2 mm)
Cylinder compressionLowest cylinder must be within 75 percent of highest cylinder
Oil pressure (engine at operating temperature)
    At idle
        1.4L engine (2015 and earlier) .... 22 psi (150 kPa)
        1.8L engine .... 18.85 psi (130 kPa)
    At 1500 rpm (hot)
        1.4L engine (2016 and later models) .... 26 to 36 psi (200 to 250 kPa)
    At 3000 rpm
        1.4L engine .... 55 to 94 psi (280 to 650 kPa)

Torque specifications

	Ft-lbs (unless otherwise indicated)	Nm

Note: *One foot-pound (ft-lb) of torque is equivalent to 12 inch-pounds (in-lbs) of torque. Torque values below approximately 15 ft-lbs are expressed in inch-pounds, since most foot-pound torque wrenches are not accurate at these smaller values.*

Connecting rod bearing cap bolts*
  1.4L engine
    2015 and earlier models

	Ft-lbs	Nm
Step 1	18	25
Step 2	Tighten an additional 45-degrees	
2016 and later models		
Step 1	18	25
Step 2	Tighten an additional 75-degrees	
1.8L engine		
Step 1	26	35
Step 2	Tighten an additional 45-degrees	
Step 3	Tighten an additional 15-degrees	
Lower crankcase bolts*		
1.4L engine - 2015 and earlier models (see illustration 10.19a)		
M6 Outer bolts		
Step 1	89 in-lbs	10
Step 2	Tighten an additional 60-degrees	
Step 3	Tighten an additional 15-degrees	
M8 Inner bolts		
Step 1	18	25
Step 2	Tighten an additional 60-degrees	
Step 3	Tighten an additional 15-degrees	
Lower crankcase perimeter bolts (see illustration 10.30a)	18	25
1.4L engine – 2016 and later models		
Inner bolts (see illustration 10.19b)		
Step 1	132 in-lbs	15
Step 2	Tighten an additional 180-degrees	
Perimeter bolts (see illustration 10.30b)		
Step 1	44 in-lbs	5
Step 2	89 in-lbs	10
Main bearing bolts, 1.8L engine* (see illustration 10.19c)		
Step 1	37	50
Step 2	Tighten an additional 45-degrees	
Step 3	Tighten an additional 15-degrees	
Crankshaft sensor reluctor wheel ring bolts - 1.4L engine	89 in-lbs	10

* Bolt(s) must be replaced.

1.10a An engine block being bored. An engine rebuilder will use special machinery to recondition the cylinder bores

1.10b If the cylinders are bored, the machine shop will normally hone the engine on a machine like this

1 General information - engine overhaul

1 Included in this portion of Chapter 2 are general information and diagnostic testing procedures for determining the overall mechanical condition of your engine.

2 The information ranges from advice concerning preparation for an overhaul and the purchase of replacement parts and/or components to detailed, step-by-step procedures covering removal and installation.

3 The following Sections have been written to help you determine whether your engine needs to be overhauled and how to remove and install it once you've determined it needs to be rebuilt. For information concerning in-vehicle engine repair, see Chapter 2A.

4 The Specifications included in this Part are general in nature and include only those necessary for testing the oil pressure, checking the engine compression, and bottom-end torque specifications. Refer to Chapter 2A for additional engine Specifications.

5 It's not always easy to determine when, or if, an engine should be completely overhauled, because a number of factors must be considered.

6 High mileage is not necessarily an indication that an overhaul is needed, while low mileage doesn't preclude the need for an overhaul. Frequency of servicing is probably the most important consideration. An engine that's had regular and frequent oil and filter changes, as well as other required maintenance, will most likely give many thousands of miles of reliable service. Conversely, a neglected engine may require an overhaul very early in its service life.

7 Excessive oil consumption is an indication that piston rings, valve seals and/or valve guides are in need of attention. Make sure that oil leaks aren't responsible before deciding that the rings and/or guides are bad. Perform a cylinder compression check to determine the extent of the work required (see Section 3). Also check the vacuum

readings under various conditions (see Section 4).

8 Check the oil pressure with a gauge installed in place of the oil pressure sending unit and compare it to this Chapter's Specifications (see Section 2). If it's extremely low, the bearings and/or oil pump are probably worn out.

9 Loss of power, rough running, knocking or metallic engine noises, excessive valve train noise and high fuel consumption rates may also point to the need for an overhaul, especially if they're all present at the same time.

10 An engine overhaul involves restoring the internal parts to the specifications of a new engine. During an overhaul, the piston rings are replaced and the cylinder walls are reconditioned (rebored and/or honed) (see illustrations 1.10a and 1.10b). If a rebore is done by an automotive machine shop, new oversize pistons will also be installed. The main bearings, connecting rod bearings and camshaft bearings are generally replaced with new ones and, if necessary, the crankshaft may be reground to restore the journals (see illustration 1.10c). Generally, the valves are serviced as well, since they're usually in

less-than-perfect condition at this point. While the engine is being overhauled, other components, such as the distributor, starter and alternator, can be rebuilt as well. The end result should be similar to a new engine that will give many trouble free miles.

Note: *Critical cooling system components such as the hoses, drivebelts, thermostat and water pump should be replaced with new parts when an engine is overhauled. The radiator should be checked carefully to ensure that it isn't clogged or leaking (see Chapter 3). If you purchase a rebuilt engine or short block, some rebuilders will not warranty their engines unless the radiator has been professionally flushed. Also, we don't recommend overhauling the oil pump - always install a new one when an engine is rebuilt.*

11 Overhauling the internal components on today's engines is a difficult and time-consuming task which requires a significant amount of specialty tools and is best left to a professional engine rebuilder (see illustrations 1.11a, 1.11b and 1.11c). A competent engine rebuilder will handle the inspection of your old parts and offer advice concerning the reconditioning or replacement of the

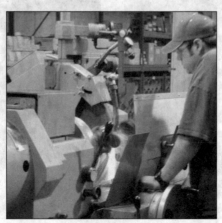

1.10c A crankshaft having a main bearing journal ground

1.11a A machinist checks for a bent connecting rod, using specialized equipment

original engine; never purchase parts or have machine work done on other components until the block has been thoroughly inspected by a professional machine shop. As a general rule, time is the primary cost of an overhaul, especially since the vehicle may be tied up for a minimum of two weeks or more. Be aware that some engine builders only have the capability to rebuild the engine you bring them while other rebuilders have a large inventory of rebuilt exchange engines in stock. Also be aware that many machine shops could take as much as two weeks time to completely rebuild your engine depending on shop workload. Sometimes it makes more sense to simply exchange your engine for another engine that's already rebuilt to save time.

1.11b A bore gauge being used to check a cylinder bore

1.11c Uneven piston wear like this indicates a bent connecting rod

2   Oil pressure check

1   Low engine oil pressure can be a sign of an engine in need of rebuilding. A low oil pressure indicator (often called an "idiot light") is not a test of the oiling system. Such indicators only come on when the oil pressure is dangerously low. Even a factory oil pressure gauge in the instrument panel is only a relative indication, although much better for driver information than a warning light. A better test is with a mechanical (not electrical) oil pressure gauge.

2   Locate the oil pressure sending unit. On 2015 and earlier 1.4L engines it is located towards the bottom of the oil filter housing (see illustration); on 2016 and later 1.4L engines it is located on the backside of the engine block towards the rear, just above the starter motor; on 1.8L engines it is located just above the exhaust manifold in the middle of the cylinder head (the exhaust manifold heat shield must be removed for access).

3   Unscrew and remove the oil pressure sending unit and screw in the hose for your oil pressure gauge. If necessary, install an adapter fitting. Use Teflon tape or thread sealant on the threads of the adapter and/or the fitting on the end of your gauge's hose.

4   Connect an accurate tachometer to the engine, according to the tachometer manufacturer's instructions.

5   Check the oil pressure with the engine running (normal operating temperature) at the specified engine speed, and compare it to this Chapter's Specifications. If it's extremely low, the bearings and/or oil pump are probably worn out.

3   Cylinder compression check

1   A compression check will tell you what mechanical condition the upper end of your engine (pistons, rings, valves, head gaskets) is in. Specifically, it can tell you if the compression is down due to leakage caused by worn piston rings, defective valves and seats or a blown head gasket. **Note:** *The engine must be at normal operating temperature and the battery must be fully charged for this check.*

2   Begin by cleaning the area around the spark plugs before you remove them (compressed air should be used, if available). The idea is to prevent dirt from getting into the cylin-

ders as the compression check is being done.

3   Remove all of the spark plugs from the engine (see Chapter 1).

4   Disable the fuel system by unplugging the electrical connector in the harness to the fuel injectors or by removing the fuel pump control module fuses (see Chapter 4).

5   Install a compression gauge in the spark plug hole (see illustration).

6   Have an assistant hold the accelerator pedal to the floor and crank the engine over at least seven compression strokes while you watch the gauge. The compression should build up quickly in a healthy engine. Low compression on the first stroke, followed by gradually increasing pressure on successive strokes, indicates worn piston rings. A low compression reading on the first stroke, which doesn't build up during successive strokes, indicates leaking valves or a blown head gasket (a cracked head could also be the cause). Deposits on the undersides of the valve heads can also cause low compression. Record the highest gauge reading obtained.

7   Repeat the procedure for the remaining cylinders and compare the results to this Chapter's Specifications.

2.2 On the 2015 and earlier 1.4L engine, the oil pressure sending unit is located on the bottom of the oil filter housing

3.5 Use a compression gauge with a threaded fitting for the spark plug hole, not the type that requires hand pressure to maintain the seal

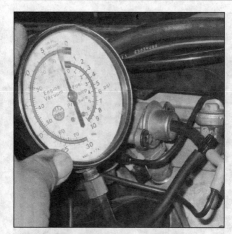

4.4 A simple vacuum gauge can be handy in diagnosing engine condition and performance

Low, steady reading   Low, fluctuating needle   Regular drops

Irregular drops   Rapid vibration

Large fluctuation   Slow fluctuation

STD-O-OBR HAYNES

4.6 Typical vacuum gauge readings

8   Add some engine oil (about three squirts from a plunger-type oil can) to each cylinder, through the spark plug hole, and repeat the test.

9   If the compression increases after the oil is added, the piston rings are definitely worn. If the compression doesn't increase significantly, the leakage is occurring at the valves or head gasket. Leakage past the valves may be caused by burned valve seats and/or faces or warped, cracked or bent valves.

10   If two adjacent cylinders have equally low compression, there's a strong possibility that the head gasket between them is blown. The appearance of coolant in the combustion chambers or the crankcase would verify this condition.

11   If one cylinder is slightly lower than the others, and the engine has a slightly rough idle, a worn lobe on the camshaft could be the cause.

12   If the compression is unusually high, the combustion chambers are probably coated with carbon deposits. If that's the case, the cylinder head(s) should be removed and decarbonized.

13   If compression is way down or varies greatly between cylinders, it would be a good idea to have a leak-down test performed by an automotive repair shop. This test will pinpoint exactly where the leakage is occurring and how severe it is.

4   Vacuum gauge diagnostic checks

1   A vacuum gauge provides inexpensive but valuable information about what is going on in the engine. You can check for worn rings or cylinder walls, leaking head or intake manifold gaskets, incorrect carburetor adjustments, restricted exhaust, stuck or burned valves, weak valve springs, improper ignition or valve timing and ignition problems.

2   Unfortunately, vacuum gauge readings are easy to misinterpret, so they should be used in conjunction with other tests to confirm the diagnosis.

3   Both the absolute readings and the rate of needle movement are important for accurate interpretation. Most gauges measure vacuum in inches of mercury (in-Hg). The following references to vacuum assume the diagnosis is being performed at sea level. As elevation increases (or atmospheric pressure decreases), the reading will decrease. For every 1,000 foot increase in elevation above approximately 2,000 feet, the gauge readings will decrease about one inch of mercury.

4   Connect the vacuum gauge directly to intake manifold vacuum, not to ported (throttle body) vacuum (see illustration). Be sure no hoses are left disconnected during the test or false readings will result.

5   Before you begin the test, allow the engine to warm up completely. Block the wheels and set the parking brake. With the transaxle in Park, start the engine and allow it to run at normal idle speed.
Warning: *Keep your hands and the vacuum gauge clear of the fans.*

6   Read the vacuum gauge; an average, healthy engine should normally produce about 17 to 22 in-Hg with a fairly steady needle (see illustration). Refer to the following vacuum gauge readings and what they indicate about the engine's condition:

7   A low steady reading usually indicates a leaking gasket between the intake manifold and cylinder head(s) or throttle body, a leaky vacuum hose, late ignition timing or incorrect camshaft timing. Check ignition

timing with a timing light and eliminate all other possible causes, utilizing the tests provided in this Chapter before you remove the timing chain cover to check the timing marks.

8   If the reading is three to eight inches below normal and it fluctuates at that low reading, suspect an intake manifold gasket leak at an intake port or a faulty fuel injector.

9   If the needle has regular drops of about two-to-four inches at a steady rate, the valves are probably leaking. Perform a compression check or leak-down test to confirm this.

10   An irregular drop or down-flick of the needle can be caused by a sticking valve or an ignition misfire. Perform a compression check or leak-down test and read the spark plugs.

11   A rapid vibration of about four in-Hg vibration at idle combined with exhaust smoke indicates worn valve guides. Perform a leak-down test to confirm this. If the rapid vibration occurs with an increase in engine speed, check for a leaking intake manifold gasket or head gasket, weak valve springs, burned valves or ignition misfire.

12   A slight fluctuation, say one inch up and down, may mean ignition problems. Check all the usual tune-up items and, if necessary, run the engine on an ignition analyzer.

13   If there is a large fluctuation, perform a compression or leak-down test to look for a weak or dead cylinder or a blown head gasket.

14   If the needle moves slowly through a wide range, check for a clogged PCV system,

6.3a After tightly wrapping water-vulnerable components, use a spray cleaner on everything, with particular concentration on the greasiest areas, usually around the valve cover and lower edges of the block. If one section dries out, apply more cleaner

6.3b Depending on how dirty the engine is, let the cleaner soak in according to the directions and hose off the grime and cleaner. Get the rinse water down into every area you can get at; then dry important components with a hair dryer or paper towels

incorrect idle fuel mixture, throttle body or intake manifold gasket leaks.

15　Check for a slow return after revving the engine by quickly snapping the throttle open until the engine reaches about 2,500 rpm and let it shut. Normally the reading should drop to near zero, rise above normal idle reading (about 5 in-Hg over) and return to the previous idle reading. If the vacuum returns slowly and doesn't peak when the throttle is snapped shut, the rings may be worn. If there is a long delay, look for a restricted exhaust system (often the muffler or catalytic converter). An easy way to check this is to temporarily disconnect the exhaust ahead of the suspected part and redo the test.

5　Engine rebuilding alternatives

1　The do-it-yourselfer is faced with a number of options when purchasing a rebuilt engine. The major considerations are cost, warranty, parts availability and the time required for the rebuilder to complete the project. The decision to replace the engine block, piston/connecting rod assemblies and crankshaft depends on the final inspection results of your engine. Only then can you make a cost effective decision whether to have your engine overhauled or simply purchase an exchange engine for your vehicle.

2　Some of the rebuilding alternatives include:

3　**Individual parts** - If the inspection procedures reveal that the engine block and most engine components are in reusable condition, purchasing individual parts and having a rebuilder rebuild your engine may be the most economical alternative. The block, crankshaft and piston/connecting rod assemblies should all be inspected carefully by a machine shop first.

4　**Short block** - A short block consists of an engine block with a crankshaft and piston/connecting rod assemblies already installed. All new bearings are incorporated and all clearances will be correct. The existing camshafts, valve train components, cylinder head and external parts can be bolted to the short block with little or no machine shop work necessary.

5　**Long block** - A long block consists of a short block plus an oil pump, oil pan, cylinder head, valve cover, camshaft and valve train components, timing sprockets and chain or gears and timing cover. All components are installed with new bearings, seals and gaskets incorporated throughout. The installation of manifolds and external parts is all that's necessary.

6　**Low mileage used engines** - Some companies now offer low mileage used engines which is a very cost effective way to get your vehicle up and running again. These engines often come from vehicles that have been in totaled in accidents or come from other countries that have a higher vehicle turn over rate. A low mileage used engine also usually has a similar warranty like the newly remanufactured engines.

7　Give careful thought to which alternative is best for you and discuss the situation with local automotive machine shops, auto parts dealers and experienced rebuilders before ordering or purchasing replacement parts.

6　Engine removal - methods and precautions

1　If you've decided that an engine must be removed for overhaul or major repair work, several preliminary steps should be taken. Read all removal and installation procedures carefully prior to committing to this job.

2　Locating a suitable place to work is extremely important. Adequate work space, along with storage space for the vehicle, will be needed. If a shop or garage isn't available, at the very least a flat, level, clean work surface made of concrete or asphalt is required.

3　Cleaning the engine compartment and engine before beginning the removal procedure will help keep tools clean and organized (see illustrations).

4　An engine hoist will also be necessary. Make sure the hoist is rated in excess of the combined weight of the engine and transaxle. Safety is of primary importance, considering the potential hazards involved in removing the engine from the vehicle.

5　A vehicle hoist will be necessary for engine removal, too, since on these models the engine and transaxle assembly must be lowered from the engine compartment, then the vehicle is raised and the powertrain unit is removed from under the vehicle. If the necessary equipment is not available, the engine will have to be removed by a qualified automotive repair facility.

6　If you're a novice at engine removal, get at least one helper. One person cannot easily do all the things you need to do to remove a big heavy engine and transaxle assembly from the engine compartment. Also helpful is to seek advice and assistance from someone who's experienced in engine removal.

7　Plan the operation ahead of time. Arrange for or obtain all of the tools and equipment you'll need prior to beginning the job (see illustrations). Some of the equipment necessary to perform engine removal and installation safely and with relative ease are (in addition to a vehicle hoist and an engine hoist) a heavy duty floor jack (preferably fitted with a transaxle jack head adapter), complete sets of wrenches and sockets as described in the front of this manual, wooden blocks, plenty of rags and

6.7a Get an engine stand sturdy enough to firmly support the engine while you're working on it. Stay away from three-wheeled models; they have a tendency to tip over more easily, so get a four-wheeled unit

6.7b A clutch alignment tool will be necessary if you're working on a model with a manual transaxle

cleaning solvent for mopping up spilled oil, coolant and gasoline.

8   Plan for the vehicle to be out of use for quite a while. A machine shop can do the work that is beyond the scope of the home mechanic. Machine shops often have a busy schedule, so before removing the engine, consult the shop for an estimate of how long it will take to rebuild or repair the components that may need work.

7   Engine - removal and installation

Warning: *Gasoline is extremely flammable, so take extra precautions when you work on any part of the fuel system. Don't smoke or allow open flames or bare light bulbs near the work area, and don't work in a garage where a gas-type appliance (such as a water heater or clothes dryer) is present. Since gasoline is carcinogenic, wear fuel-resistant gloves when there's a possibility of being exposed to fuel, and, if you spill any fuel on your skin, rinse it off immediately with soap and water. Mop up any spills immediately and do not store fuel-soaked rags where they could ignite. The fuel system is under constant pressure, so, if any fuel lines are to be disconnected, the fuel pressure in the system must be relieved first (see Chapter 4 for more information). When you perform any kind of work on the fuel system, wear safety glasses and have a Class B type fire extinguisher on hand.*
Warning: *The engine must be completely cool before beginning this procedure.*
Note: *Engine removal on these models is a difficult job, especially for the do-it-yourself mechanic working at home. Because of the vehicle's design, the manufacturer states that the engine and transaxle have to be removed as a unit from the bottom of the vehicle, not the top. With a floor jack and jackstands, the vehicle can't be raised high enough or supported safely enough for the engine/transaxle assembly to slide out from underneath. The manufacturer recommends that removal of the engine/transaxle assembly only be performed with the use of a frame-contact type vehicle hoist.*

Note: *Read through the entire Section before beginning this procedure. The engine and transaxle are removed as a unit from below, then separated outside the vehicle.*

Removal

1   Have the air conditioning refrigerant recovered by a qualified air conditioning technician.
2   Park the vehicle on a frame-contact type vehicle hoist, then engage the arms of the hoist with the jacking points of the vehicle. Raise the hoist arms until they contact the vehicle, but not so much that the wheels come off the ground. Position the steering wheel so the front wheels point straight ahead.
3   Disconnect the cable from the negative terminal of the battery (see Chapter 5), then relieve the fuel system pressure (see Chapter 4).
4   Remove the hood (see Chapter 11). Cover the fenders with fender covers.
5   Remove the air filter housing and the air intake duct (see Chapter 4).
6   On 1.4L engines, disconnect and remove the charge air cooler inlet and outlet hoses (see Chapter 4).
7   Disconnect the fuel line from the fuel rail (see Chapter 4).

8   Drain the cooling system (see Chapter 1). Support the radiator/condenser assembly to the body with wire or large plastic tie-wraps, and remove the expansion tank and its hoses.
9   Remove the upper radiator hose and disconnect the coolant hoses at the engine oil cooler, then remove the coolant reservoir (see Chapter 3).
10   Follow the heater hoses from the firewall and detach them from the pipes on the engine.
11   Clearly label and disconnect all vacuum lines, emissions hoses, wiring harness connectors and fuel lines. Masking tape and/or a touch up paint applicator work well for marking items (see illustration). Take photos or sketch the locations of components and brackets. Move the wiring harness out of the way.
12   Loosen the wheel lug nuts and the drive-axle/hub nuts (see Chapter 8), then raise the vehicle on the hoist. Remove the wheels.
13   Remove the drivebelt and drain the engine oil (see Chapter 1).
14   Remove the air conditioning compressor (see Chapter 3).
15   Take off the cover from the underhood fuse/relay box, then unbolt and set aside the underhood electrical center (see Chapter 12).

7.11 Label both ends of each wire and hose before disconnecting it

16   Remove the PCM (see Chapter 6).

17   Detach the battery cable and the electrical connectors from the alternator and starter (see Chapter 5).

18   Remove the lower radiator hose.

19   Remove the battery and battery tray (see Chapter 5), then on 2016 and later models, loosen the engine compartment fuse block encapsulated mounting bolts and lift the fuse block up slightly to disengage the retaining tabs and remove the fuse block.

Caution: *Do not try to completely remove the mounting bolts - they are encapsulated into the fuse block*

20   Unbolt the exhaust pipe from the exhaust manifold (see Chapter 2A). Disconnect the oxygen sensor electrical connectors.

21   Disconnect the shift cable(s) from the transaxle (see Chapter 7A). Also disconnect any wiring harness connectors from the transaxle and cable brackets from the engine.

22   On manual transaxle models, disconnect the hydraulic clutch fluid hose from the release cylinder.

23   Disconnect the stabilizer bar links from the stabilizer bar, the tie-rod ends from the steering knuckles, and the steering intermediate shaft from the steering gear (see Chapter 10).

Caution: *Don't allow the steering shaft to rotate after the intermediate shaft has been disconnected, as damage to the airbag clockspring could occur.*

24   Disconnect the electrical connectors from the steering gear.

25   Disconnect the control arms from the steering knuckles (see Chapter 10) and remove the driveaxles (see Chapter 8).

26   Support the engine/transaxle assembly from above with an engine hoist securely attached by heavy-duty chains to the engine lifting brackets. Place blocks of wood between the engine/transaxle and the subframe, then loosen all the engine and transaxle mount fasteners. With the hoist taking the weight off the mounts, remove the engine/transaxle mounts.

Warning: *DO NOT place any part of your body under the engine when it's supported only by a hoist or other lifting device.*

27   Recheck to be sure nothing is still connecting the engine/transaxle to the vehicle. Disconnect anything still remaining.

28   Scribe or make paint marks where the subframe meets the chassis for installation alignment purposes.

29   Lower the vehicle and support the subframe with two floor jacks - one positioned under each side of the subframe. Remove the subframe bolts (see Chapter 10).

30   With an assistant to help, carefully and slowly lower each jack until the subframe is down far enough to be slid out from under the vehicle.

31   Inspect the engine/transaxle assembly thoroughly once more to make sure that nothing is still attached, then slowly lower the powertrain down out of the engine compartment and onto the floor. Check carefully to make sure nothing is hanging up as this is done.

32   Once the powertrain is on the floor, disconnect the engine lifting chains and move the engine hoist out of the way, then raise the vehicle hoist until the vehicle clears the powertrain.

33   Reconnect the engine hoist to the engine, raise the engine/transaxle up a little and support the engine with blocks of wood. Support the transaxle with a floor jack; preferably one with a transmission adapter. Secure the transaxle to the jack with safety chains.

34   Remove the starter (see Chapter 5). On automatic transaxle models, mark the torque converter to the driveplate and remove the driveplate-to-torque converter bolts.

35   Remove the bolts and the engine-to-transaxle brace, if equipped. Remove engine-to-transaxle mounting bolts and separate the engine from the transaxle.

36   Remove the driveplate/flywheel (see Chapter 2A) and mount the engine on an engine stand (see illustration 6.3).

Installation

37   Installation is the reverse of removal, noting the following points:

a)   *Check the engine/transaxle mounts. If they're worn or damaged, replace them.*

b)   *Attach the transaxle to the engine following the procedure described in Chapter 7A or 7B.*

c)   *When installing the subframe, align the marks made during removal, then tighten the subframe mounting bolts to the torque listed in this Chapter's Specifications.*

d)   *Add coolant, oil and transaxle fluids as needed (see Chapter 1).*

e)   *Reconnect the battery (see Chapter 5).*

f)   *Run the engine and check for proper operation and leaks. Shut off the engine and recheck fluid levels.*

g)   *Have the air conditioning system recharged and leak tested, if it was discharged.*

8   Engine overhaul - disassembly sequence

1   It's much easier to remove the external components if the engine is mounted on a portable engine stand. A stand can often be rented quite cheaply from an equipment rental yard. Before the engine is mounted on a stand, the flywheel/driveplate should be removed from the engine.

2   If a stand isn't available, it's possible to remove the external engine components with it blocked up on the floor. Be extra careful not to tip or drop the engine when working without a stand.

3   If you're going to obtain a rebuilt engine, all external components must come off first, to be transferred to the replacement engine. These components include:

- *Clutch and flywheel (models with manual transaxle)*
- *Driveplate (models with automatic transaxle)*
- *Ignition system components*
- *Emissions-related components*

- *Engine mounts and mount brackets*
- *Engine rear cover (spacer plate between flywheel/driveplate and engine block)*
- *Intake/exhaust manifolds*
- *Turbocharger (1.4L engines)*
- *Fuel injection components*
- *Oil filter*
- *Ignition coil pack(s) and spark plugs*
- *Thermostat and housing assembly*
- *Water pump*

Note: *When removing the external components from the engine, pay close attention to details that may be helpful or important during installation. Note the installed position of gaskets, seals, spacers, pins, brackets, washers, bolts and other small items.*

4   If you're going to obtain a short block (assembled engine block, crankshaft, pistons and connecting rods), then remove the timing chain, cylinder head, oil pan, oil pump pick-up tube, oil pump and water pump from your engine so that you can turn in your old short block to the rebuilder as a core. See Engine rebuilding alternatives for additional information regarding the different possibilities to be considered.

9   Pistons and connecting rods - removal and installation

Removal

Note: *Prior to removing the piston/connecting rod assemblies, remove the cylinder head and oil pan (see Chapter 2A).*

1   Use your fingernail to feel if a ridge has formed at the upper limit of ring travel (about 1/4-inch down from the top of each cylinder). If carbon deposits or cylinder wear have produced ridges, they must be completely removed with a special tool (see illustration). Follow the manufacturer's instructions provided with the tool. Failure to remove the ridges before attempting to remove the piston/connecting rod assemblies may result in piston breakage.

2   After the cylinder ridges have been removed, turn the engine so the crankshaft is facing up.

3   Before the main bearing cap assembly and connecting rods are removed, check the connecting rod endplay with feeler gauges. Slide them between the first connecting rod and the crankshaft throw until the play is removed (see illustration). Repeat this procedure for each connecting rod. The endplay is equal to the thickness of the feeler gauge(s). Check with an automotive machine shop for the endplay service limit (a typical endplay limit should measure between 0.005 to 0.015 inch [0.127 to 0.381 mm]). If the play exceeds the service limit, new connecting rods will be required. If new rods (or a new crankshaft) are installed, the endplay may fall under the minimum allowable. If it does, the rods will have to be machined to restore it. If necessary, consult an automotive machine shop for advice.

9.1 Before you try to remove the pistons, use a ridge reamer to remove the raised material (ridge) from the top of the cylinders

9.3 Checking the connecting rod endplay (side clearance)

9.4 If the connecting rods and caps are not marked, use permanent ink to mark the caps to the rods by cylinder number (for example, this would be the No. 4 connecting rod)

9.13 Install the piston ring into the cylinder then push it down into position using a piston so the ring will be square in the cylinder

9.14 With the ring square in the cylinder, measure the ring end gap with a feeler gauge

9.15 If the ring end gap is too small, clamp a file in a vise as shown and file the piston ring ends - remove all raised material

4   Check the connecting rods and caps for identification marks. If they aren't plainly marked, use paint or marker to clearly identify each rod and cap (1, 2, 3, etc., depending on the cylinder they're associated with) (see illustration).

5   Remove the connecting rod cap bolts from the number one connecting rod. **Note:** *New connecting rod cap bolts must be used when reassembling the engine, but save the old bolts - they'll be used during the bearing oil clearance check during reassembly.*

6   Remove the number one connecting rod cap and bearing insert. Don't drop the bearing insert out of the cap.

7   Remove the bearing insert and push the connecting rod/piston assembly out through the top of the engine. Use a wooden dowel to push on the connecting rod. If resistance is felt, double-check to make sure that all of the ridge was removed from the cylinder.

8   Repeat the procedure for the remaining cylinders.

9   After removal, reassemble the connecting rod caps and bearing inserts in their respective connecting rods and install the cap bolts finger tight. Leaving the old bearing inserts in place until reassembly will help prevent the connecting rod bearing surfaces from being accidentally nicked or gouged.

10   The pistons and connecting rods are now ready for inspection and overhaul at an automotive machine shop.

Piston ring installation

11   Before installing the new piston rings, the ring end gaps must be checked. It's assumed that the piston ring side clearance has been checked and verified correct.

12   Lay out the piston/connecting rod assemblies and the new ring sets so the ring sets will be matched with the same piston and cylinder during the end gap measurement and engine assembly.

13   Insert the top (number one) ring into the first cylinder and square it up with the cylinder walls by pushing it in with the top of the piston (see illustration). The ring should be near the bottom of the cylinder, at the lower limit of ring travel.

14   To measure the end gap, slip feeler gauges between the ends of the ring until a gauge equal to the gap width is found (see illustration). The feeler gauge should slide between the ring ends with a slight amount of drag. A typical ring gap should fall between 0.010 and 0.020 inch [0.25 to 0.50 mm] for compression rings and up to 0.030 inch [0.76 mm] for the oil ring steel rails. If the gap is larger or smaller than specified, double-check to make sure you have the correct rings before proceeding.

15   If the gap is too small, it must be enlarged or the ring ends may come in contact with each other during engine operation, which can cause serious damage to the engine. If necessary, increase the end gaps by filing the ring ends very carefully with a fine file. Mount the file in a vise equipped with soft jaws, slip the ring over the file with the ends contacting the file face and slowly move the ring to remove material from the ends. When performing this operation, file only by pushing the ring from the outside end of the file towards the vise (see illustration).

ENGINE BEARING ANALYSIS

Debris

Babbitt bearing embedded with debris from machinings

Microscopic detail of debris

Microscopic detail of gouges

Overplated copper alloy bearing gouged by cast iron debris

Aluminum bearing embedded with glass beads

Microscopic detail of glass beads

Damaged lining caused by dirt left on the bearing back

Misassembly

Result of a lower half assembled as an upper - blocking the oil flow

Excessive oil clearance is indicated by a short contact arc

Polished and oil-stained backs are a result of a poor fit in the housing bore

Result of a wrong, reversed, or shifted cap

Overloading

Damage from excessive idling which resulted in an oil film unable to support the load imposed

Damaged upper connecting rod bearings caused by engine lugging; the lower main bearings (not shown) were similarly affected

The damage shown in these upper and lower connecting rod bearings was caused by engine operation at a higher-than-rated speed under load

Misalignment

A warped crankshaft caused this pattern of severe wear in the center, diminishing toward the ends

A poorly finished crankshaft caused the equally spaced scoring shown

A tapered housing bore caused the damage along one edge of this pair

A bent connecting rod led to the damage in the "V" pattern

Lubrication

Result of dry start: The bearings on the left, farthest from the oil pump, show more damage

Result of a low oil supply or oil starvation

Severe wear as a result of inadequate oil clearance

Corrosion

Microscopic detail of corrosion

Corrosion is an acid attack on the bearing lining generally caused by inadequate maintenance, extremely hot or cold operation, or inferior oils or fuels

Microscopic detail of cavitation

Example of cavitation - a surface erosion caused by pressure changes in the oil film

Damage from excessive thrust or insufficient axial clearance

Bearing affected by oil dilution caused by excessive blow-by or a rich mixture

9.19a Installing the spacer/expander in the oil ring groove

9.19b DO NOT use a piston ring installation tool when installing the oil ring side rails

9.22 Use a piston ring installation tool to install the number 2 and the number 1 (top) rings - be sure the directional mark on the piston ring(s) is facing toward the top of the piston

16   Excess end gap isn't critical unless it's greater than 0.040 inch (1.01 mm). Again, double-check to make sure you have the correct ring type.

17   Repeat the procedure for each ring that will be installed in the first cylinder and for each ring in the remaining cylinders. Remember to keep rings, pistons and cylinders matched up.

18   Once the ring end gaps have been checked/corrected, the rings can be installed on the pistons.

19   The oil control ring (lowest one on the piston) is usually installed first. It's composed of three separate components. Slip the spacer/expander into the groove (see illustration). If an anti-rotation tang is used, make sure it's inserted into the drilled hole in the ring groove. Next, install the upper side rail in the same manner (see illustration). Don't use a piston ring installation tool on the oil ring side rails, as they may be damaged. Instead, place one end of the side rail into the groove between the spacer/expander and the ring land, hold it firmly in place and slide a finger around the piston while pushing the rail into

the groove. Finally, install the lower side rail.

20   After the three oil ring components have been installed, check to make sure that both the upper and lower side rails can be rotated smoothly inside the ring grooves.

21   The number two (middle) ring is installed next. It's usually stamped with a mark, which must face up, toward the top of the piston. Do not mix up the top and middle rings, as they have different cross-sections.

Note: *Always follow the instructions printed on the ring package or box - different manufacturers may require different approaches.*

22   Use a piston ring installation tool and make sure the identification mark is facing the top of the piston, then slip the ring into the middle groove on the piston (see illustration). Don't expand the ring any more than necessary to slide it over the piston.

23   Install the number one (top) ring in the same manner. Make sure the mark is facing up. Be careful not to confuse the number one and number two rings.

24   Repeat the procedure for the remaining pistons and rings.

Installation

Note: *For final assembly, the pistons and rods are installed after the lower crankcase (or bedplate) has been installed and torqued in sequence.*

25   Before installing the piston/connecting rod assemblies, the cylinder walls must be perfectly clean, the top edge of each cylinder bore must be chamfered, and the crankshaft must be in place.

26   Remove the cap from the end of the number one connecting rod (refer to the marks made during removal). Remove the original bearing inserts and wipe the bearing surfaces of the connecting rod and cap with a clean, lint-free cloth. They must be kept spotlessly clean.

Connecting rod bearing oil clearance check

27   Clean the back side of the new upper bearing insert, then lay it in place in the connecting rod.

28   Make sure the tab on the bearing fits into the recess in the rod. Don't hammer the bearing insert into place and be very careful not to nick or gouge the bearing face. Don't lubricate the bearing at this time.

29   Clean the back side of the other bearing insert and install it in the rod cap. Again, make sure the tab on the bearing fits into the recess in the cap, and don't apply any lubricant. It's critically important that the mating surfaces of the bearing and connecting rod are perfectly clean and oil free when they're assembled.

30   Position the piston ring gaps at the specified intervals around the piston as shown (see illustration).

31   Lubricate the piston and rings with clean engine oil and attach a piston ring compressor to the piston. Leave the skirt protruding about 1/4-inch to guide the piston into the cylinder. The rings must be compressed until they're flush with the piston.

32   Rotate the crankshaft until the number one connecting rod journal is at BDC (Bot-

9.30 Position the piston ring end gaps as shown

Gap of Upper Side Rail

No.1 Ring Gap

Front of Engine

No. 2 Ring Gap and Spacer Expander Gap

Gap of Lower Side Rail

36060-2c-13.30 HAYNES

9.35 Use a plastic or wooden hammer handle to push the piston into the cylinder

9.37 Place Plastigage on each connecting rod bearing journal, parallel to the crankshaft centerline

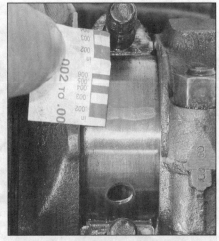

9.41 Use the scale on the Plastigage package to determine the bearing oil clearance - measure the widest part of the Plastigage and use the correct scale; it comes with both standard and metric scales

tom Dead Center) and apply a liberal coat of engine oil to the cylinder walls.

33   With the arrow on top of the piston facing the front (timing belt end or timing chain) of the engine, gently insert the piston/connecting rod assembly into the number one cylinder bore and rest the bottom edge of the ring compressor on the engine block. Install the pistons with the cavity mark(s) or arrow facing toward the timing belt or timing chain end of the engine.

34   Tap the top edge of the ring compressor to make sure it's contacting the block around its entire circumference.

35   Gently tap on the top of the piston with the end of a wooden or plastic hammer handle (see illustration) while guiding the end of the connecting rod into place on the crankshaft journal (a pair of wooden dowels would be helpful for this). The piston rings may try to pop out of the ring compressor just before entering the cylinder bore, so keep some downward pressure on the ring compressor. Work slowly, and if any resistance is felt as the piston enters the cylinder, stop immediately. Find out what's hanging up and fix it before proceeding. Do not force the piston into the cylinder - you might break a ring and/or the piston.

36   Once the piston/connecting rod assembly is installed, the connecting rod bearing oil clearance must be checked before the rod cap is permanently installed.

37   Cut a piece of the appropriate size Plastigage slightly shorter than the width of the connecting rod bearing and lay it in place on the number one connecting rod journal, parallel with the journal axis (see illustration).

38   Clean the connecting rod cap bearing face and install the rod cap. Make sure the mating mark on the cap is on the same side as the mark on the connecting rod (see illustration 9.4).

39   Install the old rod bolts, at this time, and tighten them to the torque listed in this Chapter's Specifications.

Note: *Use a thin-wall socket to avoid erroneous torque readings that can result if the socket is wedged between the rod cap and the bolt. If the socket tends to wedge itself between the fastener and the cap, lift up on it slightly until it no longer contacts the cap. DO NOT rotate the crankshaft at any time during this operation.*

40   Remove the fasteners and detach the rod cap, being very careful not to disturb the Plastigage. Discard the cap bolts at this time as they cannot be reused.

41   Compare the width of the crushed Plastigage to the scale printed on the Plastigage envelope to obtain the oil clearance (see illustration). The connecting rod oil clearance is usually about 0.001 to 0.002 inch. Consult an automotive machine shop for the clearance specified for the rod bearings on your engine.

42   If the clearance is not as specified, the bearing inserts may be the wrong size (which means different ones will be required). Before deciding that different inserts are needed, make sure that no dirt or oil was between the bearing inserts and the connecting rod or cap when the clearance was measured. Also, recheck the journal diameter. If the Plastigage was wider at one end than the other, the journal may be tapered. If the clearance still exceeds the limit specified, the bearing will have to be replaced with an undersize bearing.

Note: *When installing a new crankshaft always use a standard size bearing.*

Final installation

43   Carefully scrape all traces of the Plastigage material off the rod journal and/or bearing face. Be very careful not to scratch the bearing - use your fingernail or the edge of a plastic card.

44   Make sure the bearing faces are perfectly clean, then apply a uniform layer of clean moly-base grease or engine assembly lube to both of them. You'll have to push the piston into the cylinder to expose the face of the bearing insert in the connecting rod.

45   Slide the connecting rod back into place on the journal, install the rod cap, install the new bolts and tighten them to the torque listed in this Chapter's Specifications.

Note: *Install new connecting rod cap bolts. Do NOT reuse old bolts - they have stretched and cannot be reused.*

46   Repeat the entire procedure for the remaining pistons/connecting rods.

47   The important points to remember are:

a) *Keep the back sides of the bearing inserts and the insides of the connecting rods and caps perfectly clean when assembling them.*

b) *Make sure you have the correct piston/ rod assembly for each cylinder.*

c) *The arrow or mark on the piston must face the front (timing chain end) of the engine.*

d) *Lubricate the cylinder walls liberally with clean oil.*

e) *Lubricate the bearing faces when installing the rod caps after the oil clearance has been checked.*

48   After all the piston/connecting rod assemblies have been correctly installed, rotate the crankshaft a number of times by hand to check for any obvious binding.

49   As a final step, check the connecting rod endplay, as described in Step 3. If it was correct before disassembly and the original crankshaft and rods were reinstalled, it should still be correct. If new rods or a new crankshaft were installed, the endplay may be inadequate. If so, the rods will have to be removed and taken to an automotive machine shop for resizing.

10.1 Checking crankshaft endplay with a dial indicator

10.3 Checking the crankshaft endplay with feeler gauges at the thrust bearing journal

10   Crankshaft - removal and installation

Removal

Note: *The crankshaft can be removed only after the engine has been removed from the vehicle. It's assumed that the flywheel or driveplate, crankshaft pulley, timing belt or timing chain, oil pan, oil pump body, oil filter and piston/connecting rod assemblies have already been removed. The rear main oil seal is removed.*

1   Before the crankshaft is removed, measure the endplay. Mount a dial indicator with the indicator in line with the crankshaft and just touching the end of the crankshaft as shown (see illustration).

2   Pry the crankshaft all the way to the rear and zero the dial indicator. Next, pry the crankshaft to the front as far as possible and check the reading on the dial indicator. The distance traveled is the endplay. A typical crankshaft endplay will fall between 0.003 to 0.010 inch (0.076 to 0.254 mm). If it is greater than that, check the crankshaft thrust surfaces for wear after it's removed. If no wear is evident, new main bearings should correct the endplay.

3   If a dial indicator isn't available, feeler gauges can be used. Gently pry the crankshaft all the way to the front of the engine. Slip feeler gauges between the crankshaft and the front face of the thrust bearing or washer to determine the clearance (see illustration).

4   Loosen the lower crankcase perimeter bolts and the lower crankcase bolts 1/4-turn at a time each, until they can be removed by hand. Follow the reverse of the tightening sequence (see illustration 10.19a or 10.19b). On 1.8L engines, loosen the main bearing cap bolts 1/4-turn at a time each, until they can be removed by hand. Follow the reverse of the tightening sequence (see illustration 10.19c).

Caution: *On 1.4L engines, all lower crankcase bolts must be replaced with new ones. On 1.8L engines, all main bearing cap bolts must be replaced with new ones. Save the old bolts, however, as they will be used for the main bearing oil clearance check.*

5   On 1.4L engines, remove the lower crankcase and on 1.8L engines, remove each individual bearing cap, while keeping them in order. Try not to drop the bearing inserts if they come out with the lower crankcase or bearing caps.

6   Carefully lift the crankshaft out of the engine. It may be a good idea to have an assistant available, since the crankshaft is quite heavy and awkward to handle. On 1.4L engines, with the bearing inserts in place inside the engine block and the lower crankcase, reinstall the lower crankcase onto the engine block and tighten the bolts finger tight. On 1.8L engines, apply black RTV to the groove on each side of the rear bearing cap then install the main bearing caps with the bearing inserts onto the engine block in their original locations.

Installation

7   Crankshaft installation is the first step in engine reassembly. It's assumed at this point that the engine block and crankshaft have been cleaned, inspected and repaired or reconditioned.

8   Position the engine block with the bottom facing up.

9   Remove the mounting bolts and lift off the lower crankcase or bearing caps.

10   If they're still in place, remove the original bearing inserts from the block and from the lower crankcase. Wipe the bearing surfaces of the block and lower crankcase saddle with a clean, lint-free cloth. They must be kept spotlessly clean. This is critical for determining the correct bearing oil clearance.

Main bearing oil clearance check

11   Without mixing them up, clean the back sides of the new upper main bearing inserts (with grooves and oil holes) and lay one in each main bearing saddle in the engine block. Each upper bearing (engine block) has an oil groove and oil hole in it.

Caution: *The oil holes in the block must line up with the oil holes in the engine block inserts. The thrust washer or thrust bearing insert must be installed in the correct location.*

Caution: *Do not hammer the bearing insert into place and don't nick or gouge the bearing faces. DO NOT apply any lubrication at this time.*

Note: *The thrust bearing is located on the engine block number 3 journal. Clean the back sides of the lower main bearing inserts and lay them in the corresponding location in the lower crankcase saddles. Make sure the tab on the bearing insert fits into the recess in the block or lower crankcase saddles.*

12   Clean the faces of the bearing inserts in the block and the crankshaft main bearing journals with a clean, lint-free cloth.

13   Check or clean the oil holes in the crankshaft, as any dirt here can go only one way - straight through the new bearings.

14   Once you're certain the crankshaft is clean, carefully lay it in position in the cylinder block.

15   Before the crankshaft can be permanently installed, the main bearing oil clearance must be checked.

16   Cut several strips of the appropriate size of Plastigage. They must be slightly shorter than the width of the main bearing journal.

17   Place one piece on each crankshaft main bearing journal, parallel with the journal axis as shown (see illustration).

18   Clean the faces of the bearing inserts in the lower crankcase. Hold the bearing inserts in place and install the lower crankcase onto the crankshaft and cylinder block. DO NOT disturb the Plastigage.

10.17 Place the Plastigage onto the crankshaft bearing journal as shown

10.19a Lower crankcase bolt tightening sequence - 1.4L engine

10.19b Lower crankcase bolt tightening sequence - 2016 and later 1.4L engine

10.19c Main bearing cap bolt tightening sequence - 1.8L engine

19 Apply clean engine oil to all bolt threads prior to installation, then install all bolts finger-tight. Tighten the lower crankcase bolts or main bearing cap bolts in the sequence shown (see illustrations) progressing in steps, to the torque listed in this Chapter's Specifications. DO NOT rotate the crankshaft at any time during this operation.

20 Remove the bolts in the reverse order of the tightening sequence and carefully lift the lower crankcase straight up and off the block. Do not disturb the Plastigage or rotate the crankshaft.

21 Compare the width of the crushed Plastigage on each journal to the scale printed on the Plastigage envelope to determine the main bearing oil clearance (see illustration). Check with an automotive machine shop for the oil clearance for your engine.

22 If the clearance is not correct, the bearing inserts may be the wrong size (which means different ones will be required). Before deciding if different inserts are needed, make sure that no dirt or oil was between the bearing inserts and the caps or block when the clearance was measured. If the Plastigage was wider at one end than the other, the crankshaft journal may be tapered. If the clearance still exceeds the limit specified, the bearing insert(s) will have to be replaced with an undersize bearing insert(s).

Caution: *When installing a new crankshaft always install a standard bearing insert set.*

23 Carefully scrape all traces of the Plastigage material off the main bearing journals and/or the bearing insert faces. Remove all residue from the oil holes. Use your fingernail or the edge of a plastic card - don't nick or scratch the bearing faces.

10.21 Use the scale on the Plastigage package to determine the bearing oil clearance - measure the widest part of the Plastigage and use the correct scale; it comes with both standard and metric scales

10.30a Lower crankcase perimeter bolt tightening sequence - 2015 and earlier 1.4L engine

10.30b Lower crankcase perimeter bolt tightening sequence - 2016 and later 1.4L engine

Final installation

24   Carefully lift the crankshaft out of the cylinder block. If the crankshaft position sensor reluctor wheel ring was removed Install the ring and tighten the bolts to the torque listed in this Chapter's Specifications.

25   Clean the bearing insert faces in the cylinder block, then apply a thin, uniform layer of moly-base grease or engine assembly lube to each of the bearing surfaces. Coat the thrust faces as well as the journal face of the thrust bearing.

26   Make sure the crankshaft journals are clean, then lay the crankshaft back in place in the cylinder block.

27   Clean the bearing insert faces and apply the same lubricant to them. Clean the engine block and the mating surface of the lower crankcase thoroughly. The surfaces must be free of oil residue. Install the lower crankcase.

28   Prior to installation, apply clean engine oil to all bolt threads, wiping off any excess, then install all bolts finger-tight.

Caution: *Remember, new bolts must be used.*

29   Tighten the bolts to the torque listed in this Chapter's Specifications following the correct torque sequence (see illustration 10.19a or 10.19b).

30   If you're working on a 1.4L engine, install the lower crankcase perimeter bolts and tighten them, in sequence, to the torque listed in this Chapter's Specifications (see illustrations).

31   Recheck the crankshaft endplay with a feeler gauge or a dial indicator. The endplay should be correct if the crankshaft thrust faces aren't worn or damaged and if new bearings have been installed.

32   Rotate the crankshaft a number of times by hand to check for any obvious binding. It should rotate with a running torque of 50 in-lbs or less. If the running torque is too high, correct the problem at this time.

33   Install the new rear main oil seal (see Chapter 2A).

11   Engine overhaul - reassembly sequence

1   Before beginning engine reassembly, make sure you have all the necessary new parts, gaskets and seals as well as the following items on hand:

Common hand tools
A 1/2-inch drive torque wrench
New engine oil
Gasket sealant
Thread locking compound

2   If you obtained a short block it will be necessary to install the cylinder head, the oil pump and pick-up tube, the oil pan, the water pump, the timing belt or chain and timing cover, and the valve cover (see Chapter 2A). In order to save time and avoid problems, the external components must be installed in the following general order:

Thermostat and housing cover
Water pump
Intake and exhaust manifolds
Turbocharger (1.4L engines)
Fuel injection components
Emission control components
Spark plug wires and spark plugs
Ignition coils or coil packs
Oil filter
Engine mounts and mount brackets
Clutch and flywheel (manual transaxle)
Driveplate (automatic transaxle)

12   Initial start-up and break-in after overhaul

Warning: *Have a fire extinguisher handy when starting the engine for the first time.*

1   Once the engine has been installed in the vehicle, double-check the engine oil and coolant levels.

2   With the spark plugs out of the engine and the ignition system and fuel pump disabled, crank the engine until oil pressure registers on the gauge or the light goes out.

3   Install the spark plugs, coil pack or coils and restore the ignition system and fuel pump functions.

4   Start the engine. It may take a few moments for the fuel system to build up pressure, but the engine should start without a great deal of effort.

5   After the engine starts, it should be allowed to warm up to normal operating temperature. While the engine is warming up, make a thorough check for fuel, oil and coolant leaks.

6   Shut the engine off and recheck the engine oil and coolant levels.

7   Drive the vehicle to an area with minimum traffic, accelerate from 30 to 50 mph, then allow the vehicle to slow to 30 mph with the throttle closed. Repeat the procedure 10 or 12 times. This will load the piston rings and cause them to seat properly against the cylinder walls. Check again for oil and coolant leaks.

8   Drive the vehicle gently for the first 500 miles (no sustained high speeds) and keep a constant check on the oil level. It is not unusual for an engine to use oil during the break-in period.

9   At approximately 500 to 600 miles, change the oil and filter.

10   For the next few hundred miles, drive the vehicle normally. Do not pamper it or abuse it.

11   After 2,000 miles, change the oil and filter again and consider the engine broken in.

COMMON ENGINE OVERHAUL TERMS

B

Backlash - The amount of play between two parts. Usually refers to how much one gear can be moved back and forth without moving the gear with which it's meshed.

Bearing Caps - The caps held in place by nuts or bolts which, in turn, hold the bearing surface. This space is for lubricating oil to enter.

Bearing clearance - The amount of space left between shaft and bearing surface. This space is for lubricating oil to enter.

Bearing crush - The additional height which is purposely manufactured into each bearing half to ensure complete contact of the bearing back with the housing bore when the engine is assembled.

Bearing knock - The noise created by movement of a part in a loose or worn bearing.

Blueprinting - Dismantling an engine and reassembling it to EXACT specifications.

Bore - An engine cylinder, or any cylindrical hole; also used to describe the process of enlarging or accurately refinishing a hole with a cutting tool, as to bore an engine cylinder. The bore size is the diameter of the hole.

Boring - Renewing the cylinders by cutting them out to a specified size. A boring bar is used to make the cut.

Bottom end - A term which refers collectively to the engine block, crankshaft, main bearings and the big ends of the connecting rods.

Break-in - The period of operation between installation of new or rebuilt parts and time in which parts are worn to the correct fit. Driving at reduced and varying speed for a specified mileage to permit parts to wear to the correct fit.

Bushing - A one-piece sleeve placed in a bore to serve as a bearing surface for shaft, piston pin, etc. Usually replaceable.

C

Camshaft - The shaft in the engine, on which a series of lobes are located for operating the valve mechanisms. The camshaft is driven by gears or sprockets and a timing chain. Usually referred to simply as the cam.

Carbon - Hard, or soft, black deposits found in combustion chamber, on plugs, under rings, on and under valve heads.

Cast iron - An alloy of iron and more than two percent carbon, used for engine blocks and heads because it's relatively inexpensive and easy to mold into complex shapes.

Chamfer - To bevel across (or a bevel on) the sharp edge of an object.

Chase - To repair damaged threads with a tap or die.

Combustion chamber - The space between the piston and the cylinder head, with the piston at top dead center, in which air-fuel mixture is burned.

Compression ratio - The relationship between cylinder volume (clearance volume) when the piston is at top dead center and cylinder volume when the piston is at bottom dead center.

Connecting rod - The rod that connects the crank on the crankshaft with the piston. Sometimes called a con rod.

Connecting rod cap - The part of the connecting rod assembly that attaches the rod to the crankpin.

Core plug - Soft metal plug used to plug the casting holes for the coolant passages in the block.

Crankcase - The lower part of the engine in which the crankshaft rotates; includes the lower section of the cylinder block and the oil pan.

Crank kit - A reground or reconditioned crankshaft and new main and connecting rod bearings.

Crankpin - The part of a crankshaft to which a connecting rod is attached.

Crankshaft - The main rotating member, or shaft, running the length of the crankcase, with offset throws to which the connecting rods are attached; changes the reciprocating motion of the pistons into rotating motion.

Cylinder sleeve - A replaceable sleeve, or liner, pressed into the cylinder block to form the cylinder bore.

D

Deburring - Removing the burrs (rough edges or areas) from a bearing.

Deglazer - A tool, rotated by an electric motor, used to remove glaze from cylinder walls so a new set of rings will seat.

E

Endplay - The amount of lengthwise movement between two parts. As applied to a crankshaft, the distance that the crankshaft can move forward and back in the cylinder block.

F

Face - A machinist's term that refers to removing metal from the end of a shaft or the face of a larger part, such as a flywheel.

Fatigue - A breakdown of material through a large number of loading and unloading cycles. The first signs are cracks followed shortly by breaks.

Feeler gauge - A thin strip of hardened steel, ground to an exact thickness, used to check clearances between parts.

Free height - The unloaded length or height of a spring.

Freeplay - The looseness in a linkage, or an assembly of parts, between the initial application of force and actual movement. Usually perceived as slop or slight delay.

Freeze plug - See Core plug.

G

Gallery - A large passage in the block that forms a reservoir for engine oil pressure.

Glaze - The very smooth, glassy finish that develops on cylinder walls while an engine is in service.

H

Heli-Coil - A rethreading device used when threads are worn or damaged. The device is installed in a retapped hole to reduce the thread size to the original size.

I

Installed height - The spring's measured length or height, as installed on the cylinder head. Installed height is measured from the spring seat to the underside of the spring retainer.

J

Journal - The surface of a rotating shaft which turns in a bearing.

K

Keeper - The split lock that holds the valve spring retainer in position on the valve stem.

Key - A small piece of metal inserted into matching grooves machined into two parts fitted together - such as a gear pressed onto a shaft - which prevents slippage between the two parts.

Knock - The heavy metallic engine sound, produced in the combustion chamber as a result of abnormal combustion - usually detonation. Knock is usually caused by a loose or worn bearing. Also referred to as detonation, pinging and spark knock. Connecting rod or main bearing knocks are created by too much oil clearance or insufficient lubrication.

L

Lands - The portions of metal between the piston ring grooves.

Lapping the valves - Grinding a valve face and its seat together with lapping compound.

Lash - The amount of free motion in a gear train, between gears, or in a mechanical assembly, that occurs before movement can begin. Usually refers to the lash in a valve train.

Lifter - The part that rides against the cam to transfer motion to the rest of the valve train.

M

Machining - The process of using a machine to remove metal from a metal part.

Main bearings - The plain, or babbit, bearings that support the crankshaft.

Main bearing caps - The cast iron caps, bolted to the bottom of the block, that support the main bearings.

O

O.D. - Outside diameter.

Oil gallery - A pipe or drilled passageway in the engine used to carry engine oil from one area to another.

Oil ring - The lower ring, or rings, of a piston; designed to prevent excessive amounts of oil from working up the cylinder walls and into the combustion chamber. Also called an oil-control ring.

Oil seal - A seal which keeps oil from leaking out of a compartment. Usually refers to a dynamic seal around a rotating shaft or other moving part.

O-ring - A type of sealing ring made of a special rubberlike material; in use, the O-ring is compressed into a groove to provide the sealing action.

Overhaul - To completely disassemble a unit, clean and inspect all parts, reassemble it with the original or new parts and make all adjustments necessary for proper operation.

P

Pilot bearing - A small bearing installed in the center of the flywheel (or the rear end of the crankshaft) to support the front end of the input shaft of the transmission.

Pip mark - A little dot or indentation which indicates the top side of a compression ring.

Piston - The cylindrical part, attached to the connecting rod, that moves up and down in the cylinder as the crankshaft rotates. When the fuel charge is fired, the piston transfers the force of the explosion to the connecting rod, then to the crankshaft.

Piston pin (or wrist pin) - The cylindrical and usually hollow steel pin that passes through the piston. The piston pin fastens the piston to the upper end of the connecting rod.

Piston ring - The split ring fitted to the groove in a piston. The ring contacts the sides of the ring groove and also rubs against the cylinder wall, thus sealing space between piston and wall. There are two types of rings: Compression rings seal the compression pressure in the combustion chamber; oil rings scrape excessive oil off the cylinder wall.

Piston ring groove - The slots or grooves cut in piston heads to hold piston rings in position.

Piston skirt - The portion of the piston below the rings and the piston pin hole.

Plastigage - A thin strip of plastic thread, available in different sizes, used for measuring clearances. For example, a strip of plastigage is laid across a bearing journal and mashed as parts are assembled. Then parts are disassembled and the width of the strip is measured to determine clearance between journal and bearing. Commonly used to measure crankshaft main-bearing and connecting rod bearing clearances.

Press-fit - A tight fit between two parts that requires pressure to force the parts together. Also referred to as drive, or force, fit.

Prussian blue - A blue pigment; in solution, useful in determining the area of contact between two surfaces. Prussian blue is commonly used to determine the width and location of the contact area between the valve face and the valve seat.

R

Race (bearing) - The inner or outer ring that provides a contact surface for balls or rollers in bearing.

Ream - To size, enlarge or smooth a hole by using a round cutting tool with fluted edges.

Ring job - The process of reconditioning the cylinders and installing new rings.

Runout - Wobble. The amount a shaft rotates out-of-true.

S

Saddle - The upper main bearing seat.

Scored - Scratched or grooved, as a cylinder wall may be scored by abrasive particles moved up and down by the piston rings.

Scuffing - A type of wear in which there's a transfer of material between parts moving against each other; shows up as pits or grooves in the mating surfaces.

Seat - The surface upon which another part rests or seats. For example, the valve seat is the matched surface upon which the valve face rests. Also used to refer to wearing into a good fit; for example, piston rings seat after a few miles of driving.

Short block - An engine block complete with crankshaft and piston and, usually, camshaft assemblies.

Static balance - The balance of an object while it's stationary.

Step - The wear on the lower portion of a ring land caused by excessive side and back-clearance. The height of the step indicates the ring's extra side clearance and the length of the step projecting from the back wall of the groove represents the ring's back clearance.

Stroke - The distance the piston moves when traveling from top dead center to bottom dead center, or from bottom dead center to top dead center.

Stud - A metal rod with threads on both ends.

T

Tang - A lip on the end of a plain bearing used to align the bearing during assembly.

Tap - To cut threads in a hole. Also refers to the fluted tool used to cut threads.

Taper - A gradual reduction in the width of a shaft or hole; in an engine cylinder, taper usually takes the form of uneven wear, more pronounced at the top than at the bottom.

Throws - The offset portions of the crankshaft to which the connecting rods are affixed.

Thrust bearing - The main bearing that has thrust faces to prevent excessive endplay, or forward and backward movement of the crankshaft.

Thrust washer - A bronze or hardened steel washer placed between two moving parts. The washer prevents longitudinal movement and provides a bearing surface for thrust surfaces of parts.

Tolerance - The amount of variation permitted from an exact size of measurement. Actual amount from smallest acceptable dimension to largest acceptable dimension.

U

Umbrella - An oil deflector placed near the valve tip to throw oil from the valve stem area.

Undercut - A machined groove below the normal surface.

Undersize bearings - Smaller diameter bearings used with re-ground crankshaft journals.

V

Valve grinding - Refacing a valve in a valve-refacing machine.

Valve train - The valve-operating mechanism of an engine; includes all components from the camshaft to the valve.

Vibration damper - A cylindrical weight attached to the front of the crankshaft to minimize torsional vibration (the twist-untwist actions of the crankshaft caused by the cylinder firing impulses). Also called a harmonic balancer.

W

Water jacket - The spaces around the cylinders, between the inner and outer shells of the cylinder block or head, through which coolant circulates.

Web - A supporting structure across a cavity.

Woodruff key - A key with a radiused backside (viewed from the side).

Chapter 3
Cooling, heating and air conditioning systems

Contents

Specifications

General

Pressure cap rating	Marked on cap
Cooling system capacity..	See Chapter 1
HVAC refrigerant type..	R-134a or R-1234yf
Refrigerant capacity...	Refer to HVAC specification tag under hood

Torque specifications

Note: *One foot-pound (ft-lb) of torque is equivalent to 12 inch-pounds (in-lbs) of torque. Torque values below approximately 15 ft-lbs are expressed in inch-pounds, because most foot-pound torque wrenches are not accurate at these smaller values.*

	Ft-lbs (unless otherwise indicated)	Nm
Air conditioning compressor mounting bolts/nuts....................................	16	22
Air conditioning compressor drain plug	132 in-lbs	15
Coolant heater bolt	89 in-lbs	10
Oil cooler bolts		
2015 and earlier 1.4L engines...	15	20
2016 and later 1.4L engine		
Oil cooler-to-cylinder block (lower) bolts......................................	18	25
Oil cooler-to-water pump assembly (upper) bolts	89 in-lbs	10
1.8L engine		
Oil cooler-to-oil cooler housing bolts..	71 in-lbs	8
Oil cooler housing-to-engine block bolts.......................................	19	25
Refrigerant line manifold-to-condenser bolts	168 in-lbs	19
Refrigerant line manifold-to-compressor bolt..	168 in-lbs	19
Thermostat housing bolts		
2015 and earlier models...	71 in-lbs	8
2016 and later models..	89 in-lbs	10
Water pump bolts		
2015 and earlier 1.4L engine		
Step 1	71 in-lbs	8
Step 2 (bolts marked "A" in illustration 8.10 only)........................	Tighten an additional 30-degrees	
2016 and later 1.4L engine		
Water pump housing assembly-to-cylinder block	18	25
Water pump-to-housing assembly bolts...	89 in-lbs	10
1.8L engine	71 in-lbs	8
Water pump pulley bolts		
2015 and earlier 1.4L engine	16	22
1.8L engine*..	15	20
Water pump sprocket bolts	89 in-lbs	10
Water pump access cover bolts	89 in-lbs	10

Re-tap the threads before installing the bolts with locking compound.

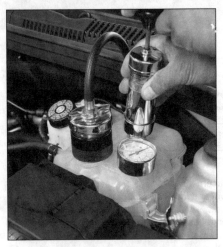

2.2 The cooling system pressure tester is connected in place of the pressure cap on the coolant expansion tank, then pumped up to pressurize the system

2.5a The combustion leak detector consists of a bulb, syringe and test fluid

2.5b Place the tester over the cooling system filler neck and use the bulb to draw a sample into the tester

1   General Information

Engine cooling system

1   The cooling system consists of a radiator, a coolant expansion tank, a pressure cap (located on the expansion tank), a thermostat, an electric cooling fan, and a water pump.

2   When the engine is cold, the thermostat restricts the circulation of coolant to the engine. When the minimum operating temperature is reached, the thermostat begins to open, allowing coolant to flow through the radiator.

Transaxle cooling system

3   Vehicles with an automatic transaxle are equipped with a transaxle fluid cooler, located inside the radiator. An auxiliary transaxle fluid cooler is located in front of the radiator.

Engine oil cooling system

4   Besides the engine and transaxle cooling systems described above, engine heat is also dissipated through an external oil cooler that's integrated into the lubrication system. The oil cooler helps keep engine and oil temperatures within design limits under extreme load conditions.

Heating system

5   The heating system consists of the heater controls, the heater core, the heater blower assembly (which houses the blower motor and the blower motor resistor), and the hoses connecting the heater core to the engine cooling system. Hot engine coolant is circulated through the heater core. When the heater mode is activated, a flap door opens to expose the heater box to the passenger compartment. A fan switch on the heater control panel activates the blower motor, which forces air through the core, heating the air.

Air conditioning system

6   The air conditioning system consists of the condenser, which is mounted in front of the radiator, the evaporator case assembly under the dash, a compressor mounted on the engine, and the plumbing connecting all of the above components.

7   A blower fan forces the warmer air of the passenger compartment through the evaporator core (sort of a radiator-in-reverse), transferring the heat from the air to the refrigerant. The liquid refrigerant boils off into low pressure vapor, taking the heat with it when it leaves the evaporator.

2   Troubleshooting

Coolant leaks

1   A coolant leak can develop anywhere in the cooling system, but the most common causes are:

a) A loose or weak hose clamp
b) A defective hose
c) A faulty pressure cap
d) A damaged radiator
e) A bad heater core
f) A faulty water pump
g) A leaking gasket at any joint that carries coolant

2   Coolant leaks aren't always easy to find. Sometimes they can only be detected when the cooling system is under pressure. Here's where a cooling system pressure tester comes in handy. After the engine has cooled completely, the tester is attached in place of the pressure cap, then pumped up to the pressure value equal to that of the pressure cap rating (see illustration). Now, leaks that only exist when the engine is fully warmed up will become apparent. The tester can be left connected to locate a nagging slow leak.

Coolant level drops, but no external leaks

3   If you find it necessary to keep adding coolant, but there are no external leaks, the probable causes include:

a) A blown head gasket
b) A leaking intake manifold gasket (only on engines that have coolant passages in the manifold)
c) A cracked cylinder head or cylinder block

4   Any of the above problems will also usually result in contamination of the engine oil, which will cause it to take on a milkshake-like appearance. A bad head gasket or cracked head or block can also result in engine oil contaminating the cooling system.

5   Combustion leak detectors (also known as block testers) are available at most auto parts stores. These work by detecting exhaust gases in the cooling system, which indicates a compression leak from a cylinder into the coolant. The tester consists of a large bulb-type syringe and bottle of test fluid (see illustration). A measured amount of the fluid is added to the syringe. The syringe is placed over the cooling system filler neck and, with the engine running, the bulb is squeezed and a sample of the gases present in the cooling system are drawn up through the test fluid (see illustration). If any combustion gases are present in the sample taken, the test fluid will change color.

6   If the test indicates combustion gas is present in the cooling system, you can be sure that the engine has a blown head gasket or a crack in the cylinder head or block, and will require disassembly to repair.

Pressure cap

Warning: *Wait until the engine is completely cool before beginning this check.*

7   The cooling system is sealed by a spring-loaded cap, which raises the boiling

2.8 Checking the cooling system pressure cap with a cooling system pressure tester

2.10 Typical thermostat:

1	Flange	5	Valve seat
2	Piston	6	Valve
3	Jiggle valve	7	Frame
4	Main coil spring	8	Secondary coil spring

2.28 The water pump weep hole is generally located on the underside of the pump

point of the coolant. If the cap's seal or spring are worn out, the coolant can boil and escape past the cap. With the engine completely cool, remove the cap and check the seal; if it's cracked, hardened or deteriorated in any way, replace it with a new one.

8   Even if the seal is good, the spring might not be; this can be checked with a cooling system pressure tester (see illustration). If the cap can't hold a pressure within approximately 1-1/2 lbs of its rated pressure (which is marked on the cap), replace it with a new one.

9   The cap is also equipped with a vacuum relief spring. When the engine cools off, a vacuum is created in the cooling system. The vacuum relief spring allows air back into the system, which will equalize the pressure and prevent damage to the radiator (the radiator tanks could collapse if the vacuum is great enough). If, after turning the engine off and allowing it to cool down you notice any of the cooling system hoses collapsing, replace the pressure cap with a new one.

Thermostat

10   Before assuming the thermostat (see illustration) is responsible for a cooling system problem, check the coolant level (see Chapter 1), drivebelt tension (see Chapter 1) and temperature gauge (or light) operation.

11   If the engine takes a long time to warm up (as indicated by the temperature gauge or heater operation), the thermostat is probably stuck open. Replace the thermostat with a new one.

12   If the engine runs hot or overheats, a thorough test of the thermostat should be performed.

13   Definitive testing of the thermostat can only be made when it is removed from the vehicle. If the thermostat is stuck in the open position at room temperature, it is faulty and must be replaced.

Caution: *Do not drive the vehicle without a thermostat. The computer may stay in open loop and emissions and fuel economy will suffer.*

14   To test a thermostat, suspend the (closed) thermostat on a length of string or wire in a pot of cold water.

15   Heat the water on a stove while observing thermostat. The thermostat should fully open before the water boils.

16   If the thermostat doesn't open and close as specified, or sticks in any position, replace it.

Cooling fan

Electric cooling fan

17   If the engine is overheating and the cooling fan is not coming on when the engine temperature rises to an excessive level, unplug the fan motor electrical connector(s) and connect the motor directly to the battery with fused jumper wires. If the fan motor doesn't come on, replace the motor.

18   If the radiator fan motor is okay, but it isn't coming on when the engine gets hot, the fan relay might be defective. A relay is used to control a circuit by turning it on and off in response to a control decision by the Powertrain Control Module (PCM). These control circuits are fairly complex, and checking them should be left to a qualified automotive technician. Sometimes, the control system can be fixed by simply identifying and replacing a bad relay.

19   Locate the fan relays in the engine compartment fuse/relay box.

20   Test the relay (see Chapter 12).

21   If the relay is okay, check all wiring and connections to the fan motor. Refer to the wiring diagrams at the end of Chapter 12. If no obvious problems are found, the problem could be the Engine Coolant Temperature (ECT) sensor or the Powertrain Control Module (PCM). Have the cooling fan system and circuit diagnosed by a dealer service

department or repair shop with the proper diagnostic equipment.

Belt-driven cooling fan

22   Disconnect the cable from the negative terminal of the battery and rock the fan back and forth by hand to check for excessive bearing play.

23   With the engine cold (and not running), turn the fan blades by hand. The fan should turn freely.

24   Visually inspect for substantial fluid leakage from the clutch assembly. If problems are noted, replace the clutch assembly.

25   With the engine completely warmed up, turn off the ignition switch and disconnect the negative battery cable from the battery. Turn the fan by hand. Some drag should be evident. If the fan turns easily, replace the fan clutch.

Water pump

26   A failure in the water pump can cause serious engine damage due to overheating.

Drivebelt-driven water pump

27   There are two ways to check the operation of the water pump while it's installed on the engine. If the pump is found to be defective, it should be replaced with a new or rebuilt unit.

28   Water pumps are equipped with weep (or vent) holes (see illustration). If a failure occurs in the pump seal, coolant will leak from the hole.

29   If the water pump shaft bearings fail, there may be a howling sound at the pump while it's running. Shaft wear can be felt with the drivebelt removed if the water pump pulley is rocked up and down (with the engine off). Don't mistake drivebelt slippage, which causes a squealing sound, for water pump bearing failure.

Timing belt-driven water pump

30   Water pumps driven by the timing belt are located underneath the timing belt cover.

31   Checking the water pump is limited because of where it is located. However, some basic checks can be made before deciding to remove the water pump. If the pump is found to be defective, it should be replaced with a new or rebuilt unit.

32   One sign that the water pump may be failing is that the heater (climate control) may not work well. Warm the engine to normal operating temperature, confirm that the coolant level is correct, then run the heater and check for hot air coming from the ducts.

33   Check for noises coming from the water pump area. If the water pump impeller shaft or bearings are failing, there may be a howling sound at the pump while the engine is running.

34   It you suspect water pump failure due to noise, wear can be confirmed by feeling for play at the pump shaft. This can be done by rocking the drive sprocket on the pump shaft up and down. To do this you will need to remove the tension on the timing chain or belt as well as access the water pump.

All water pumps

35   In rare cases or on high-mileage vehicles, another sign of water pump failure may be the presence of coolant in the engine oil. This condition will adversely affect the engine in varying degrees.

Note: *Finding coolant in the engine oil could indicate other serious issues besides a failed water pump, such as a blown head gasket or a cracked cylinder head or block.*

36   Even a pump that exhibits no outward signs of a problem, such as noise or leakage, can still be due for replacement. Removal for close examination is the only sure way to tell. Sometimes the fins on the back of the impeller can corrode to the point that cooling efficiency is diminished significantly.

Heater system

37   Little can go wrong with a heater. If the fan motor will run at all speeds, the electrical part of the system is okay. The three basic heater problems fall into the following general categories:

   a) *Not enough heat*
   b) *Heat all the time*
   c) *No heat*

38   If there's not enough heat, the control valve or door is stuck in a partially open position, the coolant coming from the engine isn't hot enough, or the heater core is restricted. If the coolant isn't hot enough, the thermostat in the engine cooling system is stuck open, allowing coolant to pass through the engine so rapidly that it doesn't heat up quickly enough. If the vehicle is equipped with a temperature gauge instead of a warning light, watch to see if the engine temperature rises to the normal operating range after driving for a reasonable distance.

39   If there's heat all the time, the control valve or the door is stuck wide open.

40   If there's no heat, coolant is probably not reaching the heater core, or the heater core is plugged. The likely cause is a collapsed or plugged hose, core, or a frozen heater control valve. If the heater is the type that flows coolant all the time, the cause is a stuck door or a broken or kinked control cable.

Air conditioning system

41   If the cool air output is inadequate:

   a) *Inspect the condenser coils and fins to make sure they're clear*
   b) *Check the compressor clutch for slippage.*
   c) *Check the blower motor for proper operation.*
   d) *Inspect the blower discharge passage for obstructions.*
   e) *Check the system air intake filter for clogging.*

42   If the system provides intermittent cooling air:

   a) *Check the circuit breaker, blower switch and blower motor for a malfunction.*
   b) *Make sure the compressor clutch isn't slipping.*
   c) *Inspect the plenum door to make sure it's operating properly.*
   d) *Inspect the evaporator to make sure it isn't clogged.*
   e) *If the unit is icing up, it may be caused by excessive moisture in the system, incorrect super heat switch adjustment or low thermostat adjustment.*

43   If the system provides no cooling air:

   a) *Inspect the compressor drivebelt. Make sure it's not loose or broken.*
   b) *Make sure the compressor clutch engages. If it doesn't, check for a blown fuse.*
   c) *Inspect the wire harness for broken or disconnected wires.*
   d) *If the compressor clutch doesn't engage, bridge the terminals of the A/C pressure switch(es) with a jumper wire; if the clutch now engages, and the system is properly charged, the pressure switch is bad.*
   e) *Make sure the blower motor is not disconnected or burned out.*
   f) *Make sure the compressor isn't partially or completely seized.*
   g) *Inspect the refrigerant lines for leaks.*
   h) *Check the components for leaks.*
   i) *Inspect the receiver-drier/accumulator or expansion valve/tube for clogged screens.*

44   If the system is noisy:

   a) *Look for loose panels in the passenger compartment.*
   b) *Inspect the compressor drivebelt. It may be loose or worn.*
   c) *Check the compressor mounting bolts. They should be tight.*
   d) *Listen carefully to the compressor. It may be worn out.*
   e) *Listen to the idler pulley and bearing and the clutch. Either may be defective.*

   f) *The winding in the compressor clutch coil or solenoid may be defective.*
   g) *The compressor oil level may be low.*
   h) *The blower motor fan bushing or the motor itself may be worn out.*
   i) *If there is an excessive charge in the system, you'll hear a rumbling noise in the high pressure line, a thumping noise in the compressor, or see bubbles or cloudiness in the sight glass.*
   j) *If there's a low charge in the system, you might hear hissing in the evaporator case at the expansion valve, or see bubbles or cloudiness in the sight glass.*

3   Air conditioning and heating system - check and maintenance

Air conditioning system

Warning: *The air conditioning system is under high pressure. Do not loosen any hose fittings or remove any components until after the system has been discharged. Air conditioning refrigerant should be properly discharged into an EPA-approved recovery/recycling unit at a dealer service department or an automotive air conditioning repair facility. Always wear eye protection when disconnecting air conditioning system fittings.*

Caution: *There can be two types of refrigerants and systems used, depending on the year of the vehicle. Both refrigerants are environmentally friendly. A sticker is located at the front of the engine compartment detailing which refrigerant is used in the vehicle's air conditioning system (either R134a or R1234yf). The refrigerants (and their appropriate oils) are not compatible with each other or other system components and must never be mixed or the components will be damaged.*

Caution: *When replacing entire components, additional refrigerant oil should be added equal to the amount that is removed with the component being replaced. Be sure to read the can before adding any oil to the system, to make sure it is compatible with the R134a or R1234yf systems.*

1   The following maintenance checks should be performed on a regular basis to ensure that the air conditioning continues to operate at peak efficiency.

   a) *Inspect the condition of the compressor drivebelt. If it is worn or deteriorated, replace it (see Chapter 1).*
   b) *Check the drivebelt tension (see Chapter 1).*
   c) *Inspect the system hoses. Look for cracks, bubbles, hardening and deterioration. Inspect the hoses and all fittings for oil bubbles or seepage. If there is any evidence of wear, damage or leakage, replace the hose(s).*
   d) *Inspect the condenser fins for leaves, bugs and any other foreign material that may have embedded itself in the fins. Use a fin comb or compressed air to remove debris from the condenser.*

3.1 The evaporator drain hose is located on the passenger's side of the unibody frame rail

3.9 Insert a thermometer in the center vent, turn on the air conditioning system and wait for it to cool down; depending on the humidity, the output air should be 35 to 40 degrees cooler than the ambient air temperature

3.11 R-134a automotive air conditioning charging kit

3.13 Air conditioning charging port locations

1 High-side charging port
2 Low-side charging port

e) *Make sure the system has the correct refrigerant charge.*

f) *If you hear water sloshing around in the dash area or have water dripping on the carpet, check the evaporator housing drain tube (see illustration) and insert a piece of wire into the opening to check for blockage.*

2   It's a good idea to operate the system for about ten minutes at least once a month. This is particularly important during the winter months because long term non-use can cause hardening, and subsequent failure, of the seals. Note that using the Defrost function operates the compressor.

3   If the air conditioning system is not working properly, proceed to Step 6 and perform the general checks outlined below.

4   Because of the complexity of the air conditioning system and the special equipment necessary to service it, in-depth troubleshooting and repairs beyond checking the refrigerant charge and the compressor clutch operation are not included in this manual. However, simple checks and component replacement procedures are provided in this Chapter. For more complete information on the air conditioning system, refer to the Haynes Automotive Heating and Air Conditioning Manual.

5   The most common cause of poor cooling is simply a low system refrigerant charge. If a noticeable drop in system cooling ability occurs, one of the following quick checks will help you determine if the refrigerant level is low.

Checking the refrigerant charge

6   Warm the engine up to normal operating temperature.

7   Place the air conditioning temperature selector at the coldest setting and put the blower at the highest setting.

8   After the system reaches operating temperature, feel the larger pipe exiting the evaporator at the firewall. The outlet pipe should be cold (the tubing that leads back to the

compressor). If the evaporator outlet pipe is warm, the system probably needs a charge.

9   Insert a thermometer in the center air distribution duct (see illustration) while operating the air conditioning system at its maximum setting - the temperature of the output air should be 35 to 40 degrees F below the ambient air temperature (down to approximately 40 degrees F). If the ambient (outside) air temperature is very high, say 110 degrees F, the duct air temperature may be as high as 60 degrees F, but generally the air conditioning is 35 to 40 degrees F cooler than the ambient air.

10   Further inspection or testing of the system requires special tools and techniques and is beyond the scope of the home mechanic.

Adding refrigerant

Caution: *Check the air conditioning system identification sticker on the front of the vehicle to verify what type system you have. There can be two types of refrigerants and systems used, depending on the year of the vehicle. Make sure any refrigerant, refrigerant oil or replacement components you purchase are designed as compatible with either R134a or R1234yf. The refrigerants, oils and components of the two systems are not compatible with each other.*

11   Purchase the appropriate R134a or R1234yf automotive charging kit at an auto parts store (see illustration). A charging kit includes a can of refrigerant, a tap valve and a short section of hose that can be attached between the tap valve and the system low side service valve.

Caution: *Never add more than one can of refrigerant to the system. If more refrigerant than that is required, the system should be evacuated and leak tested.*

12   Back off the valve handle on the charging kit and screw the kit onto the refrigerant can, making sure first that the O-ring or rub-

ber seal inside the threaded portion of the kit is in place.

13   Remove the dust cap from the low-side charging port and attach the hose's quick-connect fitting to the port (see illustration). The fittings on the charging kit are designed to fit only on the low side of the system.

Warning: *DO NOT hook the charging kit hose to the system high side!*

Warning: *Wear protective eyewear when dealing with pressurized refrigerant cans.*

14   Warm up the engine and turn On the air conditioning. Keep the charging kit hose away from the fan and other moving parts.

Note: *The charging process requires the compressor to be running. If the clutch cycles off, you can put the air conditioning switch on High and leave the car doors open to keep the clutch on and compressor working. The compressor can be kept on during the charging by removing the connector from the pressure switch and bridging it with a paper clip or jumper wire during the procedure.*

3.24 Remove the cabin air filter (see Chapter 1) and insert the nozzle of the disinfectant can into the housing

15   Turn the valve handle on the kit until the stem pierces the can, then back the handle out to release the refrigerant. You should be able to hear the rush of gas. Keep the can upright at all times, but shake it occasionally. Allow stabilization time between each addition.
Note: *The charging process will go faster if you wrap the can with a hot-water-soaked rag to keep the can from freezing up.*
16   If you have an accurate thermometer, you can place it in the center air conditioning duct inside the vehicle and keep track of the output air temperature. A charged system that is working properly should cool down to approximately 40 degrees F. If the ambient (outside) air temperature is very high, say 110 degrees F, the duct air temperature may be as high as 60 degrees F, but generally the air conditioning is 35 to 40 degrees F cooler than the ambient air.
17   When the can is empty, turn the valve handle to the closed position and release the connection from the low-side port. Reinstall the dust cap.
18   Remove the charging kit from the can and store the kit for future use with the piercing valve in the UP position, to prevent inadvertently piercing the can on the next use.

Heating systems

19   If the carpet under the heater core is damp, or if antifreeze vapor or steam is coming through the vents, the heater core is leaking. Remove it (see Section 13) and install a new unit (most radiator shops will not repair a leaking heater core).
20   If the air coming out of the heater vents isn't hot, the problem could stem from any of the following causes:
a) *The thermostat is stuck open, preventing the engine coolant from warming up enough to carry heat to the heater core. Replace the thermostat (see Section 4).*
b) *There is a blockage in the system, preventing the flow of coolant through the heater core. Feel both heater hoses at the firewall. They should be hot. If one of them is cold, there is an obstruction in one of the hoses or in the heater core, or the heater control valve is shut. Detach*

the hoses and back flush the heater core with a water hose. If the heater core is clear but circulation is impeded, remove the two hoses and flush them out with a water hose.
c) *If flushing fails to remove the blockage from the heater core, the core must be replaced (see Section 13).*

Eliminating air conditioning odors

21   Unpleasant odors that often develop in air conditioning systems are caused by the growth of a fungus, usually on the surface of the evaporator core. The warm, humid environment there is a perfect breeding ground for mildew to develop.
22   The evaporator core on most vehicles is difficult to access, and factory dealerships have a lengthy, expensive process for eliminating the fungus by opening up the evaporator case and using a powerful disinfectant and rinse on the core until the fungus is gone. You can service your own system at home, but it takes something much stronger than basic household germ-killers or deodorizers.
23   Aerosol disinfectants for automotive air conditioning systems are available in most auto parts stores, but remember when shopping for them that the most effective treatments are also the most expensive. The basic procedure for using these sprays is to start by running the system in the RECIRC mode for ten minutes with the blower on its highest speed. Use the highest heat mode to dry out the system and keep the compressor from engaging by disconnecting the wiring connector at the compressor.
24   The disinfectant can usually comes with a long spray hose. Insert the nozzle into an intake port inside the cabin, and spray according to the manufacturer's recommendations (see illustration). Try to cover the whole surface of the evaporator core, by aiming the spray up, down and sideways. Follow the manufacturer's recommendations for the length of spray and waiting time between applications.
25   Once the evaporator has been cleaned, the best way to prevent the mildew from coming back again is to make sure

your evaporator housing drain tube is clear (see illustration 3.1).

Automatic heating and air conditioning systems

26   Some vehicles are equipped with an optional automatic climate control system. This system has its own computer that receives inputs from various sensors in the heating and air conditioning system. This computer, like the PCM, has self-diagnostic capabilities to help pinpoint problems or faults within the system. Vehicles equipped with automatic heating and air conditioning systems are very complex and considered beyond the scope of the home mechanic. Vehicles equipped with automatic heating and air conditioning systems should be taken to dealer service department or other qualified facility for repair.

---

4   Thermostat - check and replacement

Check

Note: *On 1.4L engines, the thermostat is located on the right end of the engine, attached to the water pump. On 1.8L engines, it's located on the left end of the engine, attached to the cylinder head.*
1   Before assuming the thermostat is to blame for a cooling system problem, check the coolant level, drivebelt tension (see Chapter 1) and temperature gauge operation.
2   If the engine seems to be taking a long time to warm up, based on heater output or temperature gauge operation, the thermostat is probably stuck open. Replace the thermostat with a new one.
3   If the engine runs hot, use your hand to check the temperature of the radiator hose attached to the thermostat housing. If the hose isn't hot, but the engine is, the thermostat is probably stuck closed, preventing the coolant inside the engine from escaping to the radiator. Replace the thermostat.
Caution: *Don't drive the vehicle without a thermostat. The computer may stay in open loop and emissions and fuel economy will suffer.*
4   If the radiator hose is hot, it means that the coolant is flowing and the thermostat is open. Consult the Troubleshooting section at the front of this manual for cooling system diagnosis.

Replacement

Warning: *The engine must be completely cool before beginning this procedure.*
5   Disconnect the cable from the negative terminal of the battery (see Chapter 5). Drain the cooling system (see Chapter 1).
6   Disconnect the air filter outlet duct (see Chapter 4).
7   On 2015 and earlier 1.4L engines, remove the PCV vent pipe from the turbocharger. On 1.8L engines, detach the throttle body coolant hose and the heater hose from the thermostat housing.

4.8a Remove the radiator hose retaining clip. . .

4.8b. . . then twist and pull the hose away from the housing (1.4L engine)

4.9 Remove the thermostat mounting bolts (1.4L engine)

4.10 Disconnect the hose clamp and remove the hose

4.12 install a new gasket, making sure it's seated into the grooves in the housing - 1.4L engine shown

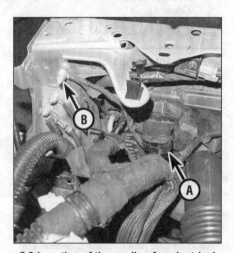

5.8 Location of the cooling fan electrical connector (A) and ground wire (B)

8   Remove the radiator hose retaining clip (1.4L engine) or clamp (1.8L engine) and detach the hose from the thermostat housing (see illustrations).
Note: *On 2016 and later 1.4L engines, disconnect the electrical connector at the thermostat housing, if equipped.*
9   Remove the fasteners and detach the thermostat housing (see illustration). If the housing is stuck, tap it with a soft-face hammer to jar it loose. Be prepared for some coolant to spill as the gasket seal is broken.
Note: *The thermostat is an integral part of the housing; the complete assembly must be replaced when servicing the thermostat.*
10   On 2015 and earlier 1.4L engines, rotate the housing, slide back the hose clamp and detach hose from the bottom of the housing (see illustration).
11   Clean the mating surfaces of the housing and cover.
12   Install a new gasket into the groove in the housing (see illustration).
13   On 2015 and earlier 1.4L engines, reconnect the hose to the base of the thermostat housing and attach the clamp.

14   Install the thermostat housing and bolts, then tighten the bolts to the torque listed in this Chapter's Specifications.
15   On 1.8L engines, reconnect the heater hose and the throttle body hose to the thermostat housing.
16   Reattach the radiator hose to the outlet pipe on the thermostat cover and install the clip (1.4L engine) or clamp (1.8L engine).
17   The remaining installation is the reverse of the removal.
18   Refill the cooling system (see Chapter 1).
19   Reconnect the battery (see Chapter 5).
20   Start the engine and allow it to reach normal operating temperature, then check for leaks and proper thermostat operation (as described in Steps 3 and 4).

5   Engine cooling fan - replacement

Warning: *To avoid possible injury or damage, DO NOT operate the engine with a damaged fan. Do not attempt to repair fan blades - replace a damaged fan with a new one.*

Warning: *The engine must be completely cool before beginning this procedure.*
1   Disconnect the cable from the negative battery terminal (see Chapter 5).
2   Remove the front bumper cover (see Chapter 11).
3   Remove the radiator support center bar fasteners and bar.
4   Remove the radiator upper air seal.
5   On 2016 and later 1.4L engines, remove the charge air cooler inlet and outlet pipes (see Chapter 4).
6   Remove the air baffles from both sides of the radiator.
7   Remove the radiator upper mounting bolts and re-position the radiator by moving it towards the front of the vehicle.
8   Disconnect the fan motor electrical connector (see illustration) and ground wire nut, then separate the harness from the clips on the fan shroud and position the harness off to the side.
9   Remove the four mounting clips and slide the fan shroud towards the right side, then tilt the left side of the fan shroud up and maneuver the fan shroud out of the vehicle.
10   Installation is the reverse of removal.

6.3 Coolant expansion tank details   **7.13 2015 and earlier, radiator upper mounting bracket bolts**

1   Air bleed hose   3   Retaining clip
2   Coolant hose

6   Coolant expansion tank - removal and installation

Warning: *Wait until the engine is completely cool before beginning this procedure.*
1   Disconnect the cable from the negative battery terminal (see Chapter 5).
2   Raise the vehicle and support it securely on jackstands, then drain approximately 1.4 quarts (1.5 liters) of coolant (see Chapter 1), so the coolant level is lower than that of the tank.
Caution: *If more than 1.4 quarts (1.5 liters) of coolant is drained, the cooling system will have to be bled (see Chapter 1, Section 20).*
3   Disconnect the hoses from the expansion tank (see illustration).
4   Remove the retaining clip from the left side of the tank..
5   Slide the tank forward to detach the tank from the mounting tangs, then lift it up and disconnect the electrical connector from the coolant level sensor on the bottom of the tank.
6   Installation is the reverse of removal.
7   Refill the cooling system (see Chapter 1).

7   Radiator - removal and installation

Warning: *Wait until the engine is completely cool before beginning this procedure.*

Removal

1   Disconnect the cable from the negative battery terminal (see Chapter 5).
2   Remove the front bumper cover (see Chapter 11), remove the grille support and cover, if equipped.
3   On 1.8L models, remove the air intake ducts.
4   Drain the cooling system (see Chapter 1). If the coolant is relatively new and in good condition, save it and reuse it.

5   Disconnect the upper and lower radiator hoses from the radiator. On the left side, loosen the hose clamp by squeezing the ends together. On the right side, remove the retaining clip and detach the hose.
6   On 1.4L models, remove the charge air cooler (see Chapter 4).
7   On 1.8L models, disconnect the electrical connector to the air conditioning pressure switch, then remove the harness from around the radiator and place the harness out of the way.
8   On 2016 and later models, disengage the air deflector clips and remove the air deflectors from each side of the radiator.
9   On automatic transaxle models, disconnect the transaxle oil cooler inlet line quick-connect fitting and separate the line from the radiator. Remove the transmission cooler line clips and pull the cooler line from radiator and the auxiliary cooler then cap the line and openings.
10   On 2015 and earlier models, remove the hood latch (see Chapter 11).
11   On 2016 and later models, disconnect the electrical connector from the air conditioning pressure sensor, then press the condenser retaining tabs towards the radiator and unclip the condenser and secure it away from the radiator. Do not let it hang on the refrigerant line - it must be supported.
12   Unclip the cooling fan shroud from the radiator and move the fan shroud away from the radiator.
13   On 2015 and earlier models, remove the radiator upper mounting bolts and remove the brackets (see illustration).
14   On 2015 and earlier models, carefully lift the radiator up and out.
15   On 2016 and later models, remove the radiator lower bracket mounting bolts from each side, then remove the radiator assembly from the vehicle. Have an assistant help support the weight of the assembly as it's removed.
16   On 2016 and later models, once the assembly is removed, slide the lower

mounts off of the radiator studs, remove the cooling fan mounting bolts and fan assembly (if not already done), then unclip the charge air cooler from the radiator.
17   Make sure the rubber radiator insulators that fit on the radiator lower mounting brackets remain in place in the body.
18   Remove bugs and dirt from the radiator with compressed air and a soft brush. Don't bend the cooling fins. Inspect the radiator for leaks and damage. If it requires repair, have a radiator shop do the work.

Installation

19   Inspect the rubber insulators for cracks and deterioration. Make sure that they're free of dirt and gravel.
20   Installation is the reverse of removal, making sure the condenser and fan shroud are seated in the radiator clips. After installation, fill the cooling system with the correct mixture of antifreeze and water (see Chapter 1).
21   Reconnect the battery (see Chapter 5).
22   Start the engine and check for leaks. Allow the engine to reach normal operating temperature, indicated by the upper radiator hose becoming hot. Recheck the coolant level and add more if required.
23   On automatic transaxle equipped vehicles, check and add fluid as needed.

8   Water pump - replacement

Warning: *The engine must be completely cool before beginning this procedure.*
1   Disconnect the cable from the negative battery terminal (see Chapter 5).
2   Remove the air filter housing (see Chapter 4).
3   Loosen the right front wheel lug nuts, raise the front of the vehicle and support it securely on jackstands. Remove the wheel.
4   Drain the cooling system (see Chapter 1).

8.7 Hold the water pump from turning by placing a wrench on the flats of the hub, then unscrew the pulley bolts

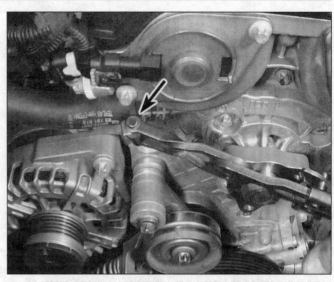

8.9 Squeeze the hose clamp with pliers and slide it back, then detach the hose from the pump

8.10 Water pump mounting bolt locations - always replace the bolts marked "A" with new ones

8.11a Use a screwdriver to pry against the pump tab to break the seal. . .

5   Remove the drivebelt (see Chapter 1).
Note: *If you're working on a 1.8L engine, loosen the water pump pulley bolts before removing the drivebelt.*

1.4L engine

2015 and earlier models

6   Remove the right-side engine mount and mount bracket (see Chapter 2A).
7   Remove the water pump pulley bolts (see illustration) and pulley.
8   Remove the thermostat (see Section 4).
9   Disconnect the heater hose from the water pump (see illustration).
10   Remove the water pump bolts (see illustration).
11   Remove the water pump and gasket from the timing chain cover (see illustrations).

8.11b. . . and remove the pump and gasket from the front cover

8.13 Water pump bolt details (1.4L engine)

1   25 mm bolt
2   52 mm bolt, with pointed end
3   60 mm bolt, without pointed end

12   Clean the bolt threads and the threaded holes in the engine and remove any corrosion or sealant. Remove all traces of old gasket material from the sealing surfaces.

13   Install a new gasket to the timing chain cover and insert the new water pump/timing chain cover bolts (marked "A" in illustration 8.10), then install the remaining bolts and tighten them loosely (see illustration). Tighten all of the water pump bolts, a little at a time in a criss-cross pattern, to the Step 1 torque listed in this Chapter's Specifications.

14   Tighten the two water pump/timing chain cover bolts ("A" in illustration 8.10) to the Step 2 torque listed in this Chapter's Specifications.

15   Reconnect the heater hose to the water pump.

16   Install the thermostat housing (see Section 4).

17   Proceed to Step 41.

2016 and later models

Note: *GM considers the water pump housing as consisting of the pulley, front housing/impeller assembly and the water pump assembly. The pump housing, thermostat housing, oil cooler assembly and the water pump assembly is mounted to the side of the engine block.*

Water pump housing

18   Remove the water pump-to-pump housing assembly bolts.

19   Disengage the engine control module wiring harness retainers and move the harness out of the way.

20   Remove the water pump and gasket from the water pump housing assembly.

21   Remove all traces of the old gasket material from the sealing surfaces.

22   Install a new gasket to the water pump assembly and install the pump and mounting bolts and tighten them hand tight.

23   Tighten the water pump housing bolts a little at a time in a criss cross pattern to the torque listed in this Chapters Specifications.

24   Proceed to Step 41.

Water pump assembly

25   Remove the charge air cooler inlet pipe (see Chapter 4).

26   Remove the turbocharger oil feed pipe (see Chapter 4).

27   Disconnect the hoses to the thermostat bypass pipe, then remove the tube mounting bolts and pipe from the back side of the water pump assembly.

28   Disengage the wiring harness retainers and move the wiring harness out of the way. It may be necessary to disconnect some of the harness electrical connectors to move the harness.

29   Remove the water pump assembly mounting bolts, then remove the water pump assembly from the side of the engine block.

Note: *The water pump assembly bolts are different lengths; make sure to note where each bolt goes when removing them.*

30   If necessary, once the water pump assembly is removed, the thermostat assembly and oil cooler can be removed from the assembly.

31   Remove all traces of the old gasket material from the sealing surfaces.

32   Install a new gasket to the cylinder block and install the pump assembly and mounting bolts (in their original locations), then tighten them hand tight.

33   Tighten the water pump assembly bolts a little at a time in a criss cross pattern to the torque listed in this Chapter's Specifications.

34   Proceed to Step 41.

1.8L engine

35   Unscrew the water pump pulley bolts and remove the pulley.

36   Unscrew the water pump mounting bolts, then remove the water pump and discard the O-ring.

37   Clean the bolt threads and the threaded holes in the engine and remove any corrosion or sealant. Clean the water pump and engine block mating surfaces.

38   Install a new O-ring into the groove on the water pump.

39   Install the water pump and bolts, tightening the bolts in a criss-cross pattern to the torque listed in this Chapter's Specifications.

40   Proceed to Step 41.

All models

41   Install the water pump pulley and tighten the bolts to the torque listed in this Chapter's Specifications.

Note: *If you're working on a 1.8L engine, tighten the pulley bolts after the drivebelt is installed (the belt will prevent the pulley from turning).*

42   The remainder of installation is the reverse of removal.

43   Refill the cooling system (see Chapter 1).

44   Reconnect the battery (see Chapter 5).

45   Operate the engine to check for leaks.

9   Engine oil cooler - removal and installation

Warning: *The engine must be completely cool before beginning this procedure.*

Removal

1   Disconnect the cable from the negative battery terminal (see Chapter 5). The engine oil cooler is integrated into the the bottom of the oil filter housing.

2   Drain the cooling system (see Chapter 1).

1.4L engine

3   Raise the vehicle and support it securely on jackstands.

4   Remove the catalytic converter (see Chapter 6).

5   Disconnect and remove the air filter housing outlet duct (see Chapter 4).

6   Disconnect the turbocharger oil feed pipe, coolant return pipe and coolant inlet pipe (see Chapter 4).

7   Disconnect the oil cooler outlet hose from the thermostat housing.

8   Disconnect then the oil pressure switch electrical connector.

9   Disconnect the inlet and outlet hoses from the oil cooler, then remove the hose bracket fasteners at the cooler and the engine block.

10   Remove the remaining two mounting bolts and remove the oil cooler.

Note: There are three oil cooler mounting bolts; one is used to hold the cooler line brackets.

1.8L engine

11   Remove the exhaust manifold (see Chapter 2A).

12   Remove the oil cooler inlet pipe bolts then remove the outlet pipe bolts from the thermostat housing and twist the outlet pipe out of the oil cooler. Be sure to replace the O-ring on the pipe.

13   Disconnect the two coolant hoses at the top of the engine oil cooler.

14   Remove the five oil cooler housing mounting bolts and remove the oil cooler assembly.

15   Remove the six oil cooler-to-oil cooler housing bolts and separate the oil cooler from the housing. Remove the oil cooler gasket.

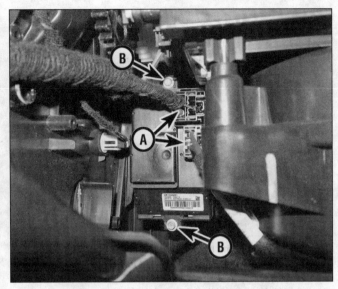

11.6 Location of the blower motor control module electrical connectors (A) and mounting screws (B)

11.10 Air duct fastener location

Installation

16   Clean the area around the engine block. Remove any debris, deposits or material from the area where the cooler mounts.

17   On 1.4L engines, install the engine oil cooler onto the engine block with new O-rings, lubricated with clean engine oil, and a new gasket.

18   On 1.8L engines, install a new gasket, then install the oil cooler to the oil cooler housing and tighten the bolts securely.

19   Connect the inlet and outlet coolant hoses and tighten the clamps.

20   The remainder of installation is the reverse of removal.

21   Reconnect the battery (see Chapter 5).

22   Change the engine oil and filter, refill the cooling system (see Chapter 1), run the engine and check for leaks.

10   Coolant temperature sending unit - check and replacement

Warning: *Wait until the engine is completely cool before beginning this procedure.*

Check

1   The coolant temperature indicator system consists of a warning light or a temperature gauge on the dash and a coolant temperature sending unit mounted on the engine. On the models covered by this manual, the Engine Coolant Temperature (ECT) sensor, which is an information sensor for the Powertrain Control Module (PCM), also functions as the coolant temperature sending unit.

2   If an overheating indication occurs, check the coolant level in the system and then make sure all connectors in the wiring harness between the sending unit and the indicator light or gauge are tight.

3   When the ignition switch is turned to START and the starter motor is turning, the indicator light (if equipped) should come on. This doesn't mean the engine is overheated; it just means that the bulb is good.

4   If the light doesn't come on when the ignition key is turned to START, the bulb might be burned out, the ignition switch might be faulty or the circuit might be open.

5   As soon as the engine starts, the indicator light should go out and remain off, unless the engine overheats. If the light doesn't go out, the wire between the sending unit and the light could be grounded; the sending unit might be defective (have it checked by a dealer service department); or the ignition switch might be faulty (see Chapter 12). Check the coolant to make sure it's correctly mixed; plain water, with no antifreeze, or coolant that's mainly water, might have too low a boiling point to activate the sending unit (see Chapter 1).

Replacement

6   See Chapter 6 for the Engine Coolant Temperature (ECT) sensor replacement procedure.

11   Blower motor control module and blower motor - replacement

Warning: *The models covered by this manual are equipped with Supplemental Restraint systems (SRS), more commonly known as airbags. Always disarm the airbag system before working in the vicinity of any airbag system component to avoid the possibility of accidental deployment of the air-*

bag, which could cause personal injury (see Chapter 12). Do not use a memory saving device to preserve the PCM's memory when working on or near airbag system components.

1   Disconnect the cable from the negative battery terminal (see Chapter 5).

2   Remove the lower insulator panel from below the passenger's side instrument panel (see Chapter 11).

Blower motor control module

Note: *The blower motor control module controls the air conditioning system, heater system and blower motor functions.*

3   Disconnect the electrical connectors to the passenger's side lower airbag, then remove the fasteners and airbag from under the glove box.

4   Remove the passengers side instrument panel end cap (see Chapter 11).

5   Remove the glove box (see Chapter 11).

6   Disconnect the electrical connectors at the blower motor control module (see illustration).

7   Remove the mounting screws and pull the module out of the housing.

8   Installation is the reverse of removal.

9   Reconnect the battery (see Chapter 5).

Blower motor

10   Remove the passenger's side floor air duct fastener (see illustration) and move the duct away from the blower motor.

Note: *To access the blower motor on 2016 and later models, the glove box must be removed (see Chapter 11).*

11   Remove the blower motor cup fasteners and cup from the the blower motor.

11.12 Blower motor details

1   Blower motor electrical connector
2   Blower motor cup fastener locations - 2 of 3 shown
3   Blower motor mounting screws

12.5 Disengage the heater/air conditioner control module retaining tabs and separate the module from the accessory bezel

1   Accessory bezel
2   Heater/air conditioner control module
3   Retaining tabs

12   Disconnect the blower motor electrical connector (see illustration).
13   Remove the blower motor fasteners and lower the blower motor assembly from the heater case.
14   Installation is the reverse of removal.
15   Reconnect the battery (see Chapter 5).

12   Heater/air conditioner control assembly - removal and installation

Warning: *The models covered by this manual are equipped with Supplemental Restraint systems (SRS), more commonly known as airbags. Always disarm the airbag system before working in the vicinity of any airbag system component to avoid the possibility of accidental deployment of the airbag, which could cause personal injury (see Chapter 12). Do not use a memory saving device to preserve the PCM's memory when working on or near airbag system components.*
Note: *The heater/air conditioner control module (display) and heater/air conditioner remote control unit both work together and independently to control the HVAC systems. The remote control unit (the computer) is a separate component in the dash, behind the heater/air conditioner control module. You can remove both components to access something else, or to remove the instrument panel, but if the control module or remote control unit must be replaced, it will have to be done by a dealer service department or other properly equipped shop because the module and control unit configuration must be programmed. Without the correct module control unit configuration, the system will not work.*
1   Disconnect the cable from the negative battery terminal (see Chapter 5).
2   Remove the dashboard center trim panel and vent assembly (see Chapter 11).

3   On 2015 and earlier models, remove the center console shift lever trim panel and storage tray (see Chapter 11).
4   Remove the instrument panel accessory bezel (see Chapter 11).
5   On 2015 and earlier models, disengage the upper and lower retaining tabs and remove the heater/air conditioner control module from the accessory bezel (see illustration).
6   On 2016 and later models, remove the heater/air conditioner control module fasteners.
7   On 2016 and later models, pull the control module out from the instrument panel, then disconnect the electrical connectors and remove the control module.
8   The remainder of installation is the reverse of removal.
9   Reconnect the battery (see Chapter 5).

13   Heater core - replacement

Warning: *The models covered by this manual are equipped with Supplemental Restraint systems (SRS), more commonly known as airbags. Always disarm the airbag system before working in the vicinity of any airbag system component to avoid the possibility of accidental deployment of the airbag, which could cause personal injury (see Chapter 12). Do not use a memory saving device to preserve the PCM's memory when working on or near airbag system components.*
Warning: *Wait until the engine is completely cool before beginning this procedure.*
Note: *On these models, the instrument panel and the cowl support brace behind the instrument panel must be removed. This requires the tagging and disconnection of many electrical connectors and working with hard-to-reach fasteners.*

Heater core
1   Drain the cooling system (see Chapter 1).
2   Remove the driver's-side knee bolster (see Chapter 11), then disconnect the electrical connector and remove the lower airbag fasteners and airbag (see Chapter 11, Section 22).
3   Remove the driver's-side center console front side panel (see Chapter 11).
4   Remove the floor air duct bolt (see illustration) from the trim panel then disconnect and remove the duct from behind the trim panel.
5   Remove the heater core cover fastener and cover from the heater case (see illustration).
6   Remove the heater core tube clamps and detach the tubes from the heater core (see illustration). Discard the O-rings.
Caution: *There will be a small amount of coolant left in the tubes and heater core. Once the tubes are removed, the coolant will drain out into the vehicle. Make sure to have a small container to catch the fluid and som rags in place to protect the carpet before disconnecting the heater core tubes.*
7   Pull the heater core out of the housing.
8   Installation is the reverse of removal. Be sure to use new O-rings on the heater core tubes.
9   Refill the cooling system (see Chapter 1).
10   Reconnect the battery (see Chapter 5).

Auxiliary heater core
Warning: *The models covered by this manual are equipped with a Supplemental Restraint System (SRS), more commonly known as airbags. Always disable the airbag system before working in the vicinity of any airbag system component to avoid the possibility of accidental deployment of the airbag, which could cause personal injury (see Chapter 12).*
Warning: *Do not use a memory saving device to preserve the ECM or radio memory*

13.4 Remove the floor duct fastener from the trim panel

13.5 Remove the bolt and detach the heater core cover

13.6 Pry the retaining clips out to release the tubes

14.6 Compressor mounting details

1	Field coil electrical connector	3	Mounting bolts (upper bolt
2	High pressure sensor		not fully visible)
	electrical connector		

when working on or near airbag system components.

Note: *The auxiliary heater core is an electric heater core mounted to the right side blower motor housing under the instrument panel on 2014 and later models. The auxiliary heater core provides heat while the engine is cold or warming up.*

11   Disconnect the cable from the negative terminal of the battery (see Chapter 5).

2014 and 2015 models

12   Remove the instrument panel (see Chapter 11).

2016 and later models

13   Disable the airbag system (see Chapter 12).

14   Remove the instrument panel lower trim panel from the passenger's side of the vehicle.

15   Remove the passenger's airbag fasteners, then carefully lower the airbag and disconnect the electrical connector.

Warning: *When carrying the airbag module, keep face of it away from your body, and when you set it down (in an isolated area), set it down with the face (trim side) pointing up.*

16   Remove the glove box assembly (see Chapter 11).

All models

17   Disconnect the air duct from the right side (see illustration 11.10).

18   Disconnect the auxiliary heater core electrical connector mounting screws

19   Remove the auxiliary heater core mounting screws and withdraw the core from the housing.

Note: *On some model is will be necessary to cut the heater core wire if it is looped through the housing brackets.*

20   Installation is the reverse of removal.

14   Air conditioning compressor - removal, installation and oil balancing

Warning: *The air conditioning system is under high pressure. DO NOT loosen any fittings or remove any components until after the system has been discharged. Air conditioning refrigerant must be properly discharged into an EPA-approved container at a dealer service department or an auto-*

motive air conditioning repair facility. Always wear eye protection when disconnecting air conditioning system fittings.

Removal

1   Have the air conditioning system discharged and recovered by a dealer service department or an automotive air conditioning shop before proceeding (see the Warning above). Disconnect the cable from the negative terminal of the battery.

Note: *If you are going to install a new compressor, inform the shop doing the work to record the amount of refrigerant oil recovered when the system is discharged (this measurement will be used when adjusting the compressor oil level during installation.*

2   Loosen the right front wheel lug nuts, raise the vehicle and support it securely on jackstands. Remove the right front wheel.

3   Remove the inner fender splash shield (see Chapter 11).

4   Remove the drivebelt (see Chapter 1).

5   On 1.4L engine models, remove the charge air cooler inlet duct (see Chapter 4).

6   Disconnect the electrical connectors from the compressor (see illustration).

15.6a Remove the refrigerant line fitting nut and separate the compressor-to-condenser line. . .

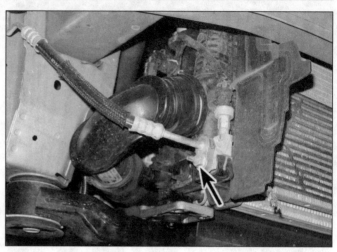

15.6b. . . and the evaporator-to-condenser line

15.8 Condenser mounting details

1   *Air deflector fasteners*
2   *Stone guard mounting clips*

7   Remove the line retaining bolt and disconnect the compressor inlet and outlet lines from the compressor. Remove and discard the old O-rings.

Note: *Once the compressor is removed, drain and measure the amount of oil from the old compressor.*

8   Remove the compressor mounting bolts and remove the compressor.

Installation

9   If a new compressor is being installed, follow the directions with the compressor regarding the measuring and adding of oil prior to installation.

10   The clutch may have to be transferred from the original to the new compressor.

11   Before reconnecting the inlet and outlet lines to the compressor, replace the O-rings and lubricate them with refrigerant oil.

12   Replace the air conditioning refrigerant desiccant (see Section 18).

13   The remainder of installation is the reverse of removal.

14   Balance the compressor oil.

Oil balancing

15   With the old compressor removed, remove the compressor drain plug and allow the oil to drain into a graduated container. Tilt

the compressor over to allow both ports to drain into the same container.

Note: *Turn the compressor shaft to make sure all of the oil drains out.*

16   Once all the oil is drained from the compressor record the amount that you measured and add the total to any amount measured when the system was evacuated in Step 1.

17   A new compressor has 1.4 oz (40 ml) of oil in it. If the total amount of oil drained is less than 1.4 oz (40 ml) no balancing is required; install the compressor and have the system evacuated, recharged and leak tested by the shop that discharged it.

18   If the total amount of oil drained is more than 1.4 oz (40 ml), oil will have to be added.

19   To balance the system, subtract 1.4 oz (40 mL) from the amount of drained and add the difference to the new compressor. Install the compressor and have the system evacuated, recharged and leak tested by the shop that discharged it.

15 Air conditioning condenser - removal and installation

Warning: *The air conditioning system is under high pressure. DO NOT loosen any fittings or remove any components until after the system*

has been discharged. Air conditioning refrigerant must be properly discharged into an EPA-approved container at a dealer service department or an automotive air conditioning repair facility. Always wear eye protection when disconnecting air conditioning system fittings.

1   Have the air conditioning system discharged by a dealer service department or by an automotive air conditioning shop before proceeding (see Warning above).

2   Disconnect the cable from the negative battery terminal (see Chapter 5).

3   Remove the air intake duct.

4   Remove the front bumper cover and radiator cover (see Chapter 11).

5   Remove the radiator support brackets (see Chapter 11, Section 8), if equipped.

6   Disconnect the refrigerant inlet and outlet lines from the condenser (see illustrations).

7   Remove the air conditioning pressure sensor (see Section 16).

8   Remove the air deflector fasteners, then disengage the condenser retaining clips and lift the condenser up and out (see illustration).

9   Before reconnecting the refrigerant lines to the condenser, coat a pair of new O-rings with refrigerant oil. Install them in the refrigerant line fittings, then tighten the condenser inlet and outlet nuts to the torque listed in this Chapter's Specifications.

10   Installation is otherwise the reverse of removal.

11   Have the system evacuated, recharged and leak tested by the shop that discharged it.

16 Air conditioning pressure sensor - replacement

Warning: *The sensor screws onto a Schrader valve, making it unnecessary to recover the refrigerant to perform this procedure. It is still a good idea to wear safety goggles though, just in case a short spurt of refrigerant escapes when removing the valve.*

1   The pressure sensor is located at bottom-right corner of the condenser, mounted

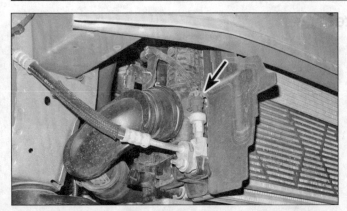

16.4 Disconnect the electrical connector from the pressure sensor (bumper cover removed for clarity) - early 1.4L model shown, later models similar

17.2 The Thermostatic Expansion Valve is located on the firewall

to the refrigerant lines. The pressure sensor detects low refrigerant line pressure, switches the compressor off, then back on again to provide higher pressure. If the pressure increases too high, the pressure cut-off switch, located in the high pressure side of the system, shuts the system off.

2   Raise the front of the vehicle and support it securely on jackstands.

3   Remove the splash guard between the bumper cover and the subframe.

Note: *The sensor is accessible by removing the splash guard, but you'll need a short wrench to unscrew it (otherwise you'll have to remove the bumper cover (see Chapter 11).*

4   Disconnect the electrical connector from the pressure sensor (see illustration).

5   Unscrew the pressure sensor.

Note: *The sensor screws onto a Schrader valve, making it unnecessary to recover the refrigerant.*

6   Lubricate the sensor O-ring with clean refrigerant oil of the correct type.

7   Screw the new sensor into place until hand tight, then tighten it securely.

8   Reconnect the electrical connector.

9   The remainder of installation is the reverse of removal.

---

17   Air conditioning thermostatic expansion valve (TXV) - general information

Warning: *The air conditioning system is under high pressure. DO NOT loosen any hose fittings or remove any components until the system has been discharged. Air conditioning refrigerant must be properly discharged into an EPA-approved recovery/recycling unit by a dealer service department or an automotive air conditioning repair facility. Always wear eye protection when disconnecting air conditioning system fittings.*

1   There are several ways that air conditioning systems convert the high-pressure liquid refrigerant from the compressor to lower-pressure vapor. The conversion

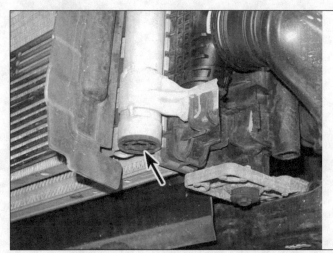

18.4 Air conditioning refrigerant desiccant cap (front bumper cover removed for clarity)

takes place at the air conditioning evaporator; the evaporator is chilled as the refrigerant passes through, cooling the airflow through the evaporator for delivery to the vents. The conversion is usually accomplished by a sudden change in the tubing size. Many vehicles have a removable controlled orifice in one of the refrigerant lines at the firewall.

2   The models covered by this manual use a Thermostatic Expansion Valve (TXV) that accomplishes the same thing as a controlled orifice (see illustration). To remove the TXV, have the air conditioning system discharged by a licensed air conditioning technician, then disconnect the refrigerant lines from the TXV at the firewall, remove the two bolts securing the valve, then remove the valve and replace the four O-rings. Installation is the reverse of removal.

---

18   Air conditioning refrigerant desiccant - replacement

Warning: *The air conditioning system is under high pressure. DO NOT loosen any fittings or remove any components until after the system has been discharged. Air con-*

ditioning refrigerant must be properly discharged into an EPA-approved container at a dealer service department or an automotive air conditioning repair facility. Always wear eye protection when servicing the air conditioning system.

Note: *These vehicles are not equipped with a traditional receiver-drier. Instead, a desiccant cartridge is built into the left side of the condenser. It should be replaced whenever the compressor is replaced or whenever a component has been replaced because of a leak in the system.*

1   Have the air conditioning system discharged by a dealer service department or by an automotive air conditioning shop before proceeding (see Warning above).

2   Raise the front of the vehicle and support it securely on jackstands.

3   Remove the splash guard between the bumper cover and the subframe.

4   Using a large Allen wrench or hex bit, unscrew the cap from the desiccant tube on the left side of the condenser (see illustration).

5   Pull the desiccant cartridge from the tube.

6   Installation is the reverse of removal. Be sure to use a new O-ring on the cap.

7   Have the system evacuated, recharged and leak tested by the shop that discharged it.

Notes

Chapter 4
Fuel and exhaust systems

Contents

Specifications

Fuel pressure

Key On, engine Off	50 to 94 psi (345 to 650 kPa)
Engine idling	43 to 58 psi (300 to 400 kPa)

Torque specifications

Note: One foot-pound (ft-lb) of torque is equivalent to 12 inch-pounds (in-lbs) of torque. Torque values below approximately 15 ft-lbs are expressed in inch-pounds, because most foot-pound torque wrenches are not accurate at these smaller values.

	Ft-lbs (unless otherwise indicated)	Nm
Fuel rail mounting bolts		
1.4L engine		
2015 and early models	62 in-lbs	7
2016 and later models	89 in-lbs	10
1.8L engine	71 in-lbs	8
Fuel injector mounting bolts* (2016 and later 1.4L models)	44 in-lbs	5
Fuel rail intermediate pipe fittings* (2016 and later 1.4L models)	22	30
Fuel rail intermediate pipe bracket bolt (2016 and later 1.4L models)	89 in-lbs	10
Fuel rail fuel pressure sensor (2016 and later 1.4L models)	24	32
High-pressure fuel pump bolts (2016 and later 1.4L models)	18	25
Throttle body mounting bolts		
2015 and early models	71 in-lbs	8
2016 and later models	89 in-lbs	10
Turbocharger		
Turbocharger/exhaust manifold-to-cylinder head nuts (2015 and earlier 1.4L engine)*	71 in-lbs	8
Turbocharger-to-cylinder head (2016 and later 1.4L engine)*		
Step 1	132 in-lbs	15
Step 2	15	20
Step 3	Tighten an additional 60-degrees	
Oil feed pipe banjo bolt*		
2015 and early models	15	20
2016 and later models	26	35
Oil feed pipe-to-block bolts*	71 in-lbs	8
Oil return pipe bolts*		
2015 and early models	71 in-lbs	8
2016 and later models	89 in-lbs	10
Coolant feed pipe banjo bolt*		
2015 and early models	22	30
2016 and later models	26	35
Coolant return pipe bolt* (2015 and earlier models)	71 in-lbs	8
Coolant return pipe-to-turbocharger banjo bolt* (2016 and later models)		
Step 1	89 in-lbs	10
Step 2	26	35
Turbocharger bypass valve solenoid mounting bolts	80 in-lbs	9

* Use new fasteners

2.2 Fuel system-related underhood fuse/relay box details

1   *Ignition main relay (supplies power to the fuel pump control module)*
2   *Fuel pump control module fuse (10 amp; receives power from the ignition main relay when the key is in the RUN position)*
3   *Fuel pump control module fuse (20 amp; always hot)*

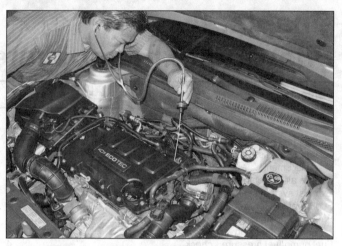

2.9 An automotive stethoscope is used to listen to the fuel injectors in operation

1   General information and precautions

Fuel system warnings

1   Gasoline is extremely flammable and repairing fuel system components can be dangerous. Consider your automotive repair knowledge and experience before attempting repairs, which may be better suited for a professional mechanic.

- *Don't smoke or allow open flames or bare light bulbs near the work area*
- *Don't work in a garage with a gas-type appliance (water heater, clothes dryer)*
- *Use fuel-resistant gloves. If any fuel spills on your skin, wash it off immediately with soap and water*
- *Clean up spills immediately*
- *Do not store fuel-soaked rags where they could ignite*
- *Prior to disconnecting any fuel line, you must relieve the fuel pressure (see Section 3)*
- *Wear safety glasses*
- *Have a proper fire extinguisher on hand*

Fuel system

2   This Chapter covers the removal and installation procedures for the important parts of the air intake, fuel and exhaust systems. Because emission control systems are integral parts of the engine management system, there are many cross-references to Chapter 6. Information on the engine management system, information sensors and output actuators is in Chapter 6.

3   The air intake system consists of the air filter housing, the air intake duct, the throttle body, on 1.4L models a turbocharger, and the intake manifold. Incoming air passes through the air filter element, the Mass Air Flow (MAF) sensor, the air intake duct, on 1.4L models the turbocharger, the throttle body, the intake manifold plenum and the intake manifold runners before being mixed with fuel sprayed into the intake ports by the fuel injectors.

4   On 2015 and earlier models the Sequential Fuel Injection (SFI) system consists of the fuel tank, an electric fuel pump/fuel level sending unit module mounted inside the tank, the fuel pressure regulator (integral with the fuel pump module), a fuel pump flow control module, the fuel rail, the fuel injectors, and the metal and flexible fuel lines that connect the various components of the SFI system.

5   All 2016 and later models are equipped with the Direct Injection (DI) system consisting of the fuel tank, an electric fuel pump/fuel level sending unit module mounted inside the tank, the fuel pressure regulator (integral with the fuel pump module), a fuel pump power control module, a high-pressure fuel pump, the fuel rail, the fuel injectors, and the metal and flexible fuel lines that connect the various components of the DI system.

6   Fuel is circulated from the fuel pump to the fuel rail through fuel lines running along the underside of the vehicle. Various sections of the fuel line are either rigid metal or nylon, or flexible fuel hose. The various sections of the fuel hose are connected either by quick-connect fittings or threaded metal fittings.

Exhaust system

7   The exhaust system consists of the exhaust manifold, catalytic converter, muffler, tailpipe and all connecting pipes, flanges and clamps. The catalytic converter is an emission control device added to the exhaust system to reduce pollutants.

2   Troubleshooting

Fuel pump

1   The fuel pump is located inside the fuel tank. Sit inside the vehicle with the windows closed, turn the ignition key to ON (not START) and listen for the sound of the fuel pump as it's briefly activated. You will only hear the sound for a second or two, but that sound tells you that the pump is working. Alternatively, have an assistant listen at the fuel filler cap.

2   If the pump does not come on, check the fuel pump control module fuses and ignition main relay (see illustration). If the fuse and relay are okay, check the wiring back to the fuel pump. If the fuse, relay and wiring are okay, the fuel pump is probably defective. If the pump runs continuously with the ignition key in the ON position, the Powertrain Control Module (PCM) is probably defective. Have the PCM checked by a professional mechanic.

Note: *On 2015 models, the fuel pump control module is referred to as the chassis control module.*

Fuel injection system

Note: *The following procedure is based on the assumption that the fuel pump is working and the fuel pressure is adequate (see Section 4).*

3   Check all electrical connectors that are related to the system. Check the ground wire connections for tightness.

4   Verify that the battery is fully charged (see Chapter 5).

5   Inspect the air filter element (see Chapter 1).

6   Check all fuses related to the fuel system (see Chapter 12).

7   Check the air induction system between the throttle body and the intake manifold for air leaks. Also inspect the condition of all vacuum hoses connected to the intake manifold and to the throttle body.

8   Remove the air intake duct from the throttle body and look for dirt, carbon, varnish, or other residue in the throttle body, particularly around the throttle plate. If it's dirty, clean it with carb cleaner, a toothbrush and a clean shop towel.

3.4 A typical fuel pressure gauge set up for relieving fuel pressure should include a screw-on adapter for the quick release fitting (1), a quick-release fitting for connecting the gauge hose to the Schrader valve (2), a bleeder valve (3) and a bleeder hose (4) that's long enough to reach the container into which you're going to drain the fuel

9   With the engine running, place an automotive stethoscope against each injector, one at a time, and listen for a clicking sound that indicates operation (see illustration).
Warning: *Stay clear of the drivebelt and any rotating or hot components.*
10   If you can hear the injectors operating, but the engine is misfiring, the electrical circuits are functioning correctly, but the injectors might be dirty or clogged. Try a commercial injector cleaning product (available at auto parts stores). If cleaning the injectors doesn't help, replace the injector(s).
11   If an injector is not operating (it makes no sound), disconnect the injector electrical connector and measure the resistance across the injector terminals with an ohmmeter. Compare this measurement to the other injectors. If the resistance of the non-operational injector is quite different from the other injectors, replace it.
12   If the injector is not operating, but the resistance reading is within the range of resistance of the other injectors, the PCM or the circuit between the PCM and the injector might be faulty.

3   Fuel pressure relief procedure

Warning: *The fuel delivery system on 2016 and later models is made up of a low-pressure system (from the fuel pump in the tank to the high-pressure fuel pump on the engine) and a high-pressure system (high-pressure fuel pump, fuel rail and injectors). Once the pressure on the low-pressure side of the system has been relieved, wait at least two hours before loosening any fuel line fittings in the high-pressure portion of the system.*
1   The fuel system is composed of: the fuel tank and tank-mounted fuel pump/fuel gauge sender unit, a high pressure fuel pump (2016 and later models), the fuel filter, the fuel injectors and the metal pipes and flexible hoses of the fuel lines between these components. All these components contain fuel, which is pressurized as soon as the ignition key is turned

to ON, and remains pressurized while the engine is running (and even after the ignition is switched off). Since the pressure remains for some time after the ignition has been switched off, it must be relieved before any fuel lines are disconnected.

2015 and earlier models
2   On most vehicles, the fuel pressure is relieved by starting the engine, then pulling a fuel pump fuse(s) (see Section 2), which disables the fuel pump and stalls the engine. However, the manufacturer doesn't recommend this method because it might set a Diagnostic Trouble Code (DTC). Instead, it recommends that you relieve system fuel pressure by draining off the residual fuel through the Schrader valve on the fuel rail (which is also used for measuring fuel pressure, as described in Section 4).
3   Remove the fuel filler cap to relieve any pressure built-up in the fuel tank.
4   The recommended setup for relieving fuel pressure (see illustration) is the same as the one that you'll need to measure fuel pressure. Your fuel pressure relief setup must include a fuel pressure gauge with a hose and fitting suitable for connecting the gauge to the Schrader valve-type test port on the fuel rail, and a bleeder valve so that you can drain off the excess fuel. You'll also need a container approved for storing fuel and a section of tubing long enough to connect the bleeder valve to the container.
5   Disconnect the cable from the negative terminal of the battery (see Chapter 5).
6   Locate the Schrader valve on the fuel rail (see illustration 4.3), then unscrew the cap and connect the gauge. Run the hose from the bleeder valve down to an approved container, then open the bleeder valve and let the excess fuel drain into the container. When the fuel ceases flowing out, close the bleeder valve, disconnect and remove your fuel pressure relief rig and screw the cap on the Schrader valve. The fuel pressure is now relieved. You may now open up the fuel system to service any component.

7   An alternative method (if you don't have a gauge with a bleeder hose) is to surround and cover the valve with shop rags, then depress the Schrader valve with a small screwdriver until the pressure is depleted.
Warning: *This procedure merely relieves the pressure in the system - but remember that fuel is still present in the system components, and take precautions accordingly before disconnecting any of them.*

2016 and later models
8   Remove the B+ fuel pump control module fuse. Start the engine and allow the engine to idle until the engine stops. The engine will stop in approximately 20–30 seconds. Disconnect the cable from the negative terminal of the battery.
Warning: *This procedure merely relieves the fuel press in the low-side of the system. Wait at LEAST two hours before working on the high-pressure side of the system. Also, remember that fuel is still present in the fuel lines and system components. It's a good idea to wrap a shop towel around all system fittings before disconnecting them.*

4   Fuel pump/fuel pressure - check

Warning: *Gasoline is extremely flammable, so take extra precautions when you work on any part of the fuel system. See Fuel system warnings in Section 1.*

Fuel pump operation check
1   The fuel pump is located inside the fuel tank, which muffles its sound when the engine is running. But you can actually hear the fuel pump. Sit inside the vehicle with the windows closed, turn the ignition key to ON (not START) and listen carefully for the sound made by the fuel pump as it's briefly turned on by the PCM to pressurize the fuel system prior to starting the engine. You will only hear the sound for a second or two, but that sound tells you that the pump is working. If you can't hear the pump, remove the fuel filler cap, depress the spring-loaded door inside the fuel filler neck, then have an assistant turn the ignition switch to ON while you listen for the sound of the pump operating for a couple of seconds.
2   If the pump does not come on when the ignition key is turned to ON, check the fuel pump fuse and relay (both of which are located in the engine compartment fuse and relay box). If the fuse and relay are okay, check the wiring back to the fuel pump (see Section 7 if you need help locating the fuel pump electrical connector). If the fuse, relay and wiring are okay, the fuel pump is probably defective. If the pump runs continuously with the ignition key in its ON position, the Powertrain Control Module (PCM) is probably defective. Have the PCM checked by a dealer service department or other qualified repair shop.

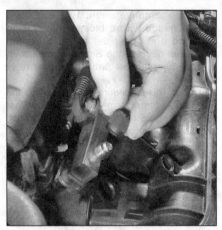

4.3 Test port on the fuel rail for fuel pressure testing (and for relieving the fuel pressure)

Fuel pressure check

Note: *On 2016 and later models, the high-side fuel pressure can only be checked using a scan tool.*

3   On 2015 and earlier models, locate the Schrader valve test port on the fuel rail, unscrew the cap and connect a fuel pressure gauge (see illustration).

4   Relieve the fuel pressure (see Section 3). After you have relieved the fuel pressure, make sure that the bleeder valve on your fuel pressure gauge is CLOSED.

5   On 2016 and later models, relieve the fuel system pressure (see Section 3), then disconnect the low-pressure fuel feed line from the high-pressure fuel pump. Using the proper adapter (GM tool no. CH-4292 or equivalent), tee-in the fuel pressure gauge between the fuel feed line and the high-pressure fuel pump.

6   Turn the ignition key to the On position (but don't start the engine). Note the gauge reading as soon as the pressure stabilizes, and compare it with the pressure listed in this Chapter's Specifications.

7   If the fuel pressure is not within specifications, check the following:

- *If the pressure is lower than the minimum specified, check for a restriction in the fuel system. If no restrictions are found, replace the fuel pump module (see Section 7).*
- *If the fuel pressure is higher than the maximum specified, replace the fuel pump module (see Section 7).*
- *If the fuel pressure is higher than the maximum specified, replace the fuel pump module (see Section 7).*

8   Turn the ignition key Off. The pressure should immediately drop to below 87 psi (600 kPa). If it doesn't, replace the fuel pump module.

9   After the initial pressure drop, verify that the fuel pressure loses no more than 5 psi (34 kPa) in one minute. If it loses more than that, there's either a leaky fuel injector or a faulty fuel pump module. This can be pinpointed by installing a shut-off valve where the fuel line

connects to the fuel rail, pressurizing the fuel system by turning the ignition key to the On position, then closing the shut-off valve. If the pressure does not bleed down anymore, a fuel injector is leaking.

10   Start the engine and allow it to idle, then check the pressure on the gauge; it should be within the range listed in this Chapter's Specifications.

11   If the pressure is too high, replace the fuel pump module (see Section 7).

12   If the pressure is too low, check for a restriction in the fuel system. If no restrictions are found, replace the fuel pump module (see Section 7).

13   Relieve the fuel pressure (see Section 3), then disconnect the fuel pressure gauge. Mop up any spilled gasoline.

14   Start the engine and verify that there are no fuel leaks.

---

5   Fuel lines and fittings - general information and disconnection

Warning: *Gasoline is extremely flammable, so take extra precautions when you work on any part of the fuel system. See Fuel system warnings in Section 1.*

1   Relieve the fuel pressure before servicing fuel lines or fittings (see Section 3). Disconnect the cable from the negative battery terminal (see Chapter 5) before proceeding.

2   The fuel supply line connects the fuel pump in the fuel tank to the fuel rail on the engine. The Evaporative emissions control (EVAP) system lines connect the fuel tank to the EVAP canister and connect the canister to the intake manifold.

3   Whenever you're working under the vehicle, be sure to inspect all fuel and evaporative emission lines for leaks, kinks, dents and other damage. Always replace a damaged fuel or EVAP line immediately.

4   If you find signs of dirt in the lines during disassembly, disconnect all lines and blow them out with compressed air. Inspect the fuel strainer on the fuel pump pick-up unit for damage and deterioration.

Steel tubing

5   It is critical that the fuel lines be replaced with lines of equivalent type and specification.

6   Some steel fuel lines have threaded fittings. When loosening these fittings, hold the stationary fitting with a wrench while turning the tube nut.

Plastic tubing

7   When replacing fuel system plastic tubing, use only original equipment replacement plastic tubing. **Caution:** When removing or installing plastic fuel line tubing, be careful not to bend or twist it too much, which can damage it. Also, plastic fuel tubing is NOT heat resistant, so keep it away from excessive heat.

Flexible hoses

8   When replacing fuel system flexible hoses, use only original equipment replacements.

9   Don't route fuel hoses (or metal lines) within four inches of the exhaust system or within ten inches of the catalytic converter. Make sure that no rubber hoses are installed directly against the vehicle, particularly in places where there is any vibration. If allowed to touch some vibrating part of the vehicle, a hose can easily become chafed and it might start leaking. A good rule of thumb is to maintain a minimum of 1/4-inch clearance around a hose (or metal line) to prevent contact with the vehicle underbody.

Disconnecting Fuel Line Fittings

10   See chart on page 4-5.

---

6   Exhaust system servicing - general information

Warning: *Allow exhaust system components to cool before inspection or repair. Also, when working under the vehicle, make sure it is securely supported on jackstands.*

Note: *On 2016 and later models, the exhaust system from the rear of the vehicle to the connection at the front exhaust pipe is one long piece. If it's necessary to remove the system, be sure to have an assistant help - it can be heavy and awkward to remove.*

1   The exhaust system consists of the exhaust manifolds, catalytic converter, muffler, tailpipe and all connecting pipes, flanges and clamps. The exhaust system is isolated from the vehicle body and from chassis components by a series of rubber hangers (see illustration). Periodically inspect these hangers for cracks or other signs of deterioration, replacing them as necessary.

6.1 Typical exhaust system hangers. Inspect regularly and replace at the first sign of damage or deterioration

Disconnecting Fuel Line Fittings

Two-tab type fitting; depress both tabs with your fingers, then pull the fuel line and the fitting apart

On this type of fitting, depress the two buttons on opposite sides of the fitting, then pull it off the fuel line

Threaded fuel line fitting; hold the stationary portion of the line or component (A) while loosening the tube nut (B) with a flare-nut wrench

Plastic collar-type fitting; rotate the outer part of the fitting

Metal collar quick-connect fitting; pull the end of the retainer off the fuel line and disengage the other end from the female side of the fitting . . .

. . . insert a fuel line separator tool into the female side of the fitting, push it into the fitting and pull the fuel line off the pipe

Some fittings are secured by lock tabs. Release the lock tab (A) and rotate it to the fully-opened position, squeeze the two smaller lock tabs (B) . . .

. . . then push the retainer out and pull the fuel line off the pipe

Spring-lock coupling; remove the safety cover, install a coupling release tool and close the tool around the coupling . . .

. . . push the tool into the fitting, then pull the two lines apart

Hairpin clip type fitting: push the legs of the retainer clip together, then push the clip down all the way until it stops and pull the fuel line off the pipe

7.4 Disconnect the electrical connectors (A). To disconnect the fuel supply (B) and vent line (C) quick-connect fittings from the fuel pump, squeeze the tabs of each retainer together and pull the fitting off the fuel pump pipe

7.5 Use a large pair of water pump pliers to loosen and unscrew the fuel pump lock ring; if the lock ring is too tight to loosen this way, carefully tap it loose with a hammer and a brass punch

7.6 After unscrewing the lock ring that secures the fuel pump to the fuel tank, make note of of the alignment mark on the tank and the aligment hole on the fuel pump module to ensure correct realignment of the pump when installing it again

7.7 Carefully remove the fuel pump/fuel level sensor module from the fuel tank; once the module has cleared the mounting hole in the tank, angle it as shown to work the fuel level sensor float and float arm through the hole without damaging anything

7.8 Remove and inspect the O-ring seal for the fuel pump mounting flange; if it's cracked, torn or deteriorated, replace it

2 Conduct regular inspections of the exhaust system to keep it safe and quiet. Look for any damaged or bent parts, open seams, holes, loose connections, excessive corrosion or other defects which could allow exhaust fumes to enter the vehicle. Do not repair deteriorated exhaust system components; replace them with new parts.
3 If the exhaust system components are extremely corroded, or rusted together, a cutting torch is the most convenient tool for removal. Consult a properly-equipped repair shop. If a cutting torch is not available, you can use a hacksaw, or if you have compressed air, there are special pneumatic cutting chisels that can also be used. Wear safety goggles to protect your eyes from metal chips and wear work gloves to protect your hands.

4 Here are some simple guidelines to follow when repairing the exhaust system:
- *Work from the back to the front when removing exhaust system components.*
- *Apply penetrating oil to the exhaust system component fasteners to make them easier to remove.*
- *Use new nuts, gaskets, hangers and clamps.*
- *Apply anti-seize compound to the threads of all exhaust system fasteners during reassembly.*
- *Be sure to allow sufficient clearance between newly installed parts and all points on the underbody to avoid overheating the floor pan and possibly damaging the interior carpet and insulation. Pay particularly close attention to the catalytic converter and heat shield.*

7 Fuel pump module - removal and installation

Warning: *Gasoline is extremely flammable, so take extra precautions when you work on any part of the fuel system. See Fuel system warnings in Section 1.*
1 Disconnect the cable from the negative battery terminal (see Chapter 5).
2 Relieve the system fuel pressure (see Section 3).
3 Remove the fuel tank (see Section 11).
4 Disconnect the fuel supply line, vent line and electrical connectors from the fuel pump/fuel level sending unit module (see illustration). Use a shop rag to soak up any spilled fuel.
5 Using a pair of large water pump pliers,

8.4 Depress the locking tab with a pointed tool and slide the sensor unit toward the top of the fuel pump until it's free of its retaining rails

9.3 Slide back the lock (A) and depress the tab (B) to unlock the release lever (C), then flip the release lever open and unplug the connector

9.4 FPFCM mounting nut (2015 and earlier models shown, later models are mounted to the battery tray)

11.7 Fuel pressure sensor electrical connector (A), fuel supply line (B) and vent line (C) quick-connect fittings

unscrew the fuel pump/fuel level sending unit module lock ring by turning it counterclockwise (see illustration). If the lock ring is tight, use a hammer and a brass punch to loosen it (don't use a steel punch, which could produce sparks when struck by the hammer). Be careful not to distort the lock ring, or it will have to be replaced. **Note:** *Lock ring removal tools are available at most auto parts stores and from specialty tool manufacturers.*

6   Note the orientation of the fuel pump in relation to the fuel tank (see illustration) to ensure that the fuel pump is correctly realigned when you install it again.

7   Remove the fuel pump/fuel level sensor module (see illustration), taking care not to damage the fuel level sensor float arm and float. You will have to angle it somewhat so the level sensor clears the tank opening. **Warning:** *There will still be fuel in the bottom of the module and it may spill. Wear gloves and eye protection.*

8   Before installing the pump, inspect the pump-to-tank seal (see illustration). It's recommended to replace the seal whenever the module has been removed.

9   Installation is the reverse of removal. Align the fuel pump/fuel level sending unit module with its hole in the tank and carefully insert it into the tank, then align the marks noted in Step 6. Make sure that you don't damage the fuel inlet strainer, the float arm or the float during installation. If the float arm is bent, the fuel level that is indicated on the fuel level gauge on the instrument cluster will be incorrect.

10   Whenever the battery has been disconnected, the Powertrain Control Module (PCM) must relearn its former driveability and performance characteristics (see Chapter 5).

8   Fuel level sensor - replacement

1   Remove the fuel pump module (see Section 7).

2   Place the fuel pump module on a clean workbench surface.

3   Disengage the fuel level sensor connector at the top of the module.

4   Depress the locking tab and slide the fuel level sensor unit from the slots on the module (see illustration).

5   Slide the fuel level sensor unit into place until you hear a click (pull on it to verify that it is locked in place).

6   The remainder of installation is the reverse of removal.

9   Fuel Pump Flow/Power Control Module (FPFCM, FPPCM) - removal and installation

Note: *The FPFCM, if replaced with a new one, must be programmed by a professional-grade scan tool in order to function properly.*

1   On 2015 and earlier models, remove the trim panel from the right side of the trunk (see Chapter 11).

2   On 2016 and later models, open the trunk or liftgate and remove the floor panel and carpeting. On some models the rear speaker must be removed.

3   Disconnect the electrical connector from the FPFCM (see illustration).

4   Remove the nut and detach the module from the bracket (see illustration).

5   Installation is the reverse of removal.

10   Fuel pressure sensor - replacement

1   See Chapter 6 for the fuel pressure sensor replacement procedure.

11   Fuel tank - removal and installation

Warning: *Gasoline is extremely flammable, so take extra precautions when you work on any part of the fuel system. See Fuel system warnings in Section 1.*

Warning: *Before disconnecting or opening any part of the fuel system, relieve the fuel system pressure (see Section 3).*

1   It's easier to remove the fuel tank when it's nearly empty. But there is no fuel tank drain plug, so if that's not possible, try to siphon out the fuel in the tank before removing the tank (see Step 5). **Note:** *On 2016 and later models, the exhaust system must be removed (see Section 6).*

2   Disconnect the cable from the negative battery terminal (see Chapter 5).

3   Relieve the fuel system pressure (see Section 3).

4   Loosen the right-rear wheel lug nuts. Raise the vehicle and support it securely on jackstands. Remove the wheel.

5   Remove the inner fender splash shield.

6   If there's still a lot of fuel in the tank, insert a small hose into the fill pipe flap and siphon or hand-pump the remaining fuel from the tank now. **Warning:** *Don't start the siphoning action by mouth! Use a siphoning kit (available at most auto parts stores).* **Note:** *On 2015 and earlier models, depending on the equipment you're using to support the tank, it may be necessary to remove the exhaust pipe and muffler insulators from the hangers and lower the exhaust pipe onto the rear axle for tank removal clearance.*

7   Disconnect the electrical connector from the fuel pressure sensor, then place a drain pan under the fuel lines and disconnect the fuel supply line and vent pipe (see illustration).

11.8 Loosen the hose clamp (A) to the fuel tank filler hose and pull the fuel filler neck hose off, then disconnect the filler pipe vent hose (B)

11.11 Locations of the fuel tank strap bolts

12.1 Air filter housing details (1.4L model shown, later models and 1.8L models similar)

1   Outlet duct clamp
2   MAF sensor electrical connector
3   Wiring harness clip

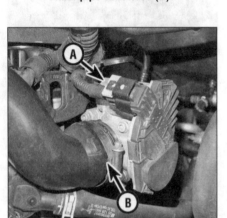

13.5 Disconnect the throttle motor electrical connector (A) and detach the charge air cooler pipe (B)

13.6 Remove the throttle body mounting bolts

8   Remove the fuel tank filler hose, vent pipe connection and the fuel tank filler vent pipe (see illustration).
9   Disconnect the fuel tank ground strap, if equipped. On 2016 and later models, remove the parking brake cable bracket retaining nuts from the fuel tank straps and secure the cables out of the way.
10   Support the fuel tank with a transmission jack, if available, or with a floor jack. If you're going to use a floor jack, put a sturdy piece of plywood between the jack head and the fuel tank to protect the tank. It's also a good idea to have an assistant to help with tank removal.
11   With the tank supported, remove the fuel tank strap bolts and lower the straps towards the rear (see illustration).
12   Lower the tank enough to have a look at the top of the tank.
13   Disconnect the electrical connector for the fuel pump module and disconnect the connector for the EVAP canister vent hose (see illustration 7.4). Disconnect the fuel tank harness from the EVAP canister.
14   Lower the tank the rest of the way, angling the right side down first until it is clear

of the chassis. Move the tank to the right until the left side of the tank clears the exhaust pipe, then remove the tank.
15   If you're replacing the tank, mark the EVAP system hoses with tape and disconnect them from the canister (see Chapter 6).
16   Installation is the reverse of removal.

12   Air filter housing - removal and installation

1   Loosen the hose clamp and detach the outlet duct from the filter housing (see illustration).
2   Disconnect the electrical connector from the Mass Air Flow (MAF) sensor and detach the wiring harness clip from the housing cover.
3   On 1.8L models with a Secondary Air Injection system, detach the secondary air injection pump hose from the air filter housing.
Note: *Some models are equipped with a drain hose attached to the bottom of the housing. Detach this hose if present.*
4   Lift up on the housing to work the mounting bosses from their mounts.
5   Installation is the reverse of removal.

13   Throttle body - removal and installation

Caution: *Do not clean the throttle motor with solvent. Also, do not use a metal brush to clean the bore of the throttle body, which is protected by a special coating. Scrubbing the bore with a stiff brush could ruin the coating. Instead, wipe out the bore with a clean shop rag and a little solvent.*
Caution: *Do not use any type of cleaner or solvent that has methyl ethyl ketone (MEK). This type of cleaner or solvent can damage many of the fuel system components. Do not spray solvent or cleaner on any of the gaskets for the throttle body.*
1   Disconnect the cable from the negative battery terminal (see Chapter 5).
2   On 2016 and later models, remove the oil filler cap and engine cover fasteners. Lift the engine cover and valve cover insulator up and off of the valve cover, then reinstall the oil filler cap. It may be necessary to remove the cover and insulator separately.
3   On 1.8L models, remove the air intake duct from the throttle body.
4   On 1.4L models, remove the charge air cooler outlet pipe from the throttle body.
5   Disconnect the throttle actuator motor electrical connector (see illustration).
Note: *To disconnect the electrical connector, slide out the lock, then depress the release tab.*
6   Remove the throttle body mounting bolts (see illustration) and remove the throttle body.
7   Remove the throttle body O-ring and inspect it. If the O-ring isn't cracked, torn or otherwise deteriorated, it's okay to reuse it. If it's damaged or worn, replace it.
8   Installation is the reverse of removal. Tighten the throttle body mounting bolts to the torque listed in this Chapter's Specifications.
9   Start the engine and verify that the throttle body operates correctly and that there are no air leaks.

14.4 To disconnect the fuel supply line from the fuel rail, release this quick-connect fitting

14.6a Use a small screwdriver or pick to pull the retaining clip back. . .

14.6b. . . then disconnect the electrical connectors from the injectors

14.7 Fuel rail mounting bolt locations (A) and ground strap (B), if equipped

14.8 After removing the fuel rail and injectors, check the injectors to make sure that there are no O-rings left in the holes (sometimes the lower O-ring on an injector come off when the injector is removed and stays in the hole)

10   Whenever the battery has been disconnected, the PCM must relearn its former driveability and performance characteristics (see Chapter 5).

14   Fuel rail and injectors - removal and installation

Warning: *Gasoline is extremely flammable, so take extra precautions when you work on any part of the fuel system. See Fuel system warnings in Section 1.*

2015 and earlier models

1   Disconnect the cable from the negative battery terminal (see Chapter 5). Remove the engine cover, if equipped, by pulling it straight up.
2   Relieve the fuel system pressure (see Section 3).

3   Remove the air intake duct and air filter housing (see Section 12).
4   Release the quick-connect fuel line fitting at the fuel rail (see illustration).
5   Disconnect the EVAP purge line from the intake manifold.
6   Disconnect the electrical connectors from the fuel injectors (see illustrations) and the MAP sensor, and unclip the electrical harness.
7   Remove the fuel rail mounting bolts (see illustration). If equipped, also detach the ground strap.
8   Remove the fuel rail and injectors as a single assembly. After removing the fuel rail and injectors, look inside each injector hole and make sure that no O-rings remain in the holes (see illustration).
9   Remove the retainer that secures each fuel injector to the fuel rail and pull out the injector (see illustration).

14.9 To release an injector retainer, free it from the small lugs on each side of the injector and pull it off

14.10 Remove and discard the old color coded O-rings from each injector and install new ones

14.44 Fuel rail/injector bolt tightening sequence - 2016 and later 1.4L engines

10   Remove the old O-rings from each injector (see illustration) and discard them. Always install new O-rings on the injectors before reassembling the injectors and the fuel rail.

11   Installation is the reverse of removal. To ensure that the new injector O-rings are not damaged when the injectors are installed into the fuel rail and into the intake manifold, lubricate them with clean engine oil. Tighten the fuel rail mounting bolts to the torque listed in this Chapter's Specifications.

12   Start the engine and verify that there are no fuel leaks.

2016 and later models

Warning: *The fuel delivery system is made up of a low-pressure system and a high-pressure system. Once the pressure on the low-pressure side of the system has been relieved, wait at least two hours before loosening any fuel line fittings in the engine compartment.*

Caution: *The manufacturer recommends replacing all of the seals on the injectors whenever they are removed from the cylinder head.*

Note: *Even if you only removed the fuel rail assembly to replace a single injector or a leaking O-ring, it's a good idea to remove all of the injectors from the fuel rail and replace all of the O-rings at the same time.*

Removal

Fuel rail assembly

13   Relieve the fuel system pressure (see Section 3).

14   Disconnect the cable from the negative battery remote terminal (see Chapter 5).

15   Remove the oil filler cap and engine cover fasteners. Lift the engine cover and valve cover insulator up and off of the valve cover, then reinstall the oil filler cap. It may be necessary to remove the cover and insulator separately.

16   Remove the ignition coils (see Chapter 5).

17   Remove the charge air cooler outlet hose (see Section 19).

18   Disconnect the harness connector from the fuel rail.

19   Disconnect the harness connector from the camshaft position sensor, then unclip the wiring harness retainers and move the harness and connectors out of the way.

20   Remove the sound insulator around the high-pressure fuel pump body.

Warning: *The sound insulator foam component must be replaced if any engine fluids have made contact with the foam. Failure to replace the sound insulator foam component that has been contaminated by engine fluids may result in an engine fire resulting in catastrophic engine damage, and possible injury or death.*

21   Using a flare-nut wrench, unscrew the intermediate high-pressure line fittings between the fuel rail and fuel pump, then remove the fuel line bracket bolt and discard the pipe (a new one must be used).

Caution: *The manufacturer states that the pipe must be replaced whenever it has been removed.*

22   Loosen the four encapsulated fuel rail-to-cylinder head bolts, do not try and remove the bolts.

23   Remove the (fuel rail side) fuel rail-to-fuel injector bolt from all the injectors. DO NOT remove bolts at the same time, a fuel leak may occur if both bolts are removed at the same time.

Caution: *The bolts are small and can easily fall into the cylinder head slot. Discard the bolts and obtain new ones for installation.*

24   Install special demounting screw no. EN-51146-1-6 to the demounting tool support no. EN-51146-1-1 and torque the tool together to 62 In-lbs (7 Nm).

Note: *Eight of assembled demounting tools will be needed.*

25   Install the assembled support tools where the injector rail line-to-injector bolts were removed and torque the tools to 62 in-lbs (7 Nm) then repeat this Step for the remaining injectors.

26   Once all the demounting tools are installed, remove the remaining fuel rail-to-fuel injector bolts, then install the remaining mounting tools in their place and torque the tools to 62 in-lbs (7 Nm).

27   Loosen the remaining four encapsulated fuel rail-to-cylinder head bolts. Again, do not try to remove the bolts.

28   Install special plate tool no. EN-51146-1-2 on top of the eight EN-51146-1-1 supports, then install the plate mounting bolts and tighten them securely. Use a back-up wrench to hold the support from rotating when the plate bolts are tightened.

29   Attach two slide hammers to the support plate. With the help of an assistant, gently tap the slide hammers upwards as evenly as possible, making sure the fuel injectors do not tilt or come out unevenly or they can bend and cause a fuel leak.

30   Once the injectors are free from the cylinder head, place the entire assembly flat on a work bench with the injectors on top and remove the side hammers, then place the plate into a vise and tighten it securely.

Caution: *Once the fuel rail and injector assembly is removed, do not allow the weight of the assembly to rest on top of the fuel injectors. Always place the assembly on a clean work surface with the fuel injectors on top.*

31   Install the special calibration tools no. EN-51146-2-5 and rotate the tools clockwise on all the injectors. The prevents the injectors from damage once they are removed.

Fuel injectors

32   To replace the fuel injector combustion seals you must use the special fuel injector kit no. EN-51146 (or equivalent) or damage to the injector seals may occur and result in a fuel leak. Follow the instructions in the tool kit to replace the combustion seals.

33   To replace an injector, remove the support plate bolts, the supports and demounting screws ONLY for the injector being replaced.

34   Disconnect the fuel injector electrical connector, then pull the injector from the fuel rail.

35   Remove the O-ring seal from the top of the injector and replace it.

Installation

36   Coat the new injector O-ring with clean engine oil install it onto the groove in the top of the injector. Insert the injector into the fuel

15.4 Heat shield mounting bolts

15.6 Oil feed pipe banjo bolt location

rail and reinstall the support tool onto the fuel rail and tighten the tool (see Step 25).

37 Remove the calibration tool, then install the new Teflon combustion seals using special fuel injector kit no. EN-51146 (or equivalent).

38 Once the new combustion seals are installed, remove the support plate and remove one support assembly from each injector.

39 Coat the new fuel injector mounting bolts with a non-hardening thread locking agent, then install the bolts and tighten them to torque listed in this Chapter's Specifications.

40 Repeat (Step 39) for the remaining fuel injector mounting bolts.

41 Make sure the injector bores in the cylinder head are clean.

42 Remove the calibration tools from the ends of the injectors and carefully insert the injectors into the bores as the fuel rail assembly is lowered onto the engine.

43 Push the injectors into their seats, then start the mounting bolts and tighten then hand tight.

44 Tighten the fuel rail mounting bolts in sequence (see illustration) to the torque listed in this Chapter's Specifications.

45 Remaining installation is the reverse of removal. Start the engine and immediately check for fuel leaks.

15 Turbocharger - removal and installation

Warning: *Wait until the engine is completely cool before beginning this procedure.*

Note: *The turbocharger is integrated into the exhaust manifold and cannot be serviced separately. The the turbocharger/exhaust manifold are removed as an assembly.*

1 Drain the engine coolant (see Chapter 1).

2 Remove the air filter housing outlet duct (see Section 12).

3 Detach the PCV hose from the turbocharger (see Chapter 6).

4 Remove the turbocharger heat shield (see illustration).

5 Disconnect the electrical connecor from the turbocharger wastegate regulator solenoid valve (see Section 18). Also detach the wiring harness from its retaining clip.

6 Place a drain pan under the engine. Remove the turbocharger oil feed pipe banjo bolt (see illustration), along with the sealing rings. Disconnect the oil feed pipe from the turbocharger.

7 Remove the turbocharger oil feed pipe-to-block bolt, then remove the pipe and gaskets.

Caution: *Care must be taken not to damage the pipe. Avoid twisting or kinking the plastic pipe. If the pipe is damaged, sufficient oil will not flow to the turbocharger, which will result in damage to the bearings.*

8 Remove the turbocharger coolant return pipe and gasket.

9 While holding the coolant feed pipe from turning, remove the coolant feed pipe banjo bolt, feed pipe and gaskets.

Note: *A special tool EN-49942 wrench is available; the wrench is made to hold the coolant feed pipe while allowing an extension and socket to be inserted through the tool to remove or install the feed pipe banjo bolt.*

10 Detach the charge air cooler inlet pipe from the turbocharger (see Section 19).

11 Remove the catalytic converter (see Chapter 6).

12 Remove the oil return pipe bolts from the bottom of the turbocharger and separate the pipe flange from the turbocharger.

13 Lower the vehicle and unbolt the turbocharger/exhaust manifold mounting nuts in reverse order of the tightening sequence (see illustration 15.15).

Note: *On 2016 and later models, there is no exhaust manifold the turbocharger bolts directly the cylinder head and the exhaust manifold is integral to the cylinder head.*

14 Remove the turbocharger and gasket from the cylinder head.

Note: *On 2016 and later models, the turbocharger gasket has been combined with a heat shield and must be replaced as an assembly.*

15 Install a new gasket over the studs, and then install the turbocharger/exhaust manifold on the studs. Install new mounting nuts and tighten the nuts in sequence (see illustration) to the torque listed in this Chapter's Specifications.

16 The remainder of installation is the reverse of removal. Use new sealing washers and tighten the oil and coolant line bolt to the torque listed in this Chapter's Specifications.

17 Refill the cooling system and change the engine oil and filter (see Chapter 1).

15.15 On 2015 and earlier turbocharger/ exhaust manifold tightening sequence

16.2 Typical turbocharger wastegate actuator details

1	Turbocharger wastegate actuator	3	Actuator rod retaining E-clip
2	Vacuum hose	4	Actuator bolts

17.1 Disconnect the vacuum hose (A) from the charge air bypass valve (B)

16 Turbocharger wastegate actuator - replacement

1   Remove the exhaust manifold/turbocharger heat shield (see illustration 15.4).
2   Disconnect the vacuum line, remove the actuator rod retaining clip and the wastegate actuator bolts. Disconnect the actuator arm, then remove the actuator (see illustration).
3   Measure the length of the actuator rod on the old wastegate actuator, then adjust, if necessary, the length of the actuator rod on the new wastegate actuator by loosening the jam nut on the rod and turning the rod end in or out, as applicable. When the proper length is obtained, tighten the jam nut securely.
4   Installation is the reverse of removal.

17 Charge air bypass valve or solenoid valve (1.4L models) - replacement

Charge air bypass valve – 2015 and earlier models

1   Remove the vacuum hose clamp and disconnect the vacuum hose from the nipple on the bypass valve, then remove the three bolts (see illustration).
Caution: *The nipple on the charge air bypass valve is easily broken off.*
2   Remove the valve.
3   Installation is the reverse of removal.

Charge air bypass valve solenoid - 2016 and later models

4   Disconnect the PCV quick-connect fitting from the air filter housing outlet duct, then loosen the duct clamps and remove the duct (see Section 12).
5   Locate the charge air bypass valve solenoid and disconnect the electrical connector from the solenoid.
6   Remove the three Allen-head mounting bolts and withdraw the solenoid from the turbocharger.
7   Installation is the reverse of removal, making sure to tighten the solenoid bolts to the torque listed in this Chapter's Specifications

18 Turbocharger wastegate regulator solenoid valve - replacement

Note: *The turbocharger wastegate regulator solenoid valve is located below the PCV hose on the turbocharger.*
1   Mark and disconnect the three vacuum lines from the solenoid valve (see illustration).
2   Push the wire retaining clip inward and disconnect the electrical connector from the solenoid valve.
3   Remove the solenoid valve mounting screw and washer and remove the valve from the turbocharger.
4   Installation is the reverse of removal.

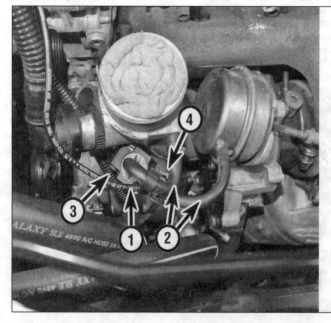

18.1 Turbocharger wastegate regulator solenoid valve details

1	Turbocharger wastegate regulator solenoid valve
2	Vacuum lines - two of three shown (third is underneath)
3	Mounting screw
4	Electrical connector

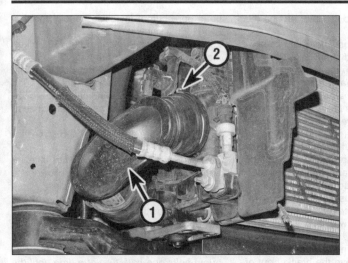

19.4 Charge air cooler inlet pipe details

1   *Charge air cooler inlet pipe*
2   *Quick connect clamp*

19.12 Charge air cooler outlet pipe details

1   *Charge air cooler outlet pipe*
2   *Quick connect clamp*

19   Charge air cooler (1.4L models) - removal and installation

Note: *The charge air cooler is also known as an intercooler.*

1   Disconnect the cable from the negative battery terminal (see Chapter 5).
2   Raise the front of the vehicle and support it securely on jackstands.
3   Remove the front bumper cover (see Chapter 11).

Air cooler inlet pipe

4   Pull the air cooler inlet pipe clamp ends apart, then detach the pipe from the charge air cooler (see illustration).
5   Loosen the clamp from the inlet pipe at the turbocharger and disconnect the pipe.
6   Remove the pipe.
7   Installation is the reverse of removal.

Air cooler outlet pipe

8   Disconnect the electrical connector from the intake air pressure and temperature sensor (see Chapter 6).
9   On 2016 and later models, remove the oil filler cap and engine cover fasteners. Lift the engine cover and valve cover insulator up and off of the valve cover, then reinstall the oil filler cap. It may be necessary to remove the cover and insulator separately.
10   On 2016 and later models, disconnect the brake booster vacuum pipe. Disconnect and cap the coolant expansion tank return hose.
11   Loosen the air cooler outlet pipe clamp at the throttle body (see illustration 13.4).
12   Pull the air cooler outlet pipe clamp ends apart, then detach the pipe from the charge air cooler (see illustration).
13   Remove the air cooler outlet pipe.
14   Installation is the reverse of removal.

Charge air cooler

15   Disconnect the air cooler inlet pipe from the charge air cooler (if necessary, see Steps 4 through 6).
16   Disconnect the air cooler outlet pipe from the charge air cooler (if necessary, see Steps 8 through 13).
17   On 2016 and later models, remove the cooling fan and shroud assembly (see Chapter 3), then disconnect the turbocharger pressure sensor electrical connector.
18   On 2015 and earlier models, disengage the clips holding the automatic transaxle cooler lines and cooler between the radiator and air conditioning condenser (see illustration). Lift the cooler up and out of way, then secure it in this position.
19   On 2015 and earlier models, lift the air conditioning condenser up to disengage it from charge air cooler, then move it away from the cooler and secure it out of the way.
20   Disengage the clips holding the charge air cooler to the radiator. On 2015 and earlier models, lift the cooler up and away from the radiator. On 2016 and later models, pull the charge air cooler back and lower the charge air cooler down and out from under the vehicle.
21   Installation is the reverse of removal.

20   High-pressure fuel pump and fuel rail fuel pressure sensor (2016 and later models) - removal and installation

Warning: *Gasoline is extremely flammable. See Fuel system warnings in Section 1.*
Warning: *The fuel delivery system is made up of a low-pressure system and a high-pressure system. Once the pressure on the low-pressure side of the system has been relieved, wait at least two hours before loosening any fuel line fittings in the engine compartment.*

1   Remove the oil filler cap and engine

19.18 Disengage the clips holding the lines (A) and lift the transaxle cooler (B) straight up from inbetween the radiator and air conditioning condenser

cover fasteners. Lift the engine cover and valve cover insulator up and off of the valve cover, then reinstall the oil filler cap. It may be necessary to remove the cover and insulator separately.

2   Relieve the fuel system pressure (see Section 3).

3   Disconnect the cable from the negative battery remote terminal (see Chapter 5).

Fuel rail fuel pressure sensor

Note: *The fuel rail fuel pressure sensor is located at the middle of the fuel rail.*

4   Disconnect the fuel pressure sensor electrical connector.

5   Unscrew and remove the sensor from the fuel rail.

Caution: *The manufacturer states that the sensor must be replaced if it has been removed.*

6   Clean the threads in the fuel rail of any gasoline. Place a single drop of oil on the new sensor threads, then install the sensor and hand tighten.

7   Remove the sensor, place another drop of clean engine oil on the threads, then reinstall the sensor and tighten it to the torque listed in this Chapter's Specifications.

8   Connect the sensor electrical connector.

9   The remainder of installation is reverse of removal.

High-pressure fuel pump

10   Remove the charge air cooler outlet hose (see Section 19).

11   Disconnect the harness connector to the fuel rail.

12   Disconnect the harness connector from the camshaft position sensor, then unclip the wiring harness retainers and move the harness and connectors out of the way.

13   Remove the sound insulator around the pump body.

Warning: *The sound insulator foam component must be replaced if any engine fluids have made contact with the foam. Failure to replace the sound insulator foam component that has been contaminated by engine fluids may result in an engine fire resulting in catastrophic engine damage, and possible injury or death.*

14   Using a flare-nut wrench, unscrew the intermediate high-pressure line fittings between the fuel rail and fuel pump, then remove the fuel line bracket bolt and discard the pipe - a new one must be used.

Caution: *The manufacturer states that the pipe must be replaced whenever it has been removed.*

15   Remove the wiring harness bracket mounting bolts and move the bracket out of the way.

16   Disconnect the electrical connector from the high-pressure fuel pump, then disconnect the wiring harness retainer and move the harness out of the way.

17   Disconnect the low pressure feed line quick-connector at the pump, then remove the low-pressure fuel feed line.

18   Remove the high-pressure fuel pump bolts a little at a time, then remove the pump, the gasket and the lifter follower. Always replace the bolts and pump gasket with new ones.

Caution: *Unscrew the bolts one half turn at a time, alternating between the two of them. If this is not done, the pump plunger will be damaged.*

19   Lubricate the lifter follower with clean engine oil, then install lifter follower into the bore in the cylinder head, aligning the guide pins with the grooves in the fuel pump

head bore before installing special tool no. EN-51365 alignment gauge.

20   Install special tool no. EN-51365 alignment gauge, then with the help of an assistant or use of a remote starter button, rotate the engine until the special tool sits flush with the cylinder head, indicating the camshaft lobe is at its lowest point (base circle of the lobe).

21   Remove the special tool and, if necessary, the valve lifter follower.

22   Lubricate the pump valve lifter follower with engine oil and insert the lifter follower into the bore aligning it with the guide pins.

23   Using a NEW O-ring gasket, set the pump into position on the bore and tighten the bolts evenly, one-half turn at a time, side-to-side.

Caution: *Alternately hand-tighten the fuel pump bolts one-half turn at a time until the pump is fully seated. Attempting to tighten down the pump unevenly may result in pump plunger damage. As the pump bolts are tightened, it will get harder to tighten the bolts until the spring in the pump is compressed.*

24   Tighten the bolts to the torque listed in this Chapter's Specifications.

25   The remainder of installation is the reverse of removal. Clean the high-pressure fuel line fittings on the pump and crossover pipe, then apply a drop of clean engine oil to the threads of each fitting. Install the NEW high-pressure intermediate fuel line, tightening the fittings to the torque listed in this Chapter's Specifications.

26   The remainder of installation is the reverse of the removal procedure.

27   Reconnect the cable to the negative battery remote terminal, then start the engine and check for fuel leaks.

Chapter 5
Engine electrical systems

Contents

Specifications

General

Firing order	1-3-4-2
Cylinder numbering (from drivebelt end to transaxle end)......................	1-2-3-4
Ignition timing	Not adjustable

Torque specifications

Note: One foot-pound (ft-lb) of torque is equivalent to 12 inch-pounds (in-lbs) of torque. Torque values below approximately 15 ft-lbs are expressed in inch-pounds, because most foot-pound torque wrenches are not accurate at these smaller values.

	Ft-lbs (unless otherwise indicated)	Nm
Ignition coil pack bolts (2015 and earlier models)	71 in-lbs	8
Ignition coil mounting bolts (2016 and later models)	89 in-lbs	10
Alternator mounting bolt/nuts		
2015 and earlier models...	18	25
2016 and later models..	16	22
Starter mounting bolt/nuts		
2015 and earlier models...	18	25
2016 and later models		
Starter mounting bolt/nut	43	58
Starter bracket-to-starter mounting bolt................................	16	22
Starter bracket-to-cylinder block bolt..................................	43	58
Ground cable bolt	16	22

1   General information and precautions

General information

Ignition system

1   The ignition system consists of the ignition control module(s), the ignition coil pack/module assembly (2015 and earlier models) or individual ignition coil(s) (2016 and later models), the spark plugs, the Camshaft Position (CMP) sensor, the Crankshaft Position (CKP) sensor, the knock sensor and the Powertrain Control Module (PCM).

2   The CKP, CMP and knock sensors are information sensors used by the PCM to control ignition timing and other engine operating parameters. The PCM also uses a number of other information sensors to make decisions regarding the correct ignition timing. These other sensors include the Throttle Position (TP) sensor, the Engine Coolant Temperature (ECT) sensor, the Mass Air Flow (MAF) sensor, the Intake Air Temperature (IAT) sensor, the Vehicle Speed Sensor (VSS) and the transmission gear position sensor or Transmission Range (TR) switch. For more information on these and other sensors, refer to Chapter 6.

Charging system

3   The charging system includes the alternator (with an integral voltage regulator), the Powertrain Control Module (PCM), the Body Control Module (BCM), a charge indicator light on the dash, the battery, a fuse or fusible link and the wiring connecting all of these components. The charging system supplies electrical power for the ignition system, the lights, the radio, etc. The alternator is driven by a drivebelt.

Starting system

4   The starting system consists of the battery, the ignition switch, the starter relay, the Powertrain Control Module (PCM), the Body Control Module (BCM), the Transmission Range (TR) switch, the starter motor and solenoid assembly, and the wiring connecting all of these components.

Precautions

5   Always observe the following precautions when working on the electrical system:

  a) *Be extremely careful when servicing engine electrical components. They are easily damaged if checked, connected or handled improperly.*

  b) *Never leave the ignition switched on for long periods of time when the engine is not running.*

  c) *Never disconnect the battery cables while the engine is running.*

  d) *Maintain correct polarity when connecting battery cables from another vehicle during jump starting - see the "Booster battery (jump) starting" in Front of this Manual, Section 7*

  e) *Always disconnect the cable from the negative battery terminal before working on the electrical system, but read the battery disconnection procedure first (see Section 3).*

6   It's also a good idea to review the safety-related information regarding the engine electrical systems located in the Safety first! Section at the front of this manual before beginning any operation included in this Chapter.

2   Troubleshooting

Ignition system

1   If a malfunction occurs in the ignition system, do not immediately assume that any particular part is causing the problem. First, check the following items:

  a) *Make sure that the cable clamps at the battery terminals are clean and tight.*

  b) *Test the condition of the battery (see Steps 21 through 24). If it doesn't pass all the tests, replace it.*

  c) *Check the ignition coil or coil pack connections.*

  d) *Check any relevant fuses in the engine compartment fuse and relay box (see Chapter 12). If they're burned, determine the cause and repair the circuit.*

Check

Warning: *Because of the high voltage generated by the ignition system, use extreme care when performing a procedure involving ignition components.*
Note: *The ignition system components on these vehicles are difficult to diagnose. In the event of ignition system failure that you can't diagnose, have the vehicle tested at a dealer service department or other qualified auto repair facility.*
Note: *For the following test, you'll need a spark tester (available at auto parts stores). If you're working on a 2006 2.2L model, you will also need spark plug wires to connect the coil high-tension terminals to the spark tester and to the other three spark plugs.*

2   If the engine turns over but won't start, verify that there is sufficient secondary ignition voltage to fire the spark plug as follows:

2015 and earlier models

3   Remove the ignition coil pack (see Section 6), then remove the spark plug boots from the coil pack (to remove the boots, simply pull them off).

4   Connect the spark plug wires to the coil high-tension terminals. Connect the spark tester to the spark plug wire for the No. 1 cylinder. Then connect the tester to the spark plug (see illustrations). Connect the other three spark plug wires to the other three spark plugs.

2016 and later models

5   Remove a coil (see Section 6) and install the tester between the boot at the lower end of the coil and the spark plug.

All models

6   Crank the engine while watching the tester. If the tester flashes, sufficient voltage is reaching the spark plug to fire it. Repeat this test on the remaining cylinders.
Caution: *Do NOT crank the engine or allow it to run for more than five seconds; running the engine for more than five seconds may set a Diagnostic Trouble Code (DTC) for a cylinder misfire.*

7   Proceed on this basis until you have verified that there's a good spark from each

2.4a Spark tester

2.4b On 2015 and earlier models, here's the setup used for checking to see if the ignition coil is sending power to the spark plug. If the coil is delivering power to the plug, the tester will flash

2.19 To test the open circuit voltage of the battery, touch the black probe of the voltmeter to the negative terminaland the red probe to the positive terminal of the battery; a fully charged battery should be at least 12.6 volts

2.21 Connect a battery load tester to the battery and check the battery condition under load following the tool manufacturer's instructions

coil terminal. If there is, then you have verified that the coils are functioning correctly.

8   If there is no spark from a coil terminal, then either the coil is bad or one or more coil boots is bad. Also inspect the coil pack electrical connector. Make sure that it's clean, tight and in good condition.

9   If all the coils are firing correctly, but the engine misfires when the coil pack is connected to the spark plugs via the boots, then one or more of the plugs might be fouled. Remove and check the spark plugs or install new ones (see Chapter 1).

10   Also inspect the boots carefully for corrosion (high resistance) or deterioration of the insulation (low resistance). If any of the boots look damaged or deteriorated, replace them as a set.

11   No further testing of the ignition system is possible without special tools. If the problem persists, have the ignition system tested by a dealer service department or other qualified repair shop.

Charging system

12   If a malfunction occurs in the charging system, do not automatically assume the alternator is causing the problem. First check the following items:

a)   *Check the drivebelt tension and condition, as described in Chapter 1. Replace it if it's worn or deteriorated.*

b)   *Make sure the alternator mounting bolts are tight.*

c)   *Inspect the alternator wiring harness and the connectors at the alternator and voltage regulator. They must be in good condition, tight and have no corrosion.*

d)   *Check the fuses in the underhood fuse/relay box. If any are burned, determine the cause, repair the circuit and replace the fuse (the vehicle will not start and/or the accessories will not work if the main fuse is blown).*

e)   *Start the engine and check the alternator for abnormal noises (a shrieking or squealing sound indicates a bad bearing).*

f)   *Check the battery. Make sure it's fully charged and in good condition (one bad cell in a battery can cause overcharging by the alternator).*

g)   *Disconnect the battery cables (negative first, then positive). Inspect the battery posts and the cable clamps for corrosion. Clean them thoroughly if necessary (see Chapter 1). Reconnect the cables (positive first, negative last).*

Alternator - check

13   Use a voltmeter to check the battery voltage with the engine off. It should be at least 12.6 volts (see illustration 2.21).

14   Start the engine and check the battery voltage again. It should now be approximately 13.5 to 15 volts.

15   If the voltage reading is more or less than the specified charging voltage, the voltage regulator is probably defective, which will require replacement of the alternator (the voltage regulator is not replaceable separately). Remove the alternator and have it bench tested (most auto parts stores will do this for you).

16   The charging system (battery) light on the instrument cluster lights up when the ignition key is turned to ON, but it should go out when the engine starts.

17   If the charging system light stays on after the engine has been started, there is a problem with the charging system. Before replacing the alternator, check the battery condition, alternator belt tension and electrical cable connections.

18   If replacing the alternator doesn't restore voltage to the specified range, have the charging system tested by a dealer service department or other qualified repair shop.

Battery - check

19   Check the battery state of charge. Visu-ally inspect the indicator eye on the top of the battery (if equipped with one); if the indicator eye is black in color, charge the battery as described in Chapter 1. Next perform an open circuit voltage test using a digital voltmeter. With the engine and all accessories Off, touch the negative probe of the voltmeter to the negative terminal of the battery and the positive probe to the positive terminal of the battery (see illustration). The battery voltage should be 12.6 volts or slightly above. If the battery is less than the specified voltage, charge the battery before proceeding to the next test. Do not proceed with the battery load test unless the battery charge is correct.

Note: *The battery's surface charge must be removed before accurate voltage measurements can be made. Turn on the high beams for ten seconds, then turn them off and let the vehicle stand for two minutes.*

20   Disconnect the negative battery cable, then the positive cable from the battery.

21   Perform a battery load test. An accurate check of the battery condition can only be performed with a load tester (see illustration). This test evaluates the ability of the battery to operate the starter and other accessories during periods of high current draw. Connect the load tester to the battery terminals. Load test the battery according to the tool manufacturer's instructions. This tool increases the load demand (current draw) on the battery.

22   Maintain the load on the battery for 15 seconds and observe that the battery voltage does not drop below 9.6 volts. If the battery condition is weak or defective, the tool will indicate this condition immediately.

Note: *Cold temperatures will cause the minimum voltage reading to drop slightly. Follow the chart given in the manufacturer's instructions to compensate for cold climates. Minimum load voltage for freezing temperatures (32 degrees F) should be approximately 9.1 volts.*

Starting system

The starter rotates, but the engine doesn't

23   Remove the starter (see Section 8). Check the overrunning clutch and bench test the starter to make sure the drive mechanism extends fully for proper engagement with the flywheel ring gear. If it doesn't, replace the starter.

24   Check the flywheel ring gear for missing teeth and other damage. With the ignition turned off, rotate the flywheel so you can check the entire ring gear.

The starter is noisy

25   If the solenoid is making a chattering noise, first check the battery (see Steps 21 through 24). If the battery is okay, check the cables and connections.

26   If you hear a grinding, crashing metallic sound when you turn the key to Start, check for loose starter mounting bolts. If they're tight, remove the starter and inspect the teeth on the starter pinion gear and flywheel ring gear. Look for missing or damaged teeth.

27   If the starter sounds fine when you first turn the key to Start, but then stops rotating the engine and emits a zinging sound, the problem is probably a defective starter drive that's not staying engaged with the ring gear. Replace the starter.

The starter rotates slowly

28   Check the battery (see Steps 21 through 24).

29   If the battery is okay, verify all connections (at the battery, the starter solenoid and motor) are clean, corrosion-free and tight. Make sure the cables aren't frayed or damaged.

30   Check that the starter mounting bolts are tight so it grounds properly. Also check the pinion gear and flywheel ring gear for evidence of a mechanical bind (galling, deformed gear teeth or other damage).

The starter does not rotate at all

31   Check the battery (see Steps 21 through 24).

32   If the battery is okay, verify all connections (at the battery, the starter solenoid and motor) are clean, corrosion-free and tight. Make sure the cables aren't frayed or damaged.

33   Check all of the fuses in the underhood fuse/relay box.

34   Check that the starter mounting bolts are tight so it grounds properly.

35   Check for voltage at the starter solenoid "S" terminal when the ignition key is turned to the start position. If voltage is present, replace the starter/solenoid assembly. If no voltage is present, the problem could be the starter relay, the Transmission Range (TR) switch (see Chapter 6) or clutch start switch (see Chapter 8), or with an electrical connector somewhere in the circuit (see the wiring diagrams at the end of Chapter 12). Also, on many modern vehicles, the Powertrain Control Module (PCM) and the Body Control Module (BCM) control the voltage signal to the starter solenoid; on such vehicles a special scan tool is required for diagnosis.

3   Battery - disconnection and reconnection

Warning: *On models with OnStar, make absolutely sure the ignition key is in the Off position and Retained Accessory Power (RAP) has been depleted before disconnecting the cable from the negative battery terminal. Also, never remove the OnStar fuse with the ignition key in any position other than Off. If these precautions are not taken, the OnStar system's backup battery will be activated, and remain activated, until it goes dead. If this happens, the OnStar system will not function as it should in the event that the main vehicle battery power is cut off (as might happen during a collision).*

Note: *To disconnect the battery for service procedures requiring power to be cut from the vehicle, first open the driver's door to disable Retained Accessory Power (RAP), then loosen the cable end bolt and disconnect the cable from the negative battery terminal. Isolate the cable end to prevent it from coming into accidental contact with the battery terminal.*

1   On 2015 and earlier models, the battery is located in the left side of the engine compartment. To disconnect the battery for service procedures that require battery disconnection, simply disconnect the cable from the negative battery terminal (see Section 4). Make sure that you isolate the cable to prevent it from coming into contact with the battery negative terminal.

2   On 2016 and later models, the battery is located in the rear of the vehicle at the right front corner of the trunk or hatch under the floor compartment panel. To disconnect the battery for service procedures that require battery disconnection, locate the remote negative cable on the side of the rear compartment, then open the protective cap, remove the cable mounting nut and slide the cable off of the stud. Be sure to isolate the cable end to prevent it from coming into contact with the body.

3   Some vehicle systems (radio, alarm system, power door locks, etc.) require battery power all the time, either to enable their operation or to maintain control unit memory (Powertrain Control Module, automatic transaxle control module, etc.), which would be lost if the battery were to be disconnected. So before you disconnect the battery, note the following points:

a)   *Before connecting or disconnecting the cable from the negative battery terminal, make sure that you turn the ignition key and the lighting switch to their OFF positions. Failure to do so could damage semiconductor components.*

b)   *On a vehicle with power door locks, it is a wise precaution to remove the key from the ignition and to keep it with you, so that it does not get locked inside if the power door locks should engage accidentally when the battery is reconnected!*

c)   *After the battery has been disconnected, then reconnected (or a new battery has been installed) on vehicles with an auto-matic transaxle, the Transaxle Control Module (TCM) will need some time to relearn its adaptive strategy. As a result, shifting might feel firmer than usual. This is a normal condition and will not adversely affect the operation or service life of the transaxle. Eventually, the TCM will complete its adaptive learning process and the shift feel of the transaxle will return to normal.*

d)   *The engine management system's PCM has some learning capabilities that allow it to adapt or make corrections in response to minor variations in the fuel system in order to optimize drivability and idle characteristics. However, the PCM might lose some or all of this information when the battery is disconnected. The PCM must go through a relearning process before it can regain its former drivability and performance characteristics. Until it relearns this lost data, you might notice a difference in drivability, idle and/or (if you have an automatic) shift "feel." To facilitate this relearning process, refer to "Enabling the PCM to relearn" below.*

Memory savers

4   Devices known as memory savers (typically, small 9-volt batteries) can be used to avoid some of the above problems. A memory saver is usually plugged into the cigarette lighter, and then you can disconnect the vehicle battery from the electrical system. The memory saver will deliver sufficient current to maintain security alarm codes and - maybe, but don't count on it! - PCM memory. It will also run unswitched (always on) circuits such as the clock and radio memory, while isolating the car battery in the event that a short circuit occurs while the vehicle is being serviced.

Warning: *If you're going to work around any airbag system components, disconnect the battery and do not use a memory saver. If you do, the airbag could accidentally deploy and cause personal injury.*

Caution: *Because memory savers deliver current to operate unswitched circuits when the battery is disconnected, make sure that the circuit that you're going to service is actually open before working on it!*

Enabling the PCM to relearn

5   After the battery has been reconnected, perform the following procedure in order to facilitate PCM relearning:

6   Start the engine and allow it to warm up to its normal operating temperature.

7   Drive the vehicle at part-throttle, under moderate acceleration and idle conditions, until normal performance returns.

8   Park the vehicle and apply the parking brake with the engine running.

9   On vehicles equipped with a manual transaxle, put the shift lever in NEUTRAL. On vehicles equipped with an automatic transaxle, put the shift lever in DRIVE.

10   Allow the engine to idle for about two minutes, or until the idle stabilizes. Make sure that the engine is at its normal operating temperature.

4.2 Battery details

1   Negative cable terminal
2   Positive cable terminal

4.3a Pry the retaining tabs to open the mega-fuse box cover. . .

4.3b. . . then remove the nut and detach the positive battery cable from its terminal

4.4 Free the retaining clips on each side of the mega-fuse box, then rotate it back out of the way, disconnecting the positive cable from its battery terminal as this is done

4.5 Unscrew the nut and remove the battery hold-down clamp

4.6 Push the top of the battery retainer to the rear (which will free the tab at the bottom), then pull the retainer up

Resetting power windows, sunroof, and Electric Power Steering (EPS)

11   Power windows: Sit in the vehicle with all of the doors closed. Operate each window (one at a time) to the fully open position, then raise the window until it is closed and hold the switch in the UP position for two seconds.
12   Sunroof: Open the sunroof completely, then close it completely.
13   Electric Power Steering (EPS): Sit in the driver's seat and start the engine. Turn the steering wheel completely counterclockwise, then completely clockwise.

4   Battery and battery tray - removal and installation

Note: Battery straps and handlers are available at most auto parts stores for reasonable prices. They make it easier to remove and carry the battery.

2015 and earlier models

1   Remove the battery cover.
2   Disconnect the cable from the negative terminal of the battery, then loosen the positive cable terminal nut (see illustration).
3   Open the battery mega-fuse box cover and remove the nut attaching the positive battery cable terminal to the mega-fuse box terminal (see illustrations).
4   Unclip the mega-fuse box and flip it back out of the way (see illustration).
5   Remove the battery hold-down clamp (see illustration).
6   If equipped, remove the battery retainer (see illustration).
Note: Not all models are equipped with a battery retainer (it depends on the size of the battery installed).
7   Lift out the battery. Be careful - it's heavy.
8   To remove the battery tray, detach the Powertrain Control Module (PCM) bracket (see Chapter 6), unscrew the three bolts (see illustration), free any wiring harness retainers, then lift it out.

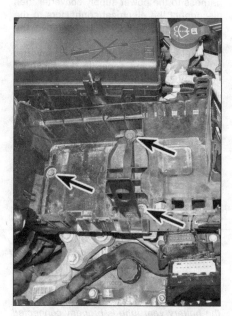

4.8 Battery tray mounting bolts

2016 and later models

Battery

9   Make sure all lights and accessories are off, the ignition is off and the ignition key is removed.

10   Open the trunk lid or hatch.

11   Lift up the rear compartment floor panel and guide the carpet/panel through the rear compartment and out of the vehicle.

12   Lift up and remove the styrofoam floor panel supports from the vehicle.

13   Open the right rear door, then fold the rear seat back forward for complete access to the battery.

14   Loosen the negative cable terminal nut and disconnect the cable from the negative terminal of the battery along with the battery sensor, then loosen the positive cable terminal nut and disconnect the cable.

15   Disconnect the battery-to-fuse block cable.

16   Disconnect the battery vent tube from the battery.

17   Remove the battery hold-down nut and retainer.

18   Lift out the battery. Be carefull - the battery is heavy.

Battery tray

19   Remove the battery (see Steps 9 through 18).

20   Remove the rear deck speaker (see Chapter 12), if equipped.

21   Using a screwdriver, disengage the fuse box cover clip and remove the cover.

22   Remove the positive battery cable retaining nut and cable from the fuse box.

23   Label the five wining harness wires to the fuse block, then remove the wiring harness nuts and the body wiring from the fuse block.

24   Unclip the fuse block from the battery tray and remove it.

25   Disconnect the electrical connector harness to the power supply converter then disconnect the electrical connectors to the power supply converter and remove the harness.

26   Release the power supply converter retaining clips and separate the converter from the battery tray.

27   Raise the rear of the vehicle and support it securely on jackstands.

28   Remove the battery tray mounting bolts from under the vehicle.

29   Remove the battery tray from the rear compartment floor.

30   Installation is the reverse of removal.

All models

31   If you are replacing the battery, make sure you get one that's identical, with the same dimensions, amperage rating, cold cranking rating, etc.

32   Installation is the reverse of removal. Connect the positive cable first and the negative cable last.

Note: *On 2016 and later models, make sure the battery vent tube is properly connected to the battery and the tube is not plugged or kinked.*

---

5   Battery cables - replacement

1   When removing the cables, always disconnect the cable from the negative battery terminal first and hook it up last, or you might accidentally short out the battery with the tool you're using to loosen the cable clamps. Even if you're only replacing the cable for the positive terminal, be sure to disconnect the negative cable from the battery first.

2   Disconnect the old cables from the battery, then trace each of them to their opposite ends and disconnect them. Be sure to note the routing of each cable before disconnecting it to ensure correct installation.

3   If you are replacing any of the old cables, take them with you when buying new cables. It is vitally important that you replace the cables with identical parts.

4   Clean the threads of the solenoid or ground connection with a wire brush to remove rust and corrosion. Apply a light coat of battery terminal corrosion inhibitor or petroleum jelly to the threads to prevent future corrosion.

5   Attach the cable to the solenoid or ground connection and tighten the mounting nut/bolt securely.

6   Before connecting a new cable to the battery, make sure that it reaches the battery post without having to be stretched.

7   Connect the cable to the positive battery terminal first, then connect the ground cable to the negative battery terminal.

---

6   Ignition coil pack or ignition coil(s) - removal and installation

Ignition coil pack - 2015 and earlier models

1   Make sure the ignition key is turned Off,

then remove the engine cover by pulling it straight up.

2   Disconnect the electrical connector from the ignition coil assembly (see illustrations).

3   Remove the ignition coil pack mounting bolts (see illustration).

4   Pull the ignition coil pack straight up, detaching the spark plug boots (see illustration).

5   If you're replacing the ignition coil pack, remove the four boots from the coil pack and inspect them for cracks, tears and deterioration. If any of the boots are damaged, replace them.

6   Before installing the boots on the ignition coil pack, coat the interior of each boot with silicone dielectric compound.

7   Installation is otherwise the reverse of removal. Tighten the ignition coil pack mounting bolts to the torque listed in this Chapter's Specifications.

Ignition coil(s) - 2016 and later models

8   Remove the oil filler cap and engine cover fasteners. Lift the engine cover and valve cover insulator up and off of the valve cover, then reinstall the oil filler cap. It may be necessary to remove the cover and insulator separately.

9   Disconnect the electrical connector(s) from the ignition coil(s).

10   Remove the ignition coil mounting fastener from the coil.

11   Grasp the coil firmly and pull it off the spark plug.

12   Repeat the same procedure for the remaining coils.

13   Installation is the reverse of removal. Tighten the coil mounting bolt(s) to the torque listed in this Chapter's Specifications.

6.2a Slide the connector lock out. . .

6.2b. . . then depress the tab to release the connector

6.3 Ignition coil pack bolts

6.4 Grasp the coil pack firmly and pull straight up; the boots should come off with the coil pack - if any of them stay with the spark plugs, pull them off the plugs

7   Alternator - removal and installation

1   Disconnect the cable from the negative battery terminal (see Section 3).

2   Raise the vehicle and support it securely on jackstands. Remove the under-vehicle splash shield.

3   On 2016 and later models, disconnect and remove the front exhaust pipe (see Chapter 4).

4   Remove the drivebelt (see Chapter 1).

5   If you're working on a 2015 or earlier 1.4L engine, remove the drivebelt tensioner lower mounting bolt, then loosen the tensioner upper bolt (see illustration). Pivot the tensioner out of the way.

6   Disconnect the electrical connectors from the alternator (see illustration).

7   Lower the vehicle and remove the alternator mounting bolts. Guide the alternator out from above (see illustration).

8   Installation is the reverse of removal. Tighten the alternator mounting bolts to the torque listed in this Chapter's Specifications.

9   Reconnect the battery (see Section 3).

7.5 Alternator mounting details (2015 and earlier 1.4L engine)

1 Drivebelt tensioner lower bolt (remove)
2 Drivebelt tensioner upper bolt (loosen)
3 Alternator mounting bolts

7.6 Disconnect the electrical connector (A) and battery positive cable nut (B)

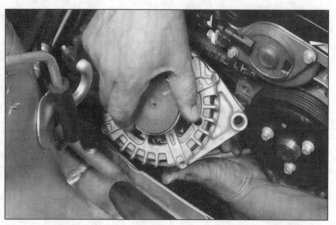

7.7 Move the alternator toward the inner fender panel and maneuver it up and out

8.4 Starter motor details

1   *Positive cable*
2   *Starter control wire ("S" terminal)*
3   *Ground cable nut and lower mounting bolt*

8.6 The upper mounting bolt can be accessed with a socket and long extension

8   Starter motor - removal and installation

1   Turn the ignition key to OFF, then disconnect the cable from the negative battery terminal (see Section 3).
2   Raise the front of the vehicle and support it securely on jackstands.

3   On 2016 and later models, disconnect and remove the front exhaust pipe (see Chapter 4).
4   Disconnect the battery cable (the larger cable) and the starter control wire from the starter motor solenoid terminals (see illustration).
5   On 2016 and later models, remove the battery ground cable bolt and cable (to access the starter lower mounting bolt), then

remove the two mounting bolts from the rear of the starter and the bracket.
6   Remove the starter motor mounting bolts (see illustration) and remove the starter motor.
7   Installation is the reverse of removal. Tighten the starter motor mounting bolts to the torque listed in this Chapter's Specifications.
8   Reconnect the battery (see Section 3).

Chapter 6
Emissions and engine control systems

Contents

Specifications

Torque specifications

Note: *One foot-pound (ft-lb) of torque is equivalent to 12 inch-pounds (in-lbs) of torque. Torque values below approximately 15 ft-lbs are expressed in inch-pounds, because most foot-pound torque wrenches are not accurate at these smaller values.*

	Ft-lbs (unless otherwise indicated)	Nm
Catalytic converter (1.4L models)		
Warm-up three-way (upper) converter		
Converter-to-turbocharger V-clamp bolt	115 in-lbs	13
Converter-to-exhaust pipe nuts	16	22
Converter bracket nuts	16	22
Secondary (lower) converter		
Front pipe-to-warm-up converter nuts	16	22
Pipe-to-muffler nuts	156 in-lbs	17
CKP sensor bolt		
2015 and earlier models	71 in-lbs	8
2016 and later models	89 in-lbs	10
1.8L engine	40 in-lbs	4.5
CMP sensor bolt		
2015 and earlier models	71 in-lbs	8
2016 and later models	89 in-lbs	10
CMP actuator solenoid valve mounting bolts		
1.4L engine		
2015 and earlier models	71 in-lbs	8
2016 and later models	89 in-lbs	10
1.8L engine	53 in-lbs	6
Fuel pressure sensor	168 in-lbs	19
Knock sensor retaining bolt		
2015 and earlier models	15	20
2016 and later models	18	25
Oxygen sensors	30	40

1 General Information

1   To prevent pollution of the atmosphere from incompletely burned and evaporating gases, and to maintain good driveability and fuel economy, a number of emission control systems are incorporated. They include the:

Catalytic converter

2   A catalytic converter is an emission control device in the exhaust system that reduces certain pollutants in the exhaust gas stream. There are two types of converters: oxidation converters and reduction converters.

3   Oxidation converters contain a monolithic substrate (a ceramic honeycomb) coated with the semi-precious metals platinum and palladium. An oxidation catalyst reduces unburned hydrocarbons (HC) and carbon monoxide (CO) by adding oxygen to the exhaust stream as it passes through the substrate, which, in the presence of high temperature and the catalyst materials, converts the HC and CO to water vapor (H_2O) and carbon dioxide (CO_2).

4   Reduction converters contain a monolithic substrate coated with platinum and rhodium. A reduction catalyst reduces oxides of nitrogen (NOx) by removing oxygen, which in the presence of high temperature and the catalyst material produces nitrogen (N) and carbon dioxide (CO_2).

5   Catalytic converters that combine both types of catalysts in one assembly are known as "three-way catalysts" or TWCs. A TWC can reduce all three pollutants.

Evaporative Emissions Control (EVAP) system

6   The Evaporative Emissions Control (EVAP) system prevents fuel system vapors (which contain unburned hydrocarbons) from escaping into the atmosphere. On warm days, vapors trapped inside the fuel tank expand until the pressure reaches a certain threshold. Then the fuel vapors are routed from the fuel tank through the fuel vapor vent valve and the fuel vapor control valve to the EVAP canister, where they're stored temporarily until the next time the vehicle is operated. When the conditions are right (engine warmed up, vehicle up to speed, moderate or heavy load on the engine, etc.) the PCM opens the canister purge valve, which allows fuel vapors to be drawn from the canister into the intake manifold. Once in the intake manifold, the fuel vapors mix with incoming air before being drawn through the intake ports into the combustion chambers where they're burned up with the rest of the air/fuel mixture. The EVAP system is complex and virtually impossible to troubleshoot without the right tools and training.

Secondary Air Injection (AIR) system

7   Some models are equipped with a secondary air injection (AIR) system. The secondary air injection system is used to reduce tailpipe emissions on initial engine start-up. The system uses an electric motor/pump assembly, relay, vacuum valve/solenoid, air shut-off valve, check valves and tubing to inject fresh air directly into the exhaust manifolds. The fresh air (oxygen) reacts with the exhaust gas in the catalytic converter to reduce HC and CO levels. The air pump and solenoid are controlled by the PCM through the AIR relay. During initial start-up, the PCM energizes the AIR relay, the relay supplies battery voltage to the air pump and the vacuum valve/solenoid, engine vacuum is applied to the air shut-off valve which opens and allows air to flow through the tubing into the exhaust manifolds. The PCM will operate the air pump until closed loop operation is reached (approximately four minutes). During normal operation, the check valves prevent exhaust backflow into the system.

Powertrain Control Module (PCM)

8   The Powertrain Control Module (PCM) is the brain of the engine management system. It also controls a wide variety of other vehicle systems. In order to program the new PCM, the dealer needs the vehicle as well as the new PCM. If you're planning to replace the PCM with a new one, there is no point in trying to do so at home because you won't be able to program it yourself.

Positive Crankcase Ventilation (PCV) system

9   The Positive Crankcase Ventilation (PCV) system reduces hydrocarbon emissions by scavenging crankcase vapors, which are rich in unburned hydrocarbons. A PCV valve or orifice regulates the flow of gases into the intake manifold in proportion to the amount of intake vacuum available.

10   The PCV system generally consists of the fresh air inlet hose, the PCV valve or orifice and the crankcase ventilation hose (or PCV hose). The fresh air inlet hose connects the air intake duct to a pipe on the valve cover. The crankcase ventilation hose (or PCV hose) connects the PCV valve or orifice in the valve cover to the intake manifold.

2   On Board Diagnosis (OBD) system

General description

1   All models are equipped with the second generation OBD-II system. This system consists of an on-board computer known as the Powertrain Control Module (PCM), and information sensors, which monitor various functions of the engine and send data to the PCM. This system incorporates a series of diagnostic monitors that detect and identify fuel injection and emissions control system faults and store the information in the computer memory. This system also tests sensors and output actuators, diagnoses drive cycles, freezes data and clears codes.

2   The PCM is the brain of the electronically controlled fuel and emissions system. It receives data from a number of sensors and other electronic components (switches, relays, etc.). Based on the information it receives, the PCM generates output signals to control various relays, solenoids (fuel injectors) and other actuators. The PCM is specifically calibrated to optimize the emissions, fuel economy and driveability of the vehicle.

3   It isn't a good idea to attempt diagnosis or replacement of the PCM or emission control components at home while the vehicle is under warranty. Because of a federally-mandated warranty which covers the emissions system components and because any owner-induced damage to the PCM, the sensors and/or the control devices may void this warranty, take the vehicle to a dealer service department if the PCM or a system component malfunctions.

Scan tool information

4   Because extracting the Diagnostic Trouble Codes (DTCs) from an engine management system is now the first step in troubleshooting many computer-controlled systems and components, a code reader, at the very least, will be required (see illustration). More powerful scan tools can also perform many of the diagnostics once associated with expensive factory scan tools (see illustration). If you're planning to obtain a generic scan tool for your vehicle, make sure that it's compatible with OBD-II systems. If you don't plan to purchase a code reader or scan tool and don't have access to one, you can have the codes extracted by a dealer service department or an independent repair shop. **Note:** *Some auto parts stores even provide this service.*

2.4a Simple code readers are an economical way to extract trouble codes when the CHECK ENGINE light comes on

2.4b Hand-held scan tools like these can extract computer codes and also perform diagnostics

Information Sensors

Accelerator Pedal Position (APP) sensor - as you press the accelerator pedal, the APP sensor alters its voltage signal to the PCM in proportion to the angle of the pedal, and the PCM commands a motor inside the throttle body to open or close the throttle plate accordingly

Camshaft Position (CMP) sensor - produces a signal that the PCM uses to identify the number 1 cylinder and to time the firing sequence of the fuel injectors

Crankshaft Position (CKP) sensor - produces a signal that the PCM uses to calculate engine speed and crankshaft position, which enables it to synchronize ignition timing with fuel injector timing, and to detect misfires

Engine Coolant Temperature (ECT) sensor - a thermistor (temperature-sensitive variable resistor) that sends a voltage signal to the PCM, which uses this data to determine the temperature of the engine coolant

Fuel tank pressure sensor - measures the fuel tank pressure and controls fuel tank pressure by signaling the EVAP system to purge the fuel tank vapors when the pressure becomes excessive

Intake Air Temperature (IAT) sensor - monitors the temperature of the air entering the engine and sends a signal to the PCM to determine injector pulse-width (the duration of each injector's on-time) and to adjust spark timing (to prevent spark knock)

Knock sensor - a piezoelectric crystal that oscillates in proportion to engine vibration which produces a voltage output that is monitored by the PCM. This retards the ignition timing when the oscillation exceeds a certain threshold

Manifold Absolute Pressure (MAP) sensor - monitors the pressure or vacuum inside the intake manifold. The PCM uses this data to determine engine load so that it can alter the ignition advance and fuel enrichment

Mass Air Flow (MAF) sensor - measures the amount of intake air drawn into the engine. It uses a hot-wire sensing element to measure the amount of air entering the engine

Oxygen sensors - generates a small variable voltage signal in proportion to the difference between the oxygen content in the exhaust stream and the oxygen content in the ambient air. The PCM uses this information to maintain the proper air/fuel ratio. A second oxygen sensor monitors the efficiency of the catalytic converter

Throttle Position (TP) sensor - a potentiometer that generates a voltage signal that varies in relation to the opening angle of the throttle plate inside the throttle body. Works with the PCM and other sensors to calculate injector pulse width (the duration of each injector's on-time)

Photos courtesy of Wells Manufacturing, except APP and MAF sensors.

3   Obtaining and clearing Diagnostic Trouble Codes (DTCs)

1   All models covered by this manual are equipped with on-board diagnostics. When the PCM recognizes a malfunction in a monitored emission or engine control system, component or circuit, it turns on the Malfunction Indicator Light (MIL) on the dash. The PCM will continue to display the MIL until the problem is fixed and the Diagnostic Trouble Code (DTC) is cleared from the PCM's memory. You'll need a scan tool to access any DTCs stored in the PCM.

2   Before outputting any DTCs stored in the PCM, thoroughly inspect ALL electrical connectors and hoses. Make sure that all electrical connections are tight, clean and free of corrosion. And make sure that all hoses are correctly connected, fit tightly and are in good condition (no cracks or tears).

Accessing the DTCs

3   The Diagnostic Trouble Codes (DTCs) can only be accessed with a code reader or scan tool. Professional scan tools are expensive, but relatively inexpensive generic code readers or scan tools (see illustrations 2.4a and 2.4b) are available at most auto parts stores. Simply plug the connector of the scan tool into the diagnostic connector (see illustration). Then follow the instructions included with the scan tool to extract the DTCs.

4   Once you have outputted all of the stored DTCs, look them up on the accompanying DTC chart.

5   After troubleshooting the source of each DTC, make any necessary repairs or replace the defective component(s).

Clearing the DTCs

6   Clear the DTCs with the code reader or scan tool in accordance with the instructions provided by the tool's manufacturer.

Diagnostic Trouble Codes

7   The accompanying tables are a list of the Diagnostic Trouble Codes (DTCs) that can be accessed by a do-it-yourselfer working at home (there are many, many more DTCs available to professional mechanics with proprietary scan tools and software, but those codes cannot be accessed by a generic scan tool). If, after you have checked and repaired the connectors, wire harness and vacuum hoses (if applicable) for an emission-related system, component or circuit, the problem persists, have the vehicle checked by a dealer service department or other qualified repair shop.

3.3 The Data Link Connector (DLC) is located at the lower edge of the dash, below the steering column

OBD-II trouble codes

Code	Code identification
P0010	Intake cam CMP, actuator circuit
P0011	Intake cam CMP, performance problem
P0013	Exhaust cam CMP, actuator circuit
P0014	Exhaust cam CMP, performance problem
P0016	CKP-to-Intake CMP, correlation problem
P0017	CKP-to-exhaust CMP, correlation problem
P0030	O2 heater control circuit (sensor 1)
P0031	O2 heater control circuit, low voltage (sensor 1)
P0032	O2 heater control circuit, high voltage (sensor 1)
P0033	1.4L, turbocharger bypass solenoid circuit
P0034	1.4L, turbocharger bypass solenoid control circuit, low voltage
P0035	1.4L, turbocharger bypass solenoid control circuit, high voltage
P0036	O2 heater control circuit (sensor 2)
P0037	O2 heater control circuit, low voltage (sensor 2)

OBD-II trouble codes (continued)

Note: *Not all trouble codes apply to all models.*

Code	Code identification
P0038	O2 heater control circuit, high voltage (sensor 2)
P0053	O2 heater resistance (sensor 1)
P0054	O2 heater resistance (sensor 2)
P0068	Throttle body airflow performance problem
P0087	Fuel Rail pressure low
P0088	Fuel Rail pressure high
P0089	Fuel pressure regulator performance problem
P0090	Fuel Pressure regulator control circuit
P0091	Fuel pressure regulator control circuit, low voltage
P0092	Fuel pressure regulator control circuit, high voltage
P0096	Intake Air temperature (IAT) sensor 2, performance problem
P0097	IAT sensor 2 circuit, low voltage, 1.8L models
P0098	IAT sensor 2 circuit, high voltage, 1.8L models
P0099	IAT sensor 2 circuit, intermittent, 1.8L models
P0101	Mass air flow or volume problem, IAT, MAF, or MAP
P0102	Mass air flow or volume air flow circuit, low input
P0103	Mass air flow or volume air flow circuit, high input
P0106	Manifold absolute pressure or barometric pressure circuit, range or performance problem
P0107	Manifold absolute pressure or barometric pressure circuit, low input
P0108	Manifold absolute pressure or barometric pressure circuit, high input
P0111	Intake Air temperature (IAT) sensor 1, performance problem
P0112	Intake air temperature circuit, low input
P0113	Intake air temperature circuit, high input
P0114	Intake Air temperature (IAT) sensor circuit, intermittent
P0116	Engine coolant temperature sensor, performance problem
P0117	Engine coolant temperature circuit, low input
P0118	Engine coolant temperature circuit, high input
P0119	Engine coolant temperature circuit, intermittent
P0120	Throttle position or pedal position sensor/switch circuit malfunction

OBD-II trouble codes (continued)

Note: *Not all trouble codes apply to all models.*

Code	Code identification
P0121	Throttle position or pedal position sensor/switch circuit, range or performance problem
P0122	Throttle position or pedal position sensor/switch circuit, low input
P0123	Throttle position or pedal position sensor/switch circuit, high input
P0125	Insufficient coolant temperature for closed loop fuel control
P0128	Coolant thermostat (coolant temperature below thermostat regulating temperature)
P0130	O2 sensor circuit malfunction (sensor 1)
P0131	O2 sensor circuit, low voltage (sensor 1)
P0132	O2 sensor circuit, high voltage (sensor 1)
P0133	O2 sensor circuit, slow response (sensor 1)
P013A	O2 sensor circuit, slow response, rich to lean (sensor 2)
P013B	O2 sensor circuit, slow response, lean to rich (sensor 2)
P013E	O2 sensor circuit, delayed response, rich to lean (sensor 2)
P013F	O2 sensor circuit, delayed response, lean to rich (sensor 2)
P015A	2 sensor circuit, delayed response, rich to lean (sensor 1)
P015B	2 sensor circuit, delayed response, lean to rich (sensor 1)
P0134	O2 sensor circuit - no activity detected (sensor 1)
P0135	O2 sensor heater circuit malfunction (sensor 1)
P0136	O2 sensor circuit malfunction (sensor 2)
P0137	O2 sensor circuit, low voltage (sensor 2)
P0138	O2 sensor circuit, high voltage (sensor 2)
P0140	O2 sensor circuit - no activity detected (sensor 2)
P0141	O2 sensor heater circuit malfunction (sensor 2)
P0171	System too lean
P0172	System too rich
P018B	Fuel system sensor performance problem
P018C	Fuel system sensor circuit, low voltage
P018D	Fuel system sensor circuit, high voltage
P0182	Fuel temperature sensor circuit, low voltage
P0183	Fuel temperature sensor circuit, high voltage

Code	Code identification
P0187	Fuel temperature sensor 2 circuit, low voltage
P0188	Fuel temperature sensor 2 circuit, high voltage
P0191	Fuel rail pressure sensor performance
P0192	Fuel rail pressure sensor circuit, low voltage
P0201	Injector circuit malfunction - cylinder no. 1
P0202	Injector circuit malfunction - cylinder no. 2
P0203	Injector circuit malfunction - cylinder no. 3
P0204	Injector circuit malfunction - cylinder no. 4
P0217	Engine coolant overtemperature
P0218	Transmission overheating condition
P0220	Throttle position or pedal position sensor/switch B circuit malfunction
P0222	Throttle position or pedal position sensor/switch B circuit, low input
P0223	Throttle position or pedal position sensor/switch B circuit, high input
P0230	Fuel pump primary circuit malfunction
P0231	Fuel pump control circuit, low voltage
P0232	Fuel pump control circuit, high voltage
P023F	Fuel pump control circuit
P0234	Turbocharger over-boost
P0236	Turbocharger boost system performance problem
P0237	Turbocharger boost sensor circuit, low voltage
P0238	Turbocharger boost sensor circuit, high voltage
P0243	Turbocharger wastegate solenoid control circuits
P0245	Turbocharger wastegate solenoid valve control circuit, low voltage
P0246	Turbocharger wastegate solenoid valve control circuit, high voltage
P025A	Fuel pump control module enable circuit
P0261	Injector 1 control circuit, low voltage
P0262	Injector 1 control circuit, high voltage
P0264	Injector 2 control circuit, low voltage
P0265	Injector 2 control circuit, high voltage
P0267	Injector 3 control circuit, low voltage
P0268	Injector 3 control circuit, high voltage

OBD-II trouble codes (continued)

Note: *Not all trouble codes apply to all models.*

Code	Code identification
P0270	Injector 4 control circuit, low voltage
P0271	Injector 4 control circuit, high voltage
P0299	Turbocharger under-boost
P0300	Random/multiple cylinder misfire detected
P0301	Cylinder 1 misfire
P0302	Cylinder 2 misfire
P0303	Cylinder 3 misfire
P0304	Cylinder 4 misfire
P0315	Crankshaft position system - variation not learned
P0324 P0325	Knock sensor no. 1 circuit malfunction (bank 1 or single sensor)
P0326	Knock sensor no. 1 circuit, range or performance problem (number 1 or single sensor)
P06B6	Control module knock sensor processor performance problem
P0327 P0328	Knock sensor no. 1 circuit, low input (number 1 or single sensor)
P0331	Knock sensor 2 performance problem
P0335	Crankshaft position sensor A circuit malfunction
P0336	Crankshaft position sensor A circuit - range or performance problem
P0340	Intake camshaft position sensor circuit, 1.8L models
P0341	Intake camshaft position sensor performance problem, 1.8L models
P0342	Intake camshaft position sensor - low voltage
P0343	Intake camshaft position sensor - high voltage
P0351	Ignition coil 1 control circuit, 1.8L models
P0352	Ignition coil 2 control circuit, 1.8L models
P0353	Ignition coil 3 control circuit, 1.8L models
P0354	Ignition coil 4 control circuit, 1.8L models
P0365	Exhaust camshaft position sensor circuit, 1.8L models
P0366	Exhaust camshaft position sensor performance problem, 1.8L models
P0367	Exhaust camshaft position sensor - low voltage
P0368	Exhaust camshaft position sensor - high voltage
P0411	Secondary Air Injection, incorrect flow

Code	Code identification
P0412	Secondary Air Injection, solenoid circuit
P0418	Secondary Air Injection, pump control circuit
P0420	Catalyst system efficiency below threshold
P0442	Evaporative emission control system, small leak detected
P0443	Evaporative emission control system, purge control valve circuit malfunction
P0446	Evaporative emission control system, vent control circuit malfunction
P0449	Evaporative emission control system, vent valve/solenoid circuit malfunction
P0451	Fuel tank pressure sensor range or performance problem
P0452	Fuel tank pressure sensor low input
P0453	Fuel tank pressure sensor high input
P0454	Fuel tank pressure sensor, circuit intermittent
P0455	Evaporative emission (EVAP) control system leak detected (large leak or no purge flow)
P0458	Evaporative emission (EVAP) purge solenoid valve control circuit, low voltage
P0459	Evaporative emission (EVAP) purge solenoid valve control circuit, high voltage
P0461	Fuel level sensor, performance problem
P0462	Fuel level sensor, low voltage
P0463	Fuel level sensor, high voltage
P0464	Fuel level sensor, circuit intermittent
P0480	Cooling fan relay 1, control circuit
P0481 P0482	Cooling fan relay 2, control circuit
P0496	Evaporative emission system - high purge flow
P0498	Evaporative emission (EVAP) vent solenoid valve control circuit, low voltage
P0499	Evaporative emission (EVAP) vent solenoid valve control circuit, high voltage
P0502	Vehicle speed sensor circuit, low input
P0503	Vehicle speed sensor circuit, Intermittent, erratic or high input
P0506	Idle control system, rpm lower than expected
P0507	Idle control system, rpm higher than expected
P0520	Engine oil pressure sensor/switch circuit malfunction
P0532	A/C refrigerant pressure sensor, low input
P0533	A/C refrigerant pressure sensor, high input
P0562	System voltage low
P0563	System voltage high

OBD-II trouble codes (continued)

Note: *Not all trouble codes apply to all models.*

Code	Code identification
P0564	Cruise control system, multi-function input signal
P0575	Cruise control circuit, switch signal
P0601	Fuel pump control module, memory check sum error
P0601	Control module read only memory performance problem (ECM)
P0602	Fuel pump control module, not programmed
P0602	(ECM) control module, not programmed
P0603	Fuel pump control module, long term memory reset
P0603	(ECM) control module, long term memory reset
P0604	Fuel pump control module, random access memory (RAM) performance problem
P0604	(ECM) control module, random access memory (RAM) performance problem
P0606	ECM processor performance problem
P062F	Control module, long term memory performance problem
P0607	Control module performance problem, 1.8L models
P0621	Generator lamp L, control circuit malfunction
P0622	Generator lamp F, control circuit malfunction
P0627	Fuel pump enable circuit problem
P0628	Fuel pump enable circuit, low voltage
P0629	Fuel pump enable circuit, high voltage
P0630	VIN is not programmed or mismatched with engine control module (ECM)
P0641	Sensor 5-volt reference 1, circuit performance problem
P06A6	Sensor 5-volt reference 1, performance problem
P0645	AC clutch relay, control circuit
P0646	AC clutch relay 1, low voltage
P0647	AC clutch relay 1, high voltage
P0650	Malfunction indicator lamp (MIL), control circuit malfunction
P0651	Sensor 5-volt reference 2, circuit performance problem
P0660	Intake manifold tuning control valve control circuit, performance problem
P0661	Intake manifold tuning control valve control circuit, low voltage
P0662	Intake manifold tuning control valve control circuit, high voltage
P0685	Ignition relay, control circuit
P0686	Ignition relay, control circuit, low voltage

Code	Code identification
P0687	Ignition relay, control circuit, high voltage
P0689	Ignition relay, feedback circuit, low voltage
P0690	Ignition relay, feedback circuit, high voltage
P0691	Cooling fan output circuit, low voltage
P069E	Fuel pump control module, requested MIL illumination
P0697	Sensor 5-volt reference 3, circuit performance problem
P06A3	Sensor 5-volt reference 4, circuit performance problem
P0700	TCM, MIL requested
P0705	Transmission range sensor, circuit malfunction (PRNDL input)
P0711	Transmission fluid temperature sensor circuit, range or performance problem
P0712	Transmission fluid temperature sensor circuit, low input
P0713	Transmission fluid temperature sensor circuit, high input
P0716	Input speed sensor circuit performance problem
P0717	Input speed sensor circuit, low voltage
P0719	Torque converter/brake switch B, circuit low
P0722	Output speed sensor, low voltage
P0723	Output speed sensor, circuit intermittent
P0724	Torque converter/brake switch B circuit, high
P0741	Torque converter clutch, circuit performance problem or stuck in off position
P0742	Torque converter clutch circuit, stuck in on position
P0751	Shift solenoid A, performance problem or stuck in off position
P0752	Shift solenoid A, stuck in on position
P0756	Shift solenoid B, performance problem or stuck in off position
P0757	Shift solenoid B, stuck in on position
P0833	Clutch switch circuit
P0842	Transmission fluid pressure sensor, circuit low voltage
P0843	Transmission fluid pressure sensor, circuit high voltage
P0961	Transmission line pressure solenoid
P0973	Shift solenoid (SS) A - control circuit low
P0974	Shift solenoid (SS) A - control circuit high
P0976	Shift solenoid (SS) B - control circuit low
P0977	Shift solenoid (SS) B - control circuit high

**4.2 Accelerator Pedal Position (APP)
sensor details**

1   *APP sensor electrical connector*
2   *Mounting bolt*

**5.1 Disconnect the sensor electrical
connector (A), then remove the sensor
retaining bolt (B) - 2015 and earlier
model intake sensor shown,
exhaust sensor identical**

4   Accelerator Pedal Position (APP) sensor - replacement

1   Turn the ignition key to OFF.
2   Disconnect the electrical connector from the APP sensor (see illustration).
3   Remove the APP sensor mounting fastener and detach the APP sensor assembly.
4   Installation is the reverse of removal.

5   Camshaft Position (CMP) sensor(s) - replacement

1.4L engine

Note: *On 2015 and earlier models, the camshaft position sensors are located on each side of the timing chain cover, just behind the camshaft position actuators. On 2016 and later models, the camshaft position (CMP) sensors are on each side of the valve cover at the front.*
1   Disconnect the sensor electrical connector, then remove the sensor retaining bolt (see illustration).
2   Remove the sensor and O-ring.
3   Installation is the reverse of removal. Lubricate the O-ring with clean engine oil prior to installing.

1.8L engine

Note: *The camshaft position sensors are located at the rear (left end) of the cylinder head. The intake CMP sensor is closest to the firewall side. The exhaust CMP sensor is closest to radiator side of the engine.*
4   Turn the ignition key to OFF.
5   Unplug the electrical connector from the CMP sensor(s) (see illustration).
6   Remove the CMP sensor retaining bolt and remove the CMP sensor(s).
7   Installation is the reverse of removal. Lubricate the O-ring with clean engine oil and tighten the CMP sensor bolt securely.

6   Crankshaft Position (CKP) sensor - replacement

Note: *After the sensor removal; engine replacement; ECM replacement; crankshaft damper replacement; or any repair that may change the crankshaft sensor to crankshaft setting, the system will need to have a "variation learn" procedure performed using the GM's TECH-2 scan tool, or a trouble code will be set.*
1   Turn the ignition key to OFF.
2   Raise the vehicle and support it securely on jackstands.

1.4L engine

Note: *The crankshaft position sensor is located on the rear side of the engine block, just above the right-side driveaxle and below the starter.*
3   Disconnect the sensor electrical connector, then remove the sensor retaining bolt (see illustration).
4   Remove the sensor and O-ring.
5   Installation is the reverse of removal. Lubricate the O-ring with clean engine oil prior to installing. Check for oil leaks immediately after starting the engine.

1.8L engine

Note: *The crankshaft position sensor is located on the rear side of the engine block, directly behind the starter motor.*
6   Remove the starter motor (see Chapter 5).
7   Disconnect the electrical connector from the CKP sensor.
8   Unscrew the CKP sensor mounting bolt and remove the sensor.
9   Even if you're planning to reuse the old CKP sensor, remove the old O-ring and discard it. Always install a new O-ring when installing the CKP sensor.
10   Installation is the reverse of removal. Tighten the CKP sensor mounting bolt securely.

**5.5 Exhaust CMP sensor (A) and intake CMP sensor (B)
(1.8L engine)**

**6.3 Disconnect the sensor electrical connector (A),
then remove the sensor retaining bolt (B)**

7.4a The engine-mounted ECT sensor is located in the coolant outlet housing on 1.4L models

1   ECT sensor electrical connector
2   Retaining clip, in the fully seated position

7.4b On 1.8L models, the engine-mounted ECT sensor is located in the thermostat housing

7.10 Radiator-mounted ECT sensor is located on the right side of the radiator

1   Electrical connector   2   Retaining clip

8.4 Knock sensor details

1   Electrical connector   2   Mounting bolt

7   Engine Coolant Temperature (ECT) sensor(s) - replacement

Warning: *Wait until the engine is completely cool before beginning this procedure.*
Note: *There are two engine coolant temperature sensors used: an upper one, located in the coolant outlet housing on 1.4L models or in the thermostat housing on 1.8L models, and a lower one, mounted in the lower right side of the radiator on both models.*
1   Turn the ignition key to OFF.
2   Drain the cooling system (see Chapter 1).

Engine-mounted ECT sensor

3   On 1.4L models, remove the charge air cooler outlet pipe (see Chapter 4).
4   Disconnect the electrical connector from the ECT sensor, which is located in the coolant outlet housing (1.4L models) or thermo-

stat housing (1.8L models) (see illustrations).
5   Pull out the retaining clip, then twist and pull the sensor from its bore.
6   Installation is the reverse of removal.
Note: *Make sure the retaining clip is fully seated.*
7   Refill the cooling system (see Chapter 1).

Radiator-mounted ECT sensor

8   Remove the front bumper cover (see Chapter 11).
9   Locate the sensor on the right side of the radiator.
10   Disconnect the sensor electrical connector, then remove the retaining clip up and pull the sensor from the radiator (see illustration).
11   Installation is the reverse of removal.
Note: *Make sure the retaining clip is fully seated.*
12   Refill the cooling system (see Chapter 1).

8   Knock sensor - replacement

Note: *The knock sensor is located on the rear side of the engine block to the rear of the starter motor.*
1   Make sure the ignition key is turned to OFF position.
2   Raise the front of the vehicle and support it securely on jackstands.
3   On 1.8L models, remove the intake manifold support bracket bolts and bracket from the bottom of the manifold.
4   Disconnect the knock sensor electrical connector (see illustration).
5   Remove the knock sensor retaining bolt.
6   Remove the knock sensor.
7   Installation is the reverse of removal. Tighten the knock sensor retaining bolt to the torque listed in this Chapter's Specifications.

9.2a MAP sensor location - 1.4L models

9.2b MAP sensor location - 1.8L models

9   Manifold Absolute Pressure (MAP) sensor - replacement

Note: *After the repair, the vehicle may not perform normally as the sensor goes through it's "learn process." It may be necessary to use the GM's TECH-2 scan tool to speed up the "learn process."*

Note: *2015 and earlier models use a MAP sensor and 2016 and later models use an IAT sensor.*

1   Turn the ignition key to OFF.
2   Disconnect the MAP sensor electrical connector (see illustrations).
3   Remove the mounting screw and pull the sensor from the intake manifold.
4   If the seal is damaged, the sensor itself must be replaced. A new sensor will come with a new seal.
5   Installation is the reverse of removal.

10   Mass Air Flow sensor - replacement

Note: *The MAF sensor is located on the air filter housing.*

Note: *After the repair, the vehicle may not perform normally as the sensor goes through it's "learn process." It may be necessary to use the GM's TECH-2 scan tool to speed up the "learn process."*

1   Turn the ignition key to OFF.
2   Disconnect the electrical connector from the sensor (see illustration).
3   Remove the mounting screws and remove the sensor.
4   Installation is the reverse of removal.

11   Vehicle Speed Sensor (VSS) - replacement

Automatic transaxle

1   The vehicle speed sensors (VSS) are mounted internally to the valve body, which is beyond the scope of this manual. It is therefore essential that problems with the VSS replacement(s) are referred to a dealer service department or other qualified repair facility for assessment and repair.

Manual transaxle

Note: *The VSS is located on the top of the transaxle. If necessary, remove the battery*

and battery tray for access (see Chapter 5).
2   Turn the ignition key to OFF.
3   Disconnect the electrical connector from the VSS sensor.
4   Disengage the electrical harness from the bracket that's attached to the VSS sensor.
5   Remove the VSS sensor bolt and remove the sensor from the top of the transaxle.
6   Remove the old O-ring from the VSS sensor and discard it. Use a new O-ring when installing the VSS sensor (even if you're planning to reuse the old VSS sensor).
7   Installation is the reverse of removal.

12   Oxygen sensors - replacement

Caution: *Because it is installed in the exhaust manifold or pipe, both of which contract when cool, an oxygen sensor might be very difficult to loosen when the engine is cold. Rather than risk damage to the sensor or its mounting threads, start and run the engine for a minute or two, then shut it off. Be careful not to burn yourself during the following procedure.*

1   Be particularly careful when servicing an oxygen sensor:
  a) *Oxygen sensors have a permanently attached pigtail and an electrical connector that cannot be removed. Damaging or removing the pigtail or electrical connector will render the sensor useless.*
  b) *Keep grease, dirt and other contaminants away from the electrical connector and the louvered end of the sensor.*
  c) *Do not use cleaning solvents of any kind on an oxygen sensor.*
  d) *Oxygen sensors are extremely delicate. Do not drop a sensor or handle it roughly.*
  e) *Make sure that the silicone boot on the sensor is installed in the correct position. Otherwise, the boot might melt and it might prevent the sensor from operating correctly.*

10.2 Mass Air Flow (MAF) sensor details (2015 and earlier 1.4L model shown)

1   *Electrical connector*
2   *Upper mounting screw - lower screw not visible*

12.5a Follow the harness from the oxygen sensor (A) to the electrical connector (B) and unplug it. . .

12.5b. . . then use an oxygen sensor socket to unscrew the upstream oxygen sensor (Sensor 1) - 1.4L model shown

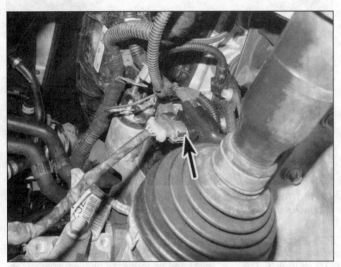

12.8 Detach the downstream O2 sensor electrical connector from the bracket, then unplug it

12.9 Use an oxygen sensor socket to unscrew the downstream oxygen sensor (Sensor 2)

Replacement

Note: *After the repair the vehicle may not perform normally as the sensor goes through its "learn process." It may be necessary to use the GM's TECH-2 scan tool to speed up the "learn process."*

Upstream oxygen sensor (Sensor 1)

Note: *On 1.4L models, oxygen sensor 1 is located at the top of the catalytic converter, just downstream of the turbocharger. On 1.8L models, it is located in the middle of the exhaust manifold.*

2   Turn the ignition key to OFF position.
3   On 1.8L models, remove the bolts securing the exhaust manifold heat shield. Remove the heat shield.
4   Disconnect the upstream oxygen sensor electrical connector, which is located near the throttle body on 1.4L models or the thermostat

housing on 1.8L models. On 1.4L models, the connector will have a CPA (connector position assurance) clip that must be pulled to disconnect the connector.
5   Using an oxygen sensor socket (available at most auto parts stores), unscrew the upstream oxygen sensor (see illustrations). If the sensor is difficult to loosen, spray some penetrant onto the sensor threads and allow it to soak in for awhile.

Downstream oxygen sensor (Sensor 2)

6   Turn the ignition key to OFF.
7   Raise the vehicle and support it securely on jackstands.
8   Disconnect the oxygen sensor electrical connector, which is located on a bracket attached to the rear of the engine block (see illustration). On some models, the connector will have a CPA (connector position assur-

ance) clip that must be pulled to disconnect the connector.
9   Unscrew the downstream oxygen sensor (see illustration), which is located behind the catalytic converter. If the sensor is difficult to loosen, spray some penetrant onto the sensor threads and allow it to soak in for awhile.

Either sensor

10   If you're going to install the old sensor, apply anti-seize compound to the threads of the sensor to facilitate future removal. If you're going to install a new oxygen sensor, it's not necessary to apply anti-seize compound to the threads. The threads on new sensors already have anti-seize compound on them.
11   Installation is otherwise the reverse of removal. Tighten the sensor to the torque listed in this Chapter's Specifications.

14.2a Slide back the lock (A), depress the tab (B) to unlock the release lever (C). . .

14.2b. . . then flip the release lever open and unplug the connector

14.3 PCM mounting nuts

15.1 To disconnect the upper end of the catalytic converter, remove the converter-to-turbocharger V-clamp bolt and clamp

13 Transmission Range (TR) switch - replacement

1   Transaxle Range (TR) switch is mounted internally to the valve body and is beyond the scope of this manual. It is therefore essential that problems with the (TR) switch are referred to a dealer service department or other qualified repair facility for assessment and repair.

14 Powertrain Control Module (PCM) - removal and installation

Caution: *To avoid electrostatic discharge damage to the PCM, handle the PCM only by its case. Do not touch the electrical terminals during removal and installation. If available, ground yourself to the vehicle with an anti-static ground strap, available at computer supply stores.*

Note: *The procedures in this section apply only to removing and installing the PCM that is already installed in your vehicle. If you need a new PCM, it must be programmed with new software and calibrations. This procedure re-*

quires the use of GM's TECH-2 scan tool and GM's latest PCM-programming software, so you WILL NOT BE ABLE TO REPLACE THE PCM AT HOME.

Note: *The PCM is a highly reliable component and rarely requires replacement. Since the PCM is the most expensive part of the engine management system, you should be absolutely positive that it has failed before replacing it. If in doubt, have the system tested by an experienced drivability technician at a dealer service department or other qualified repair shop.*

Note: *On 2015 and earlier models, the PCM is located on the left side of the engine compartment on the side of the battery box. On 2016 and later models, the PCM is located on the left side of the engine compartment next to the fuse/relay box.*

1   Disconnect the cable from the negative terminal of the battery (see Chapter 5).
2   Noting their orientation to the PCM, disconnect the three electrical connectors from the PCM (see illustrations).
3   Remove the PCM mounting nuts and remove the PCM from the bracket on the side of the battery box (see illustration).
4   Installation is the reverse of removal.

5   When the battery has been disconnected, the PCM must relearn its former drivability and performance problem characteristics (see Chapter 5).

15 Catalytic converter - replacement

1.4L models
Warm-up three-way (upper) converter
Warning: *Make sure that the exhaust system is completely cooled down before proceeding. If the vehicle has been driven recently, the catalytic converter can be hot enough to cause serious burns.*

1   Open the hood and remove the upstream oxygen sensor (see Section 12), then unscrew the converter-to-turbocharger outlet V-clamp bolt (see illustration).
Caution: *Discard the V-clamp and obtain a new one for installation.*

2   Raise the vehicle and support it securely on jackstands. Remove the under-vehicle splash shield.
3   Remove the three nuts that attach the

15.3 Remove the converter-to-exhaust pipe nuts

15.4 Three-way catalytic converter bracket nuts

15.10 Secondary (lower) catalytic converter details

1	Converter-to-muffler nuts	3	Converter support bolts
2	Secondary converter-to-warm-up converter nuts	4	Secondary converter

16.3 To remove the EVAP purge solenoid, disconnect the retaining clip (A), electrical connector (B), and the inlet and outlet quick-connect fittings (C) - 2015 and earlier 1.4L engine shown, 1.8L and later model 1.4L engine similar

front portion of the exhaust pipe (secondary converter) to the warm-up catalytic converter (see illustration).

Caution: *Discard the nuts and obtain new ones for installation.*

Note: *Prior to unscrewing the nuts, apply penetrating oil to them and allow it to soak in awhile.*

4   Remove the two converter bracket nuts (see illustration).

5   Remove the catalytic converter. If necessary, support the exhaust pipe (secondary converter) and unbolt the support bracket to reposition the pipe slightly.

6   Remove and discard the old flange gaskets.

7   Installation is the reverse of removal. Use new gaskets at both mounting flanges, a new V-clamp and new converter-to-exhaust pipe nuts. Coat the threads of the nuts and bolt with anti-seize compound to facilitate future removal. Tighten the fasteners to the torque values listed in this Chapter's Specifications.

Secondary (lower) converter

8   Raise the front of the vehicle and sup-

port it securely on jackstands. Apply penetrating oil to all of the flange nuts and allow it to soak in awhile.

9   Remove the downstream oxygen sensor (see Section 12).

10   Remove the nuts securing the front portion of the exhaust system (secondary converter) to the muffler (see illustration).

11   Remove the secondary converter-to-warm-up converter nuts.

Caution: *Discard all nuts and obtain new ones for installation.*

12   Remove the secondary converter support bolts and remove the converter/front exhaust pipe.

13   Installation is the reverse of removal. Be sure to use new gaskets and nuts, tightening the nuts to the torque listed in this Chapter's Specifications.

1.8L models

14   The catalytic converter is integrated into the exhaust manifold and cannot be serviced separately. To remove or replace the catalytic converter, see Chapter 2A.

16   Evaporative Emissions Control (EVAP) system - component replacement

EVAP canister purge solenoid

1   Turn the ignition key to OFF.

2   Locate the EVAP canister purge solenoid. It's located on the intake manifold.

3   Disconnect the canister purge solenoid electrical connector (see illustration).

4   Disconnect the inlet and outlet purge line fittings from the canister purge solenoid. Cap the lines to prevent dirt, dust and moisture from entering the EVAP system while the lines are open.

5   Slide the canister purge solenoid from its mounting tab.

6   Installation is the reverse of removal.

EVAP canister vent solenoid

7   Raise the rear of the vehicle and support it securely on jackstands.

8   Remove the EVAP canister (see Steps 12 through 16).

16.9 Disconnect this connector at the canister vent solenoid

16.14 Use a screwdriver to push in and release the hose connectors (A) and disconnect the electrical connector (B)

16.21 Location of the fuel tank pressure sensor - 1.4L models

17.2 To remove the PCV hose, move the retaining clip to the unlocked postion and pull off the hose

17.3 Squeeze the retainer and disconnect the PCV hose from the turbocharger

9   Disconnect the electrical connector at the EVAP canister vent solenoid (see illustration).
10   Remove the vent solenoid from the canister by rotating it counterclockwise.
11   Installation is the reverse of removal. When the solenoid is reinserted and rotated, the connector should point sideways.

EVAP canister

12   Raise the rear of the vehicle and support it securely on jackstands.
13   Lower the fuel tank (see Chapter 4) until the EVAP canister is accessible.
Warning: *If the fuel tank is more than half full, drain fuel from the tank until it is less than half full (see Chapter 4).*
14   Disconnect the hoses from the EVAP canister (see illustration).
Note: *For information on how to disconnect the quick-connect fittings, refer to Chapter 4 .*
15   On 1.8L models, disconnect the electrical connector from the fuel tank pressure sensor.
16   Unclip the canister from its mounting bracket.

17   Installation is the reverse of removal.

Fuel tank pressure sensor

18   Raise the vehicle and support it securely on jackstands.
19   Remove the fuel tank (see Chapter 4).

1.4L models

20   Disconnect the electrical connector from the fuel tank pressure sensor.
21   The sensor is mounted to the fuel pump module (see illustration) by rubber grommets. Rock it out of the module cover using two screwdrivers to pry under the sensor.
22   Installation is the reverse of removal.

1.8L models

23   Disconnect the electrical connector from the fuel tank pressure sensor.
24   The sensor is mounted to the EVAP canister by rubber grommets. Rock it out of the canister using two screwdrivers to pry under the sensor.
25   Installation is the reverse of removal.

17 Positive Crankcase Ventilation (PCV) system - component replacement

PCV hose

1   Remove the engine cover, if equipped.
2   Disconnect the hose from the intake manifold (see illustration).
3   On 2015 and earlier 1.4L models, disconnect the vacuum lines from the charge air bypass and wastegate actuator, then disconnect the PCV hose from the turbocharger (see illustration) and remove the hose and vacuum lines as an assembly.
4   On 2016 and later 1.4L engines, remove the PCV valve retaining bolt and pull the valve from the valve cover, then disconnect the PCV tube quick-connect fitting and remove the PCV assembly.
Note: *The PCV system components have tamper-proof connections and cannot be disassembled. The fresh air inlet duct is connected*

19.2 Location of the intake air pressure and temperature sensor

20.4 Disconnect the electircal connector from the fuel pressure sensor

to the PCV tube with a tamper-proof connection and all the components must be replaced as an assembly once they are removed.

5   On 1.8L models, disconnect the hose from the valve cover.

6   Installation is the reverse of removal.

Crankcase vent housing

7   Remove the valve cover (see Chapter 2A). The vent housing is an integral component of the valve cover and it cannot be replaced separately.

8   Installation is the reverse of removal.

18   Secondary Air Injection (AIR) system (1.8L models) - general information and pump removal and installation

General information

1   The Secondary Air Injection system assists with extra reduction of emissions during cold starts. It consists of an AIR pump mounted to the air injection assembly that conducts fresh air into the cylinder head when the PCM initiates operation of the AIR pump relay and AIR shut-off valve relay. The shut-off valve is part of an assembly that includes a system check valve and pipe assembly mounted to the cylinder head, covered by the exhaust manifold heat shield. Beyond a visual inspection of the pipe and simple circuit checks of the connector in the AIR system, checking the AIR system is best performed with a scan tool. The AIR solenoid/shut-off/pressure sensor must be replaced as an assembly only.

Secondary Air Injection pump - removal and installation

Note: The Secondary Air Injection pump is located at the right front corner of the cylinder head.

2   Disconnect the cable from the negative terminal of the battery (see Chapter 5).

3   Detach the hoses from the pump and the air filter housing.

4   Disconnect the electrical connector from the pump.

5   Remove the pump mounting nut and bolts and detach the pump from the engine.

6   Installation is the reverse of the removal procedure.

19   Intake air pressure and temperature sensor (1.4L models) - replacement

1   Located in the charge air cooler outlet pipe near the left end of the cylinder head, this four-wire sensor measures pressure and temperature between the throttle body and the turbocharger.

2   Turn the ignition key to OFF. Depress the retaining tab and disconnect the electrical connector from the sensor, then remove the retaining screw (see illustration).

3   Remove the sensor from the pipe by prying it up with a screwdriver.

4   Installation is the reverse of removal. Lubricate the O-ring with a light coating of clean engine oil prior to installation.

20   Fuel pressure sensor - replacement

Warning: This procedure will result in some fuel spillage. Read the Warning in Chapter 4, Section 1 .

Note: The fuel pressure sensor is located in the fuel line under the vehicle, near the right-front corner of the fuel tank.

1   Disconnect the cable from the negative terminal of the battery (see Chapter 5).

2   Relieve the fuel system pressure (see Chapter 4).

3   Raise the vehicle and support it securely on jackstands.

4   Disconnect the electrical connector from the fuel pressure sensor (see illustration).

5   Place a drain pan under the sensor, then unscrew the sensor from the fuel line.

6   Install a new O-ring, then install the fuel pressure sensor and tighten it securely. Reconnect the electrical connector.

7   Reconnect the battery cable. Upon starting the vehicle, immediately inspect for fuel leaks.

21   Camshaft Position (CMP) Actuator system - description and component replacement

Description

1   These models are equipped with the Camshaft Position (CMP) Actuator System. By changing camshaft timing (angle) in relation to the crankshaft, this electro-hydraulic system opens the valves earlier or later depending on operating conditions, improving engine performance, fuel economy, and lowering emissions.

2   The CMP Actuator system consists of the CMP sensors, the Powertrain Control Module (PCM), the CMP actuator solenoids and the CMP actuators. The actuators are specially designed camshaft sprockets with oil passages inside them.

3   In response to signals from the CMP sensors, the PCM signals the CMP actuator solenoids, that controls the amount of engine oil flow to the CMP actuators. The pressurized engine oil unseats a locking pin inside each actuator, then flows through a vane and rotor assembly. Each actuator has two oil passages: one to advance the camshaft and one to retard it. If the oil is directed through the advance passage, the vane and rotor assembly advances that camshaft in relation to the crankshaft position; if the oil is directed through the retard passage, the assembly retards the cam.

21.5 Insert a small screwdriver into the slots on the harness cover to release the locking clips

21.7 Remove the camshaft actuator position solenoid valve bolts, then rotate them in the direction of the arrows

1   *Intake actuator solenoid valve and rotation direction*
2   *Exhaust actuator solenoid valve and rotation direction*
3   *Solenoid valve electrical connectors*
4   *Mounting bolts*

Component replacement

CMP sensor(s)

4   See Section 5 for this procedure.

CMP actuator solenoid valves

2015 and earlier 1.4L engine

Note: *There are two CMP actuator solenoids; this procedure applies to both.*

5   Unclip the wiring harness cover from the valve cover (see illustration).

6   Disconnect the electrical connectors from the camshaft position actuator solenoid valves.

7   Remove the actuator solenoid valve mounting bolts, then rotate the intake actuator solenoid valve counterclockwise and the exhaust actuator solenoid valve clockwise until the intake solenoid valve electrical connector is at approximately the 6:30 o'clock position and the exhaust solenoid valve electrical connector is in approximately the 5:30 o'clock position (see illustration).

Caution: *The actuator position solenoid valves must be pulled straight out. If the solenoid valve is cocked or becomes stuck*

while pulling it out, the valve can be easily damaged.

8   Remove both solenoid valves from the front of the timing chain cover.

9   Inspect the solenoid valve O-ring(s) and replace if necessary.

10   Installation is the reverse of removal. Tighten the CMP actuator solenoid valve mounting bolt(s) to the torque listed in this Chapter's Specifications.

2016 and later 1.4L engine

Note: *The CMP actuator solenoids valves are located on front corners of the valve cover.*

11   Remove the oil filler cap and engine cover fasteners. Lift the engine cover and valve cover insulator up and off of the valve cover, then reinstall the oil filler cap. It may be necessary to remove the cover and insulator separately.

12   Disconnect the electrical connector from the camshaft position actuator solenoids.

13   Remove the CMP actuator solenoid mounting screws and pull the actuator out of the valve cover.

14   Inspect the actuator O-rings and replace them if they are damaged.

15   Installation is the reverse of removal. Be sure to tighten the mounting screws to the torque listed in this Chapter's Specifications.

1.8L engine

Note: *There are two CMP actuator solenoids, one for each camshaft, located in the sides of the cylinder head toward the front; this procedure applies to both.*

16   Remove the engine cover, if equipped.

17   Disconnect the electrical connector from the CMP actuator solenoid valve(s).

18   Remove the solenoid valve mounting bolt.

19   Remove the solenoid(s) from the cylinder head.

20   Inspect the CMP actuator solenoid O-ring(s) and replace if necessary.

21   Installation is the reverse of removal. Tighten the CMP actuator solenoid(s) mounting bolt(s) to the torque listed in this Chapter's Specifications.

CMP actuators

22   See Chapter 2A, Section 8 or 9 for this procedure.

Chapter 7 Part A
Manual transaxle

Contents

Specifications

General

Transaxle oil type	See Chapter 1
Transaxle oil capacity	See Chapter 1

Torque specifications

Ft-lbs (unless otherwise indicated)   **Nm**

Note: One foot-pound (ft-lb) of torque is equivalent to 12 inch-pounds (in-lbs) of torque. Torque values below approximately 15 ft-lbs are expressed in inch-pounds, because most foot-pound torque wrenches are not accurate at these smaller values.

	Ft-lbs	Nm
Carrier flange bolts (left side driveaxle)		
Step 1	15	20
Step 2	Tighten an additional 45-degrees	
Powertrain mounts	See Chapter 2A	
Shifter housing-to-floor bolts	71 in-lbs	8
Shift cable bracket-to-transaxle bolts	15	20
Transaxle-to-engine mounting bolts		
2015 and earlier models	44	60
2016 and later models		
Step 1	89 in-lbs	10
Step 2	43	58
Transaxle-to-engine lower mounting through bolt/nut	30	40

1   General Information

1   The vehicles covered by this manual are equipped with either a 6-speed manual or a 6-speed automatic transaxle. This Part of Chapter 7 contains information on the manual transaxle. All models use the M32-6 transaxle. Service procedures for the automatic transaxle are contained in Chapter 7B.

2   Because of the complexity of the manual transaxle and the specialized equipment necessary to perform most service operations, this Chapter contains only those procedures related to general diagnosis, adjustment and removal and installation procedures.

3   If the transaxle requires major repair work, it should be left to a dealer service department or an automotive or transmission repair shop. Once properly diagnosed, however, you can remove and install the transaxle yourself and save the expense, and have the repair work done by a transmission shop.

2   Back-up light switch - replacement

1   The back-up light switch is located midway up on the front side of the transaxle.

2   Disconnect the electrical connector from the back-up light switch.

3   Unscrew the switch from the case and remove the gasket. Discard the gasket.

Note: *To avoid rounding off the corners of the switch, use a socket or box-end wrench to remove the switch, not an open-end wrench.*

4   Clean the threads, apply sealant, then install a new gasket and screw in the switch, tightening it securely.

5   Reconnect the electrical connector.

6   Check the operation of the back-up lights.

3   Shift knob and shift cables - removal, installation and adjustment

Warning: *The models covered by this manual are equipped with Supplemental Restraint systems (SRS), more commonly known as airbags. Always disarm the airbag system before working in the vicinity of any airbag system component to avoid the possibility of accidental deployment of the airbag, which could cause personal injury (see Chapter 12). Do not use a memory saving device to preserve the PCM's memory when working on or near airbag system components.*

Shift knob

1   Using a small screwdriver or trim tool, disengage the shift boot retainers at the front edge of the boot, then slide the boot forward to disengage the retainers at the rear edge of the boot and lift the boot up.

2   Depress the two tabs below the retaining ring on the shift lever while lifting up on the retaining ring until the retaining ring is freed.

3   Once the retaining ring is loose, depress and lift the reverse lock-out tab at the base of the shifter until it is disengaged.

4   Remove the shift knob, reverse lock-out unit and boot as an assembly from the shift lever.

5   Lift the shift knob-to-reverse lock-out unit retaining tab and separate the knob from the lock-out unit.

6   Installation is the reverse of removal.

Shift cables

7   Disconnect the negative battery cable (see Chapter 5).

8   Remove the floor center console side trim panels and shifter bezel (see Chapter 11 Section 21).

9   Working inside the passenger compartment, lift up the shifter boot (see Steps 1 and 2).

10   Disconnect the rear air outlet duct (see illustration) from the side of the instrument panel.

11   Lift up the cable-retaining clips at the rear of the shifter assembly and release the cable ends from the shifter.

12   Remove the battery and battery tray (see Chapter 5).

13   Remove the driver's side knee bolster (see Chapter 11).

14   Mark each cable end as to the arm it connects to, then pop the shift cable ends from the transaxle shift arm and twist the cables out of their mounting bracket.

15   Pull back the carpeting and pull the cables through the grommet in the firewall.

16   Installation is the reverse of the removal procedure. Adjust the cables if necessary.

Cable adjustment

17   Lift up the cable retaining clips without disconnecting them, then release the internal cable on each cable.

18   Insert a 5 mm Allen wrench or drill bit through the hole in the shift lever and into the shifter base to lock it in place.

19   Working at the transaxle end of the cables,

press the block in at the base of the shift control housing while pushing the select lever backwards. While applying pressure on the select lever, push the block towards the control housing until both levers are locked in place.

20   Working inside the vehicle, snap the cable locking tabs down at the rear of the shifter to secure each cable. Remove the 5 mm Allen wrench or drill bit from the shift lever.

21   Working at the transaxle, push the select lever backwards slightly while pulling the block out.

Note: *When releasing the block, a snapping sound should be heard and felt.*

22   Check for proper shifting of the transaxle.

23   Remaining installation is the reverse of removal.

4   Driveaxle oil seals - replacement

1   Lubricant leaks occasionally occur due to wear of the driveaxle oil seals. Replacement of these seals is relatively easy, since the repairs can be performed without removing the transaxle from the vehicle.

2   The driveaxle oil seals are located in either sides of the transaxle, where the inner Constant Velocity (CV) joints are splined into the differential. If leakage at the seal is suspected, raise the vehicle and support it securely on jackstands. If the seal is leaking, fluid will be found on the side of the transaxle.

3   Drain the transaxle lubricant (see Chapter 1).

4   Remove the driveaxle (see Chapter 8). If you're replacing the right side driveaxle seal, also remove the intermediate shaft.

Right side seal

5   On the right side seal, carefully pry the oil seal out of the transaxle bore with a screwdriver or prybar.

6   If the oil seal cannot be removed with a screwdriver or prybar, a special oil seal removal tool (available at auto parts stores) will be required.

3.10 Push down on the adapter bellows then pull the adapter out

Left side seal

7   Unbolt the carrier flange and discard the four bolts. Replace the bolts with new ones.

8   Use a screwdriver or prybar to carefully pry the oil seal out of the carrier flange.

9   Use a small screwdriver to remove the O-ring from the groove on the rear of the carrier flange.

All models

10   Using a seal driver or a large deep socket as a drift, install the new oil seal. Drive it into the bore squarely until it is flush with the transaxle case or carrier flange. Lubricate the lip of the new seal with multi-purpose grease.

11   On the left side seal, install a new O-ring into the groove in the back side of the carrier, lubricate the O-ring with multi-purpose grease and install the carrier flange on to the transaxle then tighten the new carrier flange bolts to the torque listed in this Chapter's Specifications.

12   Install the driveaxle (see Chapter 8). Be careful not to damage the lip of the new seal.

13   Refill the transaxle with the proper lubricant (see Chapter 1).

---

5   Manual transaxle - removal and installation

Note: *The vehicle must be raised and safely supported so that it is high enough to allow the transaxle to come out the bottom of the engine compartment. Moreover, the vehicle must be supported by the uni-body and not the subframe, as subframe removal is necessary for transaxle removal. Make sure you have the right equipment before beginning.*

Note: *With all the work done to remove the transaxle, this is the best time to inspect and/ or replace the clutch assembly (see Chapter 8).*

Removal

1   Disconnect the negative battery cable (see Chapter 5).

2   On 2015 and earlier models, remove the battery and battery tray (see Chapter 5).

3   Disconnect the electrical connector for the back-up light switch, then disconnect the wire harness from the transaxle (see Section 2).

4   On 2016 and later 1.4L engines, remove the charge air cooler inlet pipe (see Chapter 4).

5   Remove the lower splash shield and both inner fender splash shields (see Chapter 11).

6   Drain some brake fluid from the clutch master cylinder reservoir, then remove the clutch hydraulic fitting at the transaxle. Plug the fittings to prevent fluid loss and contamination.

7   Remove the three upper transaxle-to-engine bolts.

8   Loosen the front wheel lug nuts and the driveaxle/hub nuts (see Chapter 8).

9   Raise the vehicle and support it securely on jackstands placed under the unibody frame rails (see Chapter 10, Section 20 for jackstand placement). Drain the transaxle lubricant (see Chapter 1).

10   With the engine supported from above by an engine support fixture or an engine hoist, remove the upper rear transaxle support, then mark the position of the left transaxle mount and remove it from the vehicle (see Chapter 2A).

Note: *If an engine support fixture is to be used, make sure it is of the type that can be adjusted up and down after the support chain(s) have been attached to the engine.*

11   Support the radiator/condenser assembly by fastening it to the upper radiator support with heavy-duty plastic tie-wraps.

12   Remove both driveaxles (see Chapter 8).

13   Support the transaxle with a transmission jack. Secure the transaxle to the jack with straps or chains so it doesn't fall off during removal.

14   Remove the starter motor (see Chapter 5).

15   Remove the subframe (see Chapter 10).

16   Remove the lower bolts that attach the transaxle to the engine.

17   Lower the engine slightly using the engine hoist or support fixture, enough to let the transaxle clear the inner fender unibody structure.

18   Make a final check that all wires, hoses, brackets and mounts have been disconnected from the transaxle, then slide the transaxle jack toward the side of the vehicle until the transaxle input shaft is clear of the engine. Make sure you keep the transaxle level as you do this.

Installation

19   Installation of the transaxle is a reversal of the removal procedure, but note the following points:

a) *Apply a thin film of high-temperature grease to the splines of the transaxle input shaft.*

b) *Tighten the transaxle mounting bolts to the torque listed in this Chapter's Specifications.*

c) *Tighten the driveaxle/hub nuts to the torque value listed in the Chapter 8 Specifications.*

d) *Tighten the subframe mounting bolts to the torque values listed in the Chapter 10 Specifications.*

e) *Tighten the wheel lug nuts to the torque listed in the Chapter 1 Specifications.*

f) *Fill the transaxle with the correct type and amount of manual transmission lubricant as described in Chapter 1.*

---

6   Manual transaxle overhaul - general information

1   Overhauling a manual transaxle is a difficult job for the do-it-yourselfer. It involves the disassembly and reassembly of many small parts. Numerous clearances must be precisely measured and, if necessary, changed with select-fit spacers and snap-rings. As a result, if transaxle problems arise, it can be removed and installed by a competent do-it-yourselfer, but overhaul should be left to a transmission repair shop. Rebuilt transaxles may be available - check with your dealer parts department and auto parts stores. At any rate, the time and money involved in an overhaul is almost sure to exceed the cost of a rebuilt unit.

2   Nevertheless, it's not impossible for an inexperienced mechanic to rebuild a transaxle if the special tools are available and the job is done in a deliberate step-by-step manner so nothing is overlooked.

3   The tools necessary for an overhaul include internal and external snap-ring pliers, a bearing puller, a slide hammer, a set of pin punches, a dial indicator and possibly a hydraulic press. In addition, a large, sturdy workbench and a vise or transaxle stand will be required.

4   During disassembly of the transaxle, make careful notes of how each piece comes off, where it fits in relation to other pieces and what holds it in place.

5   Before taking the transaxle apart for repair, it will help if you have some idea what area of the transaxle is malfunctioning. Certain problems can be closely tied to specific areas in the transaxle, which can make component examination and replacement easier. Refer to the Troubleshooting section at the front of this manual for information regarding possible sources of trouble.

Notes

Chapter 7 Part B
Automatic transaxle

Contents

Specifications

General
Lubricant type and capacity.. See Chapter 1

Torque specifications

Ft-lbs (unless otherwise indicated) **Nm**

Note: *One foot-pound (ft-lb) of torque is equivalent to 12 inch-pounds (in-lbs) of torque. Torque values below approximately 15 ft-lbs are expressed in inch-pounds, because most foot-pound torque wrenches are not accurate at these smaller values.*

	Ft-lbs	Nm
Torque converter-to-driveplate bolts	44	60
Transaxle-to-engine bolts		
2015 and earlier models		
Top three bolts	43	58
Front side bolt	52	70
2016 and later models	43	58
Engine-to-transaxle bolts/nuts		
2015 and earlier models		
Back side bolt	52	70
Lower three bolts and nut	33	45
2016 and later models	43	58
Transaxle oil cooler line nut	71 in-lbs	8
Transaxle mount fasteners	See Chapter 2A	

1   General Information

1   All information on the 6T30/6T40 automatic transaxle is included in this Part of Chapter 7. Information for the manual transaxle can be found in Chapter 7A.

2   Because of the complexity of the automatic transaxles and the specialized equipment necessary to perform most service operations, this Chapter contains only those procedures related to general diagnosis, adjustment and removal and installation procedures.

3   If the transaxle requires major repair work, it should be left to a dealer service department or an automotive or transmission repair shop. Once properly diagnosed, however, you can remove and install the transaxle yourself and save the expense, and have the repair work done by a transmission shop.

2   Diagnosis - general

1   Automatic transaxle malfunctions may be caused by five general conditions:

a) *Poor engine performance*
b) *Improper adjustments*
c) *Hydraulic malfunctions*
d) *Mechanical malfunctions*
e) *Malfunctions in the computer or its signal network*

2   Diagnosis of these problems should always begin with a check of the easily repaired items: fluid level and condition (see Chapter 1), shift cable adjustment and shift lever installation. Next, perform a road test to determine if the problem has been corrected or if more diagnosis is necessary. If the problem persists after the preliminary tests and corrections are complete, additional diagnosis should be performed by a dealer service department or other qualified transmission repair shop. Refer to the Troubleshooting section at the front of this manual for information on symptoms of transaxle problems.

Preliminary checks

3   Drive the vehicle to warm the transaxle to normal operating temperature.

4   Check the fluid level as described in Chapter 1:

a) *If the fluid level is unusually low, add enough fluid to bring it up to the proper level, then check for external leaks (see following).*
b) *If the fluid level is abnormally high, drain off the excess, and then check the drained fluid for contamination by coolant. The presence of engine coolant in the automatic transmission fluid indicates that a failure has occurred in the internal radiator oil cooler walls that separate the coolant from the transmission fluid (see Chapter 3).*
c) *If the fluid is foaming, drain it and refill the transaxle, then check for coolant in the fluid, or a high fluid level.*

5   Check for the presence of Diagnostic Trouble Codes (see Chapter 6).

Note: *If the engine is malfunctioning, do not proceed with the preliminary checks until repairs have been made and the engine runs normally.*

6   Check and adjust the shift cable, if necessary (see Section 4).

7   If hard shifting is experienced, inspect the shift cable under the center console and at the shift lever on the transaxle (see Section 4).

Fluid leak diagnosis

8   Most fluid leaks are easy to locate visually. Repair usually consists of replacing a seal or gasket. If a leak is difficult to find, the following procedure may help.

9   Identify the fluid. Make sure it's transmission fluid and not engine oil or brake fluid (automatic transmission fluid in these vehicles is a deep red color).

10   Try to pinpoint the source of the leak. Drive the vehicle several miles, then park it over a large sheet of cardboard. After a minute or two, you should be able to locate the leak by determining the source of the fluid dripping onto the cardboard.

11   Make a careful visual inspection of the suspected component and the area immediately around it. Pay particular attention to gasket mating surfaces. A mirror is often helpful for finding leaks in areas that are hard to see.

12   If the leak still cannot be found, clean the suspected area thoroughly with a degreaser or solvent, then dry it thoroughly.

13   Drive the vehicle for several miles at normal operating temperature and varying speeds. After driving the vehicle, visually inspect the suspected component again.

14   Once the leak has been located, the cause must be determined before it can be properly repaired. If a gasket is replaced but the sealing flange is bent, the new gasket will not stop the leak. The bent flange must be straightened.

15   Before attempting to repair a leak, check to make sure that the following conditions are corrected or they may cause another leak.

Note: *Some of the following conditions cannot be fixed without highly specialized tools and expertise. Such problems must be referred to a qualified transmission shop or a dealer service department.*

Seal leaks

16   If a transaxle seal is leaking, the fluid level may be too high, the vent may be plugged, the seal bore may be damaged, the seal itself may be damaged or improperly installed, the surface of the shaft protruding through the seal may be damaged or a loose bearing may be causing excessive shaft movement.

17   Periodically check the area around the sensors for leakage. If transmission fluid is evident, check the seals for damage.

Case leaks

18   If the case itself appears to be leaking, the casting is porous and will have to be repaired or replaced.

19   Make sure the oil cooler hose fittings are tight and in good condition.

3   Driveaxle oil seals - replacement

Note: *This procedure requires special tools. Read through the entire procedure before beginning. If the special tools can't be obtained (or suitable equivalents can't be fabricated), have the procedure performed at a dealer service department or other qualified repair shop.*

1   Oil leaks can occur due to wear of the driveaxle oil seals. Replacement of these seals is relatively easy, since the repairs can be performed without removing the transaxle from the vehicle.

2   The driveaxle oil seals are located in the sides of the transaxle, where the driveaxles are attached. If leakage at the seal is suspected, raise the vehicle and support it securely on jackstands. If the seal is leaking, fluid will be found on the sides of the transaxle.

3   Remove the driveaxle (see Chapter 8).

Left-side seal

4   Remove the snap-ring on the stub shaft and discard it (a new one must be used on installation).

5   Use a screwdriver or seal removal tool to carefully pry the oil seal out of the transaxle bore (see illustration).

6   Compare the old seal to the new one to be sure it's the correct one.

3.5 Using a large screwdriver or seal removal tool, carefully pry the oil seal out of the transaxle (typical)

3.8 Using a seal installer or a large deep socket as a drift, drive the new seal squarely into the bore and make sure that it's seated to the original depth (typical)

4.4 Instrument panel left-side support brace mounting bolt locations

4.6 Shift cable and bracket details
A   *Shift cable bracket*
B   *Shift cable end*

7   Coat the outside and inside diameters of the new seal with a small amount of transmission fluid.

8   Using a seal installation tool, install the new oil seal (see illustration). Drive it into the bore squarely and make sure it's seated to the original depth.

9   Install a new snap-ring on the stub shaft, then install the driveaxle (see Chapter 8).

Caution: The *seal can be easily damaged by the splines of the driveaxle.*

10   The remainder of installation is the reverse of removal. Check the transaxle fluid level, adding as necessary (see Chapter 1).

Right-side seal

11   Remove the driveaxle and, on models so equipped, the intermediate shaft (see Chapter 8, Section 8).

12   Use a screwdriver or seal removal tool to carefully pry the oil seal out of the transaxle bore (see illustration 3.5).

13   Coat the outside and inside diameters of the new seal with a small amount of transmission fluid.

14   Using a seal installation tool, install the new oil seal. Drive it into the bore squarely and make sure it's seated to the original depth.

15   Install the intermediate shaft, if equipped, and the driveaxle (see Chapter 8).

Caution: *The seal can be easily damaged by the splines of the driveaxle or intermediate shaft.*

16   The remainder of installation is the reverse of removal. Check the transaxle fluid level, adding as necessary (see Chapter 1).

---

4   Shift cable - removal, installation and adjustment

Warning: *The models covered by this manual are equipped with a Supplemental Restraint*

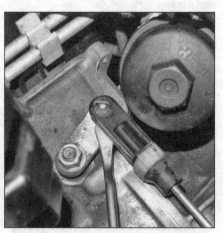

4.9 Use a flat-bladed tool to separate the shift cable from the shift lever on the transaxle

System (SRS), more commonly known as air-bags. Always disarm the airbag system before working in the vicinity of any airbag system component to avoid the possibility of accidental deployment of the airbag, which could cause personal injury (see Chapter 12).

Removal

1   In the event of hard shifting, disconnect the cable at the transaxle (see Steps 10 and 11) and operate the shifter from the driver's seat. If the shift lever moves smoothly through all positions with the cable disconnected, then the cable should be adjusted as described at the end of this Section. To remove and install the shift cable, perform the following:

2   Block the rear wheels, apply the parking brake and shift the transmission into Neutral.

3   Remove the floor center console left-side trim panel (see Chapter 11).

4   Remove the instrument panel left-side support brace bolts and brace (see illustration).

4.10 To remove the shift cable from its bracket at the transaxle, squeeze the tabs and pull the cable up from the bracket

5   Also free the driver's side carpet and push it aside for access to the cable grommet where the cable passes through the firewall.

6   Use a flat-blade screwdriver and pry the shift cable end from the shift lever pin (see illustration).

7   Squeeze the U-shaped shift cable retaining clip and slide it out of the bracket, then detach the cable from the bracket.

8   Open the hood.

9   Disconnect the shift cable end from the shift lever on the transaxle (see illustration).

10   Use needle-nose pliers to squeeze the clip on the shift cable and pull it up from its bracket (see illustration).

11   Trace the shift cable to the engine-compartment firewall, then pry the large rubber cable grommet from the firewall.

12   Carefully remove the shift cable by pulling it through the hole in the firewall from the engine compartment side.

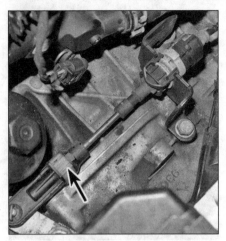

4.15 Adjustment lock tab location

5.6 Shift lever assembly mounting bolt locations – two of four bolts shown

7.15 Each transaxle cooler line is retained to the transaxle by a single nut - top line shown, other line identical

Installation

13   Installation is the reverse of removal, noting the following points:
   a) *Install the shift cable to its original path within the engine compartment and passenger cabin.*
   b) *The cable end fittings must be firmly snapped back into place onto their respective levers.*

Adjustment

14   Place the shift lever inside the car in Park. Detach the cable lock from the range select lever on the transaxle.
15   Use a small screwdriver to release the tab for the adjustment lock (see illustration).
16   Make sure there is no tension on the cable.
17   Push the white adjuster tab back into place.
18   Make sure the engine will start in the Park and Neutral positions only, and all of the gear ranges can be selected.
19   If the engine can be started in any position other than Park or Neutral, check the adjustment of the Transmission Range Switch (see Chapter 6), then adjust and check the shift cable again.

5   Shift lever - removal and installation

Warning: *The models covered by this manual are equipped with a Supplemental Restraint System (SRS), more commonly known as airbags. Always disarm the airbag system before working in the vicinity of any airbag system component to avoid the possibility of accidental deployment of the airbag, which could cause personal injury (see Chapter 12).*

1   Disconnect the cable from the negative terminal of the battery (see Chapter 5).
2   Remove the shift knob by grasping it tightly, using two hands and pulling up while twisting the knob SLIGHTLY back and forth until it is free.
3   Remove the center console (see Chapter 11).
4   Remove the shift cable end from the pin on the shift lever assembly (see Section 4).
5   Disconnect any electrical connectors to the shift lever assembly.
6   Remove the four shift lever assembly mounting bolts (see illustration) and lift the assembly out.
7   Transfer any parts as necessary if the assembly is being replaced.
8   Installation is reverse of removal. Make sure to adjust the shift cable once the shift lever has been reinstalled.

6   Transaxle Control Module (TCM) - removal and installation

1   The Transaxle Control module (TCM) is integrated into the control valve body internally in the transaxle. Diagnosis requires detailed knowledge of the transaxle's operation and construction as well as access to specialized test equipment. Because of these factors, diagnosis and repair of the Transaxle Control module (TCM) itself are beyond the scope of this manual. It is therefore essential that problems with the Transaxle Control Module (TCM) are referred to a dealer service department or other qualified repair facility for assessment and repair.

7   Automatic transaxle - removal and installation

Note: *The vehicle must be raised and supported so that it is high enough to allow the transaxle to come out the bottom of the engine compartment. Moreover, the vehicle must be supported by the uni-body and not the subframe, as subframe removal is necessary for transaxle removal.*

Removal

1   Place the vehicle in PARK with the parking brake engaged.
2   Disconnect the negative battery cable then remove the battery and battery tray (see Chapter 5).
3   Remove the under-vehicle splash shield.
4   Remove the left front inner fender splash shield and, on 2016 and later models, the front bumper (see Chapter 11).
5   Drain the cooling system (see Chapter 1).
6   Remove the upper radiator hose (see Chapter 1).
7   On 1.4L models, remove the charge air cooler outlet hose (see Chapter 4).
8   Clearly label and unplug all transaxle electrical connectors. Remove any related brackets as necessary.
9   Disconnect the shift cable from the shift lever at the transaxle (see Section 4).
10   Disconnect the Vehicle Speed Sensor (VSS) sensor (see Chapter 6).
11   Loosen the front wheel lug nuts.
12   Raise the vehicle and support it securely on jackstands.
13   Support the radiator/condenser assembly by fastening it to the upper radiator support with heavy-duty plastic tie-wraps.
14   Drain the transaxle fluid (see Chapter 1), then remove both driveaxles (see Chapter 8).
15   Remove the transaxle oil cooler lines (from the top and side of the transaxle) by removing the retaining nut, then pulling the line straight out to avoid damaging any seals (see illustration).
16   On 2016 and later models, remove the ECM (see Chapter 6), then remove the ECM mounting bracket bolts and the bracket.
17   Support the engine (from above only) using an engine hoist or engine support fixture (see Chapter 2B).
18   Remove the upper engine-to-transaxle bolts and stud.
19   Disconnect the ABS wheel speed sensor harnesses from the subframe, then remove the subframe (see Chapter 10).

7.21 Working through the starter opening, mark the relationship of the torque converter to the driveplate, then remove the torque converter-to-driveplate bolts

20   Support the transaxle with a transmission jack. Secure the transaxle to the jack with straps or chains so it doesn't fall off during removal.
21   Remove the starter (see Chapter 5).
22   Mark the relationship of the torque converter to the driveplate so they can be installed in the same relative position, then remove the torque converter-to-driveplate bolts (see illustration). Turn the crankshaft.
23   Push the torque converter into the bellhousing so it doesn't stay with the engine when the transaxle is removed.
24   Remove the lower transaxle-to-engine bolts.
25   Remove the driver's side powertrain mount (see Chapter 2A). At the left end of the transaxle, remove the mount-to-transaxle bolts. On the front and rear mounts, remove the through-bolts.
26   Make a final check that all wires, hoses, brackets and mounts have been disconnected from the transaxle. Slide the transaxle jack toward the side of the vehicle until the transaxle is clear of the engine locating dowels, then lower it. Keep the transaxle level as you do this.

Installation

27   Installation is the reverse of removal, noting the following points:
a)   *As the torque converter is reinstalled, ensure that the drive tangs at the center of the torque converter hub engage with the recesses in the automatic transaxle fluid pump inner gear. This can be confirmed by turning the torque converter while pushing it towards the transaxle. If it isn't fully engaged, it will clunk into place.*
b)   *When installing the transaxle, make sure the match-marks you made on the torque converter and driveplate line up.*
c)   *Install all of the driveplate-to-torque converter bolts before tightening any of them.*

d)   *Tighten the driveplate-to-torque converter bolts to the torque listed in this Chapter's Specifications.*
e)   *Tighten the transaxle mounting bolts to the torque listed in this Chapter's Specifications.*
f)   *Tighten the driveaxle/hub nuts to the torque value listed in the Chapter 8 Specifications.*
g)   *Tighten the wheel lug nuts to the torque listed in the Chapter 1 Specifications.*
h)   *Fill the transaxle with the correct type and amount of automatic transmission fluid as described in Chapter 1.*
i)   *Shift transaxle into all gear positions to confirm shift cable adjustment. Readjust if necessary (see Section 4).*

8   Automatic transaxle overhaul - general information

1   In the event of a problem occurring, it will be necessary to establish whether the fault is electrical, mechanical or hydraulic in nature, before any repair work can be considered. Diagnosis requires detailed knowledge of the transaxle's operation and construction as well as access to specialized test equipment. Because of these factors, diagnosis and repair of the transaxle itself are beyond the scope of this manual. It is therefore essential that problems with the automatic transaxle are referred to a dealer service department or other qualified repair facility for assessment.
2   Note that a faulty transaxle should not be removed before the vehicle has been diagnosed by a knowledgeable technician equipped with the proper tools, as troubleshooting must be performed with the transaxle installed in the vehicle.

Notes

Chapter 8
Clutch and driveaxles

Contents

Specifications

Clutch fluid type .... See Chapter 1

Torque specifications   Ft-lbs (unless otherwise indicated)   Nm

Note: *One foot-pound (ft-lb) of torque is equivalent to 12 inch-pounds (in-lbs) of torque. Torque values below approximately 15 ft-lbs are expressed in inch-pounds, because most foot-pound torque wrenches are not accurate at these smaller values.*

	Ft-lbs	Nm
Clutch pressure plate-to-flywheel bolts*		
2015 and earlier models	21	28
2016 and later models	18	25
Clutch master cylinder nuts (2015 and earlier models)	159 in-lbs	18
Clutch release cylinder/actuator bolts		
2015 and earlier models	53 in-lbs	6
2016 and later models	44 in-lbs	5
Pedal assembly mounting bolts	16	22
Driveaxle/hub nut*		
Step 1	111	150
Step 2	Loosen the nut 45-degrees (1/8 turn)	
Step 3	184	250
Intermediate shaft bearing bolt	16	22
Intermediate shaft bracket bolts	43	58
Wheel lug nuts	See Chapter 1	

Fastener(s) must be replaced.

1   General Information

1   The information in this Chapter deals with the components that transmit power to the front wheels, except for the transaxle, which is dealt with in Chapters 7A and 7B. For the purposes of this Chapter, these components are grouped into two categories: clutch and driveaxles. Separate Sections within this Chapter offer general descriptions and checking procedures for both groups.

2   Since nearly all the procedures covered in this Chapter involve working under the vehicle, make sure it's securely supported on sturdy jackstands or on a hoist where the vehicle can be easily raised and lowered.

2   Clutch - description and check

1   All vehicles with a manual transaxle have a single dry plate, diaphragm-spring type clutch. The clutch disc has a splined hub that allows it to slide along the splines of the transaxle input shaft. The clutch and pressure plate are held in contact by spring pressure exerted by the diaphragm in the pressure plate.

2   The clutch release system is operated by hydraulic pressure. The hydraulic release system consists of the clutch pedal, a master cylinder and a shared common reservoir with the brake master cylinder, a release (or slave) cylinder and the hydraulic line connecting the two components. The release cylinder and release bearing are integral parts of a single assembly, which is installed concentric to the input shaft and is bolted to the transaxle.

3   When the clutch pedal is depressed, a pushrod pushes against brake fluid inside the master cylinder, applying hydraulic pressure to the release cylinder, which pushes the release bearing against the diaphragm fingers of the clutch pressure plate.

4   Unless you're replacing components with obvious damage, do these preliminary checks to diagnose clutch problems:

3.8 Remove the clip securing the hydraulic line to the clutch master cylinder (typical)

a) *The first check should be of the fluid level in the master cylinder. If the fluid level is low, add fluid as necessary and inspect the hydraulic system for leaks. If the master cylinder reservoir is dry, bleed the system as described in Section 5 and recheck the clutch operation.*

b) *To check clutch spin-down time, run the engine at normal idle speed with the transaxle in Neutral (clutch pedal up - engaged). Disengage the clutch (pedal down), wait several seconds and shift the transaxle into Reverse. No grinding noise should be heard. A grinding noise would most likely indicate a bad pressure plate or clutch disc.*

c) *To check for complete clutch release, run the engine (with the parking brake applied to prevent vehicle movement) and hold the clutch pedal approximately 1/2-inch from the floor. Shift the transaxle between 1st gear and Reverse several times. If the shift is rough, component failure is indicated.*

d) *Visually inspect the pivot bushing at the top of the clutch pedal to make sure there's no binding or excessive play.*

3   Clutch master cylinder - removal and installation

2015 and earlier models
Removal

1   Under the dash on the driver's side, pull the plastic clip near the top of the clutch master cylinder pushrod to the pedal. Pull the clutch pedal upward to disengage it.

2   Working inside the engine compartment, remove as much fluid as you can from the brake master cylinder reservoir with a syringe, such as an old turkey baster (the clutch master cylinder is supplied with fluid from the brake fluid reservoir).

Warning: *If a baster is used, never again use it for the preparation of food.*

Warning: *Don't depress the brake pedal until the reservoir has been refilled, otherwise air may be introduced into the brake hydraulic system.*

3   Place rags under the fluid fittings and prepare caps or plastic bags to cover the ends of lines or fittings once they are disconnected.

Caution: *Brake fluid will damage paint. Cover all body parts and be careful not to spill fluid during this procedure.*

4   Disconnect the negative battery cable (see Chapter 5).

5   Remove the battery and battery tray (see Chapter 5).

6   Remove the coolant expansion tank from its mountings and reposition it, but don't disconnect the hoses (see Chapter 3).

7   Disconnect the fluid feed hose from the clutch master cylinder, plugging it to prevent spilling brake fluid.

8   Remove the line clip at the master cylinder hydraulic line fitting, then separate the hydraulic line from the cylinder (see illustration).

9   Using special pliers DT-6202-B and DT-50894 remover tool, slide the pliers over the clutch pedal then insert the DT-50894 behind the pedal engaging it with the master cylinder pushrod, squeeze the pliers against the retaining clip tabs and separate the master cylinder pushrod from the clutch pedal.

10   Remove the clutch master cylinder mounting nuts and remove the cylinder from the engine side of the fire-wall.

Installation

11   Place the master cylinder pushrod through the firewall and tighten the mounting nuts to the torque listed in this Chapter's Specifications.

12   Insert the clutch master cylinder pushrod into the retainer on the clutch pedal until there is an audible click heard. Verify the pushrod is locked into the pedal retainer by trying to pull the pushrod back out.

13   Connect the hydraulic line fitting to the end of the clutch master cylinder and install the retaining clip at the fitting.

14   Attach the fluid feed hose to the clutch master cylinder.

15   Reinstall the coolant expansion tank, battery tray and battery.

16   Fill the reservoir with brake fluid conforming to DOT 3 specifications and bleed the clutch system as outlined in Section 5.

17   Check the feel of the brake pedal. If it feels spongy when depressed, bleed the brake hydraulic system (see Chapter 9).

2016 and later models
Removal

18   Disconnect the negative battery cable (see Chapter 5).

19   Remove the cowl panel (see Chapter 11).

20   Unclip the coolant expansion tank (see Chapter 3), then secure it out of the way.

21   Disconnect the electrical connectors from the brake master cylinder.

22   Remove most of the fluid from the brake master cylinder reservoir and disconnect the hose from the clutch master cylinder, then remove the master cylinder nuts and brake booster stud bolts. Withdraw the brake master cylinder (see Chapter 9).

23   Remove the ABS ECU/hydraulic unit mounting bolt then unclip the brake lines from the retainers and move the unit back.

24   Remove the clip securing the clutch release/actuator cylinder line to the clutch master cylinder and move the line out of the way. Be sure to plug or cap the line.

25   Carefully pull the brake booster forward, then remove the pedal assembly mounting nuts from the firewall.

26   Working inside the vehicle, remove the steering column covers (see Chapter 11).

27   Remove the driver's side floor air duct fastener and remove the duct.

28   Remove the steering column (see Chapter 10).

29   Remove the accelerator pedal position (APP) sensor and pedal assembly (see Chapter 6).

30   Mark the location, then remove the brake pedal position sensor (see Chapter 9).

31   Mark the location, then remove the clutch pedal position sensor bolts and sensor.

Note: *The clutch pedal position sensor must be installed in its exact original location.*

32   Rotate the guide element 90-degrees, then remove it from the stud and push the two tabs on the pedal assembly out from the bracket.

Note: *The guide element is also called "third-hand-feature".*

33   Remove the four pedal assembly mounting bolts (two on each side).

34   Separate the wiring harness from the pedal assembly and secure it out of the way.

35   Press the tabs on the click-fit connector on the brake pedal and disconnect the brake pedal pushrod from the pedal.

Note: *The manufacturer states that the click-fit connector on the brake pedal must be replaced with a new one once the brake pedal push rod has been disconnected.*

36   Remove the pedal assembly from the vehicle.

Caution: *Place some rags inside the vehicle on the floor to prevent brake fluid from spilling onto the carpets or interior components.*

37   Using special pliers (tool no. #DT-6202-B or equivalent), insert each end of the pliers into the slots on the sides of the clutch pedal, then squeeze the pliers to disconnect the clutch master pushrod from the pedal.

38   Rotate the clutch master cylinder clockwise to unlock it from the pedal assembly, then withdraw it from the pedal assembly.

Installation

39   Insert the master cylinder into the pedal assembly, then rotate the master cylinder counterclockwise to lock into place.

40   Install the clutch master cylinder pushrod onto the clutch pedal.

41   Slide the guide element "third-hand-feature" onto the stud on the firewall.

42   Install the pedal assembly onto the firewall allowing the assembly to rest onto the guide element, then lock the tabs on the side of the pedal assembly onto the dash bracket.

43   Install the pedal assembly mounting bolts and tighten them to the torque listed in this Chapter's Specifications.

44   The remainder of installation is the reverse of removal, making sure to bleed the brakes (see Chapter 9) and clutch hydraulic system (see Section 5).

4   Clutch release cylinder - replacement

1   Disconnect the quick-connect hydraulic line fitting from the release cylinder.

Caution: *Make sure the release cylinder line seal doesn't stay in the elbow when it is removed.*

2   Remove the transaxle (see Chapter 7A).

3   Remove the fasteners securing the release cylinder to the transaxle and slide the release cylinder assembly off the transaxle input shaft.

4   Installation is the reverse of removal, noting the following points:

a)   *Lubricate the inside diameter of the bearing with a light film of high-temperature grease.*

b)   *Apply a thread locking compound to the release cylinder mounting fasteners and tighten them to the torque listed in this Chapter's Specifications.*

c)   *Install the transaxle (see Chapter 7A).*

d)   *Connect the hydraulic fitting.*

e)   *Check the fluid level in the brake fluid reservoir, adding brake fluid conforming to DOT 3 specifications until the level is correct.*

f)   *Bleed the system (see Section 5).*

5   Clutch hydraulic system - bleeding

1   These systems can only be bleed using a hydraulic brake bleeder. DO NOT try to bleed the system manual or he system will be damaged.

2   Bleed the hydraulic system whenever any part of the system has been removed or the fluid level has fallen so low that air has been drawn into the master cylinder. The bleeding procedure is very similar to bleeding a brake system.

3   Fill the brake master cylinder reservoir with new brake fluid conforming to DOT 3 specifications.

Caution: *Do not re-use any of the fluid coming from the system during the bleeding operation or use fluid which has been inside an open container for an extended period of time.*

4   Connect a brake bleeder hose to the bleeder valve fitting at the top of the transaxle.

5   Follow the instructions on the brake bleeder making sure not to pressurize the bleeder more than 29 psi (2 Bar).

6   Continue this process until all air is evacuated from the system, indicated by no air bubbles.

Note: *Wash the area with water to remove any spilled brake fluid.*

7   Check the brake fluid level again, and add some, if necessary, to bring it to the appropriate level. Check carefully for proper operation before placing the vehicle into normal service.

6   Clutch components - removal, inspection and installation

Warning: *Dust produced by clutch wear is hazardous to your health. DO NOT blow it out with compressed air and DO NOT inhale it. DO NOT use gasoline or petroleum-based solvents to remove the dust. Brake system cleaner should be used to flush the dust into a drain pan. After the clutch components are wiped clean with a rag,*

dispose of the contaminated rags and cleaner in a covered, marked container.

Removal

Note: *On 2016 and later models, the manufacturer requires the clutch pressure plate to be preloaded using special tool #DT-6263 enough to allow the clutch disc to move slightly, then measure and record that distance it took to allow the disc to move. This measurement will be used when preloading and centering the new clutch disc.*

1   Access to the clutch components is normally accomplished by removing the transaxle, leaving the engine in the vehicle. If the engine is being removed for major overhaul, check the clutch for wear and replace worn components as necessary. However, the relatively low cost of the clutch components compared to the time and trouble spent gaining access to them warrants their replacement anytime the engine or transaxle is removed, unless they are new or in near-perfect condition. The following procedures are based on the assumption the engine will stay in place.

2   Remove the transaxle from the vehicle (see Chapter 7A). Support the engine while the transaxle is out. Preferably, an engine support fixture or a hoist should be used to support it from above.

3   To support the clutch disc during removal, install a clutch alignment tool through the clutch disc hub. The tool is available at most auto parts stores.

4   Carefully inspect the flywheel and pressure plate for indexing marks. The marks are usually an X, an O or a black mark. If they cannot be found, scribe or paint marks yourself so the pressure plate and the flywheel will be in the same alignment during installation (see illustration).

5   Turning each bolt a little at a time, loosen the pressure plate-to-flywheel bolts. Work in a criss-cross pattern until all spring pressure is relieved evenly. Then hold the pressure plate securely and completely remove the bolts, followed by the pressure plate and clutch disc.

6.4 Mark the relationship of the pressure plate to the flywheel (if you're planning to re-use the old pressureplate)

Inspection

6   Ordinarily, when a problem occurs in the clutch, it can be attributed to wear of the clutch driven plate assembly (clutch disc). However, all components should be inspected at this time.

7   Inspect the flywheel for cracks, heat checking, grooves and other obvious defects. If the imperfections are slight, a machine shop can machine the surface flat and smooth, which is highly recommended regardless of the surface appearance. Refer to Chapter 2A for the flywheel removal and installation procedure.

8   Inspect the lining on the clutch disc. There should be at least 1/16-inch of lining above the rivet heads. Check for loose rivets, distortion, cracks, broken springs/dampers and other obvious damage (see illustration). As mentioned above, ordinarily the clutch disc is routinely replaced, so if in doubt about the condition, replace it with a new one.

9   The clutch release cylinder/release bearing should also be replaced along with the clutch disc (see Section 4).

10   Check the machined surfaces and the diaphragm spring fingers of the pressure plate (see illustrations). If the surface is grooved or otherwise damaged, replace the pressure plate. Also check for obvious damage, distortion, cracking, etc. Light glazing can be removed with emery cloth or sandpaper. If a new pressure plate is required, new and remanufactured units are available.

Installation

11   Before installation, clean the flywheel and pressure plate machined surfaces with brake system cleaner. It's important that no oil or grease is on these surfaces or the lining of the clutch disc. Handle the parts only with clean hands.

12   Position the clutch disc and pressure plate against the flywheel with the clutch held in place with an alignment tool (see illustration). Make sure the disc is installed properly (most replacement clutch discs will be marked "flywheel side" or something similar - if not marked, install the clutch disc with the damper springs toward the transaxle).

13   On 2016 and later models, center the clutch disc, then preload the pressure plate using special tool #DT-6263 to the measurement recorded previously. Verify the clutch disc is cen-

6.8 The clutch disc

1   *Lining - this will wear down in use*
2   *Springs or dampers - check for cracking and deformation*
3   *Splined hub - the splines must not be worn and should slide smoothly on the transmission input shaft splines*
4   *Rivets - these secure the lining and will damage the flywheel or pressure plate if allowed to contact the surfaces*

tered, install the new mounting bolts and tighten them to the torque listed in this Chapter's Specifications, then remove the special tool.

14   Tighten the pressure plate-to-flywheel bolts only finger tight, working around the pressure plate.

15   Center the clutch disc by ensuring the alignment tool extends through the splined hub and into the pilot bearing in the crankshaft. Wiggle the tool up, down or side-to-side as needed to center the disc. Install and tighten the pressure plate-to-flywheel bolts a little at a time, working in a criss-cross pattern to prevent distorting the cover. After all of the bolts are snug, tighten then to the torque listed in this Chapter's Specifications. Remove the alignment tool.

16   Install the clutch release cylinder (see Section 4).

17   Install the transaxle and all components removed previously.

7   Clutch pedal position sensor - check and replacement

1   In the passenger compartment, remove the driver's side lower trim panel (see Chapter 11).

Check

2   Verify that the engine will not start when the clutch pedal is released. Now, depress the clutch pedal - the engine should start.

3   Locate the sensor on the clutch pedal bracket and unplug the electrical connector.

4   Using an ohmmeter, verify that there is continuity between the terminals of the sensor when the pedal is depressed. There should be no continuity when the pedal is released.

EXCESSIVE WEAR

NORMAL FINGER WEAR   **EXCESSIVE FINGER WEAR**   **BROKEN OR BENT FINGERS**

6.10a Replace the pressure plate if excessive wear or damage is noted

6.10b Inspect the pressure plate surface for excessive score marks, cracks and signs of overheating

6.12 Center the clutch disc in the pressure plate with a clutch alignment tool

5   If the sensor does not work as described, replace it.

Replacement

6   Unplug the electrical connector from the sensor.

7   Remove the sensor mounting fastener and sensor.

8   Installation is the reverse of removal. The sensor is self-adjusting, so there's no need for adjustment.

Note: *The sensor must be calibrated using a GM-type scan tool.*

9   Verify that the engine doesn't start when the clutch pedal is released, and does start when the pedal is depressed.

8   Driveaxles and intermediate shaft - removal and installation

Warning: *The manufacturer recommends replacing the driveaxle/hub nuts with new ones whenever they are removed.*

Driveaxle

Removal

1   Set the parking brake. Remove the wheel cover or hubcap.

2   If you're working on a model with a manual transaxle, drain the transaxle lubricant (see Chapter 1).

3   Loosen the front wheel lug nuts, raise the vehicle and support it securely on jackstands. Remove the wheel.

4   Remove the driveaxle/hub nut (see illustration).

5   Disconnect the tie-rod end from the steering knuckle (see Chapter 10).

6   Disconnect the ABS wheel speed sensor (see Chapter 9). Separate the control arm from the steering knuckle (see Chapter 10).

7   To loosen the driveaxle from the hub splines, tap the end of the driveaxle with a soft-faced hammer. If the driveaxle is stuck in the hub splines and won't move, it may be necessary to push it from the hub with a puller.

8   Pull out on the steering knuckle and detach the driveaxle from the hub. Suspend the outer end of the driveaxle on a bungee cord or piece of wire.

9   Before you remove the driveaxle, look for lubricant leakage in the area around the differential seal. If there's evidence of a leak, you'll want to replace the seal after removing the driveaxle (see Chapter 7B).

Caution: *The seal is easily damaged by the splines on the driveaxle, which can cut the seal and cause a fluid leak.*

10   Position a prybar against the inner joint and carefully pry the joint off the transaxle side gear shaft (see illustration) or, if you're removing the right-side driveaxle, off the intermediate shaft. Do not use the driveaxle to pull on the inner joint. Doing so might damage the inner joint components. Remove the driveaxle assembly, being careful not to over-extend the inner joint or damage the axleshaft boots.

11   Should it become necessary to move the vehicle while the driveaxle is out, place

8.4 Insert a punch into one of the brake disc cooling vanes and let it rest against the caliper bracket, then unscrew the driveaxle/hub nut

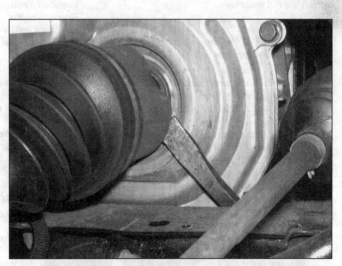

8.10 Using a large prybar, carefully pry the inner end of the driveaxle from the transaxle

8.12 Remove the old driveaxle set-ring and replace it with a new one

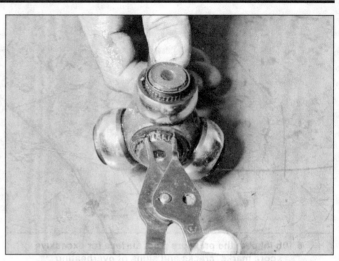

9.5 Remove the snap-ring with a pair of snap-ring pliers

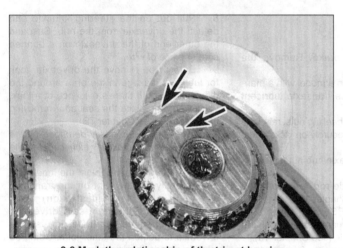

9.6 Mark the relationship of the tri-pot bearing assembly to the axleshaft

9.7 Drive the tri-pot joint off the axleshaft with a brass punch and hammer; be careful not to damage the bearing surfaces or the splines on the shaft

a large bolt with two large washers (one on each side of the hub) through the hub and tighten the nut securely.

Installation

12　Installation is the reverse of removal, noting the following points:

a) *Remove the old set-ring from the transaxle stub shaft or intermediate shaft (depending on which side you're working on) and install a new one (see illustration).*

b) *Apply a film of multi-purpose grease around the splines of the joints.*

c) *When installing the driveaxle, push it in sharply to seat the driveaxle set-ring. To make sure the set-ring is properly seated, attempt to pull the inner CV joint housing out of the transaxle by hand. If the set-ring is properly seated the inner joint will not move out.*

d) *Clean all foreign matter from the driveaxle outer CV joint threads and coat the splines with multi-purpose grease. Guide the driveaxle into the hub splines*

and install the new driveaxle/hub nut. Tighten the nut securely but not to the specified torque at this time.

e) *Reconnect the control arm and tie-rod end, then tighten the suspension fasteners to the torque listed in the Chapter 10 Specifications.*

f) *Tighten the driveaxle/hub nut to the torque listed in this Chapter's Specifications.*

g) *Install the wheel and lug nuts, then lower the vehicle.*

h) *Tighten the wheel lug nuts to the torque listed in the Chapter 10 Specifications.*

i) *Add transaxle lubricant if it was drained or if any fluid spilled out (see Chapter 1).*

Intermediate shaft

Note: *Not all models are equipped with an intermediate shaft.*

13　Remove the right-side driveaxle (see Steps 1 through 10).

14　Remove the intermediate shaft bracket bolts, remove the wheel speed sensor, then pull the intermediate shaft out of the transaxle.

15　If necessary, replace the oil seal (see Chapter 7B).

16　Installation is the reverse of removal. Install the lower bracket bolt that is closest to the drivebelt end of the engine, but do not tighten it. Install the other two bolts. Tighten the intermediate shaft bracket bolts, beginning with the upper bolt, to the torque listed in this Chapter's Specifications.

17　Install the driveaxle (see Step 12).

9　Driveaxle boot replacement

Note: *If the CV joints or boots must be replaced, explore all options before beginning the job. Complete, rebuilt driveaxles are available on an exchange basis, eliminating much time and work. Whichever route you choose to take, check on the cost and availability of parts before disassembling the vehicle.*

Inner CV joint

1　Remove the driveaxle (see Section 8).

2　Mount the driveaxle in a vise with wood-

9.10a Wrap the axleshaft splines with tape to prevent damaging the boot as it's slid onto the shaft

9.10b Install the tri-pot spider on the axleshaft (make sure your match mark is facing out and aligned with the mark on the axleshaft)

9.10c Place grease at the bottom of the CV joint housing

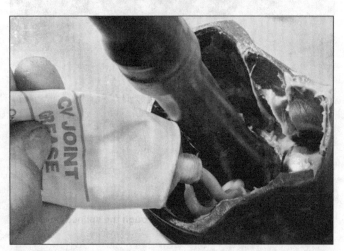

9.10d Install the boot and clamps onto the axleshaft, then insert the tri-pot into the housing, followed by the rest of the grease

lined jaws, to prevent damage to the axleshaft. Check the CV joints for excessive play in the radial direction, which indicates worn parts. Check for smooth operation throughout the full range of motion for each CV joint. If a boot is torn, the recommended procedure is to disassemble the joint, clean the components and inspect for damage due to loss of lubrication and possible contamination by foreign matter. If the CV joint is in good condition, lubricate it with CV joint grease and install a new boot.

Disassembly

3   Cut the boot clamps with side-cutters, then remove and discard them.

4   Using a screwdriver, pry up on the edge of the boot, pull it off the CV joint housing and slide it down the axleshaft, exposing the tri-pot spider assembly. Pull the CV joint housing straight off.

Note: *When removing the housing, hold the rollers in place on the spider trunnion to prevent the rollers and the needle bearings from falling free.*

5   Remove the spider assembly snap-ring with a pair of snap-ring pliers (see illustration). Some models have a second snap-ring after the spider assembly. Remove this snap-ring, as it may interfere with driving off the spider assembly.

6   Mark the tri-pot to the axleshaft to ensure that they are reassembled properly (see illustration).

7   Use a hammer and a brass drift to drive the spider assembly from the axleshaft (see illustration).

8   Slide the boot off the shaft.

Inspection

9   Thoroughly clean all components with solvent until the old CV joint grease is completely removed. Inspect the bearing surfaces of the inner tri-pots and housings for cracks, pitting, scoring and other signs of wear. If any part of the inner CV joint is worn, you must replace the entire driveaxle assembly (inner tri-pot joint, axleshaft and outer CV joint). The only components that

can be purchased separately are the boots themselves and the boot clamps.

Reassembly

10   Wrap the splines on the inner end of the axleshaft with tape to protect the boots from the sharp edges of the splines, then slide the clamps and boot onto the axleshaft (see illustration). Remove the tape and place the tri-pot spider on the axleshaft with the chamfer toward the shaft (see illustration). Tap the spider onto the shaft (aligning the marks made in Step 6) with a brass drift until it's seated, then install the snap-ring(s). Apply grease to the tri-pot assembly and inside the housing (see illustration). Insert the tri-pot into the housing and pack the remainder of the grease around the tri-pot (see illustration).

11   Slide the boot into place, making sure the raised bead on the inside of the boot is positioned in the groove on the shaft. Position the sealing boot into the groove on the tri-pot housing retaining groove.

9.12 Equalize the pressure inside the boot by inserting a screwdriver between the boot and the CV joint housing

9.17 Strike the edge of the CV joint housing sharply with a soft-face hammer to dislodge the joint from the shaft

9.22a Apply the CV joint grease through the splined hole. . .

9.22b . . . then insert a wooden dowel (slightly smaller in diameter than the hole) into the hole and push down - the dowel will force the grease into the joint. Repeat this until the joint is packed

12   Position the CV joint mid-way through its travel, then equalize the pressure in the boot (see illustration).

13   Make sure each end of the boot is seated properly, and the boot is not distorted.

14   Two types of clamps are used on the inner CV joint. If a crimp-type clamp is used, clamp the new boot clamps onto the boot with a special crimping tool (available at most automotive parts stores). Place the crimping tool over the bridge of each new boot clamp, then tighten the nut on the crimping tool until the jaws are closed. If a low-profile latching type clamp is used, place the prongs of the clamping tool (available at most automotive parts stores) in the holes of the clamp and squeeze the tool together until the top band latches behind the tabs of the lower band.

15   The driveaxle is now ready for installation (see Section 8).

Outer CV joint

Removal

16   Cut the boot clamps with side-cutters, then remove and discard them. Slide the boot away from the joint.

17   Strike the edge of the CV joint housing sharply with a soft-face hammer to dislodge the the joint from the driveaxle shaft (see illustration).

18   Slide the outer CV joint boot off the axleshaft.

Inspection

19   Thoroughly clean all components with solvent until the old CV grease is completely removed. Inspect the bearing surfaces of the inner tri-pots and housings for cracks, pitting, scoring, and other signs of wear. If any part of the outer CV joint is worn, you must replace the entire driveaxle assembly (inner CV joint, axleshaft and outer CV joint).

Reassembly

20   Slide a new sealing boot clamp and sealing boot onto the axleshaft. It's a good idea to wrap the axleshaft splines with tape to prevent damaging the boot (see illustration 9.10a).

21   Place a new bearing retainer clip onto the axleshaft.

22   Pack the outer CV joint with CV joint grease, then put the remaining grease into

the sealing boot (see illustrations).

23   Align the splines on the axleshaft with the splines on the outer CV joint assembly and using a soft-faced hammer, drive the CV joint onto the axleshaft until the CV joint is seated to the axleshaft.

24   Seat the ends of the boot on the axleshaft and the CV joint housing, then equalize the pressure in the boot (see illustration 9.12).

25   Two types of clamps are used on the outer CV joint. If a crimp-type clamp is used, clamp the new boot clamps onto the boot with a special crimping tool (available at most automotive parts stores). Place the crimping tool over the bridge of each new boot clamp, then tighten the nut on the crimping tool until the jaws are closed. If a low profile latching type clamp is used, place the prongs of the clamping tool (available at most automotive parts stores) in the holes of the clamp and squeeze the tool together until the top band latches behind the tabs of the lower band.

26   Install the driveaxle as outlined in Section 8.

Chapter 9
Brakes

Contents

Specifications

General

Brake fluid type	See Chapter 1

Disc brakes

Brake pad minimum thickness	See Chapter 1
Disc lateral runout limit	0.002 inch (0.06 mm)
Disc minimum thickness	Cast into disc
Parallelism (thickness variation) limit	0.001 inch (0.025 mm)

Drum brakes

Maximum drum diameter	Cast into drum
Shoe lining minimum thickness	See Chapter 1
Shoe lining-to-drum clearance	0.016 to 0.035 inch (0.4 to 0.9 mm)

Torque specifications

Note: *One foot-pound (ft-lb) of torque is equivalent to 12 inch-pounds (in-lbs) of torque. Torque values below approximately 15 ft-lbs are expressed in inch-pounds, because most foot-pound torque wrenches are not accurate at these smaller values.*

	Ft-lbs (unless otherwise noted)	Nm
Brake hose and brake hose banjo fitting bolt	30	40
Caliper guide pin bolts		
Front		
2015 and earlier models	21	28
2016 and later models	30	40
Rear		
2015 and earlier models	21	28
2016 and later models	27	36
Caliper mounting bracket bolts*		
Front		
15 inch disc (J67 and J93 models)		
Step 1	74	100
Step 2	Tighten an additional 60 to 75-degrees	
16 inch disc (J60 models)		
Step 1	111	150
Step 2	Tighten an additional 45 to 60-degrees	
Rear		
Step 1	74	00
Step 2	Tighten an additional 60 to 75-degrees	
Master cylinder mounting nuts*		
2015 and earlier models	37	50
2016 and later models	17	24
Power brake booster mounting bolts	15	19
Power brake booster vacuum pump-to-bracket bolt/nuts (2015 and earlier models)	66 in-lbs	7.5
Power brake booster vacuum pump bracket mounting bolts (2015 and earlier models)	15	20
Vacuum pump mounting bolts (2016 and later models)	18	25
Wheel cylinder mounting bolts	89 in-lbs	10
Wheel speed sensor bolt (all models)	53 in-lbs	6
Wheel lug nuts	See Chapter 1	

* Replace fastener(s) with new ones

1   General Information

1   The vehicles covered by this manual are equipped with hydraulically operated front and rear brake systems. The front brakes are disc type and the rear brakes are disc or drum type. Both the front and rear brakes are self adjusting. The disc brakes automatically compensate for pad wear, while the drum brakes incorporate an adjustment mechanism that is activated as the parking brake is applied.

Hydraulic system

2   The hydraulic system consists of two separate circuits. The master cylinder has separate reservoir chambers for the two circuits, and, in the event of a leak or failure in one hydraulic circuit, the other circuit will remain operative. A dynamic proportioning valve, integral with the ABS hydraulic unit, provides brake balance to each individual wheel.

Power brake booster and vacuum pump

3   The power brake booster, utilizing engine manifold vacuum, and atmospheric pressure to provide assistance to the hydraulically operated brakes, is mounted on the firewall in the engine compartment. An auxiliary vacuum pump, mounted below the power brake booster in the left side of the engine compartment, provides additional vacuum to the booster under certain operating conditions.

Parking brake

4   The parking brake operates the rear brakes only, through cable actuation. It's activated by a lever mounted in the center console.

Service

5   After completing any operation involving disassembly of any part of the brake system, always test drive the vehicle to check for proper braking performance before resuming normal driving. When testing the brakes, perform the tests on a clean, dry, flat surface. Conditions other than these can lead to inaccurate test results.

6   Test the brakes at various speeds with both light and heavy pedal pressure. The vehicle should stop evenly without pulling to one side or the other. Avoid locking the brakes, because this slides the tires and diminishes braking efficiency and control of the vehicle.

7   Tires, vehicle load and wheel alignment are factors which also affect braking performance.

Precautions

8   There are some general cautions and warnings involving the brake system on this vehicle:

a) *Use only brake fluid conforming to DOT 3 specifications.*

b) *The brake pads and linings contain fibers that are hazardous to your health if inhaled. Whenever you work on brake system components, clean all parts with brake system cleaner. Do not allow the fine dust to become airborne. Also, wear an approved filtering mask.*

c) *Safety should be paramount whenever any servicing of the brake components is performed. Do not use parts or fasteners that are not in perfect condition, and be sure that all clearances and torque specifications are adhered to. If you are at all unsure about a certain procedure, seek professional advice. Upon completion of any brake system work, test the brakes carefully in a controlled area before putting the vehicle into normal service. If a problem is suspected in the brake system, don't drive the vehicle until it's fixed.*

d) *Used brake fluid is considered a hazardous waste and it must be disposed of in accordance with federal, state and local laws. DO NOT pour it down the sink, into septic tanks or storm drains, or on the ground. Clean up any spilled brake fluid immediately and then wash the area with large amounts of water. This is especially true for any finished or painted surfaces.*

2   Troubleshooting

PROBABLE CAUSE	CORRECTIVE ACTION

No brakes - pedal travels to floor

1 Low fluid level 2 Air in system	1 and 2 Low fluid level and air in the system are symptoms of another problem a leak somewhere in the hydraulic system. Locate and repair the leak
3 Defective seals in master cylinder	3 Replace master cylinder
4 Fluid overheated and vaporized due to heavy braking	4 Bleed hydraulic system (temporary fix). Replace brake fluid (proper fix)

Brake pedal slowly travels to floor under braking or at a stop

1 Defective seals in master cylinder	1 Replace master cylinder
2 Leak in a hose, line, caliper or wheel cylinder	2 Locate and repair leak
3 Air in hydraulic system	3 Bleed the system, inspect system for a leak

Brake pedal feels spongy when depressed

1 Air in hydraulic system	1 Bleed the system, inspect system for a leak
2 Master cylinder or power booster loose	2 Tighten fasteners
3 Brake fluid overheated (beginning to boil)	3 Bleed the system (temporary fix). Replace the brake fluid (proper fix)
4 Deteriorated brake hoses (ballooning under pressure)	4 Inspect hoses, replace as necessary (it's a good idea to replace all of them if one hose shows signs of deterioration)

PROBABLE CAUSE

CORRECTIVE ACTION

Brake pedal feels hard when depressed and/or excessive effort required to stop vehicle

PROBABLE CAUSE	CORRECTIVE ACTION
1 Power booster faulty	1 Replace booster
2 Engine not producing sufficient vacuum, or hose to booster clogged, collapsed or cracked	2 Check vacuum to booster with a vacuum gauge. Replace hose if cracked or clogged, repair engine if vacuum is extremely low
3 Brake linings contaminated by grease or brake fluid	3 Locate and repair source of contamination, replace brake pads or shoes
4 Brake linings glazed	4 Replace brake pads or shoes, check discs and drums for glazing, service as necessary
5 Caliper piston(s) or wheel cylinder(s) binding or frozen	5 Replace calipers or wheel cylinders
6 Brakes wet	6 Apply pedal to boil-off water (this should only be a momentary problem)
7 Kinked, clogged or internally split brake hose or line	7 Inspect lines and hoses, replace as necessary

Excessive brake pedal travel (but will pump up)

PROBABLE CAUSE	CORRECTIVE ACTION
1 Drum brakes out of adjustment	1 Adjust brakes
2 Air in hydraulic system	2 Bleed system, inspect system for a leak

Excessive brake pedal travel (but will not pump up)

PROBABLE CAUSE	CORRECTIVE ACTION
1 Master cylinder pushrod misadjusted	1 Adjust pushrod
2 Master cylinder seals defective	2 Replace master cylinder
3 Brake linings worn out	3 Inspect brakes, replace pads and/or shoes
4 Hydraulic system leak	4 Locate and repair leak

Brake pedal doesn't return

PROBABLE CAUSE	CORRECTIVE ACTION
1 Brake pedal binding	1 Inspect pivot bushing and pushrod, repair or lubricate
2 Defective master cylinder	2 Replace master cylinder

Brake pedal pulsates during brake application

PROBABLE CAUSE	CORRECTIVE ACTION
1 Brake drums out-of-round	1 Have drums machined by an automotive machine shop
2 Excessive brake disc runout or disc surfaces out-of-parallel	2 Have discs machined by an automotive machine shop
3 Loose or worn wheel bearings	3 Adjust or replace wheel bearings
4 Loose lug nuts	4 Tighten lug nuts

Brakes slow to release

PROBABLE CAUSE	CORRECTIVE ACTION
1 Malfunctioning power booster	1 Replace booster
2 Pedal linkage binding	2 Inspect pedal pivot bushing and pushrod, repair/lubricate
3 Malfunctioning proportioning valve	3 Replace proportioning valve
4 Sticking caliper or wheel cylinder	4 Repair or replace calipers or wheel cylinders
5 Kinked or internally split brake hose	5 Locate and replace faulty brake hose

Brakes grab (one or more wheels)

PROBABLE CAUSE	CORRECTIVE ACTION
1 Grease or brake fluid on brake lining	1 Locate and repair cause of contamination, replace lining
2 Brake lining glazed	2 Replace lining, deglaze disc or drum

Troubleshooting (continued)

PROBABLE CAUSE	CORRECTIVE ACTION

Vehicle pulls to one side during braking

PROBABLE CAUSE	CORRECTIVE ACTION
1 Grease or brake fluid on brake lining	1 Locate and repair cause of contamination, replace lining
2 Brake lining glazed	2 Deglaze or replace lining, deglaze disc or drum
3 Restricted brake line or hose	3 Repair line or replace hose
4 Tire pressures incorrect	4 Adjust tire pressures
5 Caliper or wheel cylinder sticking	5 Repair or replace calipers or wheel cylinders
6 Wheels out of alignment	6 Have wheels aligned
7 Weak suspension spring	7 Replace springs
8 Weak or broken shock absorber	8 Replace shock absorbers

Brakes drag (indicated by sluggish engine performance or wheels being very hot after driving)

PROBABLE CAUSE	CORRECTIVE ACTION
1 Brake pedal pushrod incorrectly adjusted	1 Adjust pushrod
2 Master cylinder pushrod (between booster and master cylinder)	2 Adjust pushrod incorrectly adjusted
3 Obstructed compensating port in master cylinder	3 Replace master cylinder
4 Master cylinder piston seized in bore	4 Replace master cylinder
5 Contaminated fluid causing swollen seals throughout system	5 Flush system, replace all hydraulic components
6 Clogged brake lines or internally split brake hose(s)	6 Flush hydraulic system, replace defective hose(s)
7 Sticking caliper(s) or wheel cylinder(s)	7 Replace calipers or wheel cylinders
8 Parking brake not releasing	8 Inspect parking brake linkage and parking brake mechanism, repair as required
9 Improper shoe-to-drum clearance	9 Adjust brake shoes
10 Faulty proportioning valve	10 Replace proportioning valve

Brakes fade (due to excessive heat)

PROBABLE CAUSE	CORRECTIVE ACTION
1 Brake linings excessively worn or glazed	1 Deglaze or replace brake pads and/or shoes
2 Excessive use of brakes	2 Downshift into a lower gear, maintain a constant slower speed (going down hills)
3 Vehicle overloaded	3 Reduce load
4 Brake drums or discs worn too thin	4 Measure drum diameter and disc thickness, replace drums or discs as required
5 Contaminated brake fluid	5 Flush system, replace fluid
6 Brakes drag	6 Repair cause of dragging brakes
7 Driver resting left foot on brake pedal	7 Don't ride the brakes

Brakes noisy (high-pitched squeal)

PROBABLE CAUSE	CORRECTIVE ACTION
1 Glazed lining	1 Deglaze or replace lining
2 Contaminated lining (brake fluid, grease, etc.)	2 Repair source of contamination, replace linings
3 Weak or broken brake shoe hold-down or return spring	3 Replace springs
4 Rivets securing lining to shoe or backing plate loose	4 Replace shoes or pads
5 Excessive dust buildup on brake linings	5 Wash brakes off with brake system cleaner
6 Brake drums worn too thin	6 Measure diameter of drums, replace if necessary
7 Wear indicator on disc brake pads contacting disc	7 Replace brake pads
8 Anti-squeal shims missing or installed improperly	8 Install shims correctly

PROBABLE CAUSE	CORRECTIVE ACTION

Brakes noisy (scraping sound)

1 Brake pads or shoes worn out; rivets, backing plate or brake	1 Replace linings, have discs and/or drums machined (or replace) shoe metal contacting disc or drum

Brakes chatter

1 Worn brake lining	1 Inspect brakes, replace shoes or pads as necessary
2 Glazed or scored discs or drums	2 Deglaze discs or drums with sandpaper (if glazing is severe, machining will be required)
3 Drums or discs heat checked	3 Check discs and/or drums for hard spots, heat checking, etc. Have discs/drums machined or replace them
4 Disc runout or drum out-of-round excessive	4 Measure disc runout and/or drum out-of-round, have discs or drums machined or replace them
5 Loose or worn wheel bearings	5 Adjust or replace wheel bearings
6 Loose or bent brake backing plate (drum brakes)	6 Tighten or replace backing plate
7 Grooves worn in discs or drums	7 Have discs or drums machined, if within limits (if not, replace them)
8 Brake linings contaminated (brake fluid, grease, etc.)	8 Locate and repair source of contamination, replace pads or shoes
9 Excessive dust buildup on linings	9 Wash brakes with brake system cleaner
10 Surface finish on discs or drums too rough after machining	10 Have discs or drums properly machined (especially on vehicles with sliding calipers)
11 Brake pads or shoes glazed	11 Deglaze or replace brake pads or shoes

Brake pads or shoes click

1 Shoe support pads on brake backing plate grooved or	1 Replace brake backing plate excessively worn
2 Brake pads loose in caliper	2 Loose pad retainers or anti-rattle clips
3 Also see items listed under Brakes chatter	

Brakes make groaning noise at end of stop

1 Brake pads and/or shoes worn out	1 Replace pads and/or shoes
2 Brake linings contaminated (brake fluid, grease, etc.)	2 Locate and repair cause of contamination, replace brake pads or shoes
3 Brake linings glazed	3 Deglaze or replace brake pads or shoes
4 Excessive dust buildup on linings	4 Wash brakes with brake system cleaner
5 Scored or heat-checked discs or drums	5 Inspect discs/drums, have machined if within limits (if not, replace discs or drums)
6 Broken or missing brake shoe attaching hardware	6 Inspect drum brakes, replace missing hardware

Rear brakes lock up under light brake application

1 Tire pressures too high	1 Adjust tire pressures
2 Tires excessively worn	2 Replace tires
3 Defective proportioning valve	3 Replace proportioning valve

Brake warning light on instrument panel comes on (or stays on)

1 Low fluid level in master cylinder reservoir (reservoirs with fluid level sensor)	1 Add fluid, inspect system for leak, check the thickness of the brake pads and shoes
2 Failure in one half of the hydraulic system	2 Inspect hydraulic system for a leak
3 Piston in pressure differential warning valve not centered	3 Center piston by bleeding one circuit or the other (close bleeder valve as soon as the light goes out)

Troubleshooting (continued)

PROBABLE CAUSE

CORRECTIVE ACTION

Brake warning light on instrument panel comes on (or stays on) (continued)

4 Defective pressure differential valve or warning switch	4 Replace valve or switch
5 Air in the hydraulic system	5 Bleed the system, check for leaks
6 Brake pads worn out (vehicles with electric wear sensors - small probes that fit into the brake pads and ground out on the disc when the pads get thin)	6 Replace brake pads (and sensors)

Brakes do not self adjust

Disc brakes

1 Defective caliper piston seals	1 Replace calipers. Also, possible contaminated fluid causing soft or swollen seals (flush system and fill with new fluid if in doubt)
2 Corroded caliper piston(s)	2 Same as above

Drum brakes

1 Adjuster screw frozen	1 Remove adjuster, disassemble, clean and lubricate with high-temperature grease
2 Adjuster lever does not contact star wheel or is binding	2 Inspect drum brakes, assemble correctly or clean or replace parts as required
3 Adjusters mixed up (installed on wrong wheels after brake job)	3 Reassemble correctly
4 Adjuster cable broken or installed incorrectly (cable-type adjusters)	4 Install new cable or assemble correctly

Rapid brake lining wear

1 Driver resting left foot on brake pedal	1 Don't ride the brakes
2 Surface finish on discs or drums too rough	2 Have discs or drums properly machined
3 Also see Brakes drag	

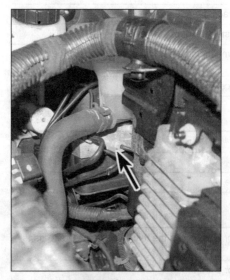

3.2 The ABS ECU/hydraulic unit is located in the left-rear corner of the engine compartment, below the coolant expansion tank

3   Anti-lock Brake System (ABS) - general information

General information

1   The anti-lock brake system is designed to maintain vehicle steerability, directional stability and optimum deceleration under severe braking conditions on most road surfaces. It does so by monitoring the rotational speed of each wheel and controlling the brake line pressure to each wheel during braking. This prevents the wheels from locking up.

2   The ABS system has three main components - the wheel speed sensors, the electronic control unit (ECU) and hydraulic unit (which are combined into one assembly) (see illustration). Four wheel speed sensors - one at each wheel - send a variable voltage signal to the control unit, which monitors these signals, compares them to its program and determines whether a wheel is about to lock up. When a wheel is about to lock up, the control unit signals the hydraulic unit to reduce hydraulic pressure (or not increase it further) at that wheel's brake caliper. Pressure modulation is handled by electrically operated solenoid valves.

3   If a problem develops within the system, an "ABS" warning light will glow on the dashboard. Sometimes, a visual inspection of the ABS system can help you locate the problem. Carefully inspect the ABS wiring harness. Pay particularly close attention to the harness and connections near each wheel. Look for signs of chafing and other damage caused by incorrectly routed wires. If a wheel sensor harness is damaged, the sensor must be replaced.

Warning: *Do NOT try to repair an ABS wiring harness. The ABS system is sensitive to even the smallest changes in resistance. Repairing the harness could alter resistance values and cause the system to malfunction. If the ABS wiring harness is damaged in any way, the damaged portion must be replaced.*

Caution: *Make sure the ignition is turned off before unplugging or reattaching any electrical connections.*

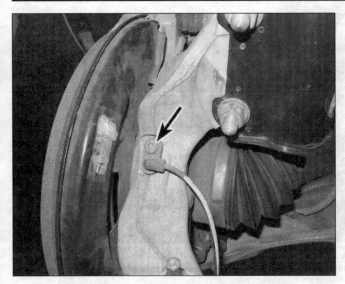

3.8a Front wheel speed sensor mounting bolt

3.8b Rear wheel speed sensor mounting bolt (disc brake model)

Diagnosis and repair

4   If a dashboard warning light comes on and stays on while the vehicle is in operation, the ABS system requires attention. Although special electronic ABS diagnostic testing tools are necessary to properly diagnose the system, you can perform a few preliminary checks before taking the vehicle to a dealer service department.

a) Check the brake fluid level in the reservoir.
b) Verify that the computer electrical connectors are securely connected.
c) Check the electrical connectors at the hydraulic control unit.
d) Check the fuses.
e) Follow the wiring harness to each wheel and verify that all connections are secure and that the wiring is undamaged.

5   If the above preliminary checks do not rectify the problem, the vehicle should be diagnosed by a dealer service department or other qualified repair shop. Due to the complex nature of this system, all actual repair work must be done by a qualified automotive technician.

Wheel speed sensor - replacement

6   Make sure the ignition key is turned to the Off position. Loosen the wheel lug nuts, raise the vehicle and support it securely on jackstands, then remove the wheel.

7   Trace the wiring harness back from the sensor, detaching it from all brackets and clips, then disconnect the electrical connector.

8   Remove the mounting bolt then pull the sensor out from the knuckle (see illustrations).

9   Installation is the reverse of removal. Tighten the sensor to the torque listed in this Chapter's Specifications.

10   Install the wheel and lug nuts, tightening them securely. Lower the vehicle and tighten the lug nuts to the torque listed in Chapter 1 Specifications.

4   Disc brake pads - replacement

Warning: *Disc brake pads must be replaced on both front or both rear wheels at the same time - never replace the pads on only one wheel. Also, the dust created by the brake system is harmful to your health. Never blow it out with compressed air and don't inhale any of it. An approved filtering mask should be worn when working on the brakes. Do not, under any circumstances, use petroleum-based solvents to clean brake parts. Use brake system cleaner only!*

Note: *Disc brake pad replacement for rear disc brakes is similar to the Steps outlined below for the front pads. See Section 5 for details of rear caliper mounting.*

All models

1   Remove the cap from the brake fluid reservoir.

2   Loosen the wheel lug nuts, raise the end of the vehicle you're working on and support it securely on jackstands. Block the wheels at the opposite end.

3   Remove the wheels. Work on one brake assembly at a time, using the assembled brake for reference if necessary.

4   Inspect the brake disc carefully as outlined in Section 6. If machining is necessary, follow the information in that Section to remove the disc, at which time the pads can be removed as well.

5   Push the piston back into its bore to provide room for the new brake pads. A C-clamp can be used to accomplish this (see illustration). As the piston is depressed to the bottom of the caliper bore, the fluid in the master cylinder will rise. Make sure that it doesn't overflow. If necessary, siphon off some of the fluid.

Caution: *On rear disc brakes, the caliper contains an integral parking brake mechanism. Do not depress the piston with the clamp any further than 1/32 inch (1 mm), or damage could be done to the parking brake mechanism.*

4.5 Before removing the caliper, depress the piston into the bottom of its bore in the caliper with a large C-clamp to make room for the new pads (front caliper only; on rear calipers, depress the piston no more than 1/32 inch [1 mm] - just enough to get the pads away from the disc)

6   Follow the accompanying photos (illustrations 4.6a through 4.6l), for the actual pad replacement procedure. Be sure to stay in order and read the caption under each illustration.

7   After the job has been completed, firmly depress the brake pedal a few times to bring the pads into contact with the disc. Check the level of the brake fluid, adding some if necessary. Check the operation of the brakes carefully before placing the vehicle into normal service.

4.6a Always wash the brakes with brake cleaner before disassembling anything

4.6b If you're working on a front brake, remove the caliper lower guide pin bolt. . .

4.6c. . . then rotate the caliper away from the disc and support it with a length of wire

4.6d If you're working on a rear brake, remove both guide pin bolts, remove the caliper and support it with a length of wire

4.6e Pull the outer brake pad from the support plates in the caliper mount

4.6f Pull the inner pad out of the caliper mount. Remove and inspect the support plates (A) - if they're damaged or fit loosely, replace them. Before installing the support plates, lightly lubricate the contact areas on the mounting bracket with silicone brake lubricant

4.6g Apply some anti-squeal compound to the backs
of the new brake pads

4.6h On rear calipers, rotate the piston with a brake piston
tool or needle-nose pliers until it's all the way at the bottom,
then align the notches in the piston with the openings
in the caliper as shown

4.6i With the support plates installed, install the inner pad -
the inner pad has a brake wear sensor, which should be
positioned at the top for front disc brakes, and at the
bottom for rear disc brakes

4.6j Install the new outer pad

4.6k Clean the caliper guide pins of dirt and grease,
then coat them with caliper lube

4.6l Install the guide pins and caliper, then install the guide pin
bolts and tighten them to the torque listed in this Chapter's
Specifications. When installing a rear caliper, align the notch
in the piston with the pin on the back of the inner brake
pad as the caliper is moved back into place

5.2 Front brake caliper details:

A Brake line banjo bolt	D Caliper mounting
B Caliper guide pin bolts	bracket bolts
C Bleeder screw	

5.9 Rear brake caliper details:

A Brake line banjo bolt	D Parking brake cable end
B Caliper guide pin bolt	E Parking brake cable
C Caliper guide pin/	retaining tab
dampener bolt	

5   Disc brake caliper - removal and installation

Warning: *Dust created by the brake system is harmful to your health. Never blow it out with compressed air and don't inhale any of it. An approved filtering mask should be worn when working on the brakes. Do not, under any circumstances, use petroleum-based solvents to clean brake parts. Use brake system cleaner only.*

Note: *If replacement is indicated (usually because of fluid leakage), it is recommended that the calipers be replaced, not overhauled. New and factory rebuilt units are available on an exchange basis, which makes this job quite easy. Always replace the calipers in pairs - never replace just one of them.*

Front

Removal

1   Loosen - but don't remove - the lug nuts on the front wheels. Raise the front of the vehicle and support it securely on jackstands. Remove the front wheels.

2   Disconnect the brake line from the caliper and plug it to keep contaminants out of the brake system and to prevent losing any more brake fluid than is necessary (see illustration).

Note: *If you're only removing the caliper for access to other components, don't disconnect the hose.*

3   Remove the caliper guide pin bolts. Detach the caliper from its mounting bracket.

Installation

4   Install the caliper by reversing the removal procedure. Remember to replace the copper sealing washers on either side of the brake line fitting with new ones. Tighten the caliper guide pin bolts and the brake line banjo fitting bolt to the torque listed in this Chapter's Specifications.

5   Bleed the brake system (see Section 11).

6   Install the wheels and lug nuts and lower the vehicle. Tighten the wheel lug nuts to the torque listed in the Chapter 1 Specifications.

Rear

Removal

7   Loosen - but don't remove - the lug nuts on the rear wheels. Raise the rear of the vehicle and support it securely on jackstands. Remove the rear wheels.

8   Disconnect the parking brake cable end from the lever on the caliper, then depress the cable retaining tab and slide the cable out of the bracket on the caliper.

9   Disconnect the brake line from the caliper and plug it to keep contaminants out of the brake system and to prevent losing any more brake fluid than is necessary (see illustration).

10   Remove the caliper guide pin bolt and dampener bolt. Detach the caliper from its mounting bracket.

Note: *Whenever the rear calipers are removed, inspect the parking brake side of the caliper for any signs of brake fluid seepage around the shaft for the parking brake lever, which passes through a seal in the caliper. The seal is not serviceable, and if there is any leakage here, the caliper must be replaced.*

Installation

11   On rear calipers, the notches in the pistons must be in the center of the caliper open-ing as viewed from above (see Section 4, if necessary).

12   Install the caliper by reversing the removal procedure. Tighten the caliper guide pin bolts and the brake line banjo fitting bolt to the torque listed in this Chapter's Specifications.

13   Bleed the brake system (see Section 11).

14   Install the wheels and lug nuts. Lower the vehicle and tighten the lug nuts to the torque listed in the Chapter 1 Specifications. On rear calipers, adjust the parking brake (see Section 14).

6   Brake disc - inspection, removal and installation

Warning: *The dust created by the brake system is harmful to your health. Never blow it out with compressed air and don't inhale any of it. An approved filtering mask should be worn when working on the brakes. Do not, under any circumstances, use petroleum-based solvents to clean brake parts. Use brake system cleaner only!*

Inspection

1   Loosen the wheel lug nuts, raise the vehicle and support it securely on jackstands. Remove the wheel and install the lug nuts to hold the disc in place against the hub flange.

Note: *If the lug nuts don't contact the disc when screwed on all the way, install washers under them. If you're checking the rear disc, release the parking brake.*

2   Remove the two caliper mounting bracket-to-steering knuckle (front) or mounting bracket-to-axle flange (rear) bolts (see

6.3 The brake pads on this vehicle were obviously neglected, as they wore down completely and cut deep grooves into the disc - wear this severe means the disc must be replaced

6.4a To check disc runout, mount a dial indicator as shown and rotate the disc

6.4b Using a swirling motion, remove the glaze from the disc surface with sandpaper or emery cloth

6.5 Use a micrometer to measure disc thickness

illustration 5.2) and remove the caliper and bracket as a unit. It isn't necessary to disconnect the brake hose. Suspend the caliper/bracket out of the way with a piece of wire.

3   Visually inspect the disc surface for score marks and other damage. Light scratches and shallow grooves are normal after use and may not always be detrimental to brake operation, but deep scoring requires disc refinishing by an automotive machine shop. Be sure to check both sides of the disc (see illustration). If pulsating has been noticed during application of the brakes, suspect disc runout.

4   To check disc runout, install the lug nuts to secure the disc to the hub, using washers if necessary. Place a dial indicator at a point about 1/2-inch from the outer edge of the disc (see illustration). Set the indicator to zero and turn the disc. The indicator reading should not exceed the specified allowable runout limit. If it does, the disc should be refinished by an automotive machine shop. If you elect not to have the discs resurfaced, remove the glaze from the surface with emery cloth or sandpa-

per, using a swirling motion (see illustration). **Note:** *Some professionals recommend resurfacing the discs when replacing brake pads regardless of the dial indicator reading, as this will impart a smooth finish and ensure a perfectly flat surface, eliminating any brake pedal pulsation or other undesirable symptoms.*

5   It's absolutely critical that the disc not be machined to a thickness under the specified minimum thickness. The minimum (or discard) thickness is cast or stamped into the disc. The disc thickness can be checked with a micrometer (see illustration).

Removal

6   Remove the disc mounting screw, then remove the disc. If the disc has never been removed, there may be wave washers on the wheel studs securing it to the hub flange. Simply cut them off and discard them. If the disc is stuck to the hub, use a mallet to knock it loose. Penetrating oil applied around the disc's hub will also help (but don't let any oil get onto the disc friction surface; clean the disc with brake cleaner after you're done).

Installation

7   Clean the inner opening in the disc, and the area of the hub on which it seats. Remove any rust with fine emery paper before reinstalling the disc.

8   Place the disc in position over the threaded studs, aligning the hole for the disc mounting screw then install the screw and tighten the screw securely.

9   Install the caliper mounting bracket and caliper, tightening the bolts to the torque values listed in this Chapter's Specifications. **Note:** *The caliper mounting bracket bolts are of a special self-locking design; do not attempt to clean the threaded holes with a tap, or the threads of the bolt with a die.*

10   Install the wheel and lug nuts, then lower the vehicle to the ground. Tighten the lug nuts to the torque listed in the Chapter 1 Specifications. Depress the brake pedal a few times to bring the brake pads into contact with the disc. Bleeding won't be necessary unless the brake hose was disconnected from the caliper. Check the operation of the brakes carefully before driving the vehicle.

7 Drum brake shoes - replacement

Warning: *Drum brake shoes must be replaced on both wheels at the same time - never replace the shoes on only one wheel. Also, the dust created by the brake system is harmful to your health. Never blow it out with compressed air and don't inhale any of it. An approved filtering mask should be worn when working on the brakes. Do not, under any circumstances, use petroleum-based solvents to clean brake parts. Use brake system cleaner only!*

1   Loosen the wheel lug nuts, raise the rear of the vehicle and support it securely on jackstands. Block the front wheels to keep the vehicle from rolling.

2   Release the parking brake.
3   Remove the wheel.
Note: *All four rear brake shoes must be replaced at the same time, but to avoid mixing up parts, work on only one brake assembly at a time.*

4   Follow the accompanying illustrations for the brake shoe replacement procedure (see illustrations 7.4a through 7.4l). Be sure to stay in order and read the caption under each illustration.
Note: *The parking brake lever is connected to the trailing shoe but cannot be disassembled from it. The shoe and lever are replaced as a unit.*
Note: *If the brake drum cannot be easily removed, make sure the parking brake is com-*

pletely released. If the drum still cannot be pulled off, the brake shoes will have to be retracted. This is done by first removing the plug from the backing plate. With the plug removed, push the lever off the adjuster star wheel with a narrow screwdriver while turning the adjuster wheel with another screwdriver, moving the shoes away from the drum. The drum should now come off.

5   Before reinstalling the drum, it should be checked for cracks, score marks, deep scratches and hard spots, which will appear as small discolored areas. If the hard spots cannot be removed with fine emery cloth or if any of the other conditions listed above exist, the drum must be taken to an automotive machine shop to have it resurfaced.

7.4a Rear drum brake assembly

1	Adjuster lever spring	5	Brake shoe lower return spring
2	Trailing brake shoe	6	Adjuster screw assembly
3	Adjuster lever	7	Leading brake shoe
4	Wheel cylinder	8	Parking brake lever

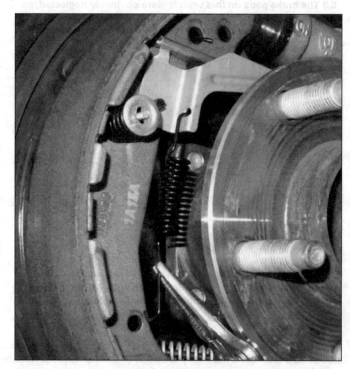

7.4b Remove the adjuster lever spring

7.4c Remove the adjuster lever from the adjuster

7.4d Using locking pliers, disconnect one end of the upper return spring from the backside of the brake shoes

7.4e Remove the adjuster from the shoes

Note: *Professionals recommend resurfacing the drums each time a brake job is done. Resurfacing will eliminate the possibility of out-of-round drums. If the drums are worn so much that they can't be resurfaced without exceeding the maximum allowable diameter (stamped into the drum), then new drums will be required. At the very least, if you elect not to have the drums resurfaced, remove the glaze from the surface with emery cloth using a swirling motion.*

6   Install the brake drum on the axle flange. Pump the brake pedal a couple of times, then turn the adjuster star wheel until the shoes rub on the drum when you turn it. Back off the star wheel adjustment a couple of clicks, pump the brake pedal a couple of

times, then turn the drum and listen for the sound of the shoes rubbing. If they are, turn the adjuster star wheel until the shoes stop rubbing.

Note: *If you have access to a brake drum gauge you can measure the shoe lining-to-drum clearance; it should be 0.016 to 0.035 inch (0.4 to 0.9 mm).*

7   Install the wheel and lug nuts, then lower the vehicle. Tighten the lug nuts to the torque listed in the Chapter 1 Specifications.

8   Make a number of forward and reverse stops and operate the parking brake to adjust the brakes until satisfactory pedal action is obtained.

9   Check the operation of the brakes carefully before driving the vehicle.

7.4f Remove the shoe hold-down springs from each shoe

7.4g Disconnect the lower return spring from each shoe and remove the shoes.

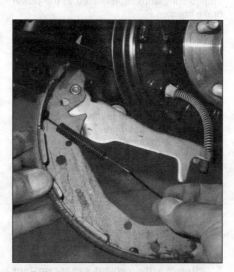

7.4h Attach the upper return spring to the trailing shoe

7.4i Install the shoes and hold-down springs

7.4j Install the lower return spring

7.4k Clean and lube the threads of the adjuster and reinstall the adjuster wheel in between the shoes. Reconnect the upper return spring to the leading shoe

7.4l Install the adjuster lever and spring, then adjust the shoes by holding the lever up while turning the star wheel (the drum should just be able to slide over the shoes)

8   Wheel cylinder - removal and installation

Note: *If replacement is indicated (usually because of fluid leakage or sticky operation), it is recommended that the wheel cylinders be replaced, not overhauled. Always replace the wheel cylinders in pairs - never replace just one of them.*

Removal

1   Block the front wheels to keep the vehicle from rolling. Loosen the rear wheel lug nuts, raise the rear of the vehicle and support it securely on jackstands.
2   Remove the wheel.
3   Release the parking brake and remove the brake drum as described in Section 7.
4   Remove the brake shoes (see Section 7).
5   Remove all dirt and foreign material from around the wheel cylinder.
6   At the rear of the backing plate, unscrew the brake line fitting, using a flare-nut wrench, if available (see illustration). Don't pull the brake line away from the wheel cylinder (it could become kinked). Remove the wheel cylinder bleeder screw with its cap.
7   Remove the wheel cylinder mounting bolts and detach the wheel cylinder from the backing plate.

Installation

8   Place the wheel cylinder in position and connect the brake line fitting finger tight. Install the wheel cylinder mounting bolts and tighten them to the torque listed in this Chapter's Specifications. Tighten the brake line fitting securely. Install the bleeder screw and cap.
9   Install the brake shoes (see Section 7).

10   Install the brake drum on the hub flange, then install the wheel and lug nuts.
11   Bleed the brake system as outlined in Section 11.
12   Lower the vehicle to the ground, then tighten the lug nuts to the torque listed in the Chapter 1 Specifications. Check the operation of the brakes carefully before driving the vehicle in traffic.

9   Master cylinder - removal and installation

Removal

1   The master cylinder is located in the engine compartment, mounted to the power brake booster.
2   Disconnect the negative battery cable (see Chapter 5).
3   Remove as much fluid as you can from the reservoir with a suction gun or an old turkey baster.
Warning: *If a baster is used, never again use it for the preparation of food.*
Warning: *Don't depress the brake pedal until the reservoir has been refilled, otherwise air may be introduced into the brake hydraulic system.*
4   On models with a manual transaxle, disconnect the clutch fluid hose from the brake master cylinder reservoir. Plug the line or wrap it with a plastic bag.
Caution: *Brake fluid will damage paint. Cover all pained surfaces around the work area and be careful not to spill fluid during this procedure.*
5   Remove the coolant expansion tank from its bracket and set it aside without disconnecting the hoses (see Chapter 3).

6   Place rags under the fluid fittings and prepare caps or plastic bags to cover the ends of the lines once they are disconnected. Loosen the fittings at the ends of the brake lines where they enter the master cylinder. To prevent rounding off the corners on these nuts, the use of a flare-nut wrench, which wraps around the nut, is preferred. Pull the brake lines slightly away from the master cylinder and plug the ends to prevent contamination.
7   Disconnect the electrical connector at the brake fluid level switch on the master cylinder reservoir (you must pull back the locking tab of the connector before removing it), then remove the nuts attaching the master cylinder to the power booster (see illustration). Pull the master cylinder off the studs and out of the engine compartment. Again, be careful not to spill the fluid as this is done.
8   If a new master cylinder is being installed, drive out the two retaining pins that hold the reservoir to the master cylinder body. Transfer the reservoir to the new master cylinder. If the same master cylinder is to be installed, check the condition of the master cylinder-to-booster seal for damage or hardness, replacing it if necessary.
Note: *Install new seals when transferring the reservoir.*

Installation

9   Bench bleed the new master cylinder before installing it. Mount the master cylinder in a vise, with the jaws of the vise clamping on the mounting flange.
10   Attach a pair of master cylinder bleeder tubes to the outlet ports of the master cylinder (see illustration).
11   Fill the reservoir with brake fluid of the recommended type (see Chapter 1).

8.6 Rear wheel cylinder details

1 Fluid line fitting	3 Mounting bolts
2 Bleed screw	

9.7 Brake master cylinder mounting details

A   Brake fluid level sensor connector
B   Brake line fittings
C   Mounting nuts

9.10 The best way to bleed air from the master cylinder before installing it on the vehicle is with a pair of bleeder tubes that direct brake fluid into the reservoir during bleeding (typical)

10.3 Using a flare-nut wrench, unscrew the threaded fitting on the brake line (A) while holding the hose end (B) with an open-end wrench, then pry the U-clip (C) off the end of the hose and separate the hose from the bracket

12   Slowly push the pistons into the master cylinder (a large Phillips screwdriver can be used for this) - air will be expelled from the pressure chambers and into the reservoir. Because the tubes are submerged in fluid, air can't be drawn back into the master cylinder when you release the pistons.

13   Repeat the procedure until no more air bubbles are present.

14   Remove the bleed tubes, one at a time, and install plugs in the open ports to prevent fluid leakage and air from entering. Install the reservoir cap.

15   Install the master cylinder over the studs on the power brake booster and tighten the new attaching nuts only finger tight at this time.

Note: *Install a new O-ring onto the sleeve of the master cylinder.*

16   Thread the brake line fittings into the master cylinder by hand until you know they are started straight. Since the master cylinder is still a bit loose, it can be moved slightly in order for the fittings to thread in easily. Do not strip the threads as the fittings are tightened.

17   Tighten the mounting nuts to the torque listed in this Chapter's Specifications, then tighten the brake line fittings securely.

18   Connect the brake fluid switch electrical connector.

19   On models with manual transaxles, connect the fluid hose from the clutch master cylinder.

Note: *On manual transaxle models, the clutch hydraulic system will have to be bled (see Chapter 8).*

20   Fill the master cylinder reservoir with fluid, then bleed the master cylinder and the brake system as described in Section 11. To bleed the cylinder on the vehicle, have an assistant depress the brake pedal and hold the pedal to the floor. Loosen the fitting to allow air and fluid to escape, then close the

fitting. Repeat this procedure on both fittings until the fluid is clear of air bubbles.

Caution: *Have plenty of rags on hand to catch the fluid - brake fluid will ruin painted surfaces. After the bleeding procedure is completed, rinse the area under the master cylinder with clean water.*

21   Test the operation of the brake system carefully before placing the vehicle into normal service.

Warning: *Do not operate the vehicle if you are in doubt about the effectiveness of the brake system. It is possible for air to become trapped in the anti-lock brake system hydraulic control unit, so, if the pedal continues to feel spongy after repeated bleedings or the BRAKE or ANTI-LOCK light stays on, have the vehicle towed to a dealer service department or other qualified shop to be bled with the aid of a scan tool.*

10   Brake hoses and lines - inspection and replacement

1   About every six months, with the vehicle raised and placed securely on jackstands, the flexible hoses which connect the steel brake lines with the front and rear brake assemblies should be inspected for cracks, chafing of the outer cover, leaks, blisters and other damage. These are important and vulnerable parts of the brake system and inspection should be complete. A light and mirror will be needed for a thorough check. If a hose exhibits any of the above defects, replace it with a new one.

Flexible hoses

2   Clean all dirt away from the ends of the hose.

3   To disconnect a brake hose from the

brake line, unscrew the metal tube nut with a flare nut wrench, then remove the U-clip from the female fitting at the bracket and remove the hose from the bracket (see illustration).

4   Disconnect the hose from the caliper, discarding the sealing washers on either side of the fitting.

5   Using new sealing washers, attach the new brake hose to the caliper or wheel cylinder.

6   To reattach a brake hose to the metal line, insert the end of the hose through the frame bracket, make sure the hose isn't twisted, then attach the metal line by tightening the tube nut fitting securely. Install the U-clip at the frame bracket.

7   Carefully check to make sure the suspension or steering components don't make contact with the hose.

8   Bleed the brake system (see Section 11).

Metal brake lines

9   When replacing brake lines, be sure to use the correct parts. Don't use copper tubing for any brake system components. Purchase steel brake lines from a dealer parts department or auto parts store.

10   Prefabricated brake line, with the tube ends already flared and fittings installed, is available at auto parts stores and dealer parts departments. These lines can be bent to the proper shapes using a tubing bender.

11   When installing the new line make sure it's well supported in the brackets and has plenty of clearance between moving or hot components.

12   After installation, check the master cylinder fluid level and add fluid as necessary. Bleed the brake system (see Section 11) and test the brakes carefully before placing the vehicle into normal operation.

11 Brake hydraulic system - bleeding

Warning: *If air has found its way into the hydraulic control unit, the system must be bled with the use of a scan tool. If the brake pedal feels spongy even after bleeding the brakes, or the ABS light on the instrument panel does not go off, or if you have any doubts whatsoever about the effectiveness of the brake system, have the vehicle towed to a dealer service department or other repair shop equipped with the necessary tools for bleeding the system.*

Warning: *Wear eye protection when bleeding the brake system. If the fluid comes in contact with your eyes, immediately rinse them with water and seek medical attention.*

Caution: *Brake fluid will damage paint. Cover all pained surfaces around the work area and be careful not to spill fluid during this procedure.*

Note: *Bleeding the brake system is necessary to remove any air that's trapped in the system when it's opened during removal and installation of a hose, line, caliper, wheel cylinder or master cylinder.*

1   It will probably be necessary to bleed the system at all four brakes if air has entered the system due to a low fluid level, or if the brake lines have been disconnected at the master cylinder.

2   If a brake line was disconnected only at a wheel, then only that caliper or wheel cylinder must be bled.

3   If a brake line is disconnected at a fitting located between the master cylinder and any of the brakes, that part of the system served by the disconnected line must be bled, beginning with the fitting closest to the master cylinder and then working downstream.

Note: *This would include the ABS EBCM/ EBTCM module.*

4   Remove any residual vacuum (or hydraulic pressure) from the power brake booster by applying the brake several times with the engine off.

5   Remove the master cylinder reservoir cap and fill the reservoir with brake fluid. Reinstall the cap.

Note: *Check the fluid level often during the bleeding operation and add fluid as necessary to prevent the fluid level from falling low enough to allow air bubbles into the master cylinder.*

6   Have an assistant on hand, as well as a supply of new brake fluid, an empty clear plastic container, a length of plastic, rubber or vinyl tubing to fit over the bleeder valve and a wrench to open and close the bleeder valve.

7   Working at the right rear wheel, loosen the bleeder screw slightly, then tighten it to a point where it's snug but can still be loosened quickly and easily.

8   Place one end of the tubing over the bleeder screw fitting and submerge the other end in brake fluid in the container (see illustration).

9   Have the assistant slowly depress the brake pedal and hold it in the depressed position.

10   While the pedal is held depressed, open the bleeder screw just enough to allow a flow of fluid to leave the valve. Watch for air bubbles to exit the submerged end of the tube. When the fluid flow slows after a couple of seconds, tighten the screw and have your assistant release the pedal.

11   Repeat Steps 9 and 10 until no more air is seen leaving the tube, then tighten the bleeder screw and proceed to the left rear wheel, the right front wheel and the left front wheel, in that order, and perform the same procedure. Check the fluid in the master cylinder reservoir frequently.

12   Never use old brake fluid. It contains moisture that can boil, rendering the brake system inoperative.

13   Refill the master cylinder with fluid at the end of the operation.

14   Check the operation of the brakes. The pedal should feel solid when depressed, with no sponginess. If necessary, repeat the entire process.

Warning: *Do not operate the vehicle if you are in doubt about the effectiveness of the brake system. It is possible for air to become trapped in the anti-lock brake system hydraulic control unit, so, if the pedal continues to feel spongy after repeated bleedings or the BRAKE or ANTI-LOCK light stays on, have the vehicle towed to a dealer service department or other qualified shop to be bled with the aid of a scan tool.*

12 Power brake booster - removal and installation

Operating check

1   Depress the brake pedal several times with the engine off and make sure that there is no change in the pedal reserve distance.

2   Depress the pedal and start the engine. If the pedal goes down slightly, operation is normal.

Airtightness check

3   Start the engine and turn it off after one or two minutes. Depress the brake pedal several times slowly. If the pedal goes down farther the first time but gradually rises after the second or third depression, the booster is airtight.

4   Depress the brake pedal while the engine is running, then stop the engine with the pedal depressed. If there is no change in the pedal reserve travel after holding the pedal for 30 seconds, the booster is airtight.

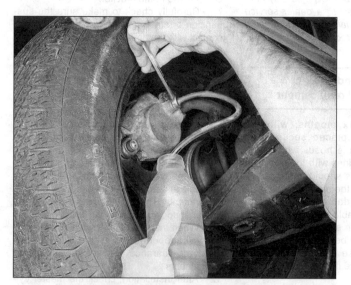

11.8 When bleeding the brakes, a hose is connected to the bleed screw at the caliper or wheel cylinder and submerged in brake fluid - air will be seen as bubbles in the tube and container (all air must be expelled before moving to the next wheel)

12.10 Disconnect the pushrod (A) from the click connector (B) on the brake pedal arm)

Removal and installation

Caution: *Brake fluid will damage paint. Cover all pained surfaces around the work area and be careful not to spill fluid during this procedure.*

5   The power brake booster is not rebuildable. If a problem develops, it must be replaced with a new one.

6   Disconnect the cable from the negative terminal of the battery (see Chapter 5). Remove the master cylinder (see Section 9).

7   Disconnect the vacuum hose check valve and electrical connector where it attaches to the power brake booster.

8   Mark and disconnect the lines to the EBCM/EBTCM (ABS) module, making sure to cap the lines and plug the openings. Disconnect the electrical connectors, then remove the mounting bolts and module.

9   In the passenger compartment, remove the driver's-side under-dash panel (see Chapter 11).

10   Disconnect the pushrod from the click connector clip securing the booster pushrod to the brake pedal arm (see illustration) and replace the click connector.

11   Remove the booster-to-firewall through bolts from inside the engine compartment.

12   Guide the booster unit away from the firewall and out of the engine compartment. Retrieve the gasket if it isn't stuck to the booster.

13   To install the booster, place it into position (using a new gasket) and tighten the bolts to the torque listed in this Chapter's Specifications.

14   Lubricate the pushrod pin on the brake pedal arm with multi-purpose grease. Connect the pushrod to the brake pedal and install a new click connector clip.

15   Reconnect the vacuum hose.

16   Install the EBCM/EBTCM module, making sure to tighten the lines securely, then connect the electrical connectors.

17   Install the master cylinder.

18   Bleed the brakes, starting with the master cylinder, then the ABS EBCM/EBTCM, then all four wheels (see Section 11).

19   Reconnect the battery.

20   Carefully test the operation of the brakes before placing the vehicle in normal service.

Warning: *Do not operate the vehicle if you are in doubt about the effectiveness of the brake system. It is possible for air to become trapped in the anti-lock brake system hydraulic control unit, so, if the pedal continues to feel spongy after repeated bleedings or the BRAKE or ANTI-LOCK light stays on, have the vehicle towed to a dealer service department or other qualified shop to be bled with the aid of a scan tool.*

13   Power brake booster vacuum pump - removal and installation

2015 and earlier models

1   Locate the brake booster vacuum pump at the left rear side of the engine compartment, below the power brake booster.

2   Disconnect the vacuum hose quick-connect fitting and electrical connector.

3   Remove the pump bracket mounting bolts and guide the assembly out of the engine compartment.

4   Once the pump and bracket assembly have been removed, remove the pump-to-bracket nuts/bolts and remove the pump from the bracket.

5   Installation is the reverse of removal.

2016 and later models

Note: *The vacuum pump is located on the left end of the cylinder head.*

6   Disconnect the quick-connect vacuum line fitting at the top of the vacuum pump.

7   Remove the charge air cooler outlet pipe (see Chapter 4).

8   Remove the vacuum pump mounting bolts, the vacuum pump and the gasket.

9   Install a new vacuum pump gasket to the cylinder head. Install the vacuum pump, aligning the vacuum pump slotted gear with the slot in the end of the camshaft.

10   Install the mounting bolts and tighten them to the torque listed in this Chapter's Specifications.

14   Parking brake - adjustment

1   These models use a self-adjusting park brake cable system which does not require any adjustment.

Notes

Chapter 10
Suspension and steering

Contents

Specifications

Torque specifications

Front suspension

	Ft-lbs (unless otherwise indicated)	Nm
Strut assembly		
Damper shaft nut*	52	70
Strut-to-body bolts or nut		
2011 models	34	45
2012 to 2015 models	48	65
2016 and later models*		
Step 1	16	22
Step 2	Tighten an additional 30 to 45-degrees	
Strut-to-steering knuckle bolts/nuts*		
2015 and earlier models		
Step 1	66	90
Step 2	Tighten an additional 60 to 70-degrees	
2016 and later models		
Step 1	74	100
Step 2	Tighten an additional 45 to 60-degrees	
Stabilizer bar		
Stabilizer bar link nuts*	48	65
Stabilizer bar bracket bolts*		
Step 1	16	22
Step 2	Tighten an additional 40-degrees	
Control arm		
Arm-to-subframe bolts/nuts*		
2015 and earlier models (front and rear)		
Step 1	52	70
Step 2	Tighten an additional 75 to 90-degrees	
2016 and later models		
Front		
Step 1	74	100
Step 2	Tighten an additional 30 to 45-degrees	
Rear		
Step 1	74	100
Step 2	Tighten an additional 90 to 105-degrees	
Rear bushing-to-control arm bolt (2015 and earlier models)*		
Step 1	41	55
Step 2	Tighten an additional 45 to 60-degrees	
Balljoint-to-steering knuckle pinch bolt/nut*		
2015 and earlier models		
Step 1	37	50
Step 2	Loosen nut 120-degrees	
Step 3	37	50
Step 4	Tighten an additional 35-degrees	
2016 and later models		
Step 1	26	35
Step 2	Tighten an additional 30 to 45-degrees	

*Fastener(s) must be replaced

Torque specifications (continued)

	Ft-lbs (unless otherwise indicated)	Nm
Hub/bearing assembly mounting bolts*		
Step 1	66	90
Step 2	Tighten an additional 60-degrees	
Step 3	Tighten an additional 15-degrees	
Subframe-to-body bolts (see illustration 20.16)*		
2015 and earlier models...	118	160
2016 and later models		
Step 1	74	100
Step 2	Tighten an additional 90 to 105-degrees	
Subframe reinforcement bracket bolts		
2015 and earlier models (rearmost bracket bolts)*		
Step 1	44	60
Step 2	Tighten an additional 45-degrees	
2016 and later models (front bolts)	43	58
Driveaxle/hub nut..	See Chapter 8	

Rear suspension

	Ft-lbs (unless otherwise indicated)	Nm
Rear axle trailing arm		
Bracket-to-body bolts*		
2015 and earlier models		
Step 1	66	90
Step 2	Tighten an additional 45-degrees	
2016 and later models		
Step 1	74	100
Step 2	Tighten an additional 30-degrees	
Bracket through bolt*		
2015 and earlier models		
Step 1	52	70
Step 2	Tighten an additional 120-degrees	
2016 and later models (compound crank)		
Step 1	74	100
Step 2	Tighten an additional 30 to 45-degrees	
2016 and later models (Watts link)		
Step 1	74	100
Step 2	Tighten an additional 180-degrees	
Rear hub/bearing bolts		
Step 1	37	50
Step 2		
2015 and earlier models	Tighten an additional 30 to 45-degrees	
2016 and later models	Tighten an additional 60 to 75-degrees	
Shock absorber		
Lower mounting bolt*		
2015 and earlier models		
Step 1	111	150
Step 2	Tighten an additional 60-degrees	
2016 and later models	74	100
Upper mounting bolts*		
2015 and earlier models	74	100
2016 and later models	16	22
Damper shaft nut*		
2015 and earlier models..	15	20
2016 and later models..	18	25
Watts links bolt/nuts*		
Bellcrank		
Step 1		
2015 and earlier models...................................	52	70
2016 and later models*	74	100
Step 2	Tighten and additional 120 to 135-degrees	
Left or right Watts links		
Watts link-to-bellcrank		
Step 1		
2015 and earlier models...............................	30	40
2016 and later models*	43	58
Step 2	Tighten an additional 60-degrees	
Watts link-to-rear axle	118	160
Watts link support beam bolts		
2015 and earlier models		
Step 1	66	90
Step 2	Tighten an additional 45 to 60-degrees	
2016 and later models*..	74	100

Fastener(s) must be replaced

Torque specifications (continued)

	Ft-lbs (unless otherwise indicated)	Nm
Steering system		
Intermediate shaft-to-steering column pinch bolt*		
2015 and earlier models	25	34
2016 and later models		
Step 1	18	25
Step 2	Tighten an additional 180 to 195-degrees	
Intermediate shaft-to-steering gear pinch bolt*	25	34
Steering column mounting fasteners*		
2015 and earlier models		
Step 1	16	22
Step 2	Tighten an additional 45-degrees	
2016 and later models*	16	22
Steering gear mounting bolts*		
Step 1		
2015 and earlier models	81	110
2016 and later models	41	55
Step 2	Tighten an additional 150 to 160-degrees	
Steering wheel bolt*		
2011 models	23	30
2012 and later models	33	45
Tie-rod end-to-steering knuckle nut*		
Step 1	26	35
Step 2	Tighten an additional 30 to 40-degrees	

Fastener(s) must be replaced

Front suspension and steering components

1	Subframe	4	Balljoint	7	Steering knuckle
2	Control arm	5	Steering gear	8	Stabilizer bar
3	Tie-rod end	6	Strut/coil spring assembly	9	Stabilizer bar link

Watts-link type rear suspension and related components

1	Rear axle	4	Coil spring	7	Right equalizer beam link
2	Axle pivot bracket and bushing	5	Left equalizer beam link	8	Equalizer beam support
3	Shock absorber	6	Center equalizer beam link (bellcrank)		

1   General Information

1   The front suspension is a MacPherson strut design. The upper end of each strut is attached to the vehicle's body strut support. The lower end of the strut is connected to the upper end of the steering knuckle. The steering knuckle is attached to a balljoint mounted on the outer end of the suspension control arm. A stabilizer bar connected to each strut and mounted to the suspension crossmember reduces body roll during cornering (see illustration).

2   There are two types of rear suspensions: a compound crank type which consists of an axle with integral trailing arms, a V-shaped, twisting cross beam, coil springs and shock absorbers, or a Watts-link type which consists of a V-shaped, twisting cross beam, coil springs, shock absorbers, equalizer beam links, an equalizer center beam link (bellcrank) and an equalizer beam support (see illustration).

3   The power-assisted rack-and-pinion steering gear is attached to the front suspension subframe. The steering gear actuates the tie-rods, which are attached to the steering knuckles. The steering column is designed to collapse in the event of an accident. The power steering system is assisted by an electric motor, rather than by hydraulic fluid circulated by an engine-driven accessory pump. This system has no fluid or pump.

4   Frequently, when working on the suspension or steering system components, you may come across fasteners that seem impossible to loosen. These fasteners on the underside of the vehicle are continually subjected to water, road grime, mud, etc., and can become rusted or frozen in place, making them extremely difficult to remove. In order to unscrew these stubborn fasteners without damaging them (or other components), use lots of penetrating oil and allow it to soak in for a while. Using a wire brush to clean exposed threads will also ease removal of the nut or

bolt and prevent damage to the threads. Sometimes a sharp blow with a hammer and punch will break the bond between a nut and bolt threads, but care must be taken to prevent the punch from slipping off the fastener and ruining the threads. Heating the stuck fastener and surrounding area with a torch sometimes helps too, but isn't recommended because of the obvious dangers associated with fire. Long breaker bars and extension, or cheater, pipes will increase leverage, but never use an extension pipe on a ratchet - the ratcheting mechanism could be damaged. Sometimes tightening the nut or bolt first will help to break it loose. Fasteners that require drastic measures to remove should always be replaced with new ones.

5   Since most of the procedures dealt with in this Chapter involve jacking up the vehicle and working underneath it, a good pair of jackstands will be needed. A hydraulic floor jack is the preferred type of jack to lift the vehicle, and it can also be used to support certain components during various operations.

Warning: *Never, under any circumstances, rely on a jack to support the vehicle while working on it. Whenever any of the suspension or steering fasteners are loosened or removed, they must be inspected and, if necessary, replaced with new ones of the same part number or of original equipment quality and design. Torque specifications must be followed for proper re-assembly and component retention. Never attempt to heat or straighten any suspension or steering components. Instead, replace any bent or damaged part with a new one.*

2   Strut assembly (front) - removal, inspection and installation

Warning: *Always replace the struts and/or coil springs in pairs - never replace just one strut or one coil spring (this could cause dangerous handling peculiarities).*

Removal

1   Loosen the wheel lug nuts, raise the vehicle and support it securely on jackstands. Remove the wheel.

2   Disconnect the stabilizer bar link from the strut (see Section 4). Also detach the brake hose from its bracket on the strut.

3   Mark the relationship of the strut to the knuckle (these marks will be used during installation to ensure the camber is returned to its original setting). Remove the strut-to-knuckle nuts (see illustration) and knock the bolts out with a hammer and punch.

4   Separate the strut from the steering knuckle. Be careful not to overextend the inner CV joint. Also, don't let the steering knuckle fall outward, as the brake hose could be damaged.

5   Remove the strut nut protective cap (see illustration) from the center of the strut assembly.

6   Using a Torx-bit and ratchet, hold the strut damper shaft from turning while using a wrench to remove the strut-to-body nut in the engine compartment (see illustration) and remove the strut.

Inspection

7   Check the strut body for leaking fluid, dents, cracks and other obvious damage that would warrant repair or replacement.

8   Check the coil spring for chips or cracks in the spring coating (this can cause premature spring failure due to corrosion). Inspect the spring seat for cuts, hardness and general deterioration.

9   If any undesirable conditions exist, proceed to the strut disassembly procedure (see Section 3).

Installation

10   Guide the strut assembly up into the fenderwell and align the assembly in the shock tower. Once the assembly is in the shock tower, install the mounting nut so the strut won't fall back through. This is most eas-

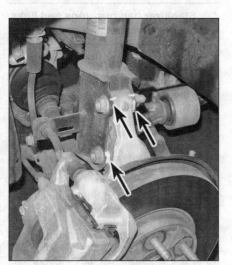

2.3 Mark the relationship of the strut to the steering knuckle at several points, then remove the strut-to-steering knuckle nuts and bolts

2.5 Remove the protective cap to expose the strut mounting nut

2.6 Hold the strut damper shaft from turning using a Torx-bit and ratchet then use a wrench to remove the strut-to-body nut

3.3 Install the spring compressor following the tool manufacturer's instructions; compress the spring until all pressure is relieved from the upper spring seat (you can verify this by wiggling the spring)

3.8 Carefully remove the compressed spring from the strut

3.10 When installing the spring, make sure the end rests against the raised stop

ily accomplished with the help of an assistant, as the strut is quite heavy and awkward.

11   Slide the steering knuckle into the strut flange and insert the two bolts. Install the nuts, aligning the marks made in Step 3, then tighten the nuts to the torque listed in this Chapter's Specifications.

12   Reattach the brake hose to the strut bracket and reconnect the stabilizer bar link.

13   Install the wheel and lug nuts, then lower the vehicle and tighten the lug nuts to the torque listed in the Chapter 1 Specifications.

14   Tighten the upper mounting nut to the torque listed in this Chapter's Specifications.

15   Have the front wheel alignment checked and, if necessary, adjusted.

3   Strut/coil spring - replacement

Warning: *The manufacturer recommends replacing the damper shaft nut with a new one whenever it is removed.*

Note: *You'll need a spring compressor for this procedure. Spring compressors are available on a daily rental basis at most auto parts stores or equipment yards.*

1   If the struts or coil springs exhibit the telltale signs of wear (leaking fluid, loss of damping capability, chipped, sagging or cracked coil springs) explore all options before beginning any work. The strut/coil spring assemblies are not serviceable and must be replaced if a problem develops. However, strut assemblies complete with springs may be available on an exchange basis, which eliminates much time and work. Whichever route you choose to take, check on the cost and availability of parts before disassembling your vehicle.

Warning: *Disassembling a strut is potentially dangerous and utmost attention must be directed to the job, or serious injury may result. Use only a high-quality spring compressor and carefully follow the manufacturer's instructions furnished with the tool. After removing the coil spring from the strut assembly, set it aside in a safe, isolated area.*

Disassembly

2   Remove the strut and spring assembly (see Section 2). Mount the strut clevis bracket portion of the strut assembly in a vise and unbolt the upper strut cap cover, exposing the damper shaft nut.

Caution: *Do not clamp any other portion of the strut assembly in the vise as it will be damaged. Line the vise jaws with wood or rags to prevent damage to the unit and don't tighten the vise excessively.*

3   Following the tool manufacturer's instructions, install the spring compressor (which can be obtained at most auto parts stores or equipment yards on a daily rental basis) on the spring and compress it sufficiently to relieve all pressure from the upper spring seat (see illustration). This can be verified by wiggling the spring.

4   While holding the strut rod from turning with a 45 Torx bit, use an offset strut socket to unscrew the damper shaft nut.

5   Remove the nut and the upper mount and bearing. Lay the parts out in the exact order in which they are removed. Check the rubber portion of the upper mount for cracking and general deterioration. If there is any separation of the rubber, replace it.

6   Remove the upper spring seat from the damper shaft. Check the rubber portion of the spring seat for cracking and hardness; replace it if necessary. Inspect the bearing in the spring seat for smooth operation. If it doesn't turn smoothly, replace it.

7   Slide the rubber bump stop off the damper shaft. Check the bump stop for cracking and general deterioration. If there is any deterioration of the rubber, replace it.

8   Carefully lift the compressed spring from the assembly (see illustration) and set it in a safe place.

Warning: *When removing the compressed spring, lift it off carefully and set it in a safe place. Keep the ends of the spring away from your body.*

Note: *If you are disassembling both struts, mark the springs LEFT and RIGHT so you don't mix them up (they're different).*

Reassembly

9   Extend the damper shaft to its full length and install the rubber bump stop.

10   Carefully place the compressed coil spring onto the lower seat of the damper, with the end of the spring resting against the raised stop (see illustration).

11   Install the bearing and upper insulator/spring seat.

12   Install the upper mount and damper shaft nut, then tighten it to the torque listed in this Chapter's Specifications. Remove the spring compressor tool.

13   Install the strut/spring assembly (see Section 2).

4   Stabilizer bar, bushings and links (front) - removal and installation

Bushings and links

1   Loosen the front wheel lug nuts, raise the front of the vehicle, support it securely on jackstands and remove the front wheels.

2   Remove and discard the nuts that attach the upper and lower ends of the stabilizer links to the strut/coil spring assembly and to the stabilizer bar (see illustrations). Detach the links.

3   Lower and support the subframe (see Section 20) enough to access the stabilizer bar mounting brackets.

4   Remove the bolts and nuts from the stabilizer bar bushing brackets (see illustration).

Note: *The stabilizer bar bushings/brackets are not available separately.*

5   Inspect the retainer bushings for cracks and tears. If either bushing is broken, damaged, distorted or worn, replace the stabilizer

4.2a Remove the nut and detach the upper link from the strut. . .

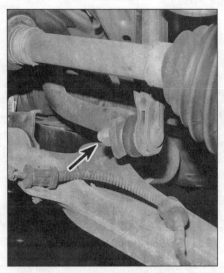

4.2b. . . then detach the link from the stabilizer bar

4.4 Remove the stabilizer bar bracket bolts

5.2a To detach the control arm balljoint from the steering knuckle, remove the nut and bolt. . .

5.2b. . . then pry the balljoint out of the steering knuckle with a large prybar, being careful to avoid nicking the boot

5.3 Control arm-to-subframe bolts
1   Front mounting through-bolt and nut
2   Rear bushing bolts

bar and bushings as a set. If the ballstuds on the links are loose or otherwise worn, replace the links.

6   Guide the stabilizer bar into place and install the bushing bracket bolts, tightening them to the torque listed in this Chapter's Specifications.

7   Install the links, tightening the link nuts to the torque listed in this Chapter's Specifications.

Stabilizer bar

8   Detach the links from the bar and remove the bushing bracket bolts (see Steps 1 through 4).

9   Twist the stabilizer bar up and remove it out through the right wheel opening.

10   Installation is the reverse of the removal procedure.

5   Control arm - removal, inspection and installation

Removal

1   Loosen the wheel lug nuts on the side to be disassembled. Apply the parking brake, raise the front of the vehicle, support it securely on jackstands and remove the wheel.

2   Remove the pinch bolt securing the balljoint to the control arm, then pry the control arm balljoint from the steering knuckle (see illustrations).

Caution: *Be careful not to damage the balljoint boot.*

3   Remove the bolts that attach the control arm to the subframe (see illustration).

4   Remove the control arm.

Inspection

5   Check the control arm for distortion and the bushings for wear, replacing parts as necessary. Do not attempt to straighten a bent control arm. If the front bushing is are cracked or show signs of wear, take the control arm to an automotive machine shop and have the bushing replaced.

6   If the rear bushing requires replacement, remove the bolt and separate the bushing from the control arm. When installing the bushing, install a new bolt and tighten it to the torque listed in this Chapter's Specifications.

Installation

7   Installation is the reverse of removal; tighten all of the fasteners to the torque values listed in this Chapter's Specifications.

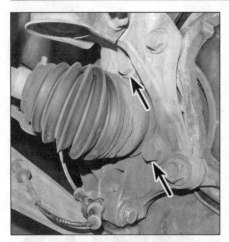

8.4 Front hub/bearing mounting bolts (two of three indicated)

9.3a Location of the rear shock absorber lower mounting bolt. . .

9.3b. . . and the upper mounting bolts

8   Install the wheel and lug nuts, lower the vehicle and tighten the lug nuts to the torque listed in the Chapter 1 Specifications.
9   It's a good idea to have the front wheel alignment checked and, if necessary, adjusted.

6   Balljoints - check and replacement

Note: *If the balljoint needs to be replaced, the control arm and balljoint must be replaced as an assembly.*
1   Raise the front of the vehicle and support it securely on jackstands. Apply the parking brake and block the rear wheels to keep the vehicle from rolling off the jackstands.
2   Place a large prybar under the balljoint and resting on the wheel, then try to pry the balljoint up while feeling for movement between the balljoint and steering knuckle. Now, pry between the control arm and the steering knuckle and try to lever the control arm down while feeling for movement between the balljoint and steering knuckle. If any movement is evident in either check, the balljoint is worn.
3   Have an assistant grasp the tire at the top and bottom and move the top of the tire in-and-out. Touch the balljoint stud nut. If any looseness is felt, suspect a worn balljoint stud or a widened hole in the steering knuckle boss. If the latter problem exists, the steering knuckle should be replaced as well as the balljoint.
4   Separate the control arm from the steering knuckle (see Section 5). Using your fingers (don't use pliers), try to twist the stud in the socket. If the stud turns, the control arm must be replaced with the balljoint (the balljoint isn't available separately).

7   Steering knuckle - removal and installation

Warning: *Dust created by the brake system is harmful to your health. Never blow it out with*

compressed air and don't inhale any of it. Do not, under any circumstances, use petroleum-based solvents to clean brake parts. Use brake system cleaner only.

Removal
1   Loosen the driveaxle/hub nut (see Chapter 8). Loosen the wheel lug nuts, raise the vehicle and support it securely on jackstands. Remove the wheel.
2   Remove the brake caliper with its bracket and support them with a piece of wire as described in Chapter 9. Remove the brake disc from the hub. Also remove the wheel speed sensor (see Chapter 9).
3   Mark the strut to the steering knuckle, then loosen, but do not remove the strut-to-steering knuckle bolt/nuts (see illustration 2.3).
4   Separate the tie-rod end from the steering knuckle arm (see Section 16).
5   Remove the balljoint-to-steering knuckle pinch bolt, then separate the balljoint from the steering knuckle (see Section 5).
6   Remove the driveaxle/hub nut and push the driveaxle from the hub as described in Chapter 8. Support the end of the driveaxle with a piece of wire.
7   The strut-to-knuckle bolts can now be removed.
8   Separate the steering knuckle from the strut.

Installation
9   Guide the knuckle and hub assembly into position, inserting the driveaxle into the hub.
10   Push the knuckle into the strut flange and install the bolts and nuts, but don't tighten them yet.
11   Connect the balljoint to the knuckle and tighten the pinch bolt/nut to the torque listed in this Chapter's Specifications.
12   Attach the tie-rod end to the steering knuckle arm (see Section 16). Tighten the strut bolts/nuts and the tie-rod end nut to the torque values listed in this Chapter's Specifications.

13   Install the wheel speed sensor.
14   Place the brake disc on the hub and install the caliper mounting bracket and caliper as outlined in Chapter 9.
15   Install the driveaxle/hub nut and tighten it securely (final tightening will be carried out when the vehicle is lowered).
16   Install the wheel and lug nuts.
17   Lower the vehicle and tighten the lug nuts to the torque listed in the Chapter 1 Specifications. Tighten the driveaxle/hub nut to the torque listed in the Chapter 8 Specifications.
18   Have the front-end alignment checked and, if necessary, adjusted.

8   Hub and bearing assembly (front) - removal and installation

Warning: *Dust created by the brake system is harmful to your health. Never blow it out with compressed air and don't inhale any of it. Do not, under any circumstances, use petroleum-based solvents to clean brake parts. Use brake system cleaner only.*
1   Loosen the driveaxle/hub nut (see Chapter 8). Loosen the wheel lug nuts, raise the vehicle and support it securely on jackstands. Remove the wheel, then remove the hub nut.
2   Remove the brake disc (see Chapter 9).
3   Remove the ABS wheel speed sensor (see Chapter 9).
4   Remove the three hub/bearing assembly mounting bolts from the inner side of the steering knuckle (see illustration).
5   Remove the hub/bearing assembly from the steering knuckle and the end of the driveaxle, taking notice of how the spacer (between the hub/bearing assembly and the knuckle) is oriented.
Caution: *Don't allow the driveaxle's inner joint to become overextended. If the driveaxle splines stick in the hub, tap the end of the driveaxle out of the hub with a soft-faced hammer, or use a puller to force it out.*
6   Installation is the reverse of removal, making sure the spacer is installed in its original manner.

11.3 Location of the Watts links

1 *Left side link*   3 *Bellcrank*
2 *Right side link*

11.10 Bellcrank details

1 *Bellcrank*   2 *Through-bolt/nut*

Warning: *Do not substitute standard fasteners for the mounting bolts, or attempt to clean up the threads on the originals. These are special self-locking bolts.*

7   Lower the vehicle and tighten the lug nuts to the torque listed in the Chapter 1 Specifications. Tighten the driveaxle/hub nut to the torque listed in the Chapter 8 Specifications.

9 Rear shock absorbers - removal and installation

Warning: *Always replace the shockabsorbers in pairs - never replace just one of them.*

1   Loosen the rear wheel lug nuts. Chock the front wheels to keep the vehicle from rolling, then raise the rear of the vehicle and support it securely on jackstands. Remove the rear wheels.
2   Use a floor jack to support the rear axle on the side you are working on. Position the jack head under the coil spring pocket.
3   Remove the shock absorber upper and lower mounting bolts (see illustrations).
4   Examine the shock for signs of fluid leakage and the shock body for signs of damage. Test the operation of the shock, while holding it in an upright position, by moving the damper shaft through a full stroke, and then through short strokes of 2 to 4 inches. In both cases, the resistance felt should be smooth and continuous. If the resistance is jerky, uneven, or if there is any visible sign of wear or damage to the shock, replacement is necessary.
5   Installation is the reverse of removal. Use new bolts and tighten them to the torque listed in this Chapter's Specifications.
Caution: *Before tightening the lower mounting bolt, raise the suspension with the floor jack to simulate normal ride height.*

10 Rear coil springs - replacement

1   Loosen the rear wheel lug nuts. Chock the front wheels to keep the vehicle from rolling, then raise the rear of the vehicle and support it securely on jackstands. Remove the rear wheels.
2   Use floor jacks to support the rear axle on each side. Place the jack heads under the coil spring pockets.
3   Mark each spring to make sure they are installed into the their original locations.
4   Remove the shock absorber lower mounting bolt on each side (see illustration 9.3a).
5   A little at a time, carefully lower both sides of the rear axle assembly, allowing it to pivot down until the coil spring tension is released.
6   The coil springs can be lifted off the pads on the rear axle assembly.
7   If the springs are being replaced, transfer the upper and lower spring pads to the new springs.
8   Installation is the reverse of removal. The springs should be installed with their colored tags toward the rear of the vehicle.

11 Watts linkage - removal and installation

Note: *GM references the Watts links as equalizer beams, the bellcrank as the equalizer center link and the Watts support beam as the equalizer support beam. When ordering replacement parts it may be necessary to refer to them under the GM referenced names.*

1   Loosen the rear wheel lug nuts. Chock the front wheels to keep the vehicle from rolling, then raise the rear of the vehicle and sup-

port it securely on jackstands. Remove the rear wheels.

Right- or left-side Watts link

2   Drill out the three rivets retaining the bellcrank heat shield to support beam and remove the heat shield.
3   Remove the Watts link end-to-rear axle bolt (see illustration) on the outer end of the link, then separate the link from the rear axle.
4   Remove the Watts link end-to-bellcrank through-bolt and nut on the inner end of the link, then separate the link from the bellcrank and remove the link from under the vehicle.
5   Place the Watts link inner end into the bellcranks and install the new through-bolt and nut then the outer end on to the rear axle and install the new mounting bolt.
Note: *On 2015 models, new Watts links are used that are slightly shorter than all other year models and are not interchangeable with the old versions. If replacing the links make sure to measure the replacement ones with the original links.*
6   Tighten the bolt/nuts to the torque listed in this this Chapter's Specifications.
7   Installation is the reverse of removal.

Bellcrank

8   Remove the rear section of the exhaust system.
9   Remove the Watts links (see Steps 1 through 5).
10   Remove the bellcrank through-bolt and nut (see illustration), then remove the bellcrank.
11   Insert the bellcrank into the opening in the Watts link support beam then install the through bolt and nut.
12   Tighten the through-bolt/nut to the torque listed in this Chapter's Specifications.
13   Installation is the reverse of removal.

11.16 Watts link support beammounting bolt locations

12.8 Rear axle bushing through-bolt (A) and bracket-to-body mounting bolts (B). Don't loosen the through-bolts unless the bushings are to be replaced

Watts link support beam

14   Remove the bellcrank (see Steps 8 through 10).

15   Disconnect the parking brake cable retainer, if equipped, and separate the cable from the support beam.

16   Remove the support beam mounting bolts (see illustration) and remove the support beam. Discard the old bolts.

17   Place the support beam against the body the install the new mounting bolts.

18   Tighten the mounting bolts to the torque listed in this Chapter's Specifications.

19   Installation is the reverse of removal.

12   Rear axle assembly - removal and installation

1   Loosen the rear wheel lug nuts. Chock the front wheels to keep the vehicle from rolling, then raise the rear of the vehicle and support it securely on jackstands. Remove the rear wheels.

13.3 Rear hub and bearing assembly bolts

2   Disconnect the brake pipes from the hoses at the trailing arms and plug the fittings to prevent entry of dirt or excessive fluid loss (see Chapter 9).

3   Disconnect the ABS electrical connectors at the rear axle.

4   Release the ends of the parking brake cables from the rear brakes (see Chapter 9). Also free the cables from any brackets on the rear axle.

5   Remove the coil springs (see Section 10).

6   Remove the outer ends of the Watts links, if equipped (see Section 11).

7   Support the rear axle with a pair of floor jacks and have an assistant on hand, or use a transmission jack on which you can chain the axle securely.

8   Remove the mounting bolts securing the axle bushing brackets to the body on each side, at the front of the trailing arms (see illustration).

Note: *If the rear axle through-bolts are removed, the final tightening must be with the vehicle at normal ride height.*

9   Carefully lower the rear axle assembly to the floor.

10   Inspect the trailing arm pivot bushings for signs of deterioration. If they are in need of replacement, take the axle assembly to an automotive machine shop to have the bushings replaced.

11   Installation is the reverse of removal, noting the following points:

a)   *Raise the rear axle assembly to approximate ride height before tightening the through-bolts (if they were removed for bushing replacement).*

b)   *Align the axle bushing brackets to the body on each side by inserting a 12 mm pin in the frontmost bolt hole on each side, through the bracket and into the body, then install and tighten the bolts.*

c)   *Tighten the fasteners to the torque listed in this Chapter's Specifications.*

d)   *Bleed the brake system (see Chapter 9).*

e)   *Tighten the wheel lug nuts to the torque listed in the Chapter 1 Specifications.*

f)   *Have the rear wheel alignment checked and, if necessary, adjusted.*

13   Hub and bearing assembly (rear) - removal and installation

Warning: *Dust created by the brake system is harmful to your health. Never blow it out with compressed air and don't inhale any of it. Do not, under any circumstances, use petroleum-based solvents to clean brake parts. Use brake system cleaner only.*

1   Loosen the rear wheel lug nuts. Chock the front wheels to keep the vehicle from rolling, then raise the rear of the vehicle and support it securely on jackstands. Remove the rear wheels.

2   Remove the brake shoes or disc brake assembly (see Chapter 9). If equipped, also detach the ABS wheel speed sensor electrical connector.

3   Remove the hub bolts (see illustration) and detach the hub from the rear axle.

4   Check the hub bearing for wear or damage. Spin it with your fingers and check for rough, loose or noisy rotation. The bearing can't be replaced separately, so if the bearing is bad or any other problems are found, replace the hub as an assembly.

5   Installation is the reverse of removal. Clean the brake backing plate on both sides and the axle flange before installing the hub/bearing assembly. Tighten the hub and bearing assembly bolts to the torque listed in this Chapter's Specifications.

6   Install the wheel and lug nuts, lower the vehicle and tighten the lug nuts to the torque listed in the Chapter 1 Specifications.

14.3 On 2015 and earlier models, the airbag is secured by spring clips that engage two posts on the airbag (one post per side); to release them, insert a blunt round tool, then repeat on the other side

14.5 Lift the airbag module off and disconnect the electrical connectors (to detach the airbag connectors, pry up the locking tabs, then pull the connectors straight off)

14.6 Steering wheel hub and steering shaft index marks

14 Steering wheel - removal and installation

Warning: *These models are equipped with a Supplemental Restraint System (SRS), more commonly known as airbags. Always disable the airbag system before working in the vicinity of any airbag system component to avoid the possibility of accidental deployment of the airbag(s), which could cause personal injury (see Chapter 12).*
Warning: *Do not use a memory saving device to preserve the PCM or radio memory when working on or near airbag system components.*
Warning: *The manufacturer recommends replacing the steering wheel retaining nut with a new one whenever it is removed.*

Removal

1   Park the vehicle with the wheels pointing straight ahead. Disconnect the cable from the negative terminal of the battery (see Chapter 5).
2   Disable the airbag system (see Chapter 12).
3   On 2015 and earlier models, starting with the steering wheel in the 3 o'clock position, detach the airbag module by inserting a blunt round tool (like a punch or the blunt end of a drill bit) into the hole on each side of the steering wheel, then push to spread the retaining clip in the hole, which will release the airbag retaining post (see illustration).
4   On 2016 and later models, remove the steering column covers (see Chapter 11), rotate the steering wheel until the curved opening on the back side of the steering wheel is on top, then insert a screwdriver into the curved opening and push down on the airbag retaining spring.
5   Lift the airbag module carefully away from the steering wheel and disconnect the electrical connectors (see illustration).
Warning: *When carrying the airbag module, keep the driver's side of it away from your*

14.8a Disconnect the electrical connectors bottom of the clockspring and multi-function switches. . .

body, and when you set it down (in an isolated area), have the driver's side facing up and away from your face.
6   Remove the steering wheel bolt, then mark the relationship of the steering wheel to the shaft (see illustration).
7   Remove the steering wheel from the steering column shaft, feeding the wiring harness through the hole in the wheel.
Caution: *While the steering wheel is removed, DO NOT turn the steering shaft. If you do so, the airbag clockspring could be damaged.*
8   If it is necessary to remove the clockspring, remove the steering column covers (see Chapter 11), unplug the electrical connectors for the clockspring (including the multi-function switch connectors), then spread the retaining tab at each side of the assembly and slide the clockspring/multifunction assembly from the steering column (see illustrations).
Note: *It is helpful to apply a piece of masking tape across the clockspring face to keep it centered while it is off the vehicle.*

14.8b. . . and the top of the clockspring and multi-function switches, then spread the clip on each side (left side shown) and slide the unit off the steering column

Installation

9   When installing the clockspring, make absolutely sure that the airbag clockspring is centered with the arrows aligned on the clockspring face. This shouldn't be a problem as long as you have not turned the steering shaft while the wheel was removed. If for some reason the shaft was turned, center the clockspring as follows:

a) *If equipped, remove the yellow locking tab from the clockspring (save it for use during installation).*
b) *Turn the hub of the clockspring clockwise until it stops (don't apply too much force, though).*
c) *Turn the hub counterclockwise, counting the number of turns until it stops (again, don't apply too much force).*
d) *Now turn the hub clockwise, half the number of turns recorded in the previous Step and align the arrows.*
e) *Install the yellow locking tab, if available. If you don't have a locking tab, prevent the clockspring hub from moving by applying a strip of tape across the clockspring body and hub. Remove the tape after the clockspring has been installed on the steering column.*

15.7 Mark the relationship of the two shafts, then remove the pinch bolt

15.8 Remove the steering column mounting nuts, and replace them with new ones

16.2 Using two wrenches, loosen the jam nut

16.3 Mark the position of the tie-rod end in relation to the threads

16.4 Disconnect the tie-rod end from the steering knuckle arm with a puller

10   Installation is the reverse of removal, noting the following points:

a) *Make sure the airbag clockspring is centered before installing the steering wheel.*

b) *When installing the steering wheel, align the marks on the shaft and the steering wheel hub.*

c) *Install then tighten a NEW steering wheel bolt to the torque listed in this Chapter's Specifications.*

d) *Install the airbag module on the steering wheel and push it into place until the retaining posts engage with the retaining springs.*

e) *Enable the airbag system (see Chapter 12).*

15   Steering column - removal and installation

Warning: *These models are equipped with airbags. Always disable the airbag system before working in the vicinity of any airbag system component to avoid the possibility of accidental deployment of the airbag(s), which*

could cause personal injury (see Chapter 12). **Warning:** *Do not use a memory saving device to preserve the PCM's memory when working on or near airbag system components.*

Removal

1   Park the vehicle with the wheels in the straight-ahead position. Disconnect the cable from the negative terminal of the battery (see Chapter 5). Disable the airbag system (see Chapter 12).
2   Remove the steering wheel (see Section 14) and the steering column covers (see Chapter 11).
3   Remove the clockspring/multi-function switch assembly (see Section 14).
4   Remove the knee bolster (see Chapter 11).
5   Disconnect the electrical connector for the shift interlock solenoid from the ignition lock cylinder.
6   Disconnect any other electrical connectors that may interfere with removal.
7   Mark the relationship of the steering column shaft to the intermediate shaft, then remove the pinch bolt (see illustration).
8   Remove the steering column mounting fasteners (see illustration), then guide the

column out from the instrument panel.
Warning: *The steering column tie strap bolts located on top of the steering column, are torque sensitive and have been tightened while the vehicle was being produced. Do not try to loosen or tighten the tie strap bolts at any time or the column may be damaged. If the column is damaged the vehicle may not perform properly resulting in a crash or personal injury.*

Installation

9   Guide the column into position, connecting the steering shaft with the intermediate shaft. Align the marks made in Step 7.
10   Install the mounting fasteners, tightening them to the torque listed in this Chapter's Specifications.
11   Install the pinch bolt and tighten it to the torque listed in this Chapter's Specifications.
12   The remainder of installation is the reverse of removal. Refer to Section 14 for the clockspring, steering wheel and airbag module installation details.

16   Tie-rod ends - removal and installation

Removal

1   Loosen the wheel lug nuts, raise the front of the vehicle and support it securely on jackstands. Apply the parking brake and block the rear wheels to keep the vehicle from rolling off the jackstands. Remove the wheel.
2   Loosen the tie-rod end jam nut (see illustration).
3   Mark the relationship of the tie-rod end to the threaded portion of the tie-rod. This will ensure the toe-in setting is restored when reassembled (see illustration).
4   Loosen the nut from the tie-rod end ballstud a few turns. Disconnect the tie-rod end ballstud from the steering knuckle arm with a puller (see illustration).
5   Remove the nut from the ballstud and discard it (use a new one during installation).

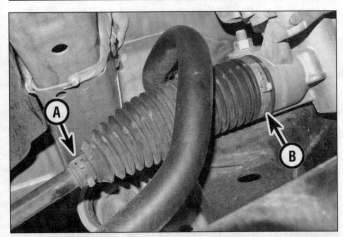

17.3 The outer ends of the steering gear boots are secured by band-type clamps (A); they're easily released with a pair of pliers. The inner ends of the steering gear boots are retained by boot clamps (B) which may be cut off and discarded

18.2 Mark the relationship of the universal joint to the steering gear input shaft, then remove the U-joint pinch bolt

Separate the tie-rod end from the steering knuckle, then unscrew the tie-rod end from the tie-rod.

Installation

6   Thread the tie-rod end onto the tie-rod to the marked position and connect the tie-rod end to the steering arm. Install a new nut on the ballstud and tighten it to the torque listed in this Chapter's Specifications.

7   Tighten the jam nut securely and install the wheel. Lower the vehicle and tighten the lug nuts to the torque listed in the Chapter 1 Specifications.

8   Have the front end alignment checked and, if necessary, adjusted.

18.6 Steering gear mounting bolts (2015 and earlier models shown, later models use three bolts)

17 Steering gear boots - removal and installation

1   Loosen the lug nuts, raise the vehicle and support it securely on jackstands. Remove the wheel.

2   Remove the tie-rod end and jam nut (see Section 16).

3   Remove the outer steering gear boot clamp with a pair of pliers (see illustration). Cut off the inner boot clamp with a pair of diagonal cutters. Slide off the boot.

4   Before installing the new boot, wrap the threads and serrations on the end of the steering rod with a layer of tape so the small end of the new boot isn't damaged.

5   Slide the new boot into position on the steering gear until it seats in the groove in the steering rod and install new clamps.

6   Remove the tape and install the tie-rod end (see Section 16).

7   Install the wheel and lug nuts. Lower the vehicle and tighten the lug nuts to the torque listed in the Chapter 1 Specifications.

8   Have the front end alignment checked and, if necessary, adjusted.

18 Steering gear - removal and installation

Warning: *Make sure the steering shaft is not turned while the steering gear is removed or you could damage the airbag system clockspring. To prevent the shaft from turning, place the ignition key in the LOCK position or thread the seat belt through the steering wheel and clip it into place.*

Warning: *Do not place any part of your body under the transaxle assembly, engine or subframe when it's supported only by a hoist or other lifting device.*

Removal

1   Disconnect the cable from the negative battery terminal (see Chapter 5). Position the wheels straight ahead, remove the ignition key and turn the steering wheel counterclockwise until the column locks.

2   Inside the vehicle, mark the relationship of the U-joint to the steering gear input shaft, then remove the pinch-bolt securing the U-joint to the steering gear input shaft (see illustration).

3   Loosen the front wheel lug nuts, raise the front of the vehicle and support it securely on jackstands. Remove both front wheels.

4   Detach the tie-rod ends from the steering knuckles (see Section 16).

5   Disconnect the electrical connectors from the steering gear.

Caution: *Electrostatic discharge can damage the internal solid state components of the steering gear. To avoid electrostatic discharge damage to the steering gear components, handle the components only by the external housing. Do not touch the electrical terminals during removal and installation. If available, ground yourself to the vehicle with an anti-static ground strap, available at computer supply stores.*

6   Remove the steering gear mounting bolts (see illustration).

7   Remove the rear transaxle mount (see Chapter 2A).

8   On 2015 and earlier models, support the rear of the subframe with a floor jack. Remove the rear subframe bolts and reinforcement bolts (see Section 18) then lower it approximately 2 inches (55 mm).

20.3 The jackstands must be placed behind the subframe, on the unibody frame rails

20.15 Remove the subframe-to-chassis mounting bolts

1	Subframe front bolts	3	Subframe
2	Subframe rear bolts		reinforcement bolts

9   On 2015 and earlier models, remove the stabilizer bar bracket bolts (see Section 4), then lift and support the right side of the bar so that the steering gear can pass underneath.

10   On 2015 and earlier models, slide the steering gear carefully out through the right side wheel opening.

11   On 2016 and later models, remove the subframe (see Section 20), then remove the stabilizer bar (see Section 4).

12   On 2016 and later models, remove and discard the steering gear mounting nuts and bolts then remove the steering gear.

13   Installation is the reverse of removal, noting the following points:

a) *Replace the steering gear mounting bolts/nuts and the intermediate shaft pinch bolt with new ones. Tighten them to the torque listed in this Chapter's Specifications.*

b) *Reconnect the negative battery cable (see Chapter 5).*

c) *Have the front end alignment checked and, if necessary, adjusted.*

19   Power steering system - general information

1   These vehicles have a power steering system that does not use power steering fluid or a hydraulic pump to circulate fluid. Instead, an electric motor applies assistance to the steering gear when needed. The system is called Electric Power Steering (EPS), and all the components are incorporated into the steering gear. Among the components are torque-sensors that determine driver input and difficulty of steering, a DC electric motor, and a Power Steering Control Module. The PSCM receives and processes information from the torque sensors, the vehicle speed

sensor (so assist is added when speeds are slowest, and vice-versa), and a steering input that tracks the amount of power assist.

2   If there is a malfunction in the EPS system, the steering will still operate, and a "PWR STR" message will be seen on the driver information display on the instrument panel.

20   Subframe - removal and installation

Warning: *The manufacturer recommends replacing the subframe bolts with new ones whenever they are removed.*

1   Disconnect the cable from the negative battery terminal (see Chapter 5).

2   Remove the lower intermediate shaft bolt and steering gear mounting bolts (see Section 18) and secure the steering gear to the body with mechanic's wire.

3   Loosen the front wheel lug nuts, raise the front of the vehicle and support it securely on jackstands (see illustration). Remove both front wheels.

4   Support the radiator and condenser from above on the condenser tabs located on each side of the condenser with plastic tie-wraps or wire, if necessary.

5   Remove the front exhaust pipe (see Chapter 4).

6   Remove the inner fender splash shield and bumper cover (see Chapter 11).

7   Remove any electrical harness clips and connectors and move the harnesses out of the way.

8   Detach the tie-rod ends from the steering knuckles (see Section 16).

9   Disconnect the stabilizer bar links from the stabilizer bar (see Section 4).

10   Roll an engine hoist into position and attach it to the engine with lengths of heavy-

duty chain. If the engine is equipped with lifting brackets, use them. If not, you'll have to fasten the chain to some substantial part of the engine - one that is strong enough to take the weight, but in a location that will provide good balance. If you're attaching the chain to a stud on the engine, or are using a bolt passing through the chain and into a threaded hole, place a washer between the nut or bolt head and the chain, and tighten the nut or bolt securely. Take up the slack in the chain, but don't lift the engine.

Warning: *DO NOT place any part of your body under the engine when it's supported only by a hoist or other lifting device.*

11   Remove the through-bolt from the front transaxle-to-subframe mount, and the mount-to-subframe bolts from the rear transaxle mount (see Chapter 2A).

12   Disconnect the control arms from the steering knuckles (see Section 5).

13   Carefully mark the position of the subframe in relation to the vehicle chassis.

14   Using two floor jacks, support the subframe. Position one jack on each side of the subframe, midway between the front and rear mounting points.

15   Remove the subframe mounting bolts (see illustration).

16   Lower the jacks until the subframe is resting on the ground.

17   Installation is the reverse of removal, noting the following points:

a) *Replace the subframe bolts with new ones. Align the reference marks on the subframe with all the bolts hand-tight, then tighten the subframe mounting bolts to the torque listed in this Chapter's Specifications.*

b) *Reconnect the negative battery cable (see Chapter 5).*

c) *Have the front end alignment checked and, if necessary, adjusted.*

21 Wheels and tires - general information

1   All vehicles covered by this manual are equipped with metric-sized fiberglass or steel belted radial tires (see illustration). Use of other size or type of tires may affect the ride and handling of the vehicle. Don't mix different types of tires, such as radials and bias belted, on the same vehicle as handling may be seriously affected. It's recommended that tires be replaced in pairs on the same axle, but if only one tire is being replaced, be sure it's the same size, structure and tread design as the other.

2   Because tire pressure has a substantial effect on handling and wear, the pressure on all tires should be checked at least once a month or before any extended trips (see Chapter 1).

3   Wheels must be replaced if they are bent, dented, leak air, have elongated bolt holes, are heavily rusted, out of vertical symmetry or if the lug nuts won't stay tight. Wheel repairs that use welding or peening are not recommended.

4   Tire and wheel balance is important in the overall handling, braking and performance of the vehicle. Unbalanced wheels can adversely affect handling and ride characteristics as well as tire life. Whenever a tire is installed on a wheel, the tire and wheel should be balanced by a shop with the proper equipment.

22 Wheel alignment - general information

1   A wheel alignment refers to the adjustments made to the wheels so they are in proper angular relationship to the suspension and the ground. Wheels that are out of proper alignment not only affect vehicle control, but also increase tire wear. The front end angles normally measured are camber, caster and toe-in (see illustration). Toe-in and camber on the front end are adjustable; if the caster is not correct, check for bent components.

2   Getting the proper wheel alignment is a very exacting process, one in which complicated and expensive machines are necessary to perform the job properly. Because of this, you should have a technician with the proper equipment perform these tasks. We will, however, use this space to give you a basic idea of what is involved with a wheel alignment so you can better understand the process and deal intelligently with the shop that does the work.

3   Toe-in is the turning in of the wheels. The purpose of a toe specification is to ensure parallel rolling of the wheels. In a vehicle

with zero toe-in, the distance between the front edges of the wheels will be the same as the distance between the rear edges of the wheels. The actual amount of toe-in is normally only a fraction of an inch. Toe-in is controlled by the tie-rod end position on the tie-rod. Incorrect toe-in will cause the tires to wear improperly by making them scrub against the road surface.

4   Camber is the tilting of the wheels from vertical when viewed from one end of the vehicle. When the wheels tilt out at the top, the camber is said to be positive (+). When the wheels tilt in at the top the camber is negative (-). The amount of tilt is measured in-degrees from vertical and this measurement is called the camber angle. This angle affects the amount of tire tread which contacts the road and compensates for changes in the suspension geometry when the vehicle is cornering or traveling over an undulating surface. Camber can be adjusted on the front end, but will require a modification of the lower strut-to-knuckle bolt hole on the strut. The strut must be disconnected from the steering knuckle, the lower mounting bolt holes elongated (from side-to-side), then reassembled. The relationship of the steering knuckle to the strut can then be altered.

5   Caster is the tilting of the front steering axis from the vertical. A tilt toward the rear is positive caster and a tilt toward the front is negative caster. Caster is not adjustable on these vehicles.

METRIC TIRE SIZES

P 185 / 80 R 13

TIRE TYPE
P-PASSENGER
T-TEMPORARY
C-COMMERCIAL

ASPECT RATIO
(SECTION HEIGHT)
(SECTION WIDTH)
70
75
80

RIM DIAMETER
(INCHES)
13
14
15

SECTION WIDTH
(MILLIMETERS)
185
195
205
ETC

CONSTRUCTION TYPE
R-RADIAL
B-BIAS - BELTED
D-DIAGONAL (BIAS)

SECTION WIDTH

SECTION HEIGHT

21.1 Metric tire size code

CAMBER ANGLE (FRONT VIEW)

CASTER ANGLE (SIDE VIEW)

TOE-IN (TOP VIEW)

22.1 Camber, caster and toe-in angles

A minus B = C (degrees camber)
D = degrees caster
E minus F = toe-in (measured in inches)
G = toe-in (expressed in degrees)

Notes

Chapter 11
Body

Contents

Specifications

Torque specifications

Note: *One foot-pound (ft-lb) of torque is equivalent to 12 inch-pounds (in-lbs) of torque. Torque values below approximately 15 ft-lbs are expressed in inch-pounds, because most foot-pound torque wrenches are not accurate at these smaller values.*

	Ft-lbs (unless otherwise indicated)	Nm
Front seat mounting bolts	33	45
Seat belt-to-seat belt tensioner bolt	44 in-lbs	5

1   General Information

Warning: *The models covered by this manual are equipped with Supplemental Restraint Systems (SRS), more commonly known as airbags. Always disable the air-* *bag system before working in the vicinity of any airbag system components to avoid the possibility of accidental deployment of the airbags, which could cause personal injury (see Chapter 12).*

1   Certain body components are particularly vulnerable to accident damage and can be unbolted and repaired or replaced. Among these parts are the hood, doors, tailgate, liftgate, bumpers and front fenders.

2   Only general body maintenance practices and body panel repair procedures within the scope of the do-it-yourselfer are included in this Chapter.

2.1a Make sure the damaged area is perfectly clean and rust free. If the touch-up kit has a wire brush, use it to clean the scratch or chip. Or use fine steel wool wrapped around the end of a pencil. Clean the scratched or chipped surface only, not the good paint surrounding it. Rinse the area with water and allow it to dry thoroughly

2.1b Thoroughly mix the paint, then apply a small amount with the touch-up kit brush or a very fine artist's brush. Brush in one direction as you fill the scratch area. Do not build up the paint higher than the surrounding paint

2   Repairing minor paint scratches

1   No matter how hard you try to keep your vehicle looking like new, it will inevitably be scratched, chipped or dented at some point. If the metal is actually dented, seek the advice of a professional. But you can fix minor scratches and chips yourself (see illustrations). Buy a touch-up paint kit from a dealer service department or an auto parts store. To ensure that you get the right color, you'll need to have the specific make, model and year of your vehicle and, ideally, the paint code, which is located on a special metal plate under the hood or in the door jamb.

3   Body repair - minor damage

Plastic body panels

1   The following repair procedures are for minor scratches and gouges. Repair of more serious damage should be left to a dealer service department or qualified auto body shop. Below is a list of the equipment and materials necessary to perform the following repair procedures on plastic body panels.

    Wax, grease and silicone removing solvent
    Cloth-backed body tape
    Sanding discs
    Drill motor with three-inch disc holder
    Hand sanding block
    Rubber squeegees
    Sandpaper
    Non-porous mixing palette
    Wood paddle or putty knife
    Wood paddle or putty knife
    Curved-tooth body file
    Flexible parts repair material

Flexible panels (bumper trim)

2   Remove the damaged panel, if necessary or desirable. In most cases, repairs can be carried out with the panel installed.

2.1c If the vehicle has a two-coat finish, apply the clear coat after the color coat has dried

3   Clean the area(s) to be repaired with a wax, grease and silicone removing solvent applied with a water-dampened cloth.
4   If the damage is structural, that is, if it extends through the panel, clean the backside of the panel area to be repaired as well. Wipe dry.
5   Sand the rear surface about 1-1/2 inches beyond the break.
6   Cut two pieces of fiberglass cloth large enough to overlap the break by about 1-1/2 inches. Cut only to the required length.
7   Mix the adhesive from the repair kit according to the instructions included with the kit, and apply a layer of the mixture approximately 1/8-inch thick on the backside of the panel. Overlap the break by at least 1-1/2 inches.
8   Apply one piece of fiberglass cloth to the adhesive and cover the cloth with additional adhesive. Apply a second piece of fiberglass cloth to the adhesive and immediately cover the cloth with additional adhesive in sufficient quantity to fill the weave.

2.1d Wait a few days for the paint to dry thoroughly, then rub out the repainted area with a polishing compound to blend the new paint with the surrounding area. When you're happy with your work, wash and polish the area

9   Allow the repair to cure for 20 to 30 minutes at 60-degrees to 80-degrees F.
10   If necessary, trim the excess repair material at the edge.
11   Remove all of the paint film over and around the area(s) to be repaired. The repair material should not overlap the painted surface.
12   With a drill motor and a sanding disc (or a rotary file), cut a "V" along the break line approximately 1/2-inch wide. Remove all dust and loose particles from the repair area.
13   Mix and apply the repair material. Apply a light coat first over the damaged area; then continue applying material until it reaches a level slightly higher than the surrounding finish.
14   Cure the mixture for 20 to 30 minutes at 60-degrees to 80-degrees F.
15   Roughly establish the contour of the area being repaired with a body file. If low areas or pits remain, mix and apply additional adhesive.

16   Block sand the damaged area with sandpaper to establish the actual contour of the surrounding surface.

17   If desired, the repaired area can be temporarily protected with several light coats of primer. Because of the special paints and techniques required for flexible body panels, it is recommended that the vehicle be taken to a paint shop for completion of the body repair.

Steel body panels

Repairing simple dents

18   When repairing dents, the first job is to pull the dent out until the affected area is as close as possible to its original shape. There is no point in trying to restore the original shape completely as the metal in the damaged area will have stretched on impact and cannot be restored to its original contours. It is better to bring the level of the dent up to a point that is about 1/8-inch below the level of the surrounding metal. In cases where the dent is very shallow, it is not worth trying to pull it out at all.

19   If the backside of the dent is accessible, it can be hammered out gently from behind using a soft-face hammer. While doing this, hold a block of wood firmly against the opposite side of the metal to absorb the hammer blows and prevent the metal from being stretched.

20   If the dent is in a section of the body which has double layers, or some other factor makes it inaccessible from behind, a different technique is required. Drill several small holes through the metal inside the damaged area, particularly in the deeper sections. Screw long, self-tapping screws into the holes just enough for them to get a good grip in the metal. Now pulling on the protruding heads of the screws with locking pliers can pull out the dent.

21   The next stage of repair is the removal of paint from the damaged area and from an inch or so of the surrounding metal. This is easily done with a wire brush or sanding disk in a drill motor, although it can be done just as effectively by hand with sandpaper. To complete the preparation for filling, score the surface of the bare metal with a screwdriver or the tang of a file or drill small holes in the affected area. This will provide a good grip for the filler material. To complete the repair, see the Section on filling and painting.

Repair of rust holes or gashes

22   Remove all paint from the affected area and from an inch or so of the surrounding metal using a sanding disk or wire brush mounted in a drill motor. If these are not available, a few sheets of sandpaper will do the job just as effectively.

23   With the paint removed, you will be able to determine the severity of the corrosion and decide whether to replace the whole panel, if possible, or repair the affected area. New body panels are not as expensive as most people think and it is often quicker to install a new panel than to repair large areas of rust.

24   Remove all trim pieces from the affected area except those which will act as a guide to the original shape of the damaged body, such as headlight shells, etc. Using metal snips or a hacksaw blade, remove all loose metal and any other metal that is badly affected by rust. Hammer the edges of the hole in to create a slight depression for the filler material.

25   Wire-brush the affected area to remove the powdery rust from the surface of the metal. If the back of the rusted area is accessible, treat it with rust inhibiting paint.

26   Before filling is done, block the hole in some way. This can be done with sheet metal riveted or screwed into place, or by stuffing the hole with wire mesh.

27   Once the hole is blocked off, the affected area can be filled and painted. See the following subsection on filling and painting.

Filling and painting

28   Many types of body fillers are available, but generally speaking, body repair kits which contain filler paste and a tube of resin hardener are best for this type of repair work. A wide, flexible plastic or nylon applicator will be necessary for imparting a smooth and contoured finish to the surface of the filler material. Mix up a small amount of filler on a clean piece of wood or cardboard (use the hardener sparingly). Follow the manufacturer's instructions on the package, otherwise the filler will set incorrectly.

29   Using the applicator, apply the filler paste to the prepared area. Draw the applicator across the surface of the filler to achieve the desired contour and to level the filler surface. As soon as a contour that approximates the original one is achieved, stop working the paste. If you continue, the paste will begin to stick to the applicator. Continue to add thin layers of paste at 20-minute intervals until the level of the filler is just above the surrounding metal.

30   Once the filler has hardened, the excess can be removed with a body file. From then on, progressively finer grades of sandpaper should be used, starting with a 180-grit paper and finishing with 600-grit wet-or-dry paper. Always wrap the sandpaper around a flat rubber or wooden block, otherwise the surface of the filler will not be completely flat. During the sanding of the filler surface, the wet-or-dry paper should be periodically rinsed in water. This will ensure that a very smooth finish is produced in the final stage.

31   At this point, the repair area should be surrounded by a ring of bare metal, which in turn should be encircled by the finely feathered edge of good paint. Rinse the repair area with clean water until all of the dust produced by the sanding operation is gone.

32   Spray the entire area with a light coat of primer. This will reveal any imperfections in the surface of the filler. Repair the imperfections with fresh filler paste or glaze filler and once more smooth the surface with sandpaper. Repeat this spray-and-repair procedure until you are satisfied that the surface of the filler and the feathered edge of the paint are

perfect. Rinse the area with clean water and allow it to dry completely.

33   The repair area is now ready for painting. Spray painting must be carried out in a warm, dry, windless and dust free atmosphere. These conditions can be created if you have access to a large indoor work area, but if you are forced to work in the open, you will have to pick the day very carefully. If you are working indoors, dousing the floor in the work area with water will help settle the dust that would otherwise be in the air. If the repair area is confined to one body panel, mask off the surrounding panels. This will help minimize the effects of a slight mismatch in paint color. Trim pieces such as chrome strips, door handles, etc., will also need to be masked off or removed. Use masking tape and several thickness of newspaper for the masking operations.

34   Before spraying, shake the paint can thoroughly, then spray a test area until the spray painting technique is mastered. Cover the repair area with a thick coat of primer. The thickness should be built up using several thin layers of primer rather than one thick one. Using 600-grit wet-or-dry sandpaper, rub down the surface of the primer until it is very smooth. While doing this, the work area should be thoroughly rinsed with water and the wet-or-dry sandpaper periodically rinsed as well. Allow the primer to dry before spraying additional coats.

35   Spray on the top coat, again building up the thickness by using several thin layers of paint. Begin spraying in the center of the repair area and then, using a circular motion, work out until the whole repair area and about two inches of the surrounding original paint is covered. Remove all masking material 10 to 15 minutes after spraying on the final coat of paint. Allow the new paint at least two weeks to harden, then use a very fine rubbing compound to blend the edges of the new paint into the existing paint. Finally, apply a coat of wax.

4   Body repair - major damage

1   Major damage must be repaired by an auto body shop specifically equipped to perform body and frame repairs. These shops have the specialized equipment required to do the job properly.

2   If the damage is extensive, the frame must be checked for proper alignment or the vehicle's handling characteristics may be adversely affected and other components may wear at an accelerated rate.

3   Due to the fact that all of the major body components (hood, fenders, etc.) are separate and replaceable units, any seriously damaged components should be replaced rather than repaired. Sometimes the components can be found in a wrecking yard that specializes in used vehicle components, often at considerable savings over the cost of new parts.

These photos illustrate a method of repairing simple dents. They are intended to supplement *Body repair - minor damage* in this Chapter and should not be used as the sole instructions for body repair on these vehicles.

1 If you can't access the backside of the body panel to hammer out the dent, pull it out with a slide-hammer-type dent puller. Tap with a hammer near the edge of the dent to help 'pop' the metal back to its original shape, about 1/8-inch below the surface of the surrounding metal

2 Using coarse-grit sandpaper, remove the paint down to the bare metal. Clean the repair area with wax/silicone remover.

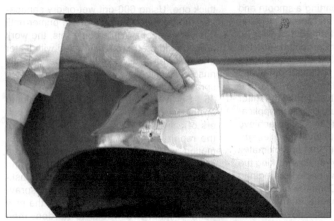

3 Following label instructions, mix up a batch of plastic filler and hardener, then quickly press it into the metal with a plastic applicator. Work the filler until it matches the original contour and is slightly above the surrounding metal

4 Let the filler harden until you can just dent it with your fingernail. File, then sand the filler down until it's smooth and even. Work down to finer grits of sandpaper - always using a board or block - ending up with 360 or 400 grit

5 When the area is smooth to the touch, clean the area and mask around it. Apply several layers of primer to the area. A professional-type spray gun is being used here, but aerosol spray primer works fine

6 Fill imperfections or scratches with glazing compound. Sand with 360 or 400-grit and re-spray. Finish sand the primer with 600 grit, clean thoroughly, then apply the finish coat. Don't attempt to rub out or wax the repair area until the paint has dried completely (at least two weeks)

5   Fastener and trim removal

1   There is a variety of plastic fasteners used to hold trim panels, splash shields and other parts in place in addition to typical screws, nuts and bolts. Once you are familiar with them, they can usually be removed without too much difficulty.

2   The proper tools and approach can prevent added time and expense to a project by minimizing the number of broken fasteners and/or parts.

3   The following illustration shows various types of fasteners that are typically used on most vehicles and how to remove and install them (see illustration). Replacement fasteners are commonly found at most auto parts stores, if necessary.

4   Trim panels are typically made of plastic and their flexibility can help during removal. The key to their removal is to use a tool to pry the panel near its retainers to release it without damaging surrounding areas or breaking-off any retainers. The

retainers will usually snap out of their designated slot or hole after force is applied to them. Stiff plastic tools designed for prying on trim panels are available at most auto parts stores (see illustration). Tools that are tapered and wrapped in protective tape, such as a screwdriver or small pry tool, are also very effective when used with care.

6   Upholstery, carpets and vinyl trim - maintenance

Upholstery and carpets

1   Every three months remove the floormats and clean the interior of the vehicle (more frequently if necessary). Use a stiff whiskbroom to brush the carpeting and loosen dirt and dust, then vacuum the upholstery and carpets thoroughly, especially along seams and crevices.

2   Dirt and stains can be removed from carpeting with basic household or automotive carpet shampoos available in spray

5.4 These small plastic pry tools are ideal for prying off trim panels

cans. Follow the directions and vacuum again, then use a stiff brush to bring back the "nap" of the carpet.

3   Most interiors have cloth or vinyl upholstery, either of which can be cleaned and maintained with a number of material-specific cleaners or shampoos available in

Fasteners

This tool is designed to remove special fasteners. A small pry tool used for removing nails will also work well in place of this tool

A Phillips head screwdriver can be used to release the center portion, but light pressure must be used because the plastic is easily damaged. Once the center is up, the fastener can easily be pried from its hole

Here is a view with the center portion fully released. Install the fastener as shown, then press the center in to set it

This fastener is used for exterior panels and shields. The center portion must be pried up to release the fastener. Install the fastener with the center up, then press the center in to set it

This type of fastener is used commonly for interior panels. Use a small blunt tool to press the small pin at the center in to release it . . .

. . . the pin will stay with the fastener in the released position

Reset the fastener for installation by moving the pin out. Install the fastener, then press the pin flush with the fastener to set it

This fastener is used for exterior and interior panels. It has no moving parts. Simply pry the fastener from its hole like the claw of a hammer removes a nail. Without a tool that can get under the top of the fastener, it can be very difficult to remove

7.3 Draw alignment marks around the hood hinges to ensure proper alignment of the hood when it's reinstalled

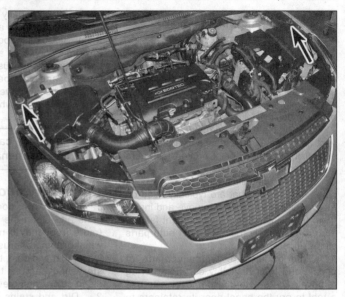

7.9 To adjust the vertical height of the leading edge of the hood so that it's flush with the fenders, turn each hood bumper clockwise (to lower the hood) or counterclockwise (to raise the hood)

auto supply stores. Follow the directions on the product for usage, and always spot-test any upholstery cleaner on an inconspicuous area (bottom edge of a backseat cushion) to ensure that it doesn't cause a color shift in the material.

4   After cleaning, vinyl upholstery should be treated with a protectant.

Note: *Make sure the protectant container indicates the product can be used on seats - some products may make a seat too slippery.*

Caution: *Do not use protectant on vinyl-covered steering wheels.*

5   Leather upholstery requires special care. It should be cleaned regularly with saddle-soap or leather cleaner. Never use alcohol, gasoline, nail polish remover or thinner to clean leather upholstery.

6   After cleaning, regularly treat leather upholstery with a leather conditioner, rubbed in with a soft cotton cloth. Never use car wax on leather upholstery.

7   In areas where the interior of the vehicle is subject to bright sunlight, cover leather seating areas of the seats with a sheet if the vehicle is to be left out for any length of time.

Vinyl trim

8   Don't clean vinyl trim with detergents, caustic soap or petroleum-based cleaners. Plain soap and water works just fine, with a soft brush to clean dirt that may be ingrained. Wash the vinyl as frequently as the rest of the vehicle.

9   After cleaning, application of a high-quality rubber and vinyl protectant will help prevent oxidation and cracks. The protectant can also be applied to weather-stripping, vacuum lines and rubber hoses, which often fail as a result of chemical degradation, and to the tires.

7   Hood - removal, installation and adjustment

Note: *The hood is somewhat awkward to remove and install; at least two people should perform this procedure.*

Removal and installation

1   Open the hood, then place blankets or pads over the fenders and cowl area of the body. This will protect the body and paint as the hood is lifted off.

2   Disconnect the windshield wiper washer hose and any cables or wires that will interfere with removal.

3   Make marks around the hood hinge to ensure proper alignment during installation (see illustration).

4   Have an assistant support the weight of the hood while you remove the hinge-to-hood nuts and lift off the hood.

5   Installation is the reverse of removal. Align the hinges with the marks made in Step 3, then tighten the nuts securely.

Adjustment

6   Fore-and-aft and side-to-side adjustment of the hood is done by moving the hood after loosening the hinge-to-body bolts. Up-and-down adjustments at the rear of the hood are made by loosening the hinge-to-hood bolts.

7   Mark around the entire hinge so you can determine the amount of movement.

8   Loosen the bolts and move the hood into correct alignment. Move it only a little at a time. Tighten the hinge bolts and carefully lower the hood to check the position.

9   Adjust the hood latch (see Section 8) and the hood bumpers on the fenders so the front of the hood, when closed, is flush with the fenders (see illustration).

10   The hood latch assembly, as well as the hinges, should be periodically lubricated with white lithium-base grease to prevent binding and wear.

8   Hood latch handle and release cable - removal and installation

Warning: *The models covered by this manual are equipped with Supplemental Restraint systems (SRS), more commonly known as airbags. Always disarm the air-bag system before working in the vicinity of any airbag system component to avoid the possibility of accidental deployment of the airbag, which could cause personal injury (see Chapter 12). Do not use a memory saving device to preserve the PCM's memory when working on or near airbag system components.*

1   Open the hood, then place blankets or pads over the fenders and cowl area of the body.

2   Remove the front bumper cover (see Section 9).

3   Remove the air inlet (see illustrations).

4   Remove the radiator grille support fasteners and support (see illustration).

5   Remove the hood latch bolts from the radiator support (see illustration).

6   Disconnect the hood latch cable by rotating the spring, providing slack. Disconnect the cable from the hook in the spring (see illustrations).

7   Inside the vehicle, use a trim tool to disengage the clips and remove the left carpet retainer/kick panel (see illustration).

8   Pull the handle downwards until is it almost straight, then unhook the handle from the body (see illustration). Free the cable end from the handle assembly.

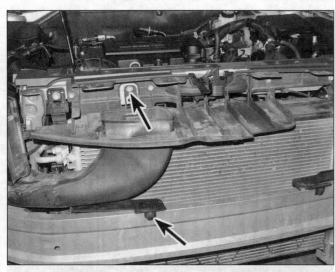

8.3a Remove the air inlet fasteners. . .

8.3b. . . then remove the air inlet support and air inlet

8.4 Radiator grille support fasteners

8.5 Hood latch mounting bolts

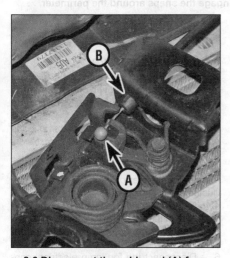

8.6 Disconnect the cable end (A) from the hook in the spring plate and release the cable mounting tab (B)

8.7 Release the clips at the door jamb and remove the carpet retainer/kick panel

8.8 Carefully pry the hood release handle from the body while sliding it downwards

**9.2 Remove the lower splash shield fasteners -
early models shown, later models similar**

9.3 Bumper cover stiffener bolt locations

9.7 Remove the fasteners at the top of the bumper cover

9.8a Carefully disengage the snaps around the perimeter. . .

9   Remove the cowl cover (see Section 12) and push the rubber release cable grommet through the firewall toward the engine. Pull the hood release cable from the interior into the engine compartment.

10   With the new cable attached to the wire or string, pull the wire or string back through the firewall until the new cable reaches the latch.

11   Check that the cable grommet is properly seated in the engine compartment firewall.

12   Working in the passenger compartment, reinstall the hood latch handle into the bracket, sliding the handle onto its bracket until the retainer clips snap into the notches in the bracket.

13   The remainder of installation is the reverse of removal.

9   Bumper covers - removal and installation

Warning: *The models covered by this manual are equipped with Supplemental Restraint systems (SRS), more commonly known as airbags. Always disarm the airbag system before working in the vicinity of any airbag system component to avoid the possibility of accidental deployment of the airbag, which could cause personal injury (see Chapter 12). Do not use a memory saving device to preserve the PCM's memory when working on or near airbag system components.*

1   Apply the parking brake, raise the vehicle and support it securely on jackstands. Use masking tape to protect the paint on adjacent panels while removing either front or rear bumper covers.

Front bumper cover

2   Remove the fasteners at the front edge of the bumper cover and remove the splash shield from under the vehicle (see illustration).

Note: *On 2016 and later models, remove the bumper cover-to-body extension fasteners and remove the extension.*

3   With the lower splash shield removed, remove the bumper cover stiffener bolts (see illustration), if equipped.

4   Remove the inner fender splash shield on each side of the vehicle (see illustration 10.2).

5   Remove the bumper cover-to-fender bolts.

6   Disconnect the fog lamp electrical connectors, if equipped.

7   Remove the fasteners along the top of the bumper cover (see illustration).

9.8b. . . then pull the bumper cover forward and off

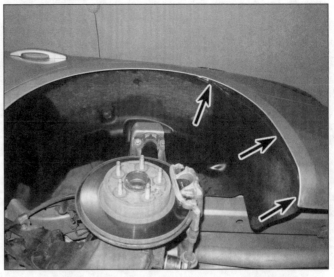

9.16 Remove the rear inner fender liner fasteners

9.17 Bumper cover-to-body fastener location

9.18 Remove the fasteners securing the cover along the bottom edge

8 Using a trim tool, unhook the snaps around the perimeter of the cover and remove the bumper cover (see illustrations).

9 Installation is the reverse of removal.

Aero shutter air deflector

10 Remove the front bumper cover.

11 Remove the aero shutter air deflector fasteners and shutter. On 2015 and earlier models, slide the deflector assembly from the bumper cover. On 2016 and later models, the shutter assembly is mounted to the bumper support brace on the vehicle instead of the bumper cover.

12 Depress the tabs around the grille opening with a flat-bladed tool, then remove the grille from the aero shutter.

13 Installation is the reverse of removal.

Rear bumper cover

14 Open the trunk lid or liftgate.

15 Disconnect the electrical connectors from the taillights, side marker lights and license plate light, then remove the taillights (see Chapter 12).

16 Remove the fasteners from the rear fenderwell splash shields (see illustration) and pull the shield back.

17 Remove the bumper cover-to-body fastener from each side (see illustration).

18 From below, remove the fasteners securing the cover along the bottom edge (see illustration).

19 Pull outward on each side of the bumper cover, while using a trim tool to disengage the retainer tabs (see illustration) around the perimeter of the cover from the rear bumper cover, then remove the bumper cover.

Caution: *It is possible to damage the rear bumper cover if all of the tabs are not disengaged before trying to remove it.*

20 Installation is the reverse of removal.

9.19 Use a trim tool to dissengage the retaining tabs around the perimeter - left side shown, remaining tabs identical

10.2 Inner fender splash shield fastener locations

10.6 Fender trim panel fastener location

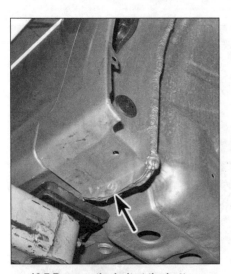

10.7 Remove the bolt at the bottom of the rocker panel

10.8 Remove the sound insulator bolt (A) then the sound insulator (B)

10.9 Location of the bolts securing the fender bracket to the body

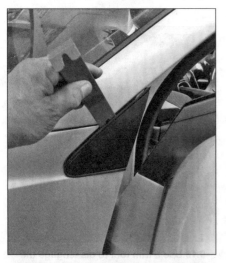

10.10a Carefully pry the trim panel out form the fender using a trim tool, then. . .

10.10b. . . remove the fender mounting bolt

10   Front fender - removal and installation

1   Loosen the front wheel lug nuts. Raise the vehicle, support it securely on jackstands and remove the front wheel. Use masking tape on adjacent body panels to prevent scratching the paint while removing the fender.

2   Remove the inner fender splash shield fasteners and remove the shield (see illustration).

3   Remove the front bumper cover (see Section 9).

4   Remove the headlight housing (see Chapter 12).

5   Remove the cowl cover (see Section 12).

6   Remove the push-pin fastener (see illustration), then side the plastic trim panel back covering the fender upper bolts and remove the trim panel.

10.11 Remove the fender mounting nut (A) and bolt (B) from inside the door opening

10.12 Fender upper mounting bolt locations

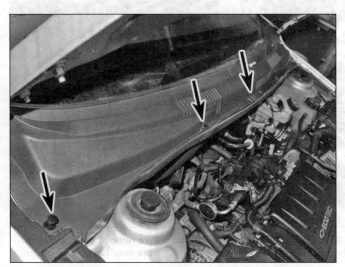

12.3a Right-side cowl cover fastener locations

12.3b Left-side cowl cover fastener locations

7   Remove the fender bolt at the bottom of the rocker panel (see illustration).

8   Remove the sound insulator panel from inside the fender (see illustration).

9   Remove the bolts securing the front of the fender bracket to the body (see illustration).

10   Open the door and remove the exterior trim panel and the mounting bolt (see illustrations).

11   With the door open, remove the nut and bolt from the rear of the fender (see illustration).

12   Remove the upper fender bolts (see illustration) and lift off the fender. It's a good idea to have an assistant support the fender while it's being moved away from the vehicle to prevent damage to the surrounding body panels.

13   Installation is the reverse of removal. Check the alignment of the fender to the hood and front edge of the door before final tightening of the fender fasteners.

11   Radiator grille - removal and installation

Upper grille

1   Remove the front bumper cover (see Section 9).

2   Remove the screws securing the grille to the bumper cover.

3   Carefully pry the grille from the bumper cover.

4   Installation is the reverse of removal.

Lower grille

5   Remove the front bumper cover (see Section 9).

6   Remove the four grille fasteners.

7   From the back of the bumper cover, depress the tabs around the grille opening with a flat-bladed tool, then remove the grille.

8   Installation is the reverse of removal.

Center grille

9   Remove the front bumper cover (see Section 9).

10   Unclip the energy absorber from the back side of the bumper cover.

11   From the back of the bumper cover, depress the tabs around the grille opening with a flat-bladed tool, then remove the grille.

12   Installation is the reverse of removal.

12   Cowl cover - removal and installation

1   Remove the wiper arms and the nuts from the wiper arm shafts (see Chapter 12).

2   Pull the hood weatherstrip up and off.

3   Remove the plastic push-pin mounting fasteners (see illustrations).

4   Lift the right-side cowl cover off first, then the left side, and disconnect the washer fluid hose.

5   Installation is the reverse of removal.

13.2 Disengage the clips and remove the sail panel

13.3 Remove the cover and the screw from the door pull cup

13.4 Release the snap securing the cover in the door handle opening, then remove the screw

13.5 Use a trim tool to release the fasteners around the door panel

13.6a Pry the end of the cable upwards to disengage the retainer. . .

13.6b. . . then remove the cable from the door handle

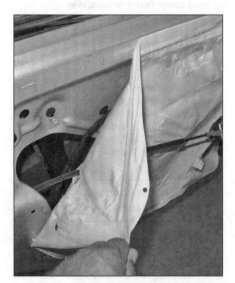

13.8 Peel back the plastic watershield, being careful not to tear it

13   Door trim panels - removal and installation

Warning: *The models covered by this manual are equipped with Supplemental Restraint systems (SRS), more commonly known as airbags. Always disarm the airbag system before working in the vicinity of any airbag system component to avoid the possibility of accidental deployment of the airbag, which could cause personal injury (see Chapter 12). Do not use a memory saving device to preserve the PCM's memory when working on or near airbag system components.*

Warning: *The manufacturer states the door panel retaining clips must be replaced with new retaining clips whenever they become loose or are removed. Failure to replace the retaining clips once they are broken or become loose may cause a severe loss of structural safety in cases of a crash, which might result in personal injury.*

Removal

Note: *Procedures for the rear doors are similar to the front doors.*

1   Disconnect the cable from the negative battery terminal (see Chapter 5).

2   Carefully pry off the sail panel (see illustration).

3   Remove the screw cover and screw from the door pull opening (see illustration).

4   At the inside door handle opening, pull the handle back and use a small screwdriver to unsnap the cap covering the retaining screw, then remove the screw (see illustration).

5   Remove the door trim panel using a trim panel removal tool (see illustration). Start from the bottom of the trim panel and work around the perimeter until all fasteners have been released from the door.

6   Lift the trim panel up to disengage the panel from the upper door ridge. Unplug any electrical connectors, disconnect the door handle release cable (see illustrations) and remove the panel.

14.6 Door mounting details

1   Door stop link mounting bolt   *2   Hinge bolts*

14.13 Adjust the door lock striker by loosening the mounting screws and gently tapping the striker in the desired direction

7   Disconnect the electrical connectors from the switch assembly.

8   For access to components inside the door, raise the window fully, then carefully peel back the plastic watershield (see illustration).

Installation

9   Prior to installation of the door trim panels, reinstall any clips in the panel which may have come out during removal.

10   Position the wire harness connectors for the power door lock switch and the power window switch (if equipped) on the back of the panel, then place the panel in position in the door. Press the door panel into place until the clips are seated.

11   The remainder of installation is the reverse of removal.

14   Door - removal, installation and adjustment

Warning: *The models covered by this manual are equipped with Supplemental Restraint systems (SRS), more commonly known as airbags. Always disarm the airbag system before working in the vicinity of any airbag system component to avoid the possibility of accidental deployment of the airbag, which could cause personal injury (see Chapter 12). Do not use a memory saving device to preserve the PCM's memory when working on or near airbag system components.*
Note: *The door is heavy and somewhat awkward to remove and install - at least two people should perform this procedure.*

Removal and installation

1   Raise the window completely in the door. Open the door all the way and support it on jacks or blocks covered with rags to prevent damaging the paint.

2   Disconnect the cable from the negative battery terminal (see Chapter 5).

3   Remove the door trim panel and watershield as described in Section 13.

4   Remove the kick panel and disconnect the electrical connectors leading to the door.

5   Detach the rubber conduit, grommet and wiring harness from the door.

6   Remove the bolt from the door stop link (see illustration).

7   Mark around the door hinge reinforcement plates with a pen or a scribe to facilitate realignment during reassembly.

8   With an assistant holding the door, remove the hinge bolts and lift the door off.

9   Installation is the reverse of removal.

10   Reconnect the battery (see Chapter 5).

Adjustment

11   Having proper door-to-body alignment is a critical part of a well-functioning door assembly. First check the door hinge pins for excessive play. Fully open the door and lift up and down on the door without lifting the body. If a door has 1/16-inch or more excessive play, the hinges should be replaced.

12   Door-to-body alignment adjustments are made by loosening the hinge-to-body bolts or hinge-to-door bolts and moving the door. Proper body alignment is achieved when the top of the doors are parallel with the roof section, the front door is flush with the fender, the rear door is flush with the rear quarter panel and the bottom of the doors are aligned with the lower rocker panel. If these goals can't be reached by adjusting the hinge-to-body or hinge-to-door bolts, body alignment shims may have to be purchased and inserted behind the hinges to achieve correct alignment.

13   To adjust the door-closed position, mark around the striker plate to provide a reference point, then check that the door latch is contacting the center of the latch striker. If not, adjust the up and down position first (see illustration).

14   Finally' adjust the latch striker sideways position so that the door outer panel is flush with the center pillar or rear quarter panel and provides positive engagement with the latch mechanism.

15   Door latch, lock cylinder and handles - removal and installation

Warning: *The models covered by this manual are equipped with Supplemental Restraint systems (SRS), more commonly known as airbags. Always disarm the airbag system before working in the vicinity of any airbag system component to avoid the possibility of accidental deployment of the airbag, which could cause personal injury (see Chapter 12). Do not use a memory saving device to preserve the PCM's memory when working on or near airbag system components.*
Caution: *Wear gloves when working inside the door openings to protect against cuts from sharp metal edges.*

Front door

1   Raise the window, then remove the door trim panel and watershield (see Section 13).

Outside door handle

Note: *This procedure only applies to the outside door handle lever. If you need to replace the outside door handle reinforcement (the actual mechanism for the outside door handle) and lock, you will need to remove it along with the door latch as a single assembly, then disconnect it from the latch (see Steps 9 through 13).*

2   Remove the trim cap for the outside handle to access the lock and handle retaining screw (see illustration).

15.2 Trim cap for outside door handle cover retaining screw

15.3 Remove the outside door handle cover and lock cylinder

15.4 To disengage the outside door handle lever from the handle reinforcement inside the door, pull it out of the door and to the rear

15.10 Remove the outside door handle reinforcement exterior retaining screw

15.11 Door latch mounting fasteners

15.12 Remove the latch, rods and handle reinforcement from the door as a unit

3   Loosen the captive screw and pull the door handle lock and cover outwards to remove it (see illustration).

4   To remove the outside door handle, pull it out of the door and to the rear to disengage it from the handle reinforcement inside the door (see illustration).

5   Remove and inspect the outside door handle seals. If the seals are cracked, torn or otherwise deteriorated, replace them.

6   Installation is the reverse of removal.

Inside door handle

Note: *The inside door handle is permanently attached to the door panel.*

7   Disconnect the actuator cable from the inside door handle (see illustrations 13.6a and 13.6b).

8   Installation is the reverse of removal.

Door latch or outside door handle reinforcement

9   Remove the outside door handle (see Steps 2 through 5).

10   Remove the outside door handle rein-

forcement exterior retaining screw (see illustration).

Note: *The outer door handle reinforcement can be removed with out removing the latch assembly if you can disconnect the lock rods from the handle inside the door. It is much easier to remove the latch and handle reinforcement as an assembly, then disconnect the rods once you have it outside the door.*

11   Remove the latch mounting fasteners (see illustration).

12   Pull out the door handle reinforcement, latch and rods from the door as a single assembly (see illustration), then disconnect the rods. Rotate the latch electrical connector lock and disconnect the electrical connector from the latch if you haven't already done so. Disconnect the inside door handle actuator cable from the latch.

13   Place the assembly on a clean workbench, then disconnect the outside handle and lock cylinder actuator rods from the latch or from the outside door handle reinforcement.

14   Installation is the reverse of removal.

Door lock cylinder

15   Remove the trim cap for the outside handle retaining screw (see illustration 15.2) and remove the screw.

16   Pull the lock cylinder out from the housing (see illustration 15.3).

17   When installing the lock cylinder, push it all the way into the outside door handle reinforcement until the end of the retaining screw can be fully seated.

18   Installation is otherwise the reverse of removal.

Rear doors

19   Raise the window, then remove the door trim panel and watershield (see Section 13). The interior door handle is removed as part of the panel procedure described in Section 13.

20   The rear outside door handle removal procedure is identical to the front outside door handle removal (see Steps 2 through 5).

16   Door window glass - removal and installation

Warning: *The models covered by this manual are equipped with Supplemental Restraint systems (SRS), more commonly known as airbags. Always disarm the airbag system before working in the vicinity of any airbag system component to avoid the possibility of accidental deployment of the airbag, which could cause personal injury (see Chapter 12). Do not use a memory saving device to preserve the PCM's memory when working on or near airbag system components.*

Caution: *Wear gloves when working inside the door openings to protect against cuts from sharp metal edges.*

Front door glass

1   Remove the door trim panel and the plastic watershield (see Section 13).

16.4 Front door glass-to-regulator bolt locations

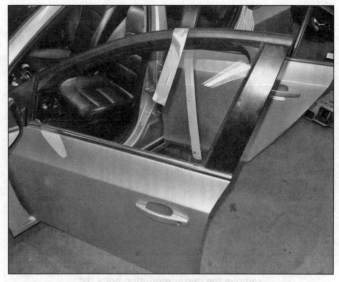

17.2 Tape the glass securely in the UP position

2   Lower the window half-way down to expose the window mounting nuts or clips.
Note: *On 2016 and later models, the window mounting bolts were replaced with large plastic retaining clips.*
3   Pry out the sealing strip from the top of the door.
4   Through holes in the door, loosen the two glass-to-regulator bolts (2015 and earlier models, see illustration) or, on 2016 and later models, use a screwdriver to push the center of the clip in, then lift the window slightly to release the clip from the retaining hole in the window support.
5   With the door open, stand at the inside of the door and pull the window up and toward the inside while rotating it slightly.
6   Installation is the reverse of removal.

Rear door glass
7   Remove the door trim panel and the plastic watershield (see Section 13).
8   Pry up the sealing strip from the top of the door.
9   Lower the window about one third, until the glass-to-regulator bolts are visible, then remove the bolts.
10   Hold the top of the window and lift the glass by pulling it up and inward.
11   Installation is the reverse of removal.

---

17   Door window glass regulator - removal and installation

Warning: *The models covered by this manual are equipped with Supplemental Restraint systems (SRS), more commonly known as airbags. Always disarm the airbag system before working in the vicinity of any airbag system component to avoid the possibility of accidental deployment of the airbag, which could cause personal injury (see Chapter 12). Do not use a memory*

17.4 Loosen the regulator-to-window glass bolts (1) and remove the bolts for the rear (2) middle and front (3) sections of the regulator

saving device to preserve the PCM's memory when working on or near airbag system components.
Caution: *Wear gloves when working inside the door openings to protect against cuts from sharp metal edges.*

Front
1   Remove the door trim panel and the plastic watershield (see Section 13).
2   Tape the glass in the Up position (see illustration). On power window models, remove the key from the ignition switch.
3   Disconnect the electrical connector from the window regulator motor.
4   The regulator assembly is comprised of a front and rear section, connected by cable. Remove the appropriate fasteners and loosen the others (see illustration).
5   Remove the window regulator/motor assembly from the door, being careful not to kink the cables connecting the two sections of the regulator assembly.

6   Lubricate the rollers and wear points on the regulator with white grease before installation.
7   Installation is the reverse of removal.

Rear
8   Remove the door trim panel and the plastic watershield (see Section 13).
9   Raise the glass and tape it in the Up position. Loosen the glass-to-regulator bolts.
10   Remove the key from the ignition switch and disconnect the electrical connector from the window regulator motor.
11   Loosen the four regulator/motor assembly mounting bolts.
12   Move the regulator so that the bolts clear the slots in the door, then remove the window regulator/motor assembly from the door.
13   Lubricate the rollers and wear points on the regulator with white grease before installation.
14   Installation is the reverse of removal.

18.3 Disconnect the electrical connector (A) and remove the mirror mounting bolts (B)

18.7 Pry the mirror glass outward carefully, until it is free of the motor

18.10 Use a trim tool to pry the trim cover off of the base

18.11 Mirror retaining screw location

19.1 Remove the inside pull down handle fasteners and handle from the trunk lid

18 Mirrors - removal and installation

Warning: *The models covered by this manual are equipped with Supplemental Restraint systems (SRS), more commonly known as airbags. Always disarm the airbag system before working in the vicinity of any airbag system component to avoid the possibility of accidental deployment of the airbag, which could cause personal injury (see Chapter 12). Do not use a memory saving device to preserve the PCM's memory when working on or near airbag system components.*

Outside mirrors

Mirror

1   On 2015 and earlier models, remove the front door interior sail panel (see Section 13). On 2016 and later models, remove the door trim panel (see Section 13).

2   Remove the foam insulator, if equipped.

3   Disconnect the electrical connector (see illustration).

4   Remove the three mirror retaining bolts and detach the mirror from the vehicle.

5   Installation is the reverse of removal.

Mirror glass

6   Push the face of the mirror in at the bottom until the mirror reaches the stop.

7   Insert a trim removal tool behind the glass until it reaches the first support rib, then pry outward carefully until the mirror glass is free (see illustration).

8   Install the mirror glass and align the mirror face to the backing plate.

9   Carefully apply pressure to the glass, using a thick pad across the glass until the mirror glass clicks in to place.

Inside mirror

10   Carefully pry the trim panel off of the mirror base (see illustration).

11   Loosen the mirror retaining screw (see

19.2 Trim panel fastener locations

19.3 Mark the position of the trunk lid bolts and remove the bolts on each side

20.2 Trunk lid latch electrical connector (A) and mounting fasteners (B)

21.2a Using a trim tool, pry the side panel out. . .

21.2b. . . to disengage the clips

illustration) and slide the mirror up and off its base. Where equipped, disconnect the electrical connector at the mirror.

12   Installation is the reverse of removal. Tighten the screw securely.

13   If the mount plate itself has come off the windshield, adhesive kits are available at auto parts stores to re-secure it. Follow the instructions included with the kit.

19   Trunk lid - removal and adjustment

Note: *The trunk lid is heavy and somewhat awkward to remove and install - at least two people should perform this procedure.*

1   Remove the mounting screw inside the pull down handle (see illustration) then use a trim tool to remove lid latch cover.

2   Pry up the centers of the trim panel retaining clips, then pry the clips out and remove the trim panel (see illustration).

3   Make marks around the trunk lid bolts to ensure proper alignment during installation (see illustration).

4   Disconnect any electrical connectors, ground wires and harness retaining clips.

5   With an assistant holding the trunk lid, remove the lid-to-hinge bolts and remove the trunk lid.

Note: *When reinstalling the trunk lid, align the lid-to-hinge fasteners with the marks made during removal.*

6   Installation is the reverse of removal.

20   Trunk lid latch - removal and installation

1   Open the trunk lid and remove the trunk lid trim panel (see Section 19).

2   Disconnect the electrical connector from the trunk latch (see illustration).

3   Remove the fasteners and detach the latch.

4   Installation is the reverse of removal.

21   Center console - removal and installation

Warning: *The models covered by this manual are equipped with Supplemental Restraint Systems (SRS), more commonly known as airbags. Always disarm the airbag system before working in the vicinity of any airbag system component to avoid the possibility of accidental deployment of the airbag, which could cause personal injury (see Chapter 12). Do not use a memory saving device to preserve the PCM's memory when working on or near airbag system components.*

1   Disconnect the cable from the negative battery terminal (see Chapter 5).

2   Use a trim tool to pry out the trim panel from each side of the console (see illustrations).

**21.3a Using a trim tool, pry the end of the shifter bezel up,
working around the perimeter. . .**

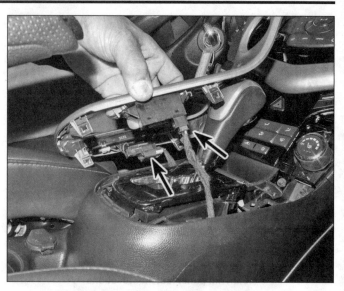

**21.3b. . . then lift the panel up and disconnect
the electrical connectors**

21.4 Console storage compartment screw locations

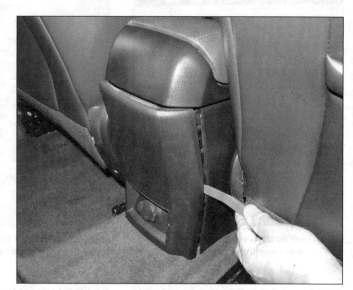

21.5a Pry the rear panel out from the console. . .

**21.5b. . . then disconnect the electrical
connector and remove the panel**

**21.6 Console trim plate screw
cover and screw**

2015 and earlier models

3   Use a trim tool to pry out the transaxle shifter bezel, then disconnect the electrical connectors from the panel (see illustrations).

4   Remove the center storage compartment screws (see illustration) and pull the storage compartment out of the console.

5   Pry out the rear panel to disengage the retaining clips, then disconnect the electrical connector (see illustrations).

6   Remove the top trim plate screw cover and remove the screw (see illustration).

7   Open the arm rest and remove the small piece of carpet at the bottom of the storage compartment and remove the mounting screws (see illustration).

8   Working around the console, remove the perimeter mounting screws (see illustrations).

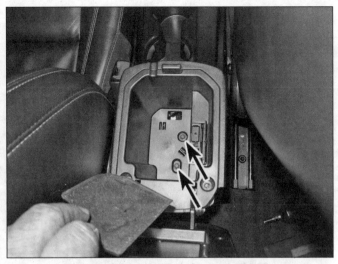

21.7 Storage compartment screw locations

21.8a Remove the mounting screws at the top...

21.8b... the front sides...

21.8c... and the rear sides

9   Lift the off the main console panel (see illustration) and disconnect the electrical connectors at the front of the console.

10   Installation is the reverse of removal.

11   Reconnect the battery (see Chapter 5).

2016 and later models

12   Remove the instrument panel fuse block access cover from the front of the console.

13   Disengage the instrument panel fuse block access cover frame fasteners at the front of the console, then carefully pry the panel away from the instrument panel.

Note: *The panel has a clip and a hooked-shaped tab that connect it to the instrument panel. Release the clip then pull the panel down and out to separate it from the instrument panel.*

14   On manual transaxle models, place the gear shift lever into the reverse position, then depress and disengage the retaining tabs around the shift boot and lift the shift boot up until the electrical connectors can be disconnected. Remove the shift boot.

15   On automatic transaxle models, disengage the clips starting at the rear of the boot and lift boot up and over the shift handle, then depress the locking tabs at the base of the shift handle. Remove the shift lever knob by moving the lever knob retainer down and remove the shift knob and boot as an assembly.

16   On models with a parking brake handle, pull up on the handle as far as possible then use a trim tool to disengage the brake lever boot retaining clips. Slide the boot over and off of the parking brake lever.

17   There are three mounting screws on both sides of the console. Slide the front seats as far forward as possible to remove the rear and middle screws, then slide the seats all the way to the rear and remove the front screws.

18   Lift the console up and disconnect any electrical connectors and remove the console.

19   Installation is the reverse of removal.

21.9 Lift the console up and off

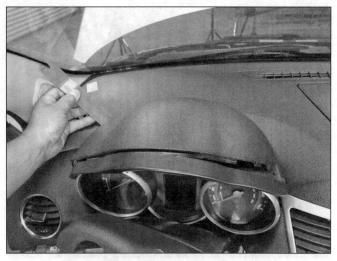

22.2 Use a plastic trim tool to pry the instrument cluster upper trim panel out

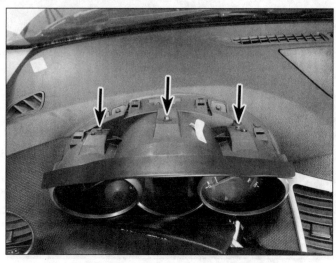

22.3 Instrument cluster lower trim panel mounting screw locations

22.12 Use a plastic trim tool to pry the center accessory trim panel out

22   Dashboard trim panels - removal and installation

Warning: *The models covered by this manual are equipped with Supplemental Restraint Systems (SRS), more commonly known as airbags. Always disarm the airbag system before working in the vicinity of any airbag system component to avoid the possibility of accidental deployment of the airbag, which could cause personal injury (see Chapter 12). Do not use a memory saving device to preserve the PCM's memory when working on or near airbag system components.*

1   Disconnect the cable from the negative battery terminal (see Chapter 5).

Instrument cluster trim panel

2015 and earlier models

2   Use a trim tool to pry up the instrument cluster upper trim panel (see illustration).
3   Remove the instrument cluster lower trim panel mounting screws (see illustration).

4   Installation is the reverse of the removal procedure. Make sure the clips are engaged properly before pushing the upper trim panel firmly into place.
5   Reconnect the battery (see Chapter 5).

2016 and later models

6   Use a trim tool and pry out the left side center trim panel, and if equipped with push button start, disconnect the electrical connector from the switch and remove the panel.
7   Carefully pry off the end trim panel from the left side of the instrument panel.
8   Locate the left side trim pad panel mounting screw that was hidden under the end trim panel and remove the screw, then carefully pry the trim pad panel out from the instrument panel.
9   Remove the mounting bolts at the base of the instrument cluster, then pull the instrument cluster trim panel out from the instrument panel.
10   Installation is the reverse of removal.
11   Reconnect the battery (see Chapter 5).

Center trim panel and vent assembly

2015 and earlier models

12   Pry the center trim panel out of the instrument panel using a plastic trim tool (see illustration).
13   If the center trim panel must be replaced, unclip the vent assemblies from the back side of the panel.
14   Installation is the reverse of removal. Make sure the clips are engaged properly before pushing the panel firmly into place.
15   Reconnect the battery (see Chapter 5).

2016 and later models

16   Use a trim tool and pry out the center trim panel from around the radio control assembly.
17   Pry the two individual vents out from the instrument panel.
18   Installation is the reverse of removal.
19   Reconnect the battery (see Chapter 5).

Knee bolster

2015 and earlier models

20   Remove the dashboard left-end trim panel (see Step 21).
21   Pry out the headlight switch (see Chapter 12) and disconnect the electrical connector.
22   Remove the knee bolster trim panel mounting fasteners (see illustration).
23   Pry the bolster panel away from the instrument panel to release the clips (see illustration).
24   Installation is the reverse of removal. Make sure the clips are engaged properly before pushing the knee bolster firmly into place.
25   Reconnect the battery (see Chapter 5).

2016 and later models

26   Remove the instrument cluster trim panel (see Steps 6 through 9).

22.22 Remove the knee bolster trim panel fasteners

22.23 Use a plastic trim tool to pry the panel out

22.35a Disconnect the glove box door stop. . .

22.35b. . . then lower the glove box door until it can be removed from the hinge

22.44 Pry off the end caps

27   Pull off the compartment access panel from the left side of the knee bolster panel.
28   Remove the fuse block access cover frame panel (see Section 21).
29   Remove the knee bolster mounting bolts.
30   Disconnect the DLC connector from the knee bolster the remove the panel.
31   Installation is the reverse of removal.
32   Reconnect the battery (see Chapter 5).

Glove box

2015 and earlier models

33   Remove the dashboard right-end trim panel (see Step 44).
34   Remove the lower insulator panel from below the passenger's side instrument panel.
35   Open the glove box and disconnect the door stops, then lower the door and lift it off of the hinge (see illustrations).

36   Remove the glove box trim panel mounting fasteners from the perimeter of the panel and remove the panel.
37   Installation is the reverse of removal. Reconnect the battery (see Chapter 5).

2016 and later models

38   Remove the instrument panel right side lower trim panel fasteners and remove the lower panel from under the glove box.
39   Carefully pry off the end trim panel from the right side of the instrument panel (see Step 44).
40   Remove the fuse block access cover frame panel (see Section 21).
41   Remove the glove box mounting screws, then disconnect the electrical connectors and remove the glove box as an assembly.
42   Installation is the reverse of removal.
43   Reconnect the battery (see Chapter 5).

Dashboard left- or right-end trim panels

44   Carefully pry off the end trim panel (see illustration).
45   Installation is the reverse of removal.

Right-side upper trim panel

2015 and earlier models

46   Remove the glove box (see Steps 33 through 36).
47   Carefully pry up the upper right trim panel.
48   Installation is the reverse of removal.

2016 and later models

49   Carefully pry off the end trim panel from the right side of the instrument panel (see Step 44).
50   Remove the fastener at the end of the trim panel.

22.53 Pry out the trim panel starting at the top, then disconnect the tether

22.54 Detach the electrical connector from the tweeter speaker, if present

22.56 Instrument panel center storage compartment fastener locations

22.61 Instrument panel accessory bezel fastener locations

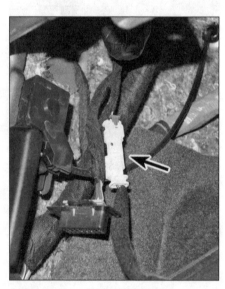

22.71a Disconnect the electrical connector from the driver's side lower airbag. . .

22.71b. . . then remove the driver's side lower airbag mounting bolts

51   Carefully pry along the top and bottom edges of the right-side trim panel and remove it. The vent can be removed from the panel from the back side.

52   Installation is the reverse of removal.

A-pillar trim panels

53   Pry out the trim panel from the top and disconnect the tether (see illustration).

Warning: *Obtain a new tether clip for installation.*

54   Pry the A-pillar trim panels back at the top then lift the bottom of the panel up and out of the dashboard. Disconnect the tweeter speaker electrical connector, if equipped (see illustration).

55   Installation is the reverse of removal.

Warning: *Be sure to use a new tether clip.*

Instrument panel center storage compartment (2015 and earlier models)

56   Open the compartment lid and remove the fasteners (see illustration).

57   Pry the storage compartment out of the instrument panel cover.

58   Installation is the reverse of removal.

Instrument panel accessory bezel (2015 and earlier models)

59   Remove the transaxle shifter bezel and center console storage compartment (see Section 21).

60   Pry the center trim panel out of the instrument panel (see Step 6).

61   Remove the instrument panel accessory bezel fasteners (see illustration) and pull the bezel from the instrument panel.

62   Disconnect the electrical connectors and remove the bezel.

63   Installation is the reverse of removal.

Main instrument panel cover

64   Remove the instrument cluster trim panels (see Steps 2 and 3).

65   Remove the center trim panel and vent assembly (see Steps 12 through 14, 16 and 17).

66   Remove the knee bolster (see Steps 20 through 23 or 26 through 30).

67   Remove the glove box (see Steps 33 through 36 or 38 through 41).

68   Remove the upper right trim panel (see Steps 23 and 24).

22.72a Remove the passenger's side airbag fasteners. . .

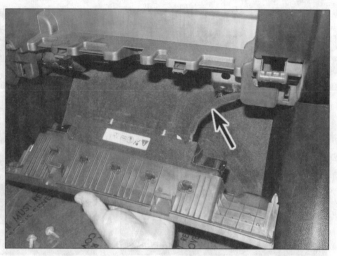

22.72b. . . then follow the harness to disconnect the passenger's side airbag electrical connector

22.73a Remove the instrument panel cover fasteners from the left side. . .

22.73b. . . the center (same on both sides). . .

69   Remove the A-pillar trim panels (see Steps 53 and 54).

70   Remove the instrument panel center storage compartment (see Steps 56 and 57).

71   Disconnect the driver's side lower airbag electrical connector (see illustration), then remove the airbag mounting bolts (see illustration) and airbag from the vehicle.

72   Remove the sound insulator panel from the passenger's side, then remove the passenger's lower airbag fasteners (see illustration) and lower the airbag until you can disconnect the electrical connector (see illustration).

73   Remove the instrument panel cover fasteners (see illustrations).

74   Release the passenger's side airbag from the instrument panel cover by pushing in on the tabs to separate the airbag module from the trim panel.

75   Remove the instrument panel cover.

76   Installation is the reverse of removal. Make sure any trim panel clips are engaged properly before pushing the panels firmly into place.

22.73c. . . upper right. . .

22.73d. . . and the right side

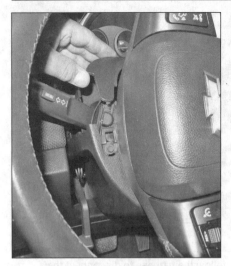

23.2 Pry up the upper steering column cover

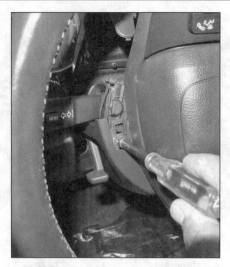

23.5a Remove the screws from the top edge on each side of the cover. . .

23.5b. . . then the mounitng screw on the bottom of the steering column lower cover

24.1 Remove the mounting bolts

24.2 Disconnect the electrical connectors under the seat

23   Steering column covers - removal and installation

Warning: *The models covered by this manual are equipped with Supplemental Restraint Systems (SRS), more commonly known as airbags. Always disarm the airbag system before working in the vicinity of any airbag system component to avoid the possibility of accidental deployment of the airbag, which could cause personal injury (see Chapter 12). Do not use a memory saving device to preserve the PCM's memory when working on or near airbag system components.*

1   Tilt the steering column to the lowest position.

2   On 2015 and earlier models, the upper column cover can be removed simply by lifting it from its clips (see illustration).

3   On 2016 and later models, remove the instrument cluster trim panel (see Section 22). Rotate the steering wheel counterclockwise 180-degrees, locate the small tab of the upper panel then use a small screwdriver to unclip the catch of the upper trim cover from the face of the lower trim panel.

4   Rotate the steering wheel clockwise 180-degrees, unclip the catch of the upper trim cover from the face of the lower trim panel then pull the upper column cover forward and up to release the remaining four clips and remove the panel.

5   With the upper cover removed, you can now access the lower cover mounting screws (see illustrations).

6   Installation is the reverse of removal.

24   Seats - removal and installation

Warning: *The models covered by this manual are equipped with Supplemental Restraint Systems (SRS), more commonly known as airbags. Always disarm the airbag system before working in the vicinity of any airbag system component to avoid the possibility of accidental deployment of*

the airbag, which could cause personal injury (see Chapter 12). Do not use a memory saving device to preserve the PCM's memory when working on or near airbag system components.

Front seat

1   Move the seat forward and remove the seat mounting bolts (see illustration).

Warning: *Discard the bolts and obtain new ones for installation.*

2   Disconnect the seatbelt wiring and any other electrical connectors under the seat (see illustration).

3   Using a small screwdriver, pry the cap out of the seatbelt tensioner (see illustration), then remove the bolt and separate the belt from the tensioner.

4   Tilt the back of the seat up and disengage the front of the seat tracks from the floor, then remove the seat from the vehicle.

5   Use the seat lever to slide the tracks forward as far as they go, then slide the front hooks on the adjusters into the floor slots.

24.3 Remove the cap from the seatbelt tensioner

25.2 Remove the rear sill fasteners, then pry up the rear sill panel

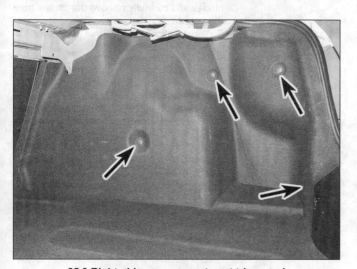

25.3 Right-side rear compartment trim panel
fastener locations - left side similar

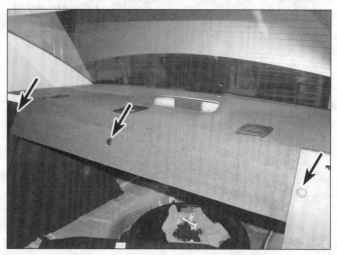

26.3 Rear package tray fastener locations

6   The remainder of installation is the reverse of removal. Tighten the seat mounting bolts and the seatbelt-to-tensioner bolt to the torque values listed in this Chapter's Specifications.
Warning: *Be sure to use new seat bolts.*

Rear seat

7   Lift corners of the rear seat cushion up to disengage the fasteners.
Note: *The rear seat cushion corners must be lifted up with force to disengage the fasteners. Once the cushion is removed, the sheet metal holding the retainers might be pulled up slightly and should be hammered down flat before installing the rear seat cushion.*

8   Remove the rear seat back side cushions by pulling the top corners out to disengage the the fastener, then lift the side cushion up and out. Repeat this procedure for the opposite side, if necessary.
Note: *The rear seat back side cushion upper corners must be pulled out with force to disengage the fasteners. Once the cushion is removed, the*

retainer may be damaged and the sheet metal holding the retainers will be pulled out slightly and should be hammered down flat before installing a new fastener or the rear seat cushion.

9   To remove the seats small (40 percent) side, lower the seat back down and slide the rear seat back off of the pivot guides.

10   To remove the seats large (60 percent) side, remove the seat belt buckle bracket nuts and buckle assembly then lower the seat back down, lift the outside end of the seat up and slide the inside end of the seat towards the door to remove it from the pivot guides.

11   Lift the seat assembly up and remove the seat through the door opening.

12   Installation is the reverse of removal.

25   Trunk trim panels - remova and installation

1   Open the trunk, then lift up and remove the floor.

2   Remove the rear sill push-pin fasteners, then carefully pry up the sill panel (see illustration).

3   Pry up the centers of the trim panel retaining clips, then pry the clips out and remove the trim panel (see illustration). If you're removing the left-side panel, also remove the convenience hook.

4   Installation is the reverse of removal.

26   Rear package tray - removal and installation

1   Remove the rear seat (see Section 24).

2   Remove the center-mount brake light (see Chapter 12).

3   Remove the plastic push-pin fasteners (see illustration) and remove the rear package tray.

4   Installation is the reverse of removal.

27   Liftgate panels, handle, latch and support struts - removal and installation

Interior trim panel

1   Using a trim tool, pry out the rear lamp assembly access covers.

2   Locate the trim panel mounting screws and remove the screws.

3   Use a trim tool to disengage the plastic trim panel fasteners around the panel and remove the panel.

4   Installation is the reverse of removal.

Outside handle

5   Open the liftgate, then remove the two handle mounting screws.

6   Pull the handle down and disconnect the electrical connector, then remove the handle.

7   To remove the liftgate release switch from the handle, depress the four locking tabs on the backside of the handle and push this with out of the handle.

8   Installation is the reverse of removal.

Liftgate latch

9   Remove the interior trim panel (see Steps 1 through 4).

10   Remove the liftgate latch mounting bolts.

11   Pull the latch down and disconnect the electrical connector, then remove the latch.

12   Installation is the reverse of removal.

Liftgate striker

13   The closing position of the liftgate can be adjusted slightly by moving the liftgate striker.

14   To access the striker, open the liftgate and carefully pry up the sill trim panel.

15   Remove the mounting bolts and striker.

16   To adjust the striker, loosen the mounting bolts, move the striker slightly, retighten the bolts and check the liftgate closing.

17   Installation is the reverse of removal.

Liftgate strut

18   There are two support struts for the lift-gate. Open the liftgate and prop it securely in the open position.

19   Release the small clip at each end of the strut, then pull the strut from the mounting ballstud.

20   Installation is the reverse of removal.

28   Liftgate – removal and installation

1   Disconnect the negative battery cable from the body in the rear floor section (see Chapter 5).

2   Disconnect the liftgate wiring harness connector.

3   Support the liftgate in the open position, then remove the liftgate supports (see Section 28).

4   Mark the location of the hinges to the body, then with the help of an assistant, remove the mounting bolts for the liftgate hinges and carefully remove the liftgate from the vehicle.

5   Installation is the reverse of removal.

Chapter 12
Chassis electrical system

Contents

1   General Information

1   The electrical system is a 12-volt, negative ground type. Power for the lights and all electrical accessories is supplied by a lead/acid battery, which is charged by the alternator.
2   This Chapter covers repair and service procedures for the various electrical components not associated with the engine. Information on the battery, alternator and starter motor can be found in Chapter 5.
3   It should be noted that when portions of the electrical system are serviced, the negative battery cable should be disconnected from the battery to prevent electrical shorts and/or fires.

2   Electrical troubleshooting - general information

1   A typical electrical circuit consists of an electrical component, any switches, relays, motors, fuses, fusible links or circuit breakers related to that component and the wiring and connectors that link the component to both the battery and the chassis. To help you pinpoint an electrical circuit problem, wiring diagrams are included at the end of this Chapter.
2   Before tackling any troublesome electrical circuit, first study the appropriate wiring diagrams to get a complete understanding of what makes up that individual circuit. Trouble spots, for instance, can often be narrowed down by noting if other components related to the circuit are operating properly. If several components or circuits fail at one time, chances are the problem is in a fuse or ground connection, because several circuits are often routed through the same fuse and ground connections.
3   Electrical problems usually stem from simple causes, such as loose or corroded connections, a blown fuse, a melted fusible link or a failed relay. Visually inspect the condition of all fuses, wires and connections in a problem circuit before troubleshooting the circuit.
4   If test equipment and instruments are going to be utilized, use the diagrams to plan ahead of time where you will make the necessary connections in order to accurately pinpoint the trouble spot.

5   The basic tools needed for electrical troubleshooting include a circuit tester or voltmeter
(a 12-volt bulb with a set of test leads can also
be used), a continuity tester, which includes a
bulb, battery and set of test leads, and a jumper
wire, preferably with a circuit breaker incorporated, which can be used to bypass electrical
components (see illustrations). Before attempting to locate a problem with test instruments,
use the wiring diagram(s) to decide where to
make the connections.

Voltage checks

6   Voltage checks should be performed if
a circuit is not functioning properly. Connect
one lead of a circuit tester to either the negative battery terminal or a known good ground.
Connect the other lead to a connector in the
circuit being tested, preferably nearest to the
battery or fuse (see illustration). If the bulb
of the tester lights, voltage is present, which
means that the part of the circuit between the
connector and the battery is problem free.
Continue checking the rest of the circuit in
the same fashion. When you reach a point at
which no voltage is present, the problem lies
between that point and the last test point with
voltage. Most of the time the problem can be
traced to a loose connection. Note: Keep in
mind that some circuits receive voltage only
when the ignition key is in the Accessory or
Run position.

Finding a short

7   One method of finding shorts in a circuit is to remove the fuse and connect a test
light or voltmeter in place of the fuse terminals. There should be no voltage present in
the circuit. Move the wiring harness from
side-to-side while watching the test light. If
the bulb goes on, there is a short to ground
somewhere in that area, probably where the
insulation has rubbed through. The same test
can be performed on each component in the
circuit, even a switch.

**2.5a The most useful tool for electrical
troubleshooting is a digital multimeter that
can check volts, amps, and test continuity**

**2.5b A simple test light is a very handy
tool for testing voltage**

Ground check

8   Perform a ground test to check whether
a component is properly grounded. Disconnect the battery and connect one lead of
a continuity tester or multimeter (set to the
ohms scale), to a known good ground. Connect the other lead to the wire or ground connection being tested. If the resistance is low
(less than 5 ohms), the ground is good. If the
bulb on a self-powered test light does not go
on, the ground is not good.

Continuity check

9   A continuity check is done to determine
if there are any breaks in a circuit - if it is
passing electricity properly. With the circuit
off (no power in the circuit), a self-powered
continuity tester or multimeter can be used
to check the circuit. Connect the test leads
to both ends of the circuit (or to the power
end and a good ground), and if the test light
comes on the circuit is passing current properly (see illustration). If the resistance is low

(less than 5 ohms), there is continuity; if the
reading is 10,000 ohms or higher, there is a
break somewhere in the circuit. The same
procedure can be used to test a switch, by
connecting the continuity tester to the switch
terminals. With the switch turned On, the
test light should come on (or low resistance
should be indicated on a meter).

Finding an open circuit

10   When diagnosing for possible open
circuits, it is often difficult to locate them by
sight because the connectors hide oxidation
or terminal misalignment. Merely wiggling a
connector on a sensor or in the wiring harness may correct the open circuit condition.
Remember this when an open circuit is indicated when troubleshooting a circuit. Intermittent problems may also be caused by oxidized
or loose connections.

11   Electrical troubleshooting is simple if
you keep in mind that all electrical circuits
are basically electricity running from the battery, through the wires, switches, relays, fuses

**2.6 In use, a basic test light's lead is clipped to a known good
ground, then the pointed probe can test connectors, wires
or electrical sockets - if the bulb lights, the circuit
being tested has battery voltage**

**2.9 With a multimeter set to the ohm scale, resistance can be
checked across two terminals - when checking for continuity,
a low reading indicates continuity, a high reading or infinity
indicates high resistance or lack of continuity**

3.1a The engine compartment fuse/relay box is mounted on the left side of the engine compartment; all fuses and relays are listed by location and function on the underside of the fuse/relay box cover

3.1b The interior fuse/relay box is behind the left closure panel of the knee bolster, with a fuse and relay guide on the back of the panel

and fusible links to each electrical component (light bulb, motor, etc.) and to ground, from which it is passed back to the battery. Any electrical problem is an interruption in the flow of electricity to and from the battery.

3   Fuses and fusible links - general information

Fuses

1   The electrical circuits of the vehicle are protected by a combination of fuses, circuit breakers and fusible links. The main fuse/relay panel is in the engine compartment (see illustration) , while the interior fuse/relay panel is located inside the passenger compartment (see illustration). Each of the fuses is designed to protect a specific circuit, and the various circuits are identified on the fuse panel itself.

2   Several sizes of fuses are employed in the fuse blocks. There are small, medium and large sizes of the same design, all with the same blade terminal design. The medium and large fuses can be removed with your fingers, but the small fuses require the use of pliers or the small plastic fuse-puller tool found in most fuse boxes.

3   If an electrical component fails, always check the fuse first. The best way to check the fuses is with a test light. Check for power at the exposed terminal tips of each fuse. If power is present at one side of the fuse but not the other, the fuse is blown. A blown fuse can also be identified by visually inspecting it (see illustration).

4   Be sure to replace blown fuses with the correct type. Fuses (of the same physical size) of different ratings may be physically interchangeable, but only fuses of the proper rating should be used. Replacing a fuse with one of a higher or lower value than specified

is not recommended. Each electrical circuit needs a specific amount of protection. The amperage value of each fuse is molded into the top of the fuse body.

5   If the replacement fuse immediately fails, don't replace it again until the cause of the problem is isolated and corrected. In most cases, this will be a short circuit in the wiring caused by a broken or deteriorated wire.

Fusible links

6   On these models, large, high-amperage fuses are used instead of traditional fusible links. They are located in the underhood fuse/relay box (see illustration 3.1a).

4   Circuit breakers - general information

1   Circuit breakers protect certain circuits, such as the power windows or heated seats. Depending on the vehicle's accessories, there may be one or two circuit breakers, located in the fuse/relay box in the engine compartment.

2   Because the circuit breakers reset automatically, an electrical overload in a circuit breaker-protected system will cause the circuit to fail momentarily, then come back on. If the circuit does not come back on, check it immediately.

3   For a basic check, pull the circuit breaker up out of its socket on the fuse panel, but just far enough to probe with a voltmeter. The breaker should still contact the sockets. With the voltmeter negative lead on a good chassis ground, touch each end prong of the circuit breaker with the positive meter probe. There should be battery voltage at each end. If there is battery voltage only at one end, the circuit breaker must be replaced.

4   Some circuit breakers must be reset manually.

BAD   GOOD

3.3 When a fuse blows, the element between the terminals melts

5   Relays - general information

Several electrical accessories in the vehicle, such as the fuel injection system, horns, starter, and fog lamps use relays to transmit the electrical signal to the component. Relays use a low-current circuit (the control circuit) to open and close a high-current circuit (the power circuit). If the relay is defective, that component will not operate properly. Most relays are mounted in the engine compartment fuse/relay box (see illustration 3.1a).

6   Electrical connectors - general information

1   Most electrical connections on these vehicles are made with multiwire plastic connectors. The mating halves of many connectors are secured with locking clips molded into the plastic connector shells. The mating halves of some

large connectors, such as some of those under the instrument panel, are held together by a bolt through the center of the connector.

2   To separate a connector with locking clips, use a small screwdriver to pry the clips apart carefully, then separate the connector halves. Pull only on the shell, never pull on the wiring harness, as you may damage the individual wires and terminals inside the connectors. Look at the connector closely before trying to separate the halves. Often the locking clips are engaged in a way that is not immediately clear. Additionally, many connectors have more than one set of clips.

3   Each pair of connector terminals has a male half and a female half. When you look at the end view of a connector in a diagram, be sure to understand whether the view shows the harness side or the component side of the connector. Connector halves are mirror images of each other, and a terminal shown on the right side end-view of one half will be on the left side end-view of the other half.

4   It is often necessary to take circuit voltage measurements with a connector connected. Whenever possible, carefully insert a small straight pin (not your meter probe) into the rear of the connector shell to contact the terminal inside, then clip your meter lead to the pin. This kind of connection is called "backprobing." When inserting a test probe into a terminal, be careful not to distort the terminal opening. Doing so can lead to a poor connection and corrosion at that terminal later. Using the small straight pin instead of a meter probe results in less chance of deforming the terminal connector.

Electrical connectors

Most electrical connectors have a single release tab that you depress to release the connector

Some electrical connectors have a retaining tab which must be pried up to free the connector

Some connectors have two release tabs that you must squeeze to release the connector

Some connectors use wire retainers that you squeeze to release the connector

Critical connectors often employ a sliding lock (1) that you must pull out before you can depress the release tab (2)

Here's another sliding-lock style connector, with the lock (1) and the release tab (2) on the side of the connector

On some connectors the lock (1) must be pulled out to the side and removed before you can lift the release tab (2)

Some critical connectors, like the multi-pin connectors at the Powertrain Control Module employ pivoting locks that must be flipped open

7.3 Disconnect the electrical connector(s) (A), then release the tabs (B) and pull the switches out

8.4 Ignition switch electrical connector (A) and mounting screw (B) locations. (C) is the lock cylinder retainer access hole

9.1 Push the switch out from the instrument panel

7   Steering column switches - replacement

Warning: *The models covered by this manual are equipped with a Supplemental Restraint System (SRS), more commonly known as airbags. Always disarm the airbag system before working in the vicinity of any airbag system component to avoid the possibility of accidental deployment of the airbag, which could cause personal injury (see Section 25).*

1   Disconnect the cable from the negative terminal of the battery (see Chapter 5).
2   Remove the steering column covers (see Chapter 11).
3   Disconnect the electrical connectors, then depress the locking tabs and remove either of the two switches from the steering column (see illustrations).
4   Installation is the reverse of removal.

8   Ignition switch, key lock cylinder and key - replacement

Warning: *The models covered by this manual are equipped with a Supplemental Restraint System (SRS), more commonly known as airbags. Always disarm the airbag system before working in the vicinity of any airbag system component to avoid the possibility of accidental deployment of the airbag, which could cause personal injury (see Section 25).*

Ignition switch

1   Disconnect the cable from the negative terminal of the battery (see Chapter 5).
2   Remove the steering column covers (see Chapter 11).
3   Turn the ignition key to the Run position.
4   Disconnect the electrical connectors from the ignition switch (see illustration).
5   Remove the two switch mounting screws and remove the ignition switch.

6   Installation is the reverse of removal. Reconnect the battery (see Chapter 5).

Key lock cylinder

7   Disconnect the cable from the negative terminal of the battery (see Chapter 5). Remove the steering column covers (see Chapter 11).
8   Insert the ignition key into the lock cylinder and rotate the key lock cylinder to the RUN position. Insert an awl or punch through the access hole to depress the retainer, then pull the cylinder out of the housing (see illustration 8.4).
9   Before installing the lock cylinder, make sure that the actuator blade inside the key lock cylinder bore is still in the RUN position. If it isn't, rotate it to this position. The key lock cylinder will not fit all the way into the bore if the actuator blade is in any other position.
10   Installation is otherwise the reverse of removal. Reconnect the battery (see Chapter 5).
11   Verify that the ignition switch operates correctly in the OFF, ACC, RUN and START positions.

Ignition key - replacing or adding

Note: *This procedure does not apply to Canadian models. On Canadian models, a scan tool is required to learn a new or additional ignition key.*

Replacing

Note: *This procedure is to be performed when replacing a lost master key (and you don't have any other keys that are programmed to work with your vehicle).*

12   Insert the key into the ignition switch lock cylinder and turn it to the ON position. Do not turn the key to the start position.
13   Watch the SECURITY message on the instrument cluster; it should go off in ten minutes.

14   Turn the ignition lock cylinder to the OFF position and wait five seconds.
15   Repeat Steps 12 through 14 two more times.
16   Start the engine to verify that the procedure was performed properly.

Adding

Note: *This procedure is to be performed when an additional key is desired (and you already have a key that works).*

17   Insert the ignition key that you already have (not the new one) into the ignition lock cylinder and turn it to the ON position. Do not turn the key to the start position.
18   Turn the key to the OFF position and remove it, then, within ten seconds, insert the new key and turn the ignition lock cylinder to the ON position.
19   The new key should now be recognized by the vehicle and should function normally.

9   Dashboard switches, accessory bezel switches and power outlet - replacement

Warning: *The models covered by this manual are equipped with a Supplemental Restraint System (SRS), more commonly known as airbags. Always disarm the airbag system before working in the vicinity of any airbag system component to avoid the possibility of accidental deployment of the airbag, which could cause personal injury (see Section 25).*

Dashboard switches

Headlight switch and rehostat

1   Open the left side storage compartment or fuse access panel door and reach through the opening and push the headlight switch assembly outfrom the instrument panel (see illustration).

9.2 Pull out the lock tab (A), then depress the retainer (B) to disconnect the electrical connector

9.6 Remove the switch mounting screws

1   Door lock switch   3   Passenger's airbag switch
2   Hazard switch

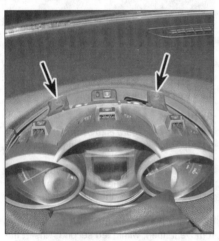

10.4a Remove the instrument cluster upper mounting screws. . .

10.4b. . . and lower mounting screws

10.5 Depress the tab then rotate the release lever over to disconnect the electrical connector

2   Disconnect the electrical connector from the switch (see illustration).

3   Installation is the reverse of removal.

Accessory bezel switches

4   The accessory bezel panel houses the hazard flasher switch, the door lock switch and the passenger's airbag indicator. To remove any of these components, you must first remove the accessory bezel trim panel (see Chapter 11).

5   Disconnect the electrical connectors from the switch(es).

6   Remove the mounting screws (see illustration) and remove the switch(es) from the backside of the accessory bezel trim panel.

7   Installation is the reverse of removal.

Power outlet

8   Using a small screwdriver pry the power outlet up and out of the center console.

9   Disconnect the electrical connector from the power outlet.

10   Installation is the reverse of removal.

Center console switch panel

11   Remove the center console top trim panel.

12   Disconnect the electrical connector to the center console switch panel.

13   Use a small screwdriver and release the retaining tabs then pull the switch out from the back side of the panel.

14   Insert the switch panel into the backside of the panel and snap the switch into place.

15   Connect the electrical connector to the switch panel.

16   Remaining installation is the reverse of removal.

---

10   Instrument cluster - removal and installation

Warning: *The models covered by this manual are equipped with a Supplemental*

Restraint System (SRS), more commonly known as airbags. Always disarm the airbag system before working in the vicinity of any airbag system component to avoid the possibility of accidental deployment of the airbag, which could cause personal injury (see Section 25).

1   Disconnect the cable from the negative terminal of the battery (see Chapter 5).

2   Remove the steering column upper trim cover (see Chapter 11).

3   Remove the instrument cluster upper and lower trim panels (see Chapter 11).

4   Remove the instrument cluster retaining screws, then remove the cluster (see illustrations).

Note: *On 2016 and later models, the retaining tab at the top of the instrument cluster must be depressed (use a plastic trim tool) before it can be removed.*

5   Disconnect the electrical connector from the cluster (see illustration).

6   Installation is the reverse of removal.

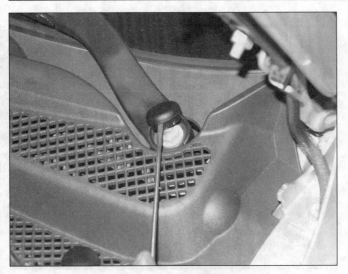

11.1a To remove the windshield wiper arms, carefully pry off each trim cap. . .

11.1b. . . and remove the wiper arm nut. Mark the arm in relation to the shaft, then remove the arm. (In some cases a small puller may be required to remove the arm from the shaft)

11.3 Windshield wiper motor electrical connector (A) and mounting bolt (B) locations

12.2 Radio control assembly mounting screw locations

12.4 Display bezel mounting fastener locations

11 Wiper motor - removal and installation

Replacement
Front

1   Pry off the windshield wiper trim caps and remove the windshield wiper retaining nuts (see illustrations). Mark the position of each wiper arm in relation to its shaft, then remove the wiper arms.
2   Remove the cowl cover (see Chapter 11).
3   Disconnect the windshield wiper motor electrical connector (see illustration).
4   Remove the windshield wiper motor and linkage assembly mounting bolts.
5   Remove the windshield wiper motor and linkage assembly from the cowl area.
6   Remove the nut securing the linkage arm to the motor, then remove the three motor mounting bolts and remove the motor.

7   Installation is the reverse of removal. Align the marks you made on the windshield wiper arms and the wiper arm shafts.

Rear

8   Using a trim tool or small screwdriver, pry the trim cap up, then remove the nut and pull the wiper arm off of the wiper motor spindle.
9   Open the rear liftgate and remove trim panel (see Chapter 11).
10   Disconnect the electrical connector from the motor, then remove the mounting bolts and lower the wiper motor from liftgate.
11   Installation is the reverse of removal.

12 Radio and speakers - removal and installation

Warning: *The models covered by this manual are equipped with a Supplemental Restraint System (SRS), more commonly known as airbags. Always disarm the airbag system before working in the vicinity of any airbag system component to avoid the possibility of accidental deployment of the airbag, which could cause personal injury (see Section 25).*

Radio control assembly

1   Remove the center trim panel and vent assembly and the instrument panel accessory bezel (see Chapter 11).
2   Remove the radio control assembly mounting screws (see illustration) and pull the controller out of the dash.
3   Disconnect the electrical connectors to the controller.
4   Remove drivers information display bezel fasteners and remove the bezel (see illustration). Disconnect the electrical connector from the display bezel.

12.5 Radio mounting fastener locations

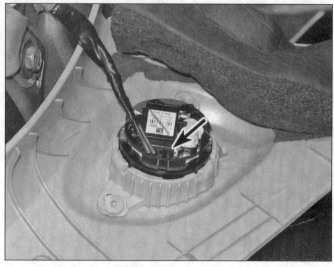

12.13 A-pillar speaker (tweeter) electrical connector location

12.25 Remove the mounting screw, then pull up the speaker and disconnect the electrical connector

Radio receiver

2015 and earlier models

5   Remove the radio mounting screws (see illustration) and pull the radio out from the dash.

6   Disconnect the antenna cable, the electrical connectors and the ground strap from the back of the radio.

7   Installation is the reverse of removal.

2016 and later models

8   Remove the trunk or rear compartment right side trim panel (see Chapter 11).

9   Disconnect the electrical connectors from the radio receiver.

10   Unclip the receiver from the mounting bracket and remove the radio receiver from the vehicle.

11   Installation is the reverse of removal.

Speakers

A-pillar speakers (tweeters)

12   Remove the A-pillar trim panel (see Chapter 11).

13   Disconnect the electrical connector from the tweeter (see illustration).

14   Carefully pry the speaker out of the mounting bracket, and remove the speaker.

15   Installation is the reverse of removal.

Instrument panel corner speakers

16   Using a plastic trim tool, carefully pry up the corner speaker grille from the instrument panel.

17   Remove the two speaker fasteners.

18   Lift the speaker out of the instrument panel, disconnect the electrical connector and remove the speaker.

19   Installation is the reverse of removal.

Instrument panel center speaker

20   Using a plastic trim tool, carefully pry up the center speaker grille from the instrument panel, then disconnect the electrical connector from the headlight automatic control light sensor.

21   Remove the two speaker fasteners.

22   Lift the speaker out of the instrument panel, disconnect the electrical connector and remove the speaker.

23   Installation is the reverse of removal.

Door speakers

24   Remove the door trim panel (see Chapter 11).

25   Remove the speaker mounting screw (see illustration).

26   Pull out the speaker and disconnect the electrical connector.

27   Installation is the reverse of removal.

Rear speakers

Note: *Not all models are equipped with rear speakers.*

2015 and earlier models

28   Remove the rear package tray (see Chapter 11).

29   Remove the mounting screws and pull the speaker housing out.

30   Disconnect the electrical connector from the speaker.

31   Installation is the reverse of removal.

2016 and later models

32   Remove the rear carpet and floor panel.

33   Remove the speaker mounting bolts.

34   Lift the speaker up from the rear floor compartment and disconnect the electrical connectors and remove the speaker.

35   Installation is the reverse of removal.

13 Antenna - removal and installation

1   Unscrew the antenna mast from its mounting base and remove it.

2   To remove the antenna base, remove the trim around the rear window.

3   Carefully pull the rear of the headliner down enough to access the antenna mounting bolt, then remove the bolt.

Caution: *Do not pull the headliner down too far, or it will leave a crease in the headliner.*

4   Remove the antenna base and disconnect the electrical connectors.

5   Installation is the reverse of removal.

14.4 When measuring the voltage at the rear window defogger grid, wrap a piece of aluminum foil around the positive probe of the voltmeter and press the foil against the wire with your finger

14.5 To determine if a heating element has broken, check the voltage at the center of each element; if the voltage is 5 or 6-volts, the element is unbroken, but if the voltage is 10 or 12-volts, the element is broken between the center and the ground side. If there is no voltage, the element is broken between the center and the positive side

14.7 To find the break, place the voltmeter negative lead against the defogger ground terminal, place the voltmeter positive lead with the foil strip against the heating element at the positive terminal end and slide it toward the negative terminal end. The point at which the voltmeter reading changes abruptly is the point at which the element is broken

14.13 To use a defogger repair kit, apply masking tape to the inside of the window at the damaged area, then brush on the special conductive coating

14 Rear window defogger - check and repair

1   The rear window defogger consists of a number of horizontal elements baked onto the glass surface.
2   Small breaks in the element can be repaired without removing the rear window.

Check

3   Turn the ignition switch and defogger system switches to the ON position. Using a voltmeter, place the positive probe against the defogger grid positive terminal and the negative probe against the ground terminal. If battery voltage is not indicated, check the fuse, defogger switch and related wiring. If voltage is indicated, but all or part of the defogger doesn't heat, proceed with the following tests.
4   When measuring voltage during the next two tests, wrap a piece of aluminum foil around the tip of the voltmeter positive probe and press

the foil against the heating element with your finger (see illustration). Place the negative probe on the defogger grid ground terminal.
5   Check the voltage at the center of each heating element (see illustration). If the voltage is 5 or 6-volts, the element is okay (there is no break). If the voltage is zero, the element is broken between the center of the element and the positive end. If the voltage is 10 to 12-volts the element is broken between the center of the element and ground. Check each heating element.
6   Connect the negative lead to a good body ground. The reading should stay the same. If it doesn't, the ground connection is bad.
7   To find the break, place the voltmeter negative probe against the defogger ground terminal. Place the voltmeter positive probe with the foil strip against the heating element at the positive terminal end and slide it toward the negative terminal end. The point at which the voltmeter deflects from several volts to

zero is the point at which the heating element is broken (see illustration).

Repair

8   Repair the break in the element using a repair kit specifically recommended for this purpose, available at most auto parts stores. Included in this kit is plastic conductive epoxy.
9   Prior to repairing a break, turn off the system and allow it to cool off for a few minutes.
10   Lightly buff the element area with fine steel wool, then clean it thoroughly with rubbing alcohol.
11   Use masking tape to mask off the area being repaired.
12   Thoroughly mix the epoxy, following the instructions provided with the repair kit.
13   Apply the epoxy material to the slit in the masking tape, overlapping the undamaged area about 3/4-inch on either end (see illustration).
14   Allow the repair to cure for 24 hours before removing the tape and using the system.

15.1a Pull out the connector lock. . .

15.1b. . . then squeeze the retainer and unplug the connector from the bulb

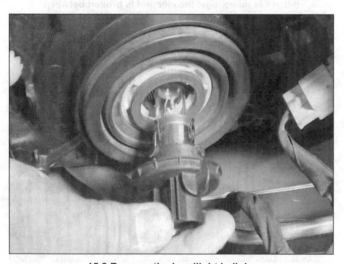

15.2 Remove the headlight bulb by turning it counterclockwise

16.1 Headlight vertical adjuster location - right-side shown, left side identical

15   Headlight bulb - replacement

Warning: *Halogen gas-filled bulbs are under pressure and can shatter if the surface is scratched or the bulb is dropped. Wear eye protection and handle the bulbs carefully, grasping only the base whenever possible. Do not touch the surface of the bulb with your fingers because the oil from your skin could cause it to overheat and fail prematurely. If you do touch the bulb surface, clean it with rubbing alcohol.*

1   Disconnect the electrical connector from the bulb (see illustrations).

Note: *When replacing the left-side bulb, you may find it necessary to remove the windshield washer reservoir neck for access (pull it straight up to remove it).*

2   Twist the headlight bulb counterclockwise and pull it out of the housing (see illustration).

3   Installation is the reverse of removal.

16   Headlights - adjustment

Note: *The headlights must be aimed correctly. If adjusted incorrectly they could blind the driver of an oncoming vehicle and cause a serious accident or seriously reduce your ability to see the road. The headlights should be checked for proper aim every 12 months and any time a new headlight is installed or front end body work is performed. It should be emphasized that the following procedure is only an interim step that will provide temporary adjustment until a properly equipped shop can adjust the headlights.*

1   The vertical adjustment screws (one per housing) are located on the top of the headlight housings (see illustration). There are no horizontal adjustment screws.

2   There are several methods for adjusting the headlights. The simplest method requires masking tape, a blank wall and a level floor.

3   Position masking tape vertically on the wall in reference to the vehicle centerline and the centerlines of both headlights (see illustration).

4   Position a horizontal tape line in reference to the centerline of all the headlights.

Note: *It might be easier to position the tape on the wall with the vehicle parked only a few inches away.*

5   Adjustment should be made with the vehicle parked 25 feet from the wall, sitting level, the gas tank half-full and no heavy load in the vehicle.

6   Starting with the low beam adjustment, position the high intensity zone so it is two inches below the horizontal line. Adjustment is made by turning the adjusting screw.

Note: *It might not be possible to position the headlight aim exactly for both high and low beams. If a compromise must be made, keep in mind that the low beams are the most used and have the greatest effect on safety.*

7   With the high beams on, the high intensity zone should be vertically centered with the exact center just below the horizontal line.

8   Have the headlights adjusted by a dealer service department or service station at the earliest opportunity.

16.3 Headlight adjustment details

17.2a Remove the headlight housing upper mounting bolts. . .

17.2b. . . and lower mounting bolts. . .

17 Headlight housing - replacement

1   Remove the front bumper cover (see Chapter 11).
2   Remove the bolts retaining the headlight housing (see illustrations).
3   Pull the headlight housing forward and disconnect the electrical connectors from the bulbs.
4   Installation is the reverse of removal.
5   Adjust the headlights (see Section 16).

18 Horn - replacement

1   Remove the front bumper cover (see Chapter 11).
2   Disconnect the electrical connector from the horn (see illustration).
3   Remove the horn mounting bracket bolt and remove the horn with its bracket.
4   Installation is the reverse of removal.

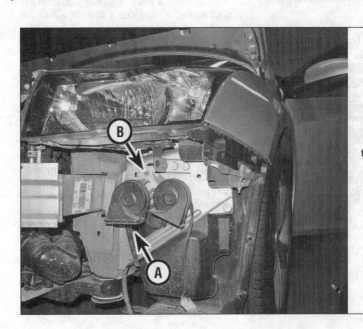

18.2 Disconnect the horn electrical connector (A) and remove the mounting nut (B)

Bulb removal

To remove many modern exterior bulbs from their holders, simply pull them out

On bulbs with a cylindrical base ("bayonet" bulbs), the socket is spring-loaded; a pair of small posts on the side of the base hold the bulb in place against spring pressure. To remove this type of bulb, push it into the holder, rotate it 1/4-turn counterclockwise, then pull it out

If a bayonet bulb has dual filaments, the posts are staggered, so the bulb can only be installed one way

To remove most overhead interior light bulbs, simply unclip them

19   Bulb replacement

Front turn signal/parking light bulbs

1   Turn the bulb holder counterclockwise, then remove it from the housing (see illustration).

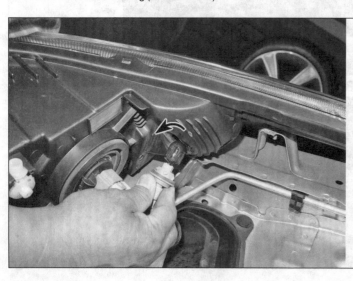

19.1 Remove the turn signal bulb by turning it counterclockwise

Note: *When replacing the left-side bulb, you may find it necessary to remove the windshield washer reservoir neck for access (pull it straight up to remove it).*

2   To remove the turn signal bulb from the bulb holder, simply pull it straight out of the socket.

3   Installation is the reverse of removal.

Fog light bulbs

4   The fog lights, if equipped, are located in the lower corners of the front bumper cover. They're easily accessed from underneath the bumper cover or through the inner fender liner.

5   Raise the front of the vehicle and place it securely on jackstands.

6   Rotate the bulb socket counterclockwise, then pull the socket and bulb out of the fog light housing.

7   Disconnect the electrical connector from the socket.

8   Remove the bulb from the socket.

9   Installation is the reverse of removal.

Front side marker bulbs

10   Remove the inner fender splash shield (see Chapter 11).

11   Disconnect the electrical connector to the bulb holder.

12   Remove the bulb holder from the housing, then remove the bulb from the holder (see illustration). Installation is the reverse of removal.

Center-mount brake light

Note: *The brake light is equipped with LED lights; the unit must be replaced as an assembly if defective.*

19.12 Remove the side marker bulb holder by turning it counterclockwise, then pull the bulb from the holder

19.13 Remove the mounting screws from inside the trunk

19.14 Pry the housing up from the front to disengage the fastener

19.15 Disconnect the electrical connector to the light

19.17 Pry open the screw covers and remove the screws

19.18 If necessary, carefully pry the tail light housing out using a plastic trim tool

13   Working inside the trunk or hatchback, remove the screws from under the brake light (see illustration).

14   Pry the housing up to disengage the fastener (see illustration).

15   On Notchback models, carefully pull the rear of the headliner down to access the center-mount brake light nuts and remove

the nuts, disconnect the electrical connector, then remove the brake light from the outside of the body.

16   On all except Notchback models, disconnect the electrical connector to the brake light (see illustration) and remove the brake from inside the vehicle, then unclip the brake light from the housing.

17   Installation is the reverse of removal.

Brake/tail/turn/sidemarker/ back-up light bulbs

18   Open the trunk and pry open the screw covers, then remove the screws (see illustration).

19.19a Tail light housing bulb details

1	Brake light/tail light bulb	3	Turn signal bulb
2	Side marker bulb	4	Back-up light bulb

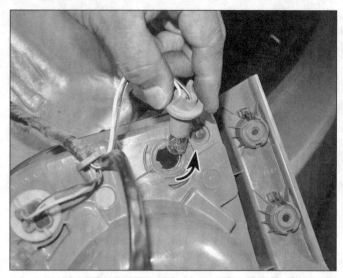

19.19b Rotate the bulb holder counterclockwise and remove the bulb holder

19.22 License plate light lens retaining screws

19.25 Use a small screwdriver to depress the tabs and pry the lens out

19   Pull the tail light housing straight back to disengage the mounting studs (see illustration).

20   On Hatchback or Notchback models, open the rear liftgate/hatch and remove the access panel on the door, then remove the retaining fasteners and pull the light assembly from the liftgate/hatch.

21   Rotate the bulb holder counterclockwise to remove the bulb that you want to replace (see illustrations).

22   Remove the bulb from its socket by pulling it straight out.

23   Installation is the reverse of removal.

License plate light bulbs

2015 and earlier models

24   Remove the screws securing the license plate lens and light to the trunk lid (see illustration).

25   To replace a bulb, rotate the bulb holder counterclockwise to remove it from the housing and pull it out.

26   Installation is the reverse of removal.

2016 and later models

27   On Hatchback or Notchback models, push the license plate lens towards the outside of the vehicle, then pull the right end out and allow the lens to come back towards the center as you are removing it.

28   Pull the bulb from the socket to replace it.

29   Slide the outer end of the lens in first and snap the inner end down until it locks into place.

Dome light, map/reading light or trunk light bulbs

30   Carefully pry the lens out (see illustration).

31   To replace the bulb(s) pull the bulb from the socket.

32   Installation is the reverse of removal.

20   Electric side view mirrors - description

Note: *These models are equipped with a Body Control Module (BCM). Several systems are linked to a centralized control module that allows simple and accurate troubleshooting, but only with a professional-grade scan tool. The Body Control Module governs the door locks, the power windows, the ignition lock and security system, the interior lights, the Daytime Running Lights system, the horn, the windshield wipers, the heating/air conditioning system and the power mirrors. In the event of malfunction with this system, have the vehicle diagnosed by a dealership service department or other qualified automotive repair facility.*

1   The electric rear view mirrors use two motors to move the glass; one for up and down

adjustments and one for left-right adjustments. Some vehicles are equipped with memory mirrors as well. These mirrors are an integral part of the power seat memory unit as well as incorporated with the Body Control Module (BCM). If there is a problem with these systems it is advised to seek out a qualified independent repair facility or your local dealer.

2   The control switch has a selector portion which sends voltage to the left or right side mirror. With the ignition in the ACC position and the engine OFF, roll down the windows and operate the mirror control switch through all functions (left-right and up-down) for both the left and right side mirrors.

3   Listen carefully for the sound of the electric motors running in the mirrors.

4   If the motors can be heard but the mirror glass doesn't move, there's probably a problem with the drive mechanism inside the mirror. Power mirrors have no user-serviceable parts inside - a defective mirror must be replaced as a unit (see Chapter 11).

5   If the mirrors don't operate and no sound comes from the mirrors, check the fuses (see Section 3).

6   If the fuses are OK, remove the mirror control switch. Have the switch continuity checked by a dealer service department or other qualified shop.

7   Check the ground connections.

8   If the mirror still doesn't work, remove the mirror and check the wires at the mirror for voltage.

9   If there's not voltage in each switch position, check the circuit between the mirror and control switch for opens and shorts. If the mirror is inoperative, try holding the switch in one of the directions and swing the door open and closed. If there is a break in the door jamb you may occasionally make contact long enough to avoid removing the mirror from the door for further testing. This will also give you some clue as to where the break is rather than testing things in one given position.

10   If there's voltage, remove the mirror and test it off the vehicle with jumper wires. Before testing check the wiring diagram for the correct leads that have to be used for each position. Applying voltage to the wrong leads can damage the mirror drive motors. Replace the mirror if it fails this test.

21 Cruise control system - general information

These models have an electrically controlled throttle body - there is no accelerator cable or cruise control cable. The accelerator pedal communicates with the throttle body through the Powertrain Control Module (PCM). See Chapters 4 and 6 for more information about the electronic throttle control system. The PCM also controls the cruise control system, which is now an integral function of the electronic throttle control system. If the system malfunctions, take it to a dealer service department or other qualified repair shop for further diagnosis.

22 Power window system - description and check

Note: *These models are equipped with a Body Control Module (BCM) incorporated with the window system. Several systems are linked to a centralized control module that allows simple and accurate troubleshooting, but only with a professional-grade scan tool. The Body Control Module governs the door locks, the power windows, the ignition lock and security system, the interior lights, the Daytime Running Lights system, the horn, the windshield wipers, the heating/air conditioning system and the power mirrors. In the event of malfunction with this system, have the vehicle diagnosed by a dealership service department or other qualified automotive repair facility.*

1   The power window system operates electric motors, mounted in the doors, which lower and raise the windows. The system consists of the control switches, the motors, regulators, glass mechanisms, the Body Control Module (BCM) and associated wiring.

2   The power windows can be lowered and raised from the master control switch by the driver or by remote switches located at the individual windows. Each window has a separate motor that is reversible. The position of the control switch determines the polarity and therefore the direction of operation.

3   The window motor circuits are protected by a fuse. Each motor is also equipped with an internal circuit breaker; this prevents one stuck window from disabling the whole system.

4   The power window system will only operate when the ignition switch has activated the Retained Accessory Power (RAP) relay. In addition, many models have a window lockout switch at the master control switch which, when activated, disables the switches at the rear windows and, sometimes, the switch at the passenger's window also. Always check these items before troubleshooting a window problem related to any of the other windows besides the drivers window. Window lock-out does not affect the driver's window.

5   These procedures are general in nature, so if you can't find the problem using them, take the vehicle to a dealer service department or to an independent repair facility that specializes in electrical repairs.

6   If the power windows won't operate, always check the fuse and circuit breaker first.

7   If only the rear windows are inoperative, or if the windows only operate from the master control switch, check the rear window lockout switch for continuity in the unlocked position. Replace it if it doesn't have continuity.

8   Check the wiring between the switches and fuse panel for continuity. Repair the wiring, if necessary.

9   If only one window is inoperative from the master control switch, try the other control switch at each individual window.

Note: *This doesn't apply to the driver's door window.*

10   If the same window works from one switch, but not the other, check the switch and/or wiring for continuity.

11   If the switch tests OK, check for a short or open in the circuit between the affected switch and the window motor.

12   If one window is inoperative from both switches, remove the switch panel from the affected door. Check for voltage at the motor (refer to Chapter 11 for door panel removal) while the switch is operated.

Note: *There are voltage and ground signals present at the switch connector. However, on 2010 and later models, there are also two data lines to the BCM that are not true positive/negative signals. Be sure you are testing the correct leads. Do not apply voltage or ground to any leads you are not sure of. Seek professional help in diagnosing any problems with the window circuits if you are unsure.*

13   If voltage is reaching the motor, disconnect the glass from the regulator (see Chapter 11). Move the window up and down by hand while checking for binding and damage. Also check for binding and damage to the regulator. If the regulator is not damaged and the window moves up and down smoothly, replace the motor. If there's binding or damage, lubricate, repair or replace parts, as necessary.

14   If voltage isn't reaching the motor, check the wiring in the circuit for continuity between the switches and the BCM, and between the BCM (if applicable) and the motors. You'll need to consult the wiring diagram in Chapter 13. If the circuit is equipped with a relay, check that the relay is grounded properly and receiving voltage.

15   Test the windows to confirm proper repairs. To verify if the motor is getting the needed voltage or ground, a simple but effective test is to sit in the car with the ignition on, open a door and look at the dome light. Then operate the switch to the faulty window. If you see the dome light dimming slightly this is a good indication that the motor is getting power and is probably a stuck motor or faulty wiring. Do not hold the switch on for very long when a motor is stuck or wiring is in question or more damage may occur. Finally, in some cases, a good rap on the door panel in the general area of the window motor - while the key is on and the window switch is depressed in the direction the window needs to move - will free up a stuck motor temporarily. You can damage the door panel or more internal components if you hit it too hard or are too aggressive.

Window express down programming

Note: *Any time the battery or window motor are disconnected, you will need to perform this procedure to reestablish the auto feature.*

16   Lower the window to its lowest position, holding the switch in the Down position for an additional five seconds.

17   Raise the window to its highest position, holding the window switch in the Up position for an additional five seconds.

18   Verify proper operation.

23.14 Carefully separate the case halves . . .   **23.15 . . . then remove the battery**

23   Power door lock and keyless entry system - description and check

Note: *These models are equipped with a Body Control Module (BCM). Several systems are linked to a centralized control module that allows simple and accurate troubleshooting, but only with a professional-grade scan tool. The Body Control Module governs the door locks, the power windows, the ignition lock and security system, the interior lights, the Daytime Running Lights system, the horn, the windshield wipers, the heating/air conditioning system and the power mirrors. In the event of malfunction with this system, have the vehicle diagnosed by a dealership service department or other qualified automotive repair facility.*

1   The power door lock system operates the door lock actuators mounted in each door. The system consists of the switches, actuators, lock and unlock relays, Body Control Module (BCM) and associated wiring. Diagnosis can usually be limited to simple checks of the wiring connections and actuators for minor faults that can be easily repaired.

2   Power door lock systems are operated by bi-directional solenoids located in the doors. The lock actuators are mounted as part of the door latch. Remove the door latch for access to the door lock actuator. The lock switches have two operating positions: Lock and Unlock. These switches send a signal to the BCM, which in turn sends a signal to the door lock relays, the relays then send the needed voltage to each of the door lock solenoids.

3   If you are unable to locate the trouble using the following general steps, consult your dealer service department or qualified independent repair shop.

4   Always check the circuit protection first. Some vehicles use a combination of circuit breakers and fuses.

5   Check for voltage at the switches. If no voltage is present, check the fuse first. If the fuse is good then check the wiring between the

fuse panel and the switches for an open lead.

6   If voltage is present, test the switch for continuity. Replace it if there's not continuity in both switch positions. There should be a voltage input and, when switch is depressed, voltage should be going out on the appropriate lead. Follow the wiring diagram for the actual wire and position on the switch. To remove the switch, use a flat-bladed trim tool to pry out the door/window switch assembly.

7   If the switch has continuity, check the wiring between the switch, BCM, door lock relay and the door lock solenoid.

8   If all but one lock solenoids operate, remove the trim panel from the affected door (see Chapter 11) and check for voltage at the solenoid while the lock switch is operated. One of the wires should have positive voltage in the Lock position; the other lead should have positive voltage in the Unlock position.

9   If the inoperative solenoid is receiving positive voltage on one lead and negative on the other, the solenoid is most likely defective. Check the connections for good contact; if the connection is good, replace the solenoid.

10   If the inoperative solenoid isn't receiving voltage or ground, check for an open or short in the wire between the lock solenoid and the relay. A good method of non-destructive testing is to squeeze the rubber corrugated tubing and search with your fingers for an individual wire. Follow the wire as far as possible and feel for any breaks in the leads.

Note: *It's not uncommon for wires to break in the portion of the harness between the body and door (opening and closing the door fatigues and eventually breaks the wires).*

11   On the models covered by this manual, power door lock system communication goes through the Body Control Module. If the above tests do not pinpoint a problem, take the vehicle to a dealer or qualified shop with the proper scan tool to retrieve trouble codes from the BCM. Replacing of some components may result in programming issues. To avoid replacing of good components always test thoroughly before any parts are deemed faulty.

Keyless entry system

12   The keyless entry system consists of a remote control transmitter that sends a coded infrared signal to a receiver, which then operates the door lock system.

13   Replace the battery when the transmitter doesn't operate the locks at a distance of ten feet. Normal range should be about 30 feet.

Key remote control battery replacement

14   Carefully separate the case halves (see illustration).

15   Replace the battery (see illustration).

16   Snap the case halves together.

Transmitter programming

17   Programming replacement transmitters requires the use of a specialized scan tool. Take the vehicle and the transmitter(s) to a dealer service department or other qualified repair shop equipped with the necessary tool to have the transmitter(s) programmed to the vehicle. Up to four key fobs can be programmed to one car. All fobs for the vehicle have to be present when reprogramming.

24   Daytime Running Lights (DRL) - general information

1   The Daytime Running Lights (DRL) system illuminates the headlights whenever the engine is running. The only exception is with the engine running and the parking brake engaged. Once the parking brake is released, the lights will remain on as long as the ignition switch is on, even if the parking brake is later applied.

2   The DRL system supplies reduced power to the headlights so they won't be too bright for daytime use, while prolonging headlight life.

25 Airbag system - general information and precautions

General information

1   All models are equipped with a Supplemental Inflatable Restraint (SIR) system, consisting of a steering wheel airbag, a passenger's-side dash airbag, driver and front passsenger knee bolster airbags, front and rear seat-back mounted airbags, and roof rail airbags. This system is designed to protect the occupants of the vehicle from serious injury in the event of a frontal or side-impact collision. It consists of an array of external and internal (inside the SDM) information sensors (decelerometers), the Inflatable Restraint Sensing and Diagnostic Module (SDM), the inflator modules in the airbag units and the wiring and connectors tying all these components together.

Airbag/inflator modules

Driver's airbag/inflator module

2   The steering wheel airbag and knee airbag inflator modules contains a housing incorporating the cushion (airbag), an initiating device, and a canister of gas-generating material. The initiator is part of the inflator module deployment loop. When a collision occurs, the SDM sends current through the deployment loop to the initiator. Current passing through the initiator ignites the material in the canister, producing a rapidly expanding gas, which inflates the airbag almost instantaneously. Seconds after the airbag inflates, it deflates almost as quickly through airbag vent holes and/or the airbag fabric.

3   When the SDM sends current to the initiator, it travels through the airbag circuit to the steering column. From there, a clockspring on the steering wheel delivers the current to the module initiator. This clockspring assembly, which is the final segment of the airbag ignition circuit, functions as the bridge between the end of the airbag circuit on the (fixed) steering column and the beginning of the circuit on the (rotating) steering wheel. It's designed to maintain a closed circuit between the steering column and the steering wheel regardless of the position of the steering wheel. For this reason, removing and installing the clockspring is critical to the performance of the driver's side airbag. For information on how to remove and install the driver's side airbag, refer to Steering wheel - removal and installation in Chapter 10.

Passenger's airbag/inflator module

4   The passenger's airbag/inflator module is mounted above the glove compartment and a second, smaller airbag module is located just below the glove compartment. When deployed by the SDM, the passenger's airbags burst through the dashboard above the glove box and below. Although these areas looks like it's simply part of the dashboard, there actually trim covers with a perforated seams that allows the cover to separate from the dash when the passenger's airbag(s) inflates.

Side impact airbag/inflator modules

5   The side-impact airbag/inflator (roof rail) modules are mounted along the outer edges of the headliner, above the door openings. They extend from the A-pillar (front windshield pillar) to the C-pillar (rear window pillar). Each module consists of a housing, an inflatable airbag, an initiator and a canister of gas-generating material. Each roof rail module employs its own side impact sensor (SIS), which contains a sensing device that monitors changes in vehicle acceleration and velocity. This data is sent to the SDM, which compares it with its program. When the data exceeds a certain threshold, the SDM determines that the vehicle has been hit hard enough on one side or the other to warrant deployment of the roof rail on that side. The SDM doesn't deploy the roof rail airbags on both sides, just on the side being hit. Then the SDM sends current to the roof rail initiator to inflate the airbag, ripping open the headliner trim as it deploys to protect the occupant(s) on the left or right side of the vehicle. Side impact airbag/inflator modules are long enough to protect the driver and a left-side rear-seat passenger, or a front seat passenger and right-side rear-seat passenger.

6   The seats are also equipped with side-impact airbags, located in the outside cushion of each front and rear seat back.

Inflatable Restraint Sensing and Diagnostic Module (SDM)

7   The SDM is the computer module that controls the airbag system. Besides a microprocessor, the SDM also includes an array of sensors. Some of them are inside the SDM itself. Other external sensors are located throughout the vehicle. All of the sensors, internal and external, send a continuous voltage signal to the SDM, which compares this data to values stored in its memory. When these signals exceed a threshold value (the SDM determines that the vehicle is decelerating more quickly than the threshold value), the SDM allows current to flow through the circuit to the appropriate airbag module(s), which initiates deployment of the airbag(s).

8   For more information about the airbag system in your vehicle, refer to your owner's manual.

Impact seat belt retractors

9   All models are equipped with pyrotechnic (explosive) units in the front seat belt retracting mechanisms for both the lap and shoulder belts. During an impact that would trigger the airbag system, the airbag control unit also triggers the seat belt retractors. When the pyrotechnic charges go off, they accelerate the retractors to instantly take up any slack in the seat belt system to more fully prepare the driver and front seat passenger for impact.

10   The airbag system should be disabled any time work is done to or around the seats. *Warning: Never strike the pillars or floorpan with a hammer or use an impact-driver tool in these areas unless the system is disabled.*

Disarming the system and other precautions

Warning: *Failure to follow these precautions could result in accidental deployment of the airbag and personal injury.*

11   Whenever working in the vicinity of the steering wheel, instrument panel or any of the other SIR system components, the system must be disarmed. To disarm the system:

   a) *Point the wheels straight ahead and turn the key to the Lock position.*
   b) *Disconnect the cable from the negative battery terminal. Refer to Chapter 5 for the disconnecting procedure.*
   c) *Wait at least two minutes for the back-up power supply to be depleted.*
   d) *Remove airbag fuse no. 17 from the underhood fuse/relay box and airbag fuse no. 15 from the under-dash fuse relay box (see Section 3).*

12   Whenever handling an airbag module, always keep the airbag opening (the upholstered side) pointed away from your body. Never place the airbag module on a bench or other surface with the airbag opening facing the surface. Always place the airbag module in a safe location with the airbag opening (the upholstered side) facing up.

13   Never measure the resistance of any SIR component or use any electrical test equipment on any of the wiring or components. An ohmmeter has a built-in battery supply that could trigger the airbag inflator.

14   Never dispose of a live airbag/inflator module. Return it to a dealer service department or other qualified repair shop for safe deployment and disposal.

15   Never use electrical welding equipment in the vicinity of any airbag components. The connectors for the system are easy to spot because they're bright yellow.

16   Like the PCM, the SDM has a malfunction indicator light, known as the AIR BAG indicator light, on the instrument cluster. When you turn the ignition key to ON, the SDM checks out all of the SIR components and circuits. If everything is okay, the AIR BAG indicator light goes off, just like the PCM's Malfunction Indicator Light (MIL). But if there's a problem somewhere, the light stays on, and will remain on until the problem is repaired and the DTC(s) cleared from the SDM's memory.

26 Wiring diagrams - general information

1   Since it isn't possible to include all wiring diagrams for every year covered by this manual, the following diagrams are those that are typical and most commonly needed.
2   Prior to troubleshooting any circuits, check the fuse and circuit breakers (if equipped) to make sure they're in good condition. Make sure the battery is properly charged and check the cable connections (see Chapter 1).
3   When checking a circuit, make sure that all connectors are clean, with no broken or loose terminals. When unplugging a connector, do not pull on the wires. Pull only on the connector housings.

Wiring Diagrams - List

1. Starting and charging systems
2. Heating and air conditioning systems
3. Engine cooling fan system
4. Power window system
5. Power door lock system
6. Windshield wiper and washer system
7. Exterior lighting system (with Daytime Running Lights) (1 of 2)
8. Exterior lighting system (with Daytime Running Lights) (2 of 2)
9. Exterior lighting system (without Daytime Running Lights)
10. Interior lighting system
11. Audio system (with graphic display)
12. Audio system (with navigation or color display)
13. Cruise control system
14. Fuses and relays (1 of 4)
15. Fuses and relays (2 of 4)
16. Fuses and relays (3 of 4)
17. Fuses and relays (4 of 4)

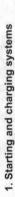

1. Starting and charging systems

*1 Vehicles with manual transmission
*2 Vehicles with automatic transmission
*3 For 1.4L engine
*4 For 1.8L engine

2. Heating and air conditioning systems

*1 For 1.4L engine
*2 For 1.8L engine
*3 Only models with HVAC - Automatic

3. Engine cooling fan system

4. Power window system

*1 Models with window operated, driver express down
*2 Models with window operated, express driver up/down

5. Power door lock system

6. Windshield wiper and washer system

7. Exterior lighting system (with Daytime Running Lights) (1 of 2)

*1 With vision – rear view
*2 Without vision – rear view

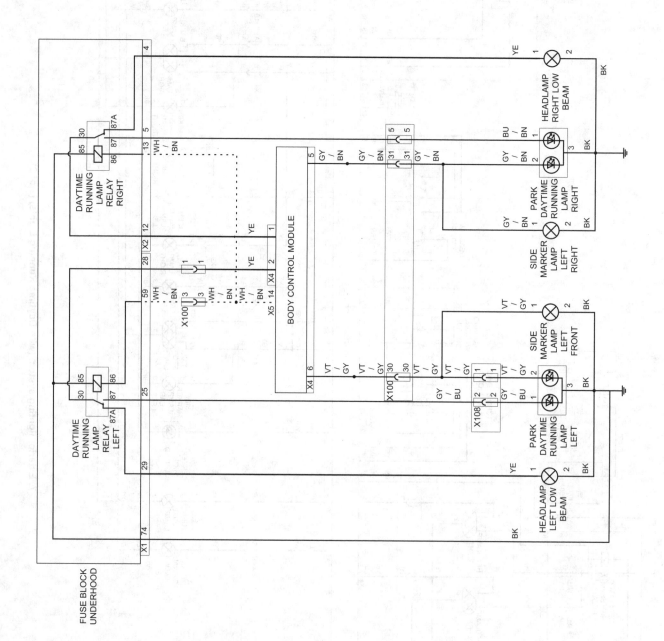

8. Exterior lighting system (with Daytime Running Lights) (2 of 2)

9. Exterior lighting system (without Daytime Running Lights)

10. Interior lighting system

11. Audio system (with graphic display)

12. Audio system (with navigation or color display)

*1 Models with BOSE sound system
*2 Models without BOSE sound system
*3 Models with audio interface
*4 Models without audio interface

13. Cruise control system

Fuse and relay box in passenger compartment

NO.	FUSE/RELAY	VALUE	DESCRIPTION
1	F1DA	10 A	Mobile phone control unit
2	F2DA	-	Not used
3	F3DA	25 A	Body control unit
4	F4DA	20 A	Radio
5	F5DA	7.5 A	Radio, Parking assistance control unit, Information display control unit, Multimedia player interface module
6	F6DA	20 A	Cigarette lighter
7	F7DA	20 A	Accessory socket
8	F8DA	30 A	Body control unit
9	F9DA	30 A	Body control unit
10	F10DA	30 A	Body control unit
11	F11DA	40 A	Blower motor control unit
12	F12DA	-	Not used
13	F13DA	25 A	Seat adjuster switch – driver
14	F14DA	7.5 A	Data link connector, Diagnostic connector
15	F15DA	10 A	Airbag diagnostic module
16	F16DA	10 A	Tailgate/boot release relay
17	F17DA	15 A	HVAC Control module, HVAC Controls switch assembly
18	F18DA	-	Not used
19	F19DA	-	Not used
20	F20DA	-	Not used
21	F21DA	15 A	Instrument cluster
22	F22DA	2 A	Ignition switch
23	F23DA	20 A	Body control unit
24	F24DA	20 A	Body control unit
25	F25DA	20 A	Steering column lock control unit
26	F26DA	-	Not used
R1	KR95B	-	Tailgate/boot release relay
R2	KR104A	-	Battery saver relay
R3	KR70	-	Accessory relay

14. Fuses and relays (1 of 4)

Fuse and relay box in engine compartment

NO.	FUSE/RELAY	VALUE	DESCRIPTION
1	F1UA	15 A	Control solenoid valve assembly
2	F2UA	15 A	Engine control unit
3	F3UA	-	Not used
4	F4UA	10 A	Evaporative emission vent solenoid valve
5	F5UA	15 A	Engine control unit, Control solenoid valve assembly
6	F6UA	30 A	Windscreen wiper relay, High-/low-speed wiper relay
7	F7UA	-	Not used
8	F8UA	-	Not used
9	F9UA	15 A	Fuel injectors, Ignition coil
10	F10UA	15 A	Engine control unit
11	F11UA	10 A	Mass air flow/intake air temperature sensor, Secondary air injection solenoid valve relay
12	F12UA	30 A	Starter relay
13	F13UA	7.5 A	Transmission control module
14	F14UA	10 A	Secondary air injection solenoid valve relay
15	F15UA	-	Not used
16	F16UA	7.5 A	Active grille air shutter actuator
17	F17UA	5 A	Airbag diagnostic module
18	F18UA	10 A	Chassis control module
19	F19UA	-	Not used
20	F20UA	-	Not used
21	F21UA	30 A	Window switches
22	F22UA	-	Not used
23	F23UA	-	Not used
24	F24UA	30 A	Window morot – driver, Window switch – driver/passenger
25	F25UA	20 A	Brake vacuum pump
26	F26UA	40 A	Electronic brake control unit (EBCM)
27	F27UA	30 A	Keyless entry control unit
28	F28UA	40 A	Rear demister
29	F29UA	-	Not used
30	F30UA	15 A	Electronic brake control unit (EBCM)
31	F31UA	20 A	Body control unit
32	F32UA	20 A	Body control unit
33	F33UA	30 A	Heated seat control unit
34	F34UA	25 A	Sunroof control unit
35	F35UA	30 A	Audio amplifier

36	F36UA	-	Not used
37	F37UA	10 A	Right headlight
38	F38UA	10 A	Left headlight
39	F39UA	-	Not used
40	F40UA	-	Not used
41	F41UA	-	Not used
42	F42UA	30 A	Cooling fan medium speed relay, cooling fan low speed relay
43	F43UA	-	Not used
44	F44UA	-	Not used
45	F45UA	40 A	Cooling fan high speed relay
46	F46UA	10 A	Cooling fan low speed relay, Cooling fan speed control relay, Cooling fan relay
47	F47UA	10 A	Heated oxygen sensor 1, Heated oxygen sensor 2, Engine coolant thermostat heater, Evaporative emission purge solenoid valve, Intake manifold tuning solenoid valve, Turbocharger bypass solenoid valve, Turbocharger wastegate solenoid valve
48	F48UA	15 A	Front fog lights
49	F49UA	-	Not used
50	F50UA	-	Not used
51	F51UA	15 A	Horns
52	F52UA	5 A	Instrument cluster
53	F53UA	10 A	Inside rearview mirror
54	F54UA	5 A	HVAC Control module, Passenger air bag disable indicator, Rearview camera
55	F55UA	7.5 A	Electric rear-view mirror switch, Driver's power window switch
56	F56UA	15 A	Windscreen washer pump
57	F57UA	15 A	Steering column lock control unit
58	F58UA	-	Not used
59	F59UA	30 A	Secondary air injection pump
60	F60UA	7.5 A	Door mirrors
61	F61UA	-	Not used
62	F62UA	10 A	Air-conditioning compressor clutch relay
63	F63UA	-	Not used
64	F64UA	5 A	Passenger presence module
65	F65UA	-	Not used
66	F66UA	-	Not used
67	F67UA	20 A	Chassis control module
68	F68UA	-	Not used
69	F69UA	5 A	Body control unit
70	F70UA	-	Not used
71	F71UA	-	Not used
R1	KR29	-	Air-conditioning compressor clutch relay
R2	KR27	-	Starter relay
R3	KR20F	-	Cooling fan relay
R4	KR12C	-	High-/low-speed wiper relay
R5	KR12B	-	Windscreen wiper relay
R6	KR26	-	Secondary air injection pressure sensor
R7	KR75	-	Engine running relay
R8	-	-	Not used

16. Fuses and relays (3 of 4)

R9	KR20P	-	Cooling fan, medium-speed relay
R10	KR20C	-	Cooling fan, low-speed relay
R11	-	-	Not used
R12	KR20E	-	Cooling fan control
R13	KR20D	-	Cooling fan, high-speed relay
R14	-	-	Not used
R15	KR73	-	Ignition main relay
R16	KR25	-	Secondary air injection pump
R17	KR5	-	Rear windscreen defroster relay
R18	KR3	-	Horn relay
R19	KR46	-	Windscreen washer pump
R20	KR48	-	Front fog light relay
R21	KR11	-	Headlight relay, main beam

Main fuses in engine compartment, on battery

NO.	FUSE	VALUE	DESCRIPTION
1	F1UD	100 A	Fuse and relay box in passenger compartment
2	F2UD	100 A	Fuse and relay box in passenger compartment
3	F3UD	80 A	Power steering control unit
4	F4UD	-	Not used
5	F5UD	250 A	Fuse and relay box in engine compartment
6	F6UD	250 A	Starter motor, Generator

Notes

Index

Haynes Automotive Manuals

NOTE: If you do not see a listing for your vehicle, please visit haynes.com for the latest product information and check out our Online Manuals!

ACURA
- 12020 **Integra** '86 thru '89 & **Legend** '86 thru '90
- 12021 **Integra** '90 thru '93 & **Legend** '91 thru '95
  Integra '94 thru '00 - see HONDA Civic (42025)
  MDX '01 thru '07 - see HONDA Pilot (42037)
- 12050 **Acura TL** all models '99 thru '08

AMC
- 14020 **Mid-size models** '70 thru '83
- 14025 **(Renault) Alliance & Encore** '83 thru '87

AUDI
- 15020 **4000** all models '80 thru '87
- 15025 **5000** all models '77 thru '83
- 15026 **5000** all models '84 thru '88
  Audi A4 '96 thru '01 - see VW Passat (96023)
- 15030 **Audi A4** '02 thru '08

AUSTIN-HEALEY
  Sprite - see MG Midget (66015)

BMW
- 18020 **3/5 Series** '82 thru '92
- 18021 **3-Series** incl. Z3 models '92 thru '98
- 18022 **3-Series** incl. Z4 models '99 thru '05
- 18023 **3-Series** '06 thru '14
- 18025 **320i** all 4-cylinder models '75 thru '83
- 18050 **1500 thru 2002** except Turbo '59 thru '77

BUICK
- 19010 **Buick Century** '97 thru '05
  Century (front-wheel drive) - see GM (38005)
- 19020 **Buick, Oldsmobile & Pontiac Full-size** (Front-wheel drive) '85 thru '05
  Buick Electra, LeSabre and Park Avenue;
  Oldsmobile Delta 88 Royale, Ninety Eight and Regency; **Pontiac** Bonneville
- 19025 **Buick, Oldsmobile & Pontiac Full-size** (Rear wheel drive) '70 thru '90
  Buick Estate, Electra, LeSabre, Limited, **Oldsmobile** Custom Cruiser, Delta 88, Ninety-eight, **Pontiac** Bonneville, Catalina, Grandville, Parisienne
- 19027 **Buick LaCrosse** '05 thru '13
  Enclave - see GENERAL MOTORS (38001)
  Rainier - see CHEVROLET (24072)
  Regal - see GENERAL MOTORS (38010)
  Riviera - see GENERAL MOTORS (38030, 38031)
  Roadmaster - see CHEVROLET (24046)
  Skyhawk - see GENERAL MOTORS (38015)
  Skylark - see GENERAL MOTORS (38020, 38025)
  Somerset - see GENERAL MOTORS (38025)

CADILLAC
- 21015 **CTS & CTS-V** '03 thru '14
- 21030 **Cadillac Rear Wheel Drive** '70 thru '93
  Cimarron - see GENERAL MOTORS (38015)
  DeVille - see GENERAL MOTORS (38031 & 38032)
  Eldorado - see GENERAL MOTORS (38030)
  Fleetwood - see GENERAL MOTORS (38031)
  Seville - see GM (38030, 38031 & 38032)

CHEVROLET
- 10305 **Chevrolet Engine Overhaul Manual**
- 24010 **Astro & GMC Safari Mini-vans** '85 thru '05
- 24013 **Aveo** '04 thru '11
- 24015 **Camaro V8** all models '70 thru '81
- 24016 **Camaro** all models '82 thru '92
- 24017 **Camaro & Firebird** '93 thru '02
  Cavalier - see GENERAL MOTORS (38016)
  Celebrity - see GENERAL MOTORS (38005)
- 24018 **Camaro** '10 thru '15
- 24020 **Chevelle, Malibu & El Camino** '69 thru '87
  Cobalt - see GENERAL MOTORS (38017)
- 24024 **Chevette & Pontiac T1000** '76 thru '87
  Citation - see GENERAL MOTORS (38020)
- 24027 **Colorado & GMC Canyon** '04 thru '12
- 24032 **Corsica & Beretta** all models '87 thru '96
- 24040 **Corvette** all V8 models '68 thru '82
- 24041 **Corvette** all models '84 thru '96
- 24042 **Corvette** all models '97 thru '13
- 24044 **Cruze** '11 thru '19
- 24045 **Full-size Sedans** Caprice, Impala, Biscayne, Bel Air & Wagons '69 thru '90
- 24046 **Impala SS & Caprice and Buick Roadmaster** '91 thru '96
  Impala '00 thru '05 - see LUMINA (24048)
- 24047 **Impala & Monte Carlo** all models '06 thru '11
  Lumina '90 thru '94 - see GM (38010)
- 24048 **Lumina & Monte Carlo** '95 thru '05
  Lumina APV - see GM (38035)
- 24050 **Luv Pick-up** all 2WD & 4WD '72 thru '82
- 24051 **Malibu** '13 thru '19
- 24055 **Monte Carlo** all models '70 thru '88
  Monte Carlo '95 thru '01 - see LUMINA (24048)
- 24059 **Nova** all V8 models '69 thru '79

- 24060 **Nova and Geo Prizm** '85 thru '92
- 24064 **Pick-ups** '67 thru '87 - Chevrolet & GMC
- 24065 **Pick-ups** '88 thru '98 - Chevrolet & GMC
- 24066 **Pick-ups** '99 thru '06 - Chevrolet & GMC
- 24067 **Chevrolet Silverado & GMC Sierra** '07 thru '14
- 24068 **Chevrolet Silverado & GMC Sierra** '14 thru '19
- 24070 **S-10 & S-15 Pick-ups** '82 thru '93, **Blazer & Jimmy** '83 thru '94,
- 24071 **S-10 & Sonoma Pick-ups** '94 thru '04, including **Blazer, Jimmy & Hombre**
- 24072 **Chevrolet TrailBlazer, GMC Envoy & Oldsmobile Bravada** '02 thru '09
- 24075 **Sprint** '85 thru '88 & **Geo Metro** '89 thru '01
- 24080 **Vans - Chevrolet & GMC** '68 thru '96
- 24081 **Chevrolet Express & GMC Savana** Full-size Vans '96 thru '19

CHRYSLER
- 10310 **Chrysler Engine Overhaul Manual**
- 25015 **Chrysler Cirrus, Dodge Stratus, Plymouth Breeze** '95 thru '00
- 25020 **Full-size Front-Wheel Drive** '88 thru '93
  K-Cars - see DODGE Aries (30008)
  Laser - see DODGE Daytona (30030)
- 25025 **Chrysler LHS, Concorde, New Yorker, Dodge** Intrepid, **Eagle Vision**, '93 thru '97
- 25026 **Chrysler LHS, Concorde, 300M, Dodge** Intrepid, '98 thru '04
- 25027 **Chrysler 300** '05 thru '18, **Dodge Charger** '06 thru '18, **Magnum** '05 thru '08 & **Challenger** '08 thru '18
- 25030 **Chrysler & Plymouth Mid-size** front wheel drive '82 thru '95
  Rear-wheel Drive - see Dodge (30050)
- 25035 **PT Cruiser** all models '01 thru '10
- 25040 **Chrysler Sebring** '95 thru '06, **Dodge Stratus** '01 thru '06 & **Dodge Avenger** '95 thru '00
- 25041 **Chrysler Sebring** '07 thru '10, **200** '11 thru '17 **Dodge Avenger** '08 thru '14

DATSUN
- 28005 **200SX** all models '80 thru '83
- 28012 **240Z, 260Z & 280Z** Coupe '70 thru '78
- 28014 **280ZX** Coupe & 2+2 '79 thru '83
  300ZX - see NISSAN (72010)
- 28018 **510 & PL521 Pick-up** '68 thru '73
- 28020 **510** all models '78 thru '81
- 28022 **620 Series Pick-up** all models '73 thru '79
  720 Series Pick-up - see NISSAN (72030)

DODGE
  400 & 600 - see CHRYSLER (25030)
- 30008 **Aries & Plymouth Reliant** '81 thru '89
- 30010 **Caravan & Plymouth Voyager** '84 thru '95
- 30011 **Caravan & Plymouth Voyager** '96 thru '02
- 30012 **Challenger & Plymouth Sapporro** '78 thru '83
- 30013 **Caravan, Chrysler Voyager & Town & Country** '03 thru '07
- 30014 **Grand Caravan & Chrysler Town & Country** '08 thru '18
- 30016 **Colt & Plymouth Champ** '78 thru '87
- 30020 **Dakota Pick-ups** all models '87 thru '96
- 30021 **Durango** '98 & '99 & **Dakota** '97 thru '99
- 30022 **Durango** '00 thru '03 & **Dakota** '00 thru '04
- 30023 **Durango** '04 thru '09 & **Dakota** '05 thru '11
- 30025 **Dart, Demon, Plymouth Barracuda, Duster & Valiant** 6-cylinder models '67 thru '76
- 30030 **Daytona & Chrysler Laser** '84 thru '89
  Intrepid - see CHRYSLER (25025, 25026)
- 30034 **Neon** all models '95 thru '99
- 30035 **Omni & Plymouth Horizon** '78 thru '90
- 30036 **Dodge & Plymouth Neon** '00 thru '05
- 30040 **Pick-ups** full-size models '74 thru '93
- 30042 **Pick-ups** full-size models '94 thru '08
- 30043 **Pick-ups** full-size models '09 thru '18
- 30045 **Ram 50/D50 Pick-ups & Raider and Plymouth Arrow Pick-ups** '79 thru '93
- 30050 **Dodge/Plymouth/Chrysler** RWD '71 thru '89
- 30055 **Shadow & Plymouth Sundance** '87 thru '94
- 30060 **Spirit & Plymouth Acclaim** '89 thru '95
- 30065 **Vans - Dodge & Plymouth** '71 thru '03

EAGLE
  Talon - see MITSUBISHI (68030, 68031)
  Vision - see CHRYSLER (25025)

FIAT
- 34010 **124 Sport Coupe & Spider** '68 thru '78
- 34025 **X1/9** all models '74 thru '80

FORD
- 10320 **Ford Engine Overhaul Manual**
- 10355 **Ford Automatic Transmission Overhaul**
- 11500 **Mustang** '64-1/2 thru '70 Restoration Guide
- 36004 **Aerostar Mini-vans** all models '86 thru '97
- 36006 **Contour & Mercury Mystique** '95 thru '00
- 36008 **Courier Pick-up** all models '72 thru '82

- 36012 **Crown Victoria & Mercury Grand Marquis** '88 thru '11
- 36014 **Edge** '07 thru '19 & **Lincoln MKX** '07 thru '18
- 36016 **Escort & Mercury Lynx** all models '81 thru '90
- 36020 **Escort & Mercury Tracer** '91 thru '02
- 36022 **Escape** '01 thru '17, **Mazda Tribute** '01 thru '11, & **Mercury Mariner** '05 thru '11
- 36024 **Explorer & Mazda Navajo** '91 thru '01
- 36025 **Explorer & Mercury Mountaineer** '02 thru '10
- 36026 **Explorer** '11 thru '17
- 36028 **Fairmont & Mercury Zephyr** '78 thru '83
- 36030 **Festiva & Aspire** '88 thru '97
- 36032 **Fiesta** all models '77 thru '80
- 36034 **Focus** all models '00 thru '11
- 36035 **Focus** '12 thru '14
- 36045 **Fusion** '06 thru '14 & **Mercury Milan** '06 thru '11
- 36048 **Mustang V8** all models '64-1/2 thru '73
- 36049 **Mustang II** 4-cylinder, V6 & V8 models '74 thru '78
- 36050 **Mustang & Mercury Capri** '79 thru '93
- 36051 **Mustang** all models '94 thru '04
- 36052 **Mustang** '05 thru '14
- 36054 **Pick-ups & Bronco** '73 thru '79
- 36058 **Pick-ups & Bronco** '80 thru '96
- 36059 **F-150** '97 thru '03, **Expedition** '97 thru '17, **F-250** '97 thru '99, **F-150 Heritage** '04 & **Lincoln Navigator** '98 thru '17
- 36060 **Super Duty Pick-ups & Excursion** '99 thru '10
- 36061 **F-150** full-size '04 thru '14
- 36062 **Pinto & Mercury Bobcat** '75 thru '80
- 36063 **F-150** full-size '15 thru '17
- 36064 **Super Duty Pick-ups** '11 thru '16
- 36066 **Probe** all models '89 thru '92
  Probe '93 thru '97 - see MAZDA 626 (61042)
- 36070 **Ranger & Bronco II** gas models '83 thru '92
- 36071 **Ranger** '93 thru '11 & **Mazda Pick-ups** '94 thru '09
- 36074 **Taurus & Mercury Sable** '86 thru '95
- 36075 **Taurus & Mercury Sable** '96 thru '07
- 36076 **Taurus** '08 thru '14, **Five Hundred** '05 thru '07, **Mercury Montego** '05 thru '07 & **Sable** '08 thru '09
- 36078 **Tempo & Mercury Topaz** '84 thru '94
- 36082 **Thunderbird & Mercury Cougar** '83 thru '88
- 36086 **Thunderbird & Mercury Cougar** '89 thru '97
- 36090 **Vans** all V8 Econoline models '69 thru '91
- 36094 **Vans** full size '92 thru '14
- 36097 **Windstar** '95 thru '03, **Freestar & Mercury Monterey** Mini-van '04 thru '07

GENERAL MOTORS
- 10360 **GM Automatic Transmission Overhaul**
- 38001 **GMC Acadia** '07 thru '16, **Buick Enclave** '08 thru '17, **Saturn Outlook** '07 thru '10 & **Chevrolet Traverse** '09 thru '17
- 38005 **Buick Century, Chevrolet Celebrity, Oldsmobile Cutlass Ciera & Pontiac 6000** all models '82 thru '96
- 38010 **Buick Regal** '88 thru '04, **Chevrolet Lumina** '88 thru '04, **Oldsmobile Cutlass Supreme** '88 thru '97 & **Pontiac Grand Prix** '88 thru '07
- 38015 **Buick Skyhawk, Cadillac Cimarron, Chevrolet Cavalier, Oldsmobile Firenza, Pontiac J-2000 & Sunbird** '82 thru '94
- 38016 **Chevrolet Cavalier & Pontiac Sunfire** '95 thru '05
- 38017 **Chevrolet Cobalt** '05 thru '10, **HHR** '06 thru '11, **Pontiac G5** '07 thru '09, **Pursuit** '05 thru '06 & **Saturn ION** '03 thru '07
- 38020 **Buick Skylark, Chevrolet Citation, Oldsmobile Omega, Pontiac Phoenix** '80 thru '85
- 38025 **Buick Skylark** '86 thru '98, **Somerset** '85 thru '87, **Oldsmobile Achieva** '85 thru '91, **Calais** '85 thru '91, & **Pontiac Grand Am** all models '85 thru '98
- 38026 **Chevrolet Malibu** '97 thru '03, **Classic** '04 thru '05, **Oldsmobile Alero** '99 thru '03, **Cutlass** '97 thru '00, & **Pontiac Grand Am** '99 thru '03
- 38027 **Chevrolet Malibu** '04 thru '12, **Pontiac G6** '05 thru '10 & **Saturn Aura** '07 thru '10
- 38030 **Cadillac Eldorado, Seville, Oldsmobile Toronado & Buick Riviera** '71 thru '85
- 38031 **Cadillac Eldorado, Seville, DeVille, Fleetwood, Oldsmobile Toronado & Buick Riviera** '86 thru '93
- 38032 **Cadillac DeVille** '94 thru '05, **Seville** '92 thru '04 & **Cadillac DTS** '06 thru '10
- 38035 **Chevrolet Lumina APV, Oldsmobile Silhouette & Pontiac Trans Sport** all models '90 thru '96
- 38036 **Chevrolet Venture** '97 thru '05, **Oldsmobile Silhouette** '97 thru '04, **Pontiac Trans Sport** '97 thru '98 & **Montana** '99 thru '05
- 38040 **Chevrolet Equinox** '05 thru '17, **GMC Terrain** '10 thru '17 & **Pontiac Torrent** '06 thru '09

GEO
  Metro - see CHEVROLET Sprint (24075)
  Prizm - '85 thru '92 see CHEVY (24060), '93 thru '02 see TOYOTA Corolla (92036)
- 40030 **Storm** all models '90 thru '93
  Tracker - see SUZUKI Samurai (90010)

(Continued on other side)

Haynes Automotive Manuals (continued)

NOTE: If you do not see a listing for your vehicle, please visit haynes.com for the latest product information and check out our Online Manuals!

GMC
Acadia - see GENERAL MOTORS (38001)
Pick-ups - see CHEVROLET (24027, 24068)
Vans - see CHEVROLET (24081)

HONDA
42010 Accord CVCC all models '76 thru '83
42011 Accord all models '84 thru '89
42012 Accord all models '90 thru '93
42013 Accord all models '94 thru '97
42014 Accord all models '98 thru '02
42015 Accord '03 thru '12 & Crosstour '10 thru '14
42016 Accord '13 thru '17
42020 Civic 1200 all models '73 thru '79
42021 Civic 1300 & 1500 CVCC '80 thru '83
42022 Civic 1500 CVCC all models '75 thru '79
42023 Civic all models '84 thru '91
42024 Civic & del Sol '92 thru '95
42025 Civic '96 thru '00, CR-V '97 thru '01
& Acura Integra '94 thru '00
42026 Civic '01 thru '11 & CR-V '02 thru '11
42027 Civic '12 thru '15 & CR-V '12 thru '16
42030 Fit '07 thru '13
42035 Odyssey all models '99 thru '10
Passport - see ISUZU Rodeo (47017)
42037 Honda Pilot '03 thru '08, Ridgeline '06 thru '14
& Acura MDX '01 thru '07
42040 Prelude CVCC all models '79 thru '89

HYUNDAI
43010 Elantra all models '96 thru '19
43015 Excel & Accent all models '86 thru '13
43050 Santa Fe all models '01 thru '12
43055 Sonata all models '99 thru '14

INFINITI
G35 '03 thru '08 - see NISSAN 350Z (72011)

ISUZU
Hombre - see CHEVROLET S-10 (24071)
47017 Rodeo '91 thru '02, Amigo '89 thru '94 & '98 thru '02
& Honda Passport '95 thru '02
47020 Trooper '84 thru '91 & Pick-up '81 thru '93

JAGUAR
49010 XJ6 all 6-cylinder models '68 thru '86
49011 XJ6 all models '88 thru '94
49015 XJ12 & XJS all 12-cylinder models '72 thru '85

JEEP
50010 Cherokee, Comanche & Wagoneer Limited
all models '84 thru '01
50011 Cherokee '14 thru '19
50020 CJ all models '49 thru '86
50025 Grand Cherokee all models '93 thru '04
50026 Grand Cherokee '05 thru '19
& Dodge Durango '11 thru '19
50029 Grand Wagoneer & Pick-up '72 thru '91
Grand Wagoneer '84 thru '91, Cherokee &
Wagoneer '72 thru '83, Pick-up '72 thru '88
50030 Wrangler all models '87 thru '17
50035 Liberty '02 thru '12 & Dodge Nitro '07 thru '11
50050 Patriot & Compass '07 thru '17

KIA
54050 Optima '01 thru '10
54060 Sedona '02 thru '14
54070 Sephia '94 thru '01, Spectra '00 thru '09,
Sportage '05 thru '20
54077 Sorento '03 thru '13

LEXUS
ES 300/330 - see TOYOTA Camry (92007, 92008)
ES 350 - see TOYOTA Camry (92009)
RX 300/330/350 - see TOYOTA Highlander (92095)

LINCOLN
MKX - see FORD (36014)
Navigator - see FORD Pick-up (36059)
59010 Rear-Wheel Drive Continental '70 thru '87,
Mark Series '70 thru '92 & Town Car '81 thru '10

MAZDA
61010 GLC (rear-wheel drive) '77 thru '83
61011 GLC (front-wheel drive) '81 thru '85
61012 Mazda3 '04 thru '11
61015 323 & Protogé '90 thru '03
61016 MX-5 Miata '90 thru '14
61020 MPV all models '89 thru '98
Navajo - see Ford Explorer (36024)
61030 Pick-ups '72 thru '93
Pick-ups '94 thru '09 - see Ford Ranger (36071)
61035 RX-7 all models '79 thru '85
61036 RX-7 all models '86 thru '91
61040 626 (rear-wheel drive) all models '79 thru '82
61041 626 & MX-6 (front-wheel drive) '83 thru '92
61042 626 '93 thru '01 & MX-6/Ford Probe '93 thru '02
61043 Mazda6 '03 thru '13

MERCEDES-BENZ
63012 123 Series Diesel '76 thru '85
63015 190 Series 4-cylinder gas models '84 thru '88
63020 230/250/280 6-cylinder SOHC models '68 thru '72
63025 280 123 Series gas models '77 thru '81
63030 350 & 450 all models '71 thru '80
63040 C-Class: C230/C240/C280/C320/C350 '01 thru '07

MERCURY
64200 Villager & Nissan Quest '93 thru '01
All other titles, see FORD Listing.

MG
66010 MGB Roadster & GT Coupe '62 thru '80
66015 MG Midget, Austin Healey Sprite '58 thru '80

MINI
67020 Mini '02 thru '13

MITSUBISHI
68020 Cordia, Tredia, Galant, Precis & Mirage '83 thru '93
68030 Eclipse, Eagle Talon & Plymouth Laser '90 thru '94
68031 Eclipse '95 thru '05 & Eagle Talon '95 thru '98
68035 Galant '94 thru '12
68040 Pick-up '83 thru '96 & Montero '83 thru '93

NISSAN
72010 300ZX all models including Turbo '84 thru '89
72011 350Z & Infiniti G35 all models '03 thru '08
72015 Altima all models '93 thru '06
72016 Altima '07 thru '12
72020 Maxima all models '85 thru '92
72021 Maxima all models '93 thru '08
72025 Murano '03 thru '14
72030 Pick-ups '80 thru '97 & Pathfinder '87 thru '95
72031 Frontier '98 thru '04, Xterra '00 thru '04,
& Pathfinder '96 thru '04
72032 Frontier & Xterra '05 thru '14
72037 Pathfinder '05 thru '14
72040 Pulsar all models '83 thru '86
72042 Roque all models '08 thru '20
72050 Sentra all models '82 thru '94
72051 Sentra & 200SX all models '95 thru '06
72060 Stanza all models '82 thru '90
72070 Titan pick-ups '04 thru '10, Armada '05 thru '10
& Pathfinder Armada '04
72080 Versa all models '07 thru '19

OLDSMOBILE
73015 Cutlass V6 & V8 gas models '74 thru '88
For other OLDSMOBILE titles, see BUICK,
CHEVROLET or GENERAL MOTORS listings.

PLYMOUTH
For PLYMOUTH titles, see DODGE listing.

PONTIAC
79008 Fiero all models '84 thru '88
79018 Firebird V8 models except Turbo '70 thru '81
79019 Firebird all models '82 thru '92
79025 G6 all models '05 thru '09
79040 Mid-size Rear-wheel Drive '70 thru '87
Vibe '03 thru '10 - see TOYOTA Corolla (92037)
For other PONTIAC titles, see BUICK,
CHEVROLET or GENERAL MOTORS listings.

PORSCHE
80020 911 Coupe & Targa models '65 thru '89
80025 914 all 4-cylinder models '69 thru '76
80030 924 all models including Turbo '76 thru '82
80035 944 all models including Turbo '83 thru '89

RENAULT
Alliance & Encore - see AMC (14025)

SAAB
84010 900 all models including Turbo '79 thru '88

SATURN
87010 Saturn all S-series models '91 thru '02
Saturn Ion '03 thru '07- see GM (38017)
Saturn Outlook - see GM (38001)
87020 Saturn L-series all models '00 thru '04
87040 Saturn VUE '02 thru '09

SUBARU
89002 1100, 1300, 1400 & 1600 '71 thru '79
89003 1600 & 1800 2WD & 4WD '80 thru '94
89080 Impreza '02 thru '11, WRX '02 thru '14,
& WRX STI '04 thru '14
89100 Legacy all models '90 thru '99
89101 Legacy & Forester '00 thru '09
89102 Legacy '10 thru '16 & Forester '12 thru '16

SUZUKI
90010 Samurai/Sidekick & Geo Tracker '86 thru '01

TOYOTA
92005 Camry all models '83 thru '91
92006 Camry '92 thru '96 & Avalon '95 thru '96
92007 Camry, Avalon, Solara, Lexus ES 300 '97 thru '01

92008 Camry, Avalon, Lexus ES 300/330 '02 thru '06
& Solara '02 thru '08
92009 Camry, Avalon & Lexus ES 350 '07 thru '17
92015 Celica Rear-wheel Drive '71 thru '85
92020 Celica Front-wheel Drive '86 thru '99
92025 Celica Supra all models '79 thru '92
92030 Corolla all models '75 thru '79
92032 Corolla all rear-wheel drive models '80 thru '87
92035 Corolla all front-wheel drive models '84 thru '92
92036 Corolla & Geo/Chevrolet Prizm '93 thru '02
92037 Corolla '03 thru '19, Matrix '03 thru '14,
& Pontiac Vibe '03 thru '10
92040 Corolla Tercel all models '80 thru '82
92045 Corona all models '74 thru '82
92050 Cressida all models '78 thru '82
92055 Land Cruiser FJ40, 43, 45, 55 '68 thru '82
92056 Land Cruiser FJ60, 62, 80, FZJ80 '80 thru '96
92060 Matrix '03 thru '11 & Pontiac Vibe '03 thru '10
92065 MR2 all models '85 thru '87
92070 Pick-up all models '69 thru '78
92075 Pick-up all models '79 thru '95
92076 Tacoma '95 thru '04, 4Runner '96 thru '02
& T100 '93 thru '08
92077 Tacoma all models '05 thru '18
92078 Tundra '00 thru '06 & Sequoia '01 thru '07
92079 4Runner all models '03 thru '09
92080 Previa all models '91 thru '95
92081 Prius all models '01 thru '12
92082 RAV4 all models '96 thru '12
92085 Tercel all models '87 thru '94
92090 Sienna all models '98 thru '10
92095 Highlander '01 thru '19
& Lexus RX330/330/350 '99 thru '19
92179 Tundra '07 thru '19 & Sequoia '08 thru '19

TRIUMPH
94007 Spitfire all models '62 thru '81
94010 TR7 all models '75 thru '81

VW
96008 Beetle & Karmann Ghia '54 thru '79
96009 New Beetle '98 thru '10
96016 Rabbit, Jetta, Scirocco & Pick-up
gas models '75 thru '92 & Convertible '80 thru '92
96017 Golf, GTI & Jetta '93 thru '98, Cabrio '95 thru '02
96018 Golf, GTI, Jetta '99 thru '05
96019 Jetta, Rabbit, GLI, GTI & Golf '05 thru '11
96020 Rabbit, Jetta & Pick-up diesel '77 thru '84
96021 Jetta '11 thru '18 & Golf '15 thru '19
96023 Passat '98 thru '05 & Audi A4 '96 thru '01
96030 Transporter 1600 all models '68 thru '79
96035 Transporter 1700, 1800 & 2000 '72 thru '79
96040 Type 3 1500 & 1600 all models '63 thru '73
96045 Vanagon Air-Cooled all models '80 thru '83

VOLVO
97010 120, 130 Series & 1800 Sports '61 thru '73
97015 140 Series all models '66 thru '74
97020 240 Series all models '76 thru '93
97040 740 & 760 Series all models '82 thru '88
97050 850 Series all models '93 thru '97

TECHBOOK MANUALS
10205 Automotive Computer Codes
10206 OBD-II & Electronic Engine Management
10210 Automotive Emissions Control Manual
10215 Fuel Injection Manual '78 thru '85
10225 Holley Carburetor Manual
10230 Rochester Carburetor Manual
10305 Chevrolet Engine Overhaul Manual
10320 Ford Engine Overhaul Manual
10330 GM and Ford Diesel Engine Repair Manual
10331 Duramax Diesel Engines '01 thru '19
10332 Cummins Diesel Engine Performance Manual
10333 GM, Ford & Chrysler Engine Performance Manual
10334 GM Engine Performance Manual
10340 Small Engine Repair Manual, 5 HP & Less
10341 Small Engine Repair Manual, 5.5 thru 20 HP
10345 Suspension, Steering & Driveline Manual
10355 Ford Automatic Transmission Overhaul
10360 GM Automatic Transmission Overhaul
10405 Automotive Body Repair & Painting
10410 Automotive Brake Manual
10411 Automotive Anti-lock Brake (ABS) Systems
10420 Automotive Electrical Manual
10425 Automotive Heating & Air Conditioning
10435 Automotive Tools Manual
10445 Welding Manual
10450 ATV Basics

Over a 100 Haynes
motorcycle manuals
also available

10/22

Haynes North America, Inc. • (805) 498-6703 • www.haynes.com